Economics and its Discontents

To David M. Gordon, Hyman Minsky and William Vickrey, dissenters who will be sorely missed

Economics and its Discontents

Twentieth Century Dissenting Economists

Edited by

Richard P.F. Holt

Associate Professor of Economics, Southern Oregon University, USA

Steven Pressman

Professor of Economics and Finance, Monmouth University, USA

Edward Elgar

Cheltenham, UK · Northampton, MA, USA

Published by
Edward Elgar Publishing Limited
8 Lansdown Place
Cheltenham
Glos GL50 2HU
UK

Edward Elgar Publishing, Inc
6 Market Street
Northampton
Massachusetts 01060
USA

HB
171
.E2487
1998
Sept .1999

A catalogue record for this book
is available from the British Library

Library of Congress Cataloging in Publication Data

Economics and its discontents: twentieth century dissenting
    economists / edited by Richard P.F. Holt, Steven Pressman.
        Includes bibliographical references.
        1. Economics. 2. Economists. I. Holt, Richard P.F., 1953–
    II. Pressman, Steven.
    HB171.E2487 1998
    330—dc21
                                                                97–35417
                                                                    CIP

ISBN 1 85898 272 3

Printed and bound in Great Britain by Bookcraft (Bath) Ltd.

Contents

Contributors

Jeff E. Biddle is Associate Professor of Economics at Michigan State University, USA

Peter J. Boettke is Associate Professor of Economics and Finance at Manhattan College, USA

Victoria Chick is Professor of Economics at University College, London, UK

Charles M.A. Clark is Associate Professor of Economics and Finance at St. John's University, USA

David Colander is Christian A. Johnson Distinguished Professor of Economics at Middlebury College, USA

Zohreh Emami is Associate Professor of Economics at Alverno College, USA

Ross B. Emmett is Assistant Professor of Economics at Augustana College, Canada

Mathew Forstater is Assistant Professor of Economics at Gettysburg College, USA

Richard P.F. Holt is Associate Professor of Economics at Southern Oregon University, USA

J.E. King is Professor of Economics at La Trobe University, Australia

Heinz D. Kurz is Professor of Economics at the University of Graz, Austria

David Latzko is Assistant Professor of Economics at Wilkes University, USA

Frederic Lee is Reader in Economics at DeMontfort University, UK

Laurence S. Moss is Professor of Economics at Babson College, USA

Elizabeth A. Paulin is Associate Professor of Economics at LaSalle University, USA

Steven Pressman is Professor of Economics and Finance at Monmouth University, USA

Christine Rider is Professor of Economics and Finance at St. John's University, USA

Neri Salvadori is Professor of Economics at the University of Pisa, Italy.

Warren J. Samuels is Professor of Economics at Michigan State University, USA

Malcolm Sawyer is Professor of Economics at the University of Leeds, UK

Introduction: dissent in twentieth century economics

Richard P.F. Holt and Steven Pressman

In the late 1940s, President Harry S. Truman actively sought out a one-armed economist to give him advice. The problem, he lamented, was that whenever he asked one of his economic advisers for help and suggestions their response was always 'On the one hand ... and the other hand ...'. About thirty-five years later, President Ronald Reagan expressed a similar dissatisfaction with his economic advisers, quipping that if you line up all the economists in the world end to end they would not reach a conclusion.

These two jokes about economists reflect the popular perception of economists and the economics profession. Yet the reality is rather different from these popular perceptions. Economists actually agree more than they disagree; and they tend to agree more on fundamentals (how the economy works and how to do economics) and disagree more over magnitudes (how much the economy will slow down if interest rates rise) and means (what is the best way to cut taxes, reduce the deficit, and so on). Surveys of economists show that an extremely large percentage of the profession support free trade, oppose minimum wages because they increase unemployment among unskilled workers, and favour taxes on pollutants rather than government regulations mandating certain solutions to the problem of pollution, such as electric cars (Frey et al. 1984).

This strong consensus, however, has not become unanimity. On virtually every issue there remains a sizeable minority (10 per cent or more) of economists who oppose the views of the majority. And these dissenters are not all extremists, or 'economic quacks'. Many are respected figures. This book is about these twentieth century dissenters, and about dissent within the discipline of economics. It addresses how and why various economists disagree with the majority views of their colleagues, and the nature of dissent or disagreement within the economics profession.

Dissent can take many shapes and forms, as the chapters in this book show. Dissent can be over how economics gets taught (Robinson). It can be disagreement with the deductive methodology of economic analysis (Bergmann, Buchanan and Friedman). It can be dissatisfaction with the lack of attention economists pay to the real-world behaviour of individuals and the outside forces that affect this behaviour (Commons, Means and Veblen), the narrow and limited assumptions that economists make (Hayek, Lowe and Schelling), or the inappropriate attempt of economics to dominate all the social sciences (Knight). There are economists who have expressed their dissatisfaction primarily with the theoretical core of traditional economics (Kalecki, Keynes and Sraffa), and economists whose dissent primarily concerns the policy conclusions reached by standard economic analysis (Hobson, Kaldor and Lange). Also, as one might expect, several figures dissent along several dimensions at once.

The chapters that follow, and this book itself, assumes that such disagreement among economists is healthy. It can counter problems of overconfidence and 'groupthink' (Plous 1993). It can also help to keep economists from making serious mistakes in how they view the world and in how they do economics.

In the late twentieth century, economics has come under heavy attack from both within the profession (Heilbroner and Milberg 1995) and from outside it (Cassidy 1996). Business people view economists as aloof number crunchers who are unable to understand the real problems facing business firms. Colander and Klamer (1987) have found that graduate students are greatly dissatisfied with their economic education, and feel that they are learning a lot of sophisticated mathematical techniques, but little or nothing about how real economies work. While the knives of economic analysis have become sharper, the next generation of economists are learning a set of tools that cut less deeply. The common complaints raised about economists are thus likely to be heard more often and more loudly in the future.

There is also the problem of declining enrolments in economics courses and a sharp fall in the percentage of college students choosing to major in economics. This has become a matter of survival. If students will not take economics courses and will not major in economics, what will happen to economists?

Finally, the percentage of female economists remains significantly lower than female representation in other academic disciplines, and this is not just a matter of the mathematical nature of economics. As a recent article in the *Journal of Economic Perspectives* (Kahn 1995) pointed out, the representation of women in mathematics is greater than the representation of women in economics.

All these problems show that something is wrong within the economics profession despite its agreement on most issues. A study of dissenting figures, we believe, can help shed light on the root causes of these problems as well as point the way to a better economics.

Contrary to what many economists might think or would like to think, dissent has played an important role in the history of economic thought. Like other disciplines, economics has developed over time as a result of economists pursuing new lines of inquiry and questioning old truths and beliefs. Adam Smith, Thomas Robert Malthus and David Ricardo would have been considered dissenting economists during their time as they tried to understand the broad new features of capitalism as it emerged during the late eighteenth century. Likewise, the marginalists were dissenters when they questioned the classical perspective. Every generation, in fact, needs dissenters who question past truths and keep the discipline of economics from ossifying.

The dissenting voices set forth in this volume represent a broad spectrum within twentieth century economics; and the entries that comprise this book demonstrate that dissent in the profession goes beyond ideology. Dissenters in the profession can come from a radical, or liberal or conservative framework. What they seem to have in common is a dissatisfaction with economics as it is presently practised, how it explains the world, and the type of questions the typical economist asks.

The dissenters, whose ideas and theories are presented in this volume, seem to be saying that there is a better way to do economics and a better way to be an economist. Each of these dissenters, in some sense, has helped keep the economics profession honest by his or her constant questioning of traditional thinking. This book salutes and celebrates these economic dissenters who exemplify the very best of the discipline. If economics is again to be a respected field and a highly regarded profession, it is to these dissenters that we need to look towards as pointing the way forward.

NOTE

The editors thank all the authors for their flexibility and willingness to work hard in order to improve the quality of this volume. Also, special thanks are due to Diana Prout for typing numerous chapters, and parts of chapters, in this volume.

REFERENCES

Cassidy, J. (1996), 'The decline of economics', *The New Yorker*, 2 December, 50–60.
Colander, D. and A. Klamer (1987), 'The making of an economist', *Journal of Economic Perspectives*, **1**, Fall, 95–111.

Frey, B.S., W.W. Pommerehre, F. Schneider and G. Gilbert (1984), 'Consensus and dissension among economists: an empirical inquiry', *American Economic Review*, **74**, December, 986–94.

Heilbroner, R. and W. Milberg (1995), *The Crisis of Vision in Modern Economic Thought*, New York: Cambridge University Press.

Kahn, S. (1995), 'Women in the economics profession', *Journal of Economic Perspectives*, **9**, Fall, 193–205.

Plous, S. (1993), *The Psychology of Judgment and Decision Making*, New York: McGraw-Hill.

1. The seditious dissent of Barbara R. Bergmann

Elizabeth A. Paulin

INTRODUCTION

A dissenting economist is one who disagrees. He or she is the Marxist, the institutionalist, the Sraffian, the Post Keynesian who assails neoclassical economics; the neoclassical economist who in turn rejects alternative paradigms; the Marxist feminist who takes issue with the traditional Marxian conception of production; and the neoclassical economist who challenges some aspect of that theory. In fact, in one way or another we are all dissenting economists; for as everyone knows, economists never agree.

Such a sweeping definition is rather sterile, however, for it rules out the existence of non-dissenting economists. We thus need another definition; one that specifies an object of dissent, a Goliath from which economic Davids dissent. The obvious choice for such a Goliath is the reigning economic orthodoxy which, of course, varies across time and space. In the West, we can point to Goliath the mercantilist; Goliath the Physiocrat; Goliath the classical economist, the Keynesian and the neoclassicist. We can also point to Davids who became Goliaths (J.M. Keynes) and Davids who did not (Thorstein Veblen).

But identifying a Goliath takes us only part way to defining a dissenting economist. For the nature, the extent and the implications of dissent vary widely. Among those who challenge today's economic Goliath – the neoclassical paradigm – there exists, at one extreme, constructive dissent. Constructive dissent is designed to strengthen the existing orthodoxy without disturbing its core metaphysical and epistemological beliefs. Such was the dissent of the rational expectations school, which (in the late 1960s and 1970s) challenged the way neoclassical economists understood the formation of expectations. This type of dissent was also levelled against the orthodoxy by the human capital school in the 1960s, ultimately changing the way neoclassical economists analysed the demand

for education. And today we find this dissent among some feminist economists who seek to refashion the tools of neoclassical analysis to better
incorporate the impact of gender (as a social construct) on economic
phenomena (Woolley 1993).

At the other extreme, there exists seditious dissent, dissent that challenges the metaphysical and epistemological beliefs upon which orthodox
theory rests. Seditious dissent seeks not to strengthen, but rather to
undermine and replace, the existing orthodoxy. This is where we find the
Keynesian dissent from the classical school, the institutional dissent from
neoclassical economics, and the Marxian dissent from both.

Given the role of core beliefs in distinguishing the two types of dissent,
it behooves us to look more closely at those beliefs before we assign
Barbara Bergmann a place among the dissenting economists of the twentieth century.

The core philosophical beliefs underpinning neoclassical economics
derive from the classical liberalism of John Locke and Jean Rousseau,
two 'Davids-turned-Goliaths' in the realm of political philosophy. In
rejecting the dominant orthodoxy known as patriarchalism, these eighteenth century philosophers formulated a concept of human nature that
lies at the heart of today's economic Goliath.[1]

Locke and Rousseau argued that humans are distinguished from other
animals by their ability to reason, both morally (individuals can decide
for themselves what is right and good and preferable) and prudentially
(they can calculate the best way of achieving their desired ends).
According to Jaggar (1983), this focus on rationality led contemporary
liberal philosophers (and neoclassical economists) to a belief in normative dualism – the idea that the mind is separate from the body and
superior to it. Physical attributes and the physical environment are
regarded as irrelevant in determining the essence of human beings, since
the physical is common to all animals.

Normative dualism and the assumption of human rationality underlie
the belief in abstract individualism, where rationality is conceived of as
independent of the individual's physical, social and cultural surroundings.
Such a view of the individual leads orthodox economists to use Robinson
Crusoe prototypes in constructing 'rational economic man'. A solitary,
abstract individual is put at the centre of neoclassical theory, one who
always seeks to maximize happiness, subject to resource constraints. His
productivity (and hence access to resources) is solely a function of his
investment in human capital. His reasoning is not clouded by race, sex,
age, class, culture, religion, or any other factors evident in his physical
environment. And what is true of 'him' is, by default, true of 'her'.

Jaggar (1983, p. 40) argues that the metaphysical assumption of abstract individualism rationalizes another liberal tenet, that of political solipsism, 'the liberal assumption that human individuals are essentially solitary, with needs and interests that are separate from if not in opposition to those of other individuals'. The importance of this doctrine for othodox economics cannot be underestimated, for it specifies the framework for formulating questions about the allocation of scarce resources. Given political solipsism, we cannot ask why altruistic, cooperating groups might degenerate into selfish, competitive individuals. Instead, we must ask under what conditions selfish, competitive individuals will interact and form contracts with one another, and what the outcomes of those interactions will be. This is illustrated most clearly with the neoclassical New Home Economics, which seeks to explain why solitary economic agents form families, share resources and have children (see Becker 1973, 1981). Political solipsism blinds these theorists to the fact that as infants we are born dependent on others with needs and interests that are inseparable from others. The question of how we turn that essentially social existence into a solitary and competitive one is a question political solipsism does not allow.

Abstract individualism and normative dualism also rationalize political scepticism, the ability (or more accurately, the inability) of society to establish political institutions that can promote human welfare. As liberal political philosophers argued, since each individual has different preferences and different ideas about achieving desired ends, government intervention in human affairs – which necessitates choosing one end over another – is, by definition, inequitable and hence unjustifiable. Thus, the best society is one where each individual has the freedom to decide for him- or herself (using prudential reason) what is preferable.

In its purest form, constructive dissent accepts all these beliefs; seditious dissent, in its purest form, does not. Yet, the dissent voiced by economists is rarely pure. Instead, many who dissent embrace some liberal tenets but reject others – a point that will be made clearer by our focus on Barbara Bergmann.

The next section discusses Bergmann's critique of neoclassical methodology, and introduces her alternative method. We then describe Bergmann's work as a feminist economist, her dissent from the neoclassical paradigm, and her alternative view of the labour market. The final section concludes by arguing that Bergmann's dissent, while not purely seditious, is a close kin.

BERGMANN'S METHODOLOGY

> If we are talking about understanding the real world, the subject matter of economics is a lot closer to anthropology than to mathematics. That fact should inform our methodological practice. (Bergmann 1987b, p. 194).

For Bergmann, the purpose of economics is to gain useful knowledge about how the economy actually works. The key word here is 'useful'. Economic knowledge *must* be useful, and it becomes useful only when it enables us to accurately predict economic phenomena and derive solutions to real economic problems. In this regard, Bergmann sounds strikingly like the neoclassical economist Milton Friedman (1953, p. 3), who writes: 'The ultimate goal of a positive science is the development of a "theory" or "hypothesis" that yields valid and meaningful (i.e., not truistic) predictions about phenomena not yet observed'. However, for Bergmann, most theories and hypotheses generated by neoclassical economists do not yield useful knowledge. In other words, they do not yield 'valid and meaningful   predictions about phenomena not yet observed'.

To illustrate this point Bergmann directs us to several studies of capital investment published in Fromm (1971). Each study addressed the same question: the impact of tax incentives on investment behaviour. Bergmann quotes from one of the discussants:

> The four analyses presented in this book are all marked by high quality. Each applies sophisticated econometric tools to the empirical and theoretical analysis of an important problem; each does so in a professional and convincing manner; each sheds light where before there was darkness. *If it were not for the inconvenient fact that the four analyses happen to concern the same problem and happen to contradict each other's findings, there would be little to discuss.* (Bergmann 1974d, p. 18; emphasis added)

Bergmann claims that such contradictory findings are far too common in economics. Furthermore, she argues, this problem will never be resolved as long as economists continue to practise the 'methodology of musing'.

Neoclassical economists' methodology of musing derives directly from the paradigm's metaphysical core. It is a methodology emphasizing the human ability to reason and adheres closely to the concept of normative dualism. Knowledge derived from introspection is judged as best and rewarded accordingly. Knowledge gained from direct contact with the physical world carries less prestige. Indeed, in the search for economic knowledge direct contact with the physical world is seen as unnecessary, if not misleading.

As Bergmann describes it, neoclassical economists begin with a basic set of 'factual crumbs' derived from casual observation – more income is preferred to less, lower prices generate greater demand, and so on. Then, like mathematicians, they generate knowledge by 'just sitting in [their] offices and thinking' (1989b, p. 31). As a consequence, they become preoccupied with the 'adding up' process – first, the way in which individual 'decisions, actions and interactions ... "add up," ... to prices and production levels of particular commodities, [and] wages rates for particular types of labor in particular labor markets'; and second, the way in which the outcomes from individual markets, "add up" to more global aggregates such as unemployment rates, GDP, and the wholesale price index' (1974d, p. 19). These are the parts of economic analysis that allow economists to sit in their offices and muse; the parts that allow them to show off their quantitative skills. (As Bergmann so colourfully puts it, these are the parts that in the minds of neoclassical economists separate 'the sheep from the goats'.)

One might think that neoclassical economists would be interested in arriving at a better understanding of the processes forming the basis of their analysis. But this would require economists to gather information about how individuals actually arrive at their decisions. Neoclassical economists shun this 'less glamorous assignment' because it requires direct contact with the physical world. Instead, they make up ostensibly feasible assumptions about economic decision-making and then muse about the logical results. For example, when the New Classical economists introduced the notion of rational expectations into the discussion of economic decision-making, they made no effort to understand how expectations are formed (Bergmann 1989b). Nor did they make any effort to determine the accuracy of economic agents' forecasts of the future. Mainstream theorists (whose own economic forecasts are known for their fallibility) simply assumed that, on average, rational economic agents would not repeatedly make erroneous forecasts.

For Bergmann, this example represents the fundamental problem with the methodology of musing:

> I believe one of the habits of mind which is inhibiting the formation of useful economic knowledge is the unwillingness and inability of economists to collect for themselves information about behavior which should be of professional interest to them – the behavior of men and women when they act as economic agents. (Bergmann 1974d, p. 18).

Instead, the methodology of musing allows economists to make any assumptions about human behaviour and decision-making that are necessary to build their increasingly mathematical economic models. Consequently, they offer a variety of possible explanations for economic phenomena and a variety of predictions, as occurred in the previously mentioned studies of tax incentives on investment behaviour.

If mainstream economists had an incontrovertible method for choosing the best model they might be able to get around this problem. But the methodology of musing does not allow for such an evaluative tool. Given the way neoclassical economists generate theoretical knowledge, they see no need to evaluate their assumptions by confronting them with actual cases. Rather, they prefer to evaluate the results derived from the adding-up process – results which can be subjected to classical hypothesis testing. Success then becomes synonymous with statistical significance.

Economists know that, all else equal, the likelihood of obtaining statistically significant results increases with the number of observations. Because the time and money needed to collect sufficient data are enough to dissuade economists from gathering it on their own, they use data that others have compiled for different purposes in order to test their regression models. If the results are statistically significant, the predictions are judged to be valid. But, the second-hand data that we gather are never exactly what we want. Consequently, our models are circumscribed by data availability, and the construction of a well-specified and unbiased model is always in question. Furthermore, in testing hypotheses one never runs just one regression. We try various specifications by adding and deleting variables and by changing the functional form, and only report those that most closely fit our hypothesized results (that is, the ones that come from our musings). And if, despite our best creative efforts, we do not get the desired empirical results, we bemoan the fact that the data did not meet our needs or put together what Karl Popper contemptuously referred to as a set of 'ad-hoc auxiliary assumptions' or 'immunizing stratagems' (cited in Blaug 1980, p. 18), which are never directly tested.

As a case in point, Bergmann describes the reaction of neoclassical theorists whose best efforts to account for sex-based wage differentials in terms of human capital accumulation fall short of the mark.

> Those unhappy with the unanimous verdict of the regression studies ... pin their hopes on getting more and better information about workers. If only the right variables could be added to the equation, the full extent of women's lower quality as employees relative to men would be revealed, and the measured sex effect on wages reduced to insignificant levels, they say. ... Gary S. Becker (1985) ... now thinks (wage differentials are) mostly due to differences in the amount of housework men and women workers do. Men spend their off-the-job hours in rest and recreation ... Becker says that men come to the job with more energy, and that explains their higher pay. ... Becker's idea is no more than a conjecture; he presents no evidence at all that women are less energetic in their work than men. (Bergmann 1989a, pp. 45, 48)

Instead of musing about the causes of wage differentials Bergmann (1974d, p. 23) exhorts us to discover how 'things work in the real world', to ask pointed questions about the behaviour of economic agents, and to actually observe. Once we have our first-hand knowledge of how the economy works we then need to develop a non-fictional account of actual behaviour. This account can then be used as the building block for our theories. In this way, we can reduce the preponderance of contradictory results and generate useful knowledge. For without direct observation, there is no way to prove that one person's musing is any better than another's and, given the way we evaluate our musings, no way to prove whose predictions are best. Furthermore, Bergmann argues, direct observation will force us to change how we add up. We shall be compelled to move away from simple cause-and-effect model designs, and to others that take into account the interactions of individuals as they make decisions that impact on one another.

Bergmann suggests four avenues that should be more fully explored: experimental economics, participant observation, survey research and computer simulation. The first three methods involve discovering how the world really works. The last, computer simulation, is an adding-up methodology that allows the researcher to model the interactions of economic agents based upon what is learned (through experiment, observation or survey) about the way economic agents actually behave.

To illustrate how the experimental research method can be used in economics we turn to an experiment Bergmann (1988) designed to determine how people form expectations of the future. She first created several computer-generated time series, which varied systematically according to preordained characteristics such as the number of turning-points, the direction of the last segment in the series, and the distance from the last turning-point in the series. The time series charts were then distributed to a group of students, who were asked to predict the future direction of the time series by choosing among five different trend lines. The experimental results revealed that students' predictions were upwardly biased. In addition, respondents' ability to correctly forecast the future direction of the series proved weak, thereby directly challenging neoclassical assumptions about decision-making.

Bergmann warns us that by making wrong assumptions about human behaviour we not only jeopardize our predictions of economic phenomena, but we may also blind ourselves to other behaviour that has a direct bearing on the operation of the economy. For example, by assuming that expectations are formed rationally we run the risk of overlooking behaviour that attempts to protect us from the uncertainty associated with the future. If this latter behaviour has a direct impact on economic outcomes (and Bergmann believes it does) then it should be of primary interest to economists and incorporated into our models of the economy.

Consistent with her methodological beliefs, Bergmann (1973, 1974a, c) suggests that we make greater use of simulation to model microeconomic behaviour. Simulation, like econometrics, is a tool to analyse an economic system. However, unlike econometrics, where the system is modelled with one or more equations which must be solved simultaneously, simulation proceeds sequentially, just like the actual system (Smith 1968). For example, consider a simple micro-simulation model of the labour market that Bergmann (1990b) constructed for expository purposes. She begins with a market comprising individual workers and employers, each of whom has certain characteristics (for example, employment status, number of job openings). She then models the behaviour of each worker and employer, and their interactions, in a way that mirrors the actual operation of the labour market:

> First, employers decide on the stock of jobs they wish to have filled this week. Some workers will be laid off, others will quit. ... After the separations have occurred, the unemployed ... search for job vacancies; some are chosen at random to come to an interview, and some of these agree to become employed. (Bergmann 1990b, p. 103)

The design is then programmed into the computer with a series of statements and equations, and the system is put in motion by letting the economic agents act. At set intervals, outcomes of the interactions of the market participants are observed and used to calculate the unemployment rate and the average duration of unemployment. Bergmann then introduces unemployment insurance into the model in order to show how a simulation model can provide more insight into the determination of unemployment levels and duration than traditional models.

The accuracy of these simulations depends crucially on how well the mathematical equations describe the behaviour of firms, workers and markets. This is where experimental economics, participant observation and survey research are useful.

Simulation models are to conventional econometric models what induction is to deduction. Economists, like Bergmann, who generalize from numerical results are sometimes subject to the scorn of neoclassical economists who like to remind us about the fallacy of induction. Bergmann is well aware of the shortcomings and drawbacks of simulation models. None the less, she argues that 'treating the simulation methodology itself as entirely taboo cuts out a lot of valuable possibilities for exploration. Economists need more tools in our kits, not fewer' (Bergmann 1990b, p. 102).

BERGMANN'S FEMINISM

While Bergmann has done considerable work with micro-simulation models, she is best known for her work as a feminist economist. Feminist economics is a method of analysis that incorporates both economic and feminist theory into its analytical framework.[2] But just as there is no single theory to which all economists subscribe, there is no single feminist theory to which all feminists adhere. While all feminists seek to uncover the causes and consequences of women's oppression (with the ultimate goal of eradicating that oppression), feminists – like economists – do not all interpret the world in identical fashion (Tong 1989). Consequently, nor do feminist economists.

Bergmann's work as a feminist economist closely corresponds with the branch of liberal feminism known as 'welfare liberalism'. As its name implies, liberal feminism first developed out of the same liberal political tradition which underlies neoclassical economics. Liberal feminists in the late eighteenth and early nineteenth centuries (such as Mary Wollstonecraft, Harriet Taylor Mill and John Stuart Mill) accepted the liberal philosophers' conception of human nature, and their assumptions of abstract individualism, normative dualism, political solipsism and political scepticism. But they did not accept excluding (white) women by custom and by law from the rights and opportunities that this philosophy rationalized for (white) men. Since patriarchalism was rejected in the public sphere, they believed, it should also be rejected in the private sphere. They argued that like men, women had a capacity for rationality and should be afforded the opportunity to develop that capacity and develop fully as persons. Consequently, women merited the same civil rights and educational opportunities as men.

During the second wave of feminism, which began in the 1960s, liberal feminists continued their prior push for political, legal and educational equality. In addition, they placed increasing emphasis on equality of opportunity in the economic sphere. Remaining philosophically committed to abstract individualism, today's classical liberal feminists take the position that equal opportunity requires nothing more (but also nothing less) than removing discriminatory laws and policies that prevent women from competing with men on a level playing field. Equal opportunity requires that the rules of the game be the same for everyone. Once this occurs, if women are still underrepresented in certain jobs, occupations and industries and still earn a fraction of what men make, then so be it.

This is where welfare liberal feminists, like Barbara Bergmann, break with classical liberals. They argue that for women to compete equally with men for jobs and promotions, and for women to be compensated fairly, more will have to be done than providing a level playing field.

For these feminists, the assumption of abstract individualism is replaced by concrete individualism – the notion that our 'emotions, beliefs, abilities, and interests can ... be articulated and understood (only) with ... reference ... to the social context' within which we exist (Tong 1989, p. 36). Thus, an employer attempting to maximize profits (an exercise of prudential reasoning) may none the less deny qualified women access to certain occupations because of a socially-sanctioned belief that women are naturally suited for some occupations but not others. If the way we think and the way we reason is integrally tied to our social context (a rejection of political solipsism), and if that social context is one where women are subordinated to men, then women's equality will require that the social context be changed. This means that government must take a more active role in forcing employers to open occupations to women and pay women fairly (the antithesis of political scepticism). Rejecting the neoclassical model as a way to analyse women's position in the home and the labour market is consistent with that feminism.

BERGMANN'S CRITIQUE OF THE NEOCLASSICAL MODEL

The New Home Economics

We begin with Bergmann's critique of the New Home Economics which came out of the Chicago School in the early 1960s. While Betty Friedan (1974) was interviewing white, suburban housewives and uncovering the angst and unhappiness generated from the 'feminine mystique', Chicago economists were advancing theories of the family to prove (through deductive reasoning) that women's traditional roles in the home were utility maximizing. Applying human capital theory and Becker's (1965) theory of time allocation to the study of marriage, fertility decisions and the division of labour in the home, Chicago economists provided the world with an economic defence of the traditional, Victorian family.

According to the New Home Economics, wives have a comparative advantage in home production while husbands have a comparative advantage in market production.[3] The efficient allocation of resources (in this case time and human capital) requires that each specialize in those tasks in which they have a comparative advantage and then trade.

Bergmann attacks the New Home Economics for using circular reasoning to justify the traditional division of labour. The comparative advantage argument takes men's greater earning power as given. Yet, in explaining why women earn comparatively less, advocates of the New

Home Economics argue that women do not invest as much as men in human capital. And the reason women do not invest as much in human capital is because they expect to take major responsibility for production in the home. Thus, women's responsibilities in the home result from their low wages; and women's low wages result from their work in the home.

Bergmann does not disagree that women have traditionally held a comparative advantage in home production. She does, however, disagree with the New Home Economics about the causes and consequences of this. For Bergmann, women's comparative advantage in the home is due to socialization, their accommodation to the status quo, and discrimination in the market and in educational institutions (note the influence of welfare liberal feminism). Eliminating discrimination will go a long way towards abolishing women's comparative disadvantage in the market. Eliminating discrimination will also go a long way towards eliminating its consequences: 'Women's economic specialization has been a source of limitation, boredom, deprivation for many of them and of powerlessness for virtually all of them' (Bergmann 1986, p. 7).

In the New Home Economics, however, unhappiness among family members cannot exist as long as there is at least one altruist among them. An altruist (assumed to be the husband) is one whose utility depends positively on the well-being of another member of the family (the wife) and whose behaviour is changed by his altruism. An altruistic husband can consume less family income and still maintain the same level of utility if his lower consumption results in more consumption opportunities for his wife. Using indifference curve analysis, Becker shows that if another family member chooses to act selfishly (for instance, a wife who takes a job that somehow reduces her husband's and thus her family's income) then not only will her altruistic husband be worse off, but so will she. A rational economic agent will not undertake such selfish behaviour, thus the happiness of all family members is assured.

Bergmann considers this story of family life preposterous because of the way an altruistic husband is defined and because the conclusion does not fit the facts. Suppose that the altruistic husband specializes in market production while his wife completely specializes in home production. According to the New Home Economics, he is an altruist if he shares some of his income with his wife, no matter how trivial the amount. He could spend every payday at the corner tavern and stumble home with only a fraction of his original earnings; but as long as he brings some money home to his wife he is, according to Becker, an altruist. And since he is an altruist no one in the family will behave to reduce family happiness. Yet, Bergmann reminds us, we know alcoholism destroys families and is a significant problem in the US and other countries. We also know that physical and sexual abuse, drug addiction, adultery and troublesome children are problems too prevalent to be dismissed as mere exceptions to the norm.

Consistent with her methodological beliefs, Bergmann argues that economic knowledge *in order to be useful* must explain this behaviour and provide solutions to the problems that result. The New Home Economics does neither. Like neoclassical theory, it is built on factual crumbs (for example, individuals will marry if they expect to be happier than they would being single) and simplifying assumptions. Elaborate models are constructed using the methodology of musing and then preposterous conclusions are drawn out.[4]

The Neoclassical Theory of Discrimination

We noted above that Bergmann regarded discrimination as one reason for women's comparative advantage in the home. For neoclassical economists, however, discrimination cannot persist in a competitive market economy. This conclusion (another preposterous one according to Bergmann) is drawn from Becker (1957), who shows that discrimination is incompatible with profit maximization. Competition will drive any firm that discriminates out of business. But as Bergmann (1989a, p. 50) points out:

> The applicability of (Becker's) theory to a real situation (as opposed to its validity as a piece of deductive logic) depends on three assumptions that may or may not be true in any particular time or place: (1) that there are large numbers of people who are willing and able to openly violate social customs, which they themselves support and enjoy, for purposes of making money, (2) that violating customs does not entail costs that cancel out the advantage of cheap wages, and (3) that competition is intense enough to put out of business those who refrain from violating customs.

Once again, Bergmann challenges neoclassical theory by considering the real as opposed to the abstract. She asks us to consider the multitude of court cases and EEOC (Equal Employment Opportunity Commission) complaints received annually which reflect just a fraction of the employers who are unwilling or unable to violate social customs. And competition among firms does not seem to drive discriminating employers out of business. Case study after case study suggests just the opposite. From Chase Manhattan Bank to Hertz Rental Car Agency to Pizza Hut, economically successful firms have been shown in court to discriminate against women. On the other hand, 'no one has ever reported seeing a firm that discriminated reduced to ruin by a less bigoted competitor' (Bergmann 1986, p. 139).

Bergmann does not claim that discrimination is the only cause of women's second-class status in the labour market. She recognises that some women accept traditional roles and do not invest much in education or training. Some drop out of the labour force to have children, and are unwilling to devote themselves to their careers. However, Bergmann warns us not to think that discrimination is minimal because it may not be the only cause of lower female wages. In fact, discrimination and accommodation are mutually reinforcing. Employers discriminate against women by segregating them into low-paying female-dominated jobs. This makes women economically dependent on the men in their lives and provides an economic incentive for accommodating to tradition. Those women who accommodate to tradition avoid jobs that stray too far from their assigned domestic roles and drop out of the labour force when they have children. These behaviours reinforce employer stereotypes and lead them to evaluate each woman as a member of a well-defined group rather than evaluating each woman independently on her merits (as they do men). Thus employers track the women they hire into low-paying dead-end jobs, and generate their own self-fulfilling prophecy.

Human Capital Theory

Despite much evidence to the contrary, neoclassical economists remain committed to the argument that discrimination cannot persist in a market economy. Occupational segregation and low pay (the two most commonly discussed consequences of discrimination) are seen to result from women's own rational decisions. The fact that women, on average, make fewer human capital investments than men, and are more likely to exhibit detrimental labour market behaviour (more labour force intermittency, unwillingness to take jobs that require a great deal of travel or long hours of work, and so on), has been taken by neoclassical economists as the sole cause of women's low pay and occupational segregation.

Bergmann (1986, p. 74) agrees that *some* differences in earnings between women and men can be accounted for by differences in human capital. But study after study finds that while human capital differences can account for some, they cannot account for all of the wage differences between women and men. Part of the problem, of course, is that empirical models fail to include all of the human capital factors affecting wages. Consequently, neoclassical economists are correct in claiming that the omission of variables such as college major and attitude towards work may lead us to underestimate the amount of the wage gap that can be accounted for. However, as Bergmann points out there is another set of variables omitted from the equations: 'Data demonstrating men's greater tendency to alcohol abuse, drug abuse, smoking, bad driving, resort to violence, criminal records, bankruptcies, back problems, [and] history of heart attacks' (Bergmann 1989a, p. 45). The omission of these variables may well lead to an underestimate of that portion of the wage gap attributable to discrimination.

Bergmann also cautions that discrimination against women may be underestimated because women and men may receive different rewards and suffer different penalties for the same choices. For example, if females get penalized more than males for labour force intermittency, then differential rates of intermittency do not, in and of themselves, tell the whole story. Rather, part of the problem lies with the differential and discriminatory way women are treated.

Finally, Bergmann points to the fact that human capital factors themselves, such as on-the-job training and seniority, can be affected by market discrimination. For example, we know that quit rates are negatively correlated with wages. If women receive low wages due to discrimination, then (all else equal) they will have higher quit rates than men. It begs the question to explain women's low wages by pointing out that higher quit rates among women result in less on-the-job training and lower seniority levels, which then result in lower wages. The question we should ask is why women have higher quit rates in the first place. Neoclassical economists do not ask this question because the answer requires them to resort once again to circular reasoning.

Throughout her critique of the neoclassical paradigm, Bergmann repeatedly asks us to look at the empirical evidence from a variety of angles before we accept the claims of any economist; and she warns us to avoid the all-or-nothing conclusions that neoclassical economists find so attractive. In some ways, her critique can be described as institutionalist. Yet, while Bergmann (1974d, p. 23) shares the institutionalist concern for facts, she is critical of their 'downgrading of economic theory':

> While observation is a necessary condition for the success of our science, the part of economics I have referred to as the 'adding up' – the analysis of how the actions and interactions of the decision-making units combine into the macro-result – is as necessary as observation of the facts about decision-making. We cannot wait until 'we have studied the data' to begin work on building our understanding of the 'adding up' process.

Thus, we turn now to Bergmann's adding-up process in the labour market. It is a view that clearly illustrates her rejection of the normative dualism, abstract individualism, political solipsism and political scepticism inherent in neoclassical economics. In rejecting the neoclassical model, which 'takes no account at all of the psychological and social aspects of economic relations', Bergmann (1989c, p. 67) aligns herself with those feminists and economists who argue that our moral and prudential reasoning cannot be separated from the social, cultural and economic environments within which we develop.

BERGMANN'S ANALYSIS OF THE LABOUR MARKET

Labour markets have two main functions – they set wages and other terms of employment, and they allocate labour among occupations, jobs and employers. According to Bergmann (1987b), these functions are carried out primarily through the workings of supply and demand as each is affected by the social relations among people of different races and sex.

Within the individual firm, productivity (and hence profitability) is crucially related to the social relations among workers. When the social relations of production are harmonious, employees work cooperatively with one another and we get higher productivity. When social relations are hostile, resentment of others may result in communication breakdowns, substandard on-the-job training of new employees by more experienced ones, sexual harassment and possibly even sabotage. An employer can increase the likelihood of harmonious social relations by structuring production in such a way that the social arrangements reflect those that exist in society at large. If societal norms give white men higher status than women and people of colour, then productivity concerns will dictate a similar set of social relations in the workplace. As such, the employer has an economic incentive to practice discrimination in the form of occupational segregation. 'Employers who may want to hire blacks and women because of their cheapness may find it easier to do if they carve out for them territory which is least desirable for white males. Thus, employers may purposely structure jobs that are dull, dirty, dangerous, and dead-end so as to have jobs that white males do not covet and do not make trouble over' (Bergmann and Darity 1981, p. 161).

Such behaviour on the part of individual employers 'adds-up' to occupational segregation in the labour market as a whole and partly accounts for the low wages received by women workers. Although wages are primarily determined by supply and demand, this does not mean that those wages are fair or efficient.

Discrimination keeps the men's and women's labor markets separate from each other. The exclusion of women from a big share of all the jobs in the economy is what creates two labor markets where there should be only one. The discriminatory assignment of jobs, to one sex or the other is what sets the level of demand in each market. So the fact that supply and demand affect wages does not prove that wages are fair, or even economically sensible. (Bergmann 1986, p. 126)

The demand for labour by firms is, of course, inversely related to the wage that must be paid. The level of demand is also related to estimates of how workers in those jobs will contribute to the firm's total product. Demand can be reduced, that is, a firm will be willing to pay less for any given number of workers, if the firm restructures jobs such that they require little human capital. The demand curve for labour in these occupations will 'lie below' the demand for labour in other occupations.

Adding up the demand for labour by all firms results in a market demand for labour. If there were no occupational segregation, both female and male workers would face this single market demand curve. But since occupational segregation does exist, we have a demand for women's labour and a demand for men's labour. Given that the occupations open to women require less human capital and are thus less productive than many occupations open to men, the demand for women's labour will lie below the demand for men's labour.[5]

Occupational segregation also affects the supply of labour. When employers demand only women for certain occupations and only men for others, this effectively splits the labour supply into separate markets. Although there may be fewer women than men supplying labour, the crowding of women into a limited number of occupations will cause their supply to be higher relative to the demand for their labour. Consequently, their wages will be less.

> The employer who looks to the market for the wage scales to apply to the predominantly male and female occupations within his or her own establishment is looking at and adopting within that establishment the result of almost universally discriminatory behaviour on the part of fellow employers. (Bergmann, 1990a, 71)

We cannot, therefore, conclude that these wages are just or fair.

Even in seemingly integrated occupations, evidence shows that jobs in these occupations are segregated by employers, and women generally earn less. For example, one firm might hire men for purposes of accounting and bookkeeping while another might hire women. The firm that employs men hires them from the male labour market, where wages are higher. The firm that employs women hires them from the female labour market where wages are lower. Consequently, the wages of male accountants and bookkeepers are higher than their female counterparts whose jobs (although not occupations) are segregated by sex. This situation occurs frequently and, according to Bergmann, accounts for more of the sex differential in wages *within occupations* than differences in human capital accumulation.

Finally, Bergmann also notes that the causality just described, where occupational segregation leads to wage differentials between women and men, may also flow in the opposite direction. Since employers are sensitive to the social relations of production, they may desire to make certain that the men in their establishments are more highly paid than the women. The easiest way to maintain that pay differential, and hence avoid disrupting the social relations of production, is to place women and men in different jobs.

The strategies Bergmann prescribes for improving women's status in the labour market are grounded in her economics and her feminism. She believes that government involvement in the economy can improve societal well-being and consequently should be used to do so. Two of the most controversial strategies she advocates are affirmative action and pay equity (Bergmann 1987c, 1989a and 1996).[6] In defence of affirmative action, Bergmann points out that

> the arguments against affirmative action are that such plans unfairly exclude the more qualified, and that they harm the intended beneficiaries more than they help them. These complaints are largely based on the unstated assumption that discrimination is absent. Given that current hiring and promotion practices are by no means fair in many cases the alternative to affirmative action is not perfect fairness, but an automatic and unfair preference for the type of person for whom the job was traditionally earmarked. If there is discrimination and no affirmative action, the candidates excluded for reasons of race or sex may be as well qualified or more so than those hired. (Bergmann 1989a, p. 53)

While Bergmann argues that affirmative action, if pursued aggressively and successfully, will eventually increase wages for all women, she none the less recognizes that from a practical standpoint this may be a long time in coming. Consequently, many women, especially those in female-dominated jobs and occupations, will continue to be one pay packet away from poverty. To help eliminate poverty among women, Bergmann advocates the strategy of pay equity directed at employers who pay lower wages to workers in female-dominated jobs than they do to those in comparably valued male-dominated jobs.

As a welfare liberal feminist, Bergmann believes strongly that for women to be liberated, all women need to enter the workforce. These views are consistent with those espoused by Betty Friedan (1974). But while Friedan moderated her views, and later argued that it was not necessary for women to leave the home in order to be liberated (only that they have the choice to do so), Bergmann has not wavered in her views. She believes, quite strongly that women who stay home to take care of husband, house and kids hurt the movement towards women's equality. It is this view that has shaped her policy positions on welfare reform (Bergmann 1987a, Bergmann and Hartmann 1995).

CONCLUSION

Barbara Bergmann does not reject all of what neoclassical economics has to offer. She takes from the neoclassical tool kit what is useful; and she discards what is not (that is, that which blatantly contradicts what we know to be true).

Her analysis of the labour market attempts to develop a theory that will generate useful knowledge. She is not attempting to devise a theory deduced from a set of metaphysical beliefs and factual crumbs. In fact, the theory that she does develop leads her to reject many of the metaphysical beliefs held by neoclassical economists, in particular beliefs in normative dualism, abstract individualism, political solipsism and political scepticism.

For this reason, Bergmann falls closer to the seditious end of the spectrum of dissent than to the constructive end. Her dissent can, in many ways, be likened to that of John Maynard Keynes. Like Keynes, Bergmann has proven herself to be a practical, common-sense economist concerned with developing useful economic knowledge that enables us to predict economic phenomena accurately and derive solutions to everyday economic problems.

NOTES

1. It is important to note that Locke and Rousseau's rejection of patriarchalism was limited to the public sphere and applied only to the relations among white men (Butler 1995). In the third section of this chapter we will see that this limited applicability of early liberal thought gave rise to the liberal feminism of the 1800s, the fundamental roots of which influence the thinking of some feminist economists today – Barbara Bergmann among them.
2. Some feminist economists also incorporate theoretical developments in other fields such as psychology, sociology and anthropology.
3. Becker (1981) points to women's unique capacity to bear children and men's higher market wages as evidence of this fact.
4. For Bergmann, one of the most notorious conclusions is from Becker's theory of marriage (1973) where he states: 'laws that prevent men from taking more than one wife no more benefit women than the laws in South Africa that restrict the ratio of black to white workers benefit blacks' (Becker 1973, pp. 334–5). Yet as Bergmann points out, 'We know that the proposition is false because in societies that allow polygamy, women tend to have abysmal status ... something is going on here that is not captured by supply and demand curves' (1995, p. 145).
5. It should also be pointed out that demand is also affected by how employers perceive the value of the jobs to the firm. Evidence suggests that jobs held by women and minorities are perceived to have lower value just because of who is holding them.
6. Bergmann advocates other market-based strategies to level the playing field for women. These strategies include legislative initiatives for ending discrimination against part-time workers and for eradicating sexual harassment from the workplace. She also advocates a 'publicly funded, high-quality child-care system that would be available without cost to single parents' and a reduction in the standard work day (Bergmann and Hartmann 1995).

REFERENCES

Becker, G.S. (1957), *The Economics of Discrimination*, Chicago: University of Chicago Press.
Becker, G.S. (1965), 'A theory of the allocation of time', *Economic Journal*, **75** (299), September, 493–517.
Becker, G.S. (1973), 'A theory of marriage', in T.W. Schultz (ed.), *Economics of the Family: Marriage, Children, and Human Capital*, Chicago: University of Chicago Press, pp. 299–344.
Becker, G.S. (1981), *A Treatise on the Family*, Cambridge, MA: Harvard University Press.
Becker, G.S. (1985), 'Human capital, effort, and the sexual division of labor', *Journal of Labor Economics*, **3**, January, S33–S58.
Bergmann, B. (1973), 'Combining microsimulation and regression: a "prepared" regression of poverty incidence on unemployment and growth', *Econometrica*, **41** (5), September, 955–63.
Bergmann, B. (1974a), 'Empirical work on the labor market: is there any alternative to regression running?', Paper and Proceedings of the Industrial Relations Research Association, 27th annual Winter Meeting, 243–51.
Bergmann, B. (1974b), 'Occupational segregation, wages and profits when employers discriminate by race or sex', *Eastern Economic Journal*, **1** (1–2), April–July, 103–110.
Bergmann, B. (1974c), 'A microsimulation of the macroeconomy with explicitly represented money flows', *Annals of Economic and Social Measurement*, **3** (3), 475–89.
Bergmann, B. (1974d), 'Have economists failed?', *Eastern Economic Journal*, **1** (4), October, 16–24.
Bergmann, B. (1986), *The Economic Emergence of Women*, New York: Basic Books.
Bergmann, B. (1987a), 'A fresh start on welfare reform', *Challenge*, **30** (5), November/December, 44–50.
Bergmann, B. (1987b), '"Measurement" or finding things out in economics', *Journal of Economic Education*, **18** (2), Spring, 191–201.
Bergmann, B. (1987c), 'Pay equity – surprising answers to hard questions', *Challenge*, **30** (2), May/June, 45–51.
Bergmann, B. (1988), 'An experiment on the formation of expectations', *Journal of Economic Behaviour and Organization*, **9**, 137–51.
Bergmann, B. (1989a), 'Does the market for women's labor need fixing?', *Journal of Economic Perspectives*, **3** (1), Winter, 43–60.
Bergmann, B. (1989b), 'Why do most economists know so little about the economy?', in S. Bowles, R. Edwards and W.G. Shepherd (eds) *Unconventional Wisdom: Essays on Economics in Honor of John Kenneth Galbraith*, Boston: Houghton Mifflin, pp. 29–37.
Bergmann, B. (1989c), 'What the common economic arguments against comparable worth are worth', *Journal of Social Issues*, **45** (4), 67–80.
Bergmann, B. (1990a), 'Feminism and economics', *Women's Studies Quarterly*, **18** (3/4), Fall/Winter, 68–74.
Bergmann, B. (1990b), 'Micro-to-macro simulation: a primer with a labor market example', *Journal of Economic Perspectives*, **4** (1), Winter, 99–116.
Bergmann, B. (1994), 'Curing child poverty in the United States', *American Economic Review*, **84** (2), May, 76–80.

Bergmann, B. (1995), 'Becker's theory of the family: preposterous conclusions', *Feminist Economics*, **1** (1), Spring, 141–50.

Bergmann, B. (1996), *In Defense of Affirmative Action*, New York: Basic Books.

Bergmann, B. and W. Darity, Jr. (1981), 'Social relations in the workplace and employer discrimination', *Papers and Proceedings of the Industrial Relations Research Association*, pp. 155–62.

Bergmann, B. and H.I. Hartmann (1995) 'A program to help working parents', *The Nation*, 1 May, 592–95.

Blaug, M. (1980), *The Methodology of Economics*, Cambridge: Cambridge University Press.

Butler, M.A. (1995), 'Early liberal roots of feminism: John Locke and the attack on patriarchy', in N. Tuana and R. Tong (eds), *Feminism and Philosophy,* Boulder: Westview Press, pp. 27–47.

Friedan, B. (1974), *The Feminine Mystique*, New York: Dell.

Friedman, M. (1953), 'The methodology of positive economics', in *Essays in Positive Economics*, Chicago: University of Chicago Press, pp. 3–43.

Fromm, G. (ed.) (1971), *Tax Incentives and Capital Spending*, Washington: Brookings Institution.

Jaggar, A.M. (1983), *Feminist Politics and Human Nature*, Totowa, New Jersey: Rowman & Allanheld.

Smith, J. (1968), *Computer Simulation Models*, New York: Hafner Publishing Company.

Tong, R. (1989), *Feminist Thought: A Comprehensive Introduction*, Boulder: Westview Press.

Woolley, F. (1993), 'The Feminist Challenge to Neoclassical Economics', *Cambridge Journal of Economics*, **17** (4), 485–500.

2. James M. Buchanan and the rebirth of political economy

Peter J. Boettke*

> If not an economist, what am I? An outdated freak whose functional role in the general scheme of things has passed into history? Perhaps I should accept such an assessment, retire gracefully, and, with alcoholic breath, hoe my cabbages. Perhaps I could do so if the modern technicians had indeed produced 'better' economic mousetraps. Instead of evidence of progress, however, I see a continuing erosion of the intellectual (and social) capital that was accumulated by 'political economy' in its finest hours. James Buchanan (1979, p. 279)

INTRODUCTION

It is somewhat odd to consider anyone who has received the Nobel Prize to be an outsider. Outsider status is usually reserved for those who toil in obscurity. Buchanan attended the University of Chicago, taught at the University of Virginia, published articles in the *American Economic Review* and *Journal of Political Economy,* was named Distinguished Fellow of the American Economic Association, and received National Science Foundation as well as private foundation grants to develop public choice economics. His former students have taught at some of the finest institutions of higher learning (Cornell, Penn, Cal Tech and the University of Virginia) and have held high public office (Director of the Federal Trade Commission, Director of the Office of Management and Budget and Under Secretary of the Treasury). Why should such a well-connected character be included in a volume about dissenters?

Brave individuals who buck the intellectual trends of their time (usually at great professional cost) to pursue truth grace these pages, not those who have garnered so many rewards. But Buchanan's career, like some crucial aspects of his thought itself, is at tension with itself. True, he taught at the University of Virginia, but he left there because of internal university political troubles and has taught at lesser-known schools for the past thirty or so years.[1] The public choice revolution began at the

University of Virginia in the 1960s; but it was at Virginia Tech in the 1970s that the revolution took hold and at George Mason University in the 1980s that victory was achieved on several theoretical fronts in public economics. Buchanan has spent a good part of his career as an insider who thought like an outsider, and as an outsider who possessed an insider's claim on the professional establishment. As he has argued, he never would have received the Nobel Prize if the committee consisted of *American* economists, for his work was by far appreciated more in Europe than at home in the US research community.

Buchanan is not the only Nobel Laureate to suffer this fate; Friedrich Hayek, Gunnar Myrdal, Herbert Simon, Ronald Coase and Douglass North were all awarded the prize despite rejecting the conventional economic wisdom in terms of methodology, politics and field of study. Buchanan, however, was special in one sense – he took great pride in his Southern heritage and the intellectual challenge he represented to the mainstream economic profession. As he himself put it:

> how many farm boys from Middle Tennessee, educated in tiny, poor, and rural public schools and at a struggling state-financed teachers college, have received the Nobel Prize? How many scholars who have worked almost exclusively at southern universities have done so, in any scientific discipline? How many of my economist peers who are laureates have eschewed the use of both formal mathematical techniques and the extended resort to empirical testing? (Buchanan 1992, p. 164)

Buchanan has made original contributions to methodology, social philosophy and public policy economics, as well as the discipline of political science. I shall limit my discussion to three areas that define him as a major dissenter from the mainstream of professional opinion in economics. First, Buchanan burst the romantic vision of politics that dominated political science, and the economic treatment of market failure and public economics in general, during the 1950s to 1970s. Second, Buchanan challenged the formalism of modern economics with a restated, consistent subjectivism. Finally, Buchanan reintroduced economics to its sister discipline of moral philosophy and laid the foundation for a modern political economy.

DEFINING DISSENT

The *Oxford English Dictionary* defines secular dissent as disagreement with a proposal or resolution; the opposite of consent. The meaning here is best understood within the context of political discourse. But, science is not politics. In politics, the goal is to reach consensus; in science the idea is to get at truth (however imperfectly we strive to attain that goal). Hence, the religious meaning of dissent might be more appropriate for economics.

The idea of modern economics as a secular religion has been explored both as satire and serious scholarship. Leijonhufvud (1981, p. 359) exposes the rituals and the social structure of the economics profession in a satirical fashion to make the serious point that 'Among the younger generations, it is now rare to find an individual with any conception of the history of the Econ. Having lost their past, the Econ are without confidence in the present and without purpose and direction for the future'. On the other hand, Robert Nelson (1991, p.2) documents how economics became the theology of the modern age. Eliminating evil is no longer the divine prerogative; ensuring economic progress *is* because our modern secular religion teaches that 'If all important material needs could be fully satisfied ... the main cause of past wars, hatreds, and other banes of human history would be ended. There would be far less basis for envy, jealousy, and other sources of evil thoughts and actions'.

If Leijonhufvud and Nelson are even partially correct, then perhaps looking at economics as a religious community within the institutions of higher education and protected by the social structure and norms of the profession would be a useful starting-point from which to deal with the question of dissent. Within this religious community, how are nonconformists dealt with? Daniel Defoe's pamphlet 'Shortest way with the dissenters' (an exercise in the literary hoax) recommended that dissenters either be put to death or exiled. The guardians of the consensus praised Defoe's analysis of the situation. Once it was revealed that the author himself was a dissenter, these guardians were so upset that their bigotry was exposed that Defoe was put in the pillory. While the high priests of modern economics do not champion such extreme measures, exile from the profession is not uncommon. Nonconformity within a certain range of questions is common in modern economics, but the range has a narrow width, as does the possible set of answers. McCloskey (1995, p.14) has succinctly made this point:

> the typical, and narrow, American Department of Economics these days, ranges all the way from M to N. If one stands too close to such a range one can become convinced that it is 'wide'. But it does not stretch to Israel Kirzner or Barbara Bergmann or Jim Buchanan or Tom Weisskopf.

A dissenter in economics is thus one who resists the dominant economic religion. They can do this by (1) eschewing mathematical modelling and econometric testing, and thus the basic *language* and *toolkit* of contemporary scientific economics; (2) articulating a philosophical case against modern economics; and (3) rejecting the professional strictures against normative theorizing and see policy relevance as a virtue. Any one of these positions would constitute a dissent from the current orthodoxy; holding all three is surely grounds for expulsion. It is all three, however, which characterize the work of James Buchanan.

The sociological question of why some ideas 'stick' and others do not is particularly relevant for this discussion. An effective dissenter has to be Kuhn's (1959) 'divergent thinker' – one firmly rooted in the contemporary scientific tradition who has adopted a 'convergent thinking' approach to science. Thus, the successful scientist displays the characteristics of a traditionalist and an iconoclast simultaneously.[2] This 'essential tension' between convergent and divergent thinking is a striking characteristic of Buchanan, and it explains the paradox concerning his professional status. Because Buchanan was grounded in the conformity of neoclassicism, his dissent struck a cord in part of the profession and generated a paradigmatic shift in the way public economics was done.

AN OVERVIEW OF BUCHANAN'S CONTRIBUTION

Buchanan's personal biography can be found in his entertaining *Better Than Plowing* (1992). Born in rural Tennessee, educated at the local public school and then the local college, Middle Tennessee State Teachers' College (where he paid for his college fees and books by milking dairy cows), a year of graduate study in economics at the University of Tennessee (where he learned little economics, but much about life), Naval duty during World War II, and then (with the aid of the GI subsidy) a PhD in economics from the University of Chicago. A libertarian socialist on his arrival at Chicago, Buchanan was 'converted' to classical liberalism after six weeks of price theory with Frank Knight. Libertarian values remained, but Buchanan now understood that the market (not government) was the more consistent with those values. Also at Chicago, Buchanan discovered Knut Wicksell's principle of just taxation. The final intellectual influence was the Italian tradition of public finance that Buchanan was exposed to during a Fulbright Fellowship year. This tradition emphasized real as opposed to ideal politics.

From Knight, Buchanan got his theoretical framework, and the idea that economics is not a science. From Wicksell, Buchanan learned that politics must be understood in an exchange framework. Efficiency in the public sector could be guaranteed only under a rule of unanimity for collective choices. From the Italians, Buchanan learned that public finance must postulate a theory of the state, and that it would be best to reject utilitarianism and Hegelian idealism in postulating such a theory. Once these three elements were brought together, the framework for Buchanan's contributions to public sector economics was set. All that remained was to work out the implications.[3]

Sandmo (1990, pp. 62–3) has argued that Buchanan's 'main achievements have been to introduce his fellow economists to new ways of thinking about economics, in particular about the public sector and the interaction between economics and politics'. By recasting public finance in the light of this Knight/Wicksell/Italian connection, Buchanan was able to challenge the received wisdom of his day on several fronts.[4]

Buchanan (1958) challenged the accepted Keynesian doctrine on both methodological and analytical grounds. The level of aggregation in Keynesian fiscal theory, for example, violated the political norms of democratic society, and fundamentally misconstrued the nature of the debt burden. Focusing on the aggregate unit, fiscal theorists were unable to address the problem of who pays for the creation of public goods and when the payments will be made. The problem was an elementary one – the principles of opportunity cost and economic decision-making were forgotten.

The controversy over the burden of debt forced Buchanan to re-examine the conceptual foundations of economic science. This led to his slim volume *Cost and Choice* (1969). The opportunity cost logic of economics would lead to surprising results on a broad range of issues, from the burden of debt to issues concerning the military draft to the problem of externalities to the choice context of bureaucratic decision-making. Compelling his fellow economists to re-examine the conceptual foundations of their discipline characterizes Buchanan's outsider status. The burden of debt debate, in other words, was typical of Buchanan's career; he was viewed as an outsider because he asked economists to pay attention to the most elementary principles of their discipline. By announcing that the modern technical Emperor has no clothes, Buchanan served an important intellectual function beyond his substantive contribution to the issue.[5]

During the 1970s, Buchanan's work became more philosophical. *The Limits of Liberty* (1975) presents the contractarian perspective in political economy. This was followed by several collections of essays (Buchanan 1977, 1986, 1991). In recent years Buchanan (and Yoon 1994) has addressed issues around increasing returns and the positive role of the work ethic. Unlike other scholars working on the technical and policy implications of increasing returns, Buchanan focused on the effects of increasing returns on specific institutions and practices. His concern was to understand Adam Smith's argument about increasing returns from specialization, and how the institutional environment channels human inclinations to 'truck, barter and exchange' in order to realize the gains from increasing returns.

There is a surprising unity in Buchanan's research programme throughout his career. The basic propositions which guide his work can be summarized neatly (see Buchanan 1979, pp. 280–82).

1. Economics is a 'science', but it is a 'philosophical' science, and the strictures against scientism offered by Knight and Friedrick Hayek should be heeded.
2. Economics is about choice and processes of adjustment, not states of rest. Equilibrium models are only useful when we recognize their limits.
3. Economics is about exchange, not about maximizing. Exchange and arbitrage should be the central focus of economic analysis.
4. Economics is about individual actors, not collective entities. Only individuals choose.
5. Economics is about a game played within rules.
6. Economics cannot be studied properly outside of politics. The choices among different rules of the game cannot be ignored.
7. The most important function of economics as a discipline is its didactic role in explaining the principle of spontaneous order.
8. Economics is elementary.

From his early critique of social choice theory and welfare economics to his most recent writings on constitutional design, Buchanan stresses these eight points.

Finally, it is important to recognize the methodological schema that Buchanan employs to address questions in political economy and how this schema allows him to weave these eight propositions into a coherent framework for social theory. Buchanan emphasizes that we must distinguish between pre- and post-constitutional levels of analysis. Pre-constitutional analysis concerns the rules of the game, while post-constitutional analysis examines the strategies players adopt within a set of defined rules. Political economy, properly understood, involves moving back and forth between these two levels. Successful application of modern political economy to the world of public policy demands a *constitutional* perspective. In this regard, Buchanan introduces the vital distinction between 'policy within politics' and systematic changes in the rules of the game. Lasting reform results not from policy changes within the existing rules, but rather from changing the rules of governance. Thus, far from being a conservative intellectual, Buchanan is an intellectual radical seeking to get at the root cause of social and political ills.

THE END OF ROMANCE

According to ancient legend, a Roman Emperor was asked to judge a singing contest between two participants. After hearing the first contestant, the Emperor gave the prize to the second on the assumption that the second could be no worse than the first. Of course, this assumption could have been wrong; the second singer might have been worse. The theory of market failure committed the same mistake as the Emperor. Demonstrating that the market economy failed to live up to the ideals of general competitive equilibrium was one thing, but to gleefully assert that public action could costlessly correct the failure was quite another matter. Unfortunately, much analytical work proceeded in such a manner. Many scholars burst the bubble of this romantic vision of the political sector during the 1960s. But it was Buchanan and Gordon Tullock who deserve the credit for shifting scholarly focus.

Before public choice, economic theory frequently postulated an objective welfare function which 'society' sought to maximize, and assumed that political actors were motivated to pursue that objective welfare function. The Buchanan/Tullock critique pointed out: (1) that no objective welfare function exists, (2) that even if one existed societies do not choose (only individuals do), and (3) that individuals within the political sector, just as in the private sector, base their choices on their private assessment of costs and benefits.[6]

The major insights of modern political economy all flow from these three elementary propositions – the vote motive; the logic of dispersed costs and concentrated benefits; the shortsightedness bias in policy; and the constitutional perspective in policy evaluation. Politics must be endogenous in any reasonable model of economic policy-making. But the intellectual spirit of the 1950s and early 1960s was one of zealous optimism about the nature of politics. Buchanan's warning of democratic folly, and the need for constitutional constraint, did not sit well with the intellectual idealist of the day. In the wake of the Vietnam War, and then Watergate, as well as the failed economic policies that emerged from both Democratic and Republican administrations, it is now difficult to imagine a non-cynical view of politics. This is not an endorsement of apathy and malcontent with politicians. Nowhere in the Buchanan body of work is it suggested that politicians are any worse than the rest of us. Rather, his work simply stressed that politicians are just like the rest of us – neither sinners nor saints, but a bit of both.

Methodologically, Buchanan employed the assumption of economic man within politics not to describe the motivation of any particular political actor, but rather as a modelling strategy. As pointed out above,

Buchanan learned from the Italians (and from Wicksell) that one must postulate a theory of the state. By postulating the revenue-maximizing Leviathan, Buchanan was able to address the political rules of the game that would constrain the behaviour of individuals within politics. In particular, if government officials are revenue maximizing, then the question becomes what rules of the game are necessary to transform revenue maximizing behaviour into wealth-maximizing behaviour? This is a question of constitutional design. In two books with Geoffrey Brennan, *The Power to Tax* (1980) and *The Reason of Rules* (1985), Buchanan employed the economic man assumption to establish rules that guard against 'worst-case' scenarios in politics. Even if rulers were sinners, it would be important to design a constitution that would compel these sinners to act more like saints.

But to develop an idealized constitutional political structure (a vision of a workable utopia), one had to first deconstruct the idealist/romantic vision of politics, where unconstrained democracy is envisioned as a workable model of self-rule and substitute a more realist vision of political processes. Buchanan (and Tullock) accomplished this with the aid of elementary economic reasoning, most notably the idea that only individuals choose, that in making their choices they weigh costs and benefits, and that the way individuals perceive costs and benefits depends on the institutional context within which they must choose. Simple concepts, applied consistently and persistently, often generate surprising results that must be repeatedly stressed.

SUBJECTIVISM AND THE ELEMENT PRINCIPLES OF ECONOMICS

Ironically, modern economists were reluctant to accept the 'economic way of thinking', in particular, the central role of exchange and the notion of subjective tradeoffs. In his 1963 Presidential Address to the Southern Economic Association, Buchanan (1979, pp. 17–37) argued that economists should put the contribution of constrained maximization in perspective. Resource allocation was *not* the central problem of economics. Economists should, Buchanan urged, concentrate on the human propensity to truck, barter and exchange, and the institutional arrangements that emerge as a result of this propensity.

If this step is not taken, it is too easy for error to sneak into economic analysis and become embedded at the most fundamental level. The allocation definition of economics 'makes it all too easy to slip across the bridge between personal and individual utility of decisions and "social" aggregates' (Buchanan 1979, pp. 22–3). Economists know that crossing the bridge is difficult, and Lionel Robbins was successful in keeping many from summing utilities in order to get across the bridge. But Robbins was only partially successful, for economists still thought that as long as they specified their social welfare function they could 'maximize to their own hearts' content'. Buchanan pointed out that this intellectual exercise is illegitimate; economists *should not* engage in this activity.

The Buchanan critique of optimizing models is not about the introduction of value judgements via the social welfare function; nor is it a critique of formalization *per se*. Rather, the critique is that the subject matter of economics is lost in these exercises in applied mathematics, and that where the subject matter seems to creep back into the analysis it is mischaracterized. The mutual advantage that can be realized through exchange in specified institutional settings is the one important truth of political economy, Buchanan insists; modern economics has threatened our ability to understand this truth.

Consider, for example, Buchanan's critique of the model of perfect competition in the light of his plea for exchange *activity* to occupy the central place in economic theorizing. Perfectly competitive general equilibrium eliminates all social content from individual decision-making. The individual confronts an array of externally determined variables, and the choice problem is transformed into a mechanical problem of computation. Within such a world there is only one equilibrium point, and so the model cannot capture the dynamics of competition or the trading behaviour that would prod a system to equilibrium. Buchanan (1979, pp. 29–30, original emphasis) summarizes the point nicely:

A market is not competitive by assumption or by construction. A market *becomes* competitive, and competitive rules *come to be* established as institutions emerge to place limits on individual behavior patterns. It is this *becoming* process, brought about by the continuous pressure of human behavior in exchange, that is the central part of our discipline, if we have one, not the dry rot of postulated perfection. A solution to a general-equilibrium set of equations is not predetermined by exogenously determined rules. A general solution, if there is one, *emerges* as a result of a whole network of evolving exchanges, bargains, trades, side payments, agreements, contracts which, finally at some point, ceases to renew itself. At each stage in this evolution toward solution there are *gains* to be made, there are exchanges possible, and this being true, the direction of movement is modified.

It is for these reasons that the model of perfect competition is of such limited explanatory value except when changes in variables exogenous to the system are introduced. There is no place in the structure of the model for internal change, change that is brought about by men who continue to be haunted by the Smithean propensity. But surely the dynamic element in the economic system is precisely this continual evolution of the exchange process, as [Joseph] Schumpeter recognized in his treatment of entrepreneurial function.

Subjectivist economics compels theorists to avoid the pitfalls of abstraction. It grounds economic analysis in the choices of individuals, and demands that empirical analysis pay attention to the institutional context of choice and how agents perceive their institutional constraints. The mechanical model of allocational computation, and its corollary (the model of perfect competition) eliminates genuine choice from study, just as the focus on aggregate data ignores the ideas, desires, beliefs and cultural practices that motivate historical actors.

Buchanan's great contribution to subjectivist thought was to demonstrate how a consistently subjectivist position would lead to a different perspective on many issues. The contribution was to challenge the very notion of an objective social welfare function that was to be maximized. On a more concrete microeconomic analytical level, Buchanan was able to demonstrate how the burden of debt is passed on to future generations rather than consumed at the current moment in terms of real resources. In the burden of debt controversy, Buchanan criticized both the theory of functional finance and the traditional theory of public finance, which holds that the real cost of debt is incurred at the moment when the resources are employed.[7] The theory of functional finance was challenged on two grounds. First, it failed to postulate a model of political actors, and as a result, failed to recognize that political actors would lack the incentive to run surpluses during good economic times. In bad times, of course, the incentive to run deficits is there, but why would a politician ever want to reduce expenditures and raise revenue during good times? The policy of functional finance, if pursued as designed, would reverse the logic of politics by concentrating costs and dispersing benefits during times of plenty; but this is incentive incompatible with electoral politics. Second, the Keynesian orthodoxy failed to take into account the generational transfer of the debt burden. Of course, this intergenerational transfer reinforced the political logic because the least informed and least organized interest group would be the as-yet born, and thus the constituency any politician can afford to ignore.

Buchanan's emphasis on the tight relationship between the act of choice and the notion of cost compelled him to criticize the traditional theory of public debt as well as the Keynesian theory of functional finance. During war, for example, it was typically argued that the opportunity cost of debt-financed public goods was the alternative use for which those resources would have otherwise been put. Steel was used to produce guns, not automobiles.

By introducing the distinction between choice-influencing and choice-influenced costs, Buchanan was able to show the fundamental error in traditional theory. It is true that resource use is shifted, but debt instruments entail obligations to service that debt. Buchanan (1969, p. 64) argued that

> in the decision-maker's subjective evaluation ... costs are concentrated in the moment of choice and not in the later periods during which the actual outlays must be made. But the choice-influencing, subjective costs exist only because of the decision-makers recognition that it will be necessary to make future-period outlays.

The choice-influenced costs of debt-financing (that is, the utility forgone as a result of the choice) are borne solely in the future.

Cost, Buchanan insisted, must be understood as the subjective assessment of tradeoffs by individuals if it is going to have any meaning in a theory of decision-making. A final example, which may drive the point home, is Buchanan's critique of Pigovian taxes as correctives. The Pigovian remedy was to bring marginal private costs (subjectively understood) into line with marginal social costs (objectively understood). The problem, Buchanan pointed out, was that the analyst had to specify the conditions under which objectively measurable costs could be ascertained by economic and policy actors. In general competitive equilibrium, measurable costs serve as a reasonable proxy for the subjectively held assessment of tradeoffs. But in general competitive equilibrium there are also no deviations between marginal private costs and marginal social costs. In other words, Buchanan (like Ronald Coase) pointed out that either Pigovian tax remedies are possible and redundant, or impossible to set because the conditions presupposed for their establishment either eliminate their necessity or (if absent) preclude their enactment.[8]

The neoclassical project, where the subjective half of the 1870s revolution in value theory is emphasized as strongly as the marginalist half, leads to a different sort of economic science. In a broad brush summary, it leads to a conception of economic science as a philosophical science, and not a technocratic one. Unlike other critics of modern economics (such as Institutionalists or Post Keynesians), the subjectivist tradition retains a commitment to universality, an emphasis on marginalism, and seeks to study how a systematic order emerges as the unintended consequence of individual choice. However, the subjectivist joins the Institutionalist by highlighting the institutional context of choice, and the Post Keynesian by recognizing that the market order can break down and that theoretical problems result from treating time and ignorance seriously.

Subjectivism demands a major restructuring of economic theory. In addition to a renewed appreciation of the nature of choice, the context of choice comes to occupy a central stage within the subjectivist research programme. There can be little doubt that Buchanan has been among the most important figures in resurrecting a broader notion of political economy; this conception is grounded in his appreciation of the subjective nature of choice and its implications for social order. In other words, subjectivism is the foundation of Buchanan's thought.

ECONOMICS, SOCIAL PHILOSOPHY AND CONSTITUTIONAL POLITICAL ECONOMY

Positivism and formalism promised to lift economics from its immature past when ethical concerns and the ambiguities of philosophy and natural language clouded the thinking of its leading figures. Submission to empirical reality would compel those with a scientific mind to surrender ideological beliefs, and mathematical reasoning would eliminate the ability of theorists to slip in unwarranted assumptions. But these promises were false. Empirical reality is complex and must be sifted through a theoretical lens for us to make sense. In addition, mathematical reasoning might be precise but irrelevant. Mathematical modelling ensures *syntactic* clarity, but it does not guarantee *semantic* clarity. The model may be logically precise, but lack meaning.

Both the empiricist and formalist aspiration were misapplied in the study of man. One cannot cast out of scientific court the very things (beliefs, desires, expectations) that motivate the subject of study without distorting the object of study. To put it another way, while eliminating anthropomorphism from the physical sciences was a noble cause, eliminating anthropomorphism from the study of man eliminated the very thing that was supposed to be studied.

Along with figures such as Hayek, G.L.S. Shackle, Ludwig Lachmann and Israel Kirzner, Buchanan fought persistently against the disappearance of man from economic analysis.[9] By insisting that economic processes always exist within a political/legal/social context, Buchanan begged economists to focus attention on the rule structure within which individual strategies would manifest themselves. Reform, he insisted, would not come from tinkering with individuals and their strategies, but only from changes in the rules of the game. By introducing the methodological schema of pre- and post-constitutional analysis, Buchanan was able to demonstrate the positive-scientific value of social philosophy for economics. He proposed both a positive analysis of normative issues and a recognition that political economists engage in normative analysis whether we want to admit it or not.

First, Buchanan proposed that pre-constitutional analysis (the realm of social philosophy) could help economics understand two things:

(1) the principle of voluntary exchange; and (2) the effect of strategies, given a set of rules, on the social and philosophic judgement of the rules themselves. Economists need to ask what rules of the game people would voluntarily agree to behind a veil of uncertainty, and then examine how alternative rules would engender patterns of behaviour and consequences for the economic game.[10] Going back and forth between the examination of pre- and post-constitutional choice constitutes the research pro-gramme of modern political economy (and the integration of social and moral philosophy with economic science).

By introducing the theoretical construct of the veil of uncertainty, Buchanan was able to highlight the relevance of the Paretian norm for political economy. In the pre-constitutional moment, no bargain concern-ing the rules of the game would be agreed to unless all parties expected to be made better off by adopting the rules in question. Since individuals were uncertain about where they would be situated in the post-constitu-tional environment, they would not agree to bargains that clearly valued one subgroup over any other. In this manner, the rights of the majority would surely be constrained by the interests of the minority. The concern here (following Wicksell) was with balancing the costs of decision exter-nalities in politics with the costs of decision-making. If a voting rule was such that a small minority could win, then that minority could impose costs on others and accrue benefits for themselves through the power of the state. To avoid this externality problem one could propose unanimity as the only rule, but unanimity entails increased costs associated with decision-making. Conceptual unanimity emerged as the decision rule minimizing the total costs of political decision-making, which again high-lighted the relevance of the Paretian principle for understanding political agreement over the rules.

In the post-constitutional environment, players of the political/eco-nomic game treat the rules as constraints and devise optimal strategies in response to them. Rules of the game that promise a 'good' life, but gener-ate incentives leading to patterns of behaviour not associated with the 'good' life are perhaps rules in need of change. Buchanan (1991) has argued that classical political economy discovered that as long as the state provided and maintained appropriate rules of the game, individuals could pursue their own interests and simultaneously enjoy the values of liberty, prosperity and peace. The classical liberal vision, however, was never implemented, and it failed to capture the imagination of intellectuals for more than a generation or two. Buchanan conjectures that this failure was due to the absence of a theory of justice in classical liberal political economy. Twentieth century attempts to develop a model of social justice in order to correct this weakness have generated failed experiments in socialism and the social democratic welfare state. The failure of socialism and the welfare state can be directly attributed to the incentive incompatibility of the rules of these games with the strategies of the work ethic and personal responsibility, behaviour associated with economic prosperity and social cooperation – or at least this is the type of argument that Buchanan's work would suggest. The veracity of this claim is not the issue here; rather I want to use it as an example of how Buchanan's work provides a positive analysis of how we choose among rules.

The Limits of Liberty contains Buchanan's (1975) most articulate statement of his political philosophic project. The subtitle of the book ('Between anarchy and Leviathan') neatly sums up Buchanan's research purpose. Frustrated with the failure of the classical liberal political philosophy to constrain the growth of government, some free market theorists (notably Murray Rothbard and David Friedman) suggested in the 1960s and 1970s that the market could provide endogenously the infrastructure that would govern its operation: anarcho-capitalism. In addition, Hayek's work was being interpreted myopically by classical liberal scholars throughout the 1970s and 1980s as a blanket indictment of rational constructivism.[11]

Buchanan shared the frustration of libertarians with the growth of the state in the twentieth century. A large part of the growth of the state had to do with the Romantic vision of politics that had captured the imagination of American liberals. In addition, from a technical perspective many arguments for government intervention were grounded in a poor understanding of economics and an even worse understanding of the political processes. Much of the critique of the market was generated by those who failed to grasp the basic principles of spontaneous order analysis. Buchanan believed that rational analysis and the construction of the appropriate institutions of governance could emerge from the pens of economists and could reform the system in a 'desirable' direction.[12] Freedom was to be found in the constitutional contract, not in the absence of government (despite the philosophical attractiveness of anarchism) or in the submission to the forces of evolution. Anarchism promised de-evolution into Hobbesian war of all against all, and evolutionism promised nothing but the elevation of tradition to that of the sacred.

Buchanan put forth a modern argument for the state to establish governance structures, at the same time that he hoped to delineate the powers of the state. In this respect, Buchanan was pursuing the Madisonian project of empowering and then constraining government. In *The Limits of Liberty*, Buchanan (1975, pp. 68–70) distinguished between the 'protective state' and the 'productive state'. The protective state enforces the rights that emerged out of the pre-constitutional moment. In this capacity, the state is external to contracting parties and does not attempt to 'produce' anything other than contract enforcement. The productive state, on the other hand, produces collective goods. These two roles of the state are conceptually distinct, and failure to consistently distinguish these roles leads to confusion. The law, for example, is not an object of choice in the post-constitutional moment, whereas the supply and demand of public goods is subject to a process of collective choice.

With the development of the theory of the rent-seeking society, the productive state had to be further distinguished from what could be termed the redistributive state (see Buchanan, Tollison and Tullock 1980). The productive state adds value by coordinating the plans of actors who are unable to do this through individual action. The redistributive state, however, simply transfers value from one party to another through collective action. The logic of politics, unfortunately, biases the process of collective action in a manner which often transforms the productive state into the redistributive state, even against the best intentions of economic and political actors. This is one reason why Buchanan limits his reform proposals to the pre-constitutional level; once the post-constitutional level is reached, changing the players will do little to effectuate lasting change. Reform is only possible, in Buchanan's system, at the level of the rules.

By focusing attention on the rules of political economy, Buchanan has opened up the discourse in economics to again deal with moral questions and the tradition of political philosophy.

CONCLUSION

As I have attempted to demonstrate, Buchanan dissented from mainstream economic thinking throughout his career. He was a non-Keynesian when Keynesianism was in vogue; he pursued a subjectivist research programme when the majority of the profession lost sight of the subjectivist roots of the neoclassical revolution; he rejected the formal models of utility maximization and perfect competition when these models represented the tool-kit of any respectable economist; and he reintroduced moral concerns into economics at a time when economists were content to worship at the shrine of scientism.

When Buchanan won the Nobel Prize in 1986, many rejoiced that an outsider could win the award. Buchanan himself interpreted this support (in the face of negative reaction from the popular press) as a penchant to root for the underdog. Surely, this sentiment underlaid the good wishes and hardy congratulations that Buchanan received. But the award represented more than that to many people. It represented a recognition that economics was too important to be left to the technicians and ideological eunuchs (two terms that Buchanan (1986, p. 14) has employed to describe modern economists). Over the past 50 years, economics has weeded out of scientific concern precisely those questions deserving serious scholarly attention. Buchanan pursued a research programme more akin to his classical predecessors than to modern economists inspired by Paul Samuelson or Robert Lucas. For those of us who see economics as part of a broad interdisciplinary search for truth about man and the social organization of exchange and production, any nod in the direction of heterodox thinkers is interpreted as a sign that the economics profession may be regaining its 'collective sanity'.[13]

Of course, our hopes are often dashed as soon as we discuss the prize with colleagues or graduate students who wonder where the lemma lies in the work of a Buchanan. But hope remains that economists will realize that our discipline possesses a cultural heritage and social capital that has been eroded by the blind quest for scientistic precision. In reviewing Samuelson's *Foundations* many years ago, Boulding (1948, p. 247) wrote:

> Conventions of generality and mathematical elegance may be ... barriers to the attainment and diffusion of knowledge. ... It may well be that the slovenly and literary borderland between economics and sociology will be the most fruitful building ground during the years to come and that mathematical economics will remain too flawless in its perfection to be very fruitful.

Boulding's words are even more telling today now that we have seen the fruits of the formalist revolution in economic theory and how it has cut economics off from the social theoretic discourse on the human condition. Buchanan was one of the few who, despite his deep commitment to the logic of economic argumentation, resisted the formalist revolution and strove to fit modern economics into the classical political economy project. One can disagree with this or that aspect of the project, but the scholarly enterprise demands our respect, admiration and, most definitely, our emulation.

NOTES

* I would like to thank James Buchanan, Jack High, Israel Kirzner, Mario Rizzo and Karen Vaughn for comments on an earlier draft of this Chapter. In addition, I would especially like to thank Steven Pressman for his comments and suggestions for improvement. Financial assistance from the Austrian Economics Program at New York University is gratefully acknowledged. Responsibility for remaining errors is mine.

1. See Cushman (1994) for a discussion of the Virginia episode and the rise of rational choice political science and the reaction it has generated.

2. A change of heart in old age is not enough, that would just be attributed to softness of brain or sour grapes. No, the dissenter must be consistent from early on, yet couch the dissent in a manner that gets attention.

3. On Buchanan's contributions to economics, see Atkinson (1987), Boettke (1987), Romer (1988) and Sandmo (1990). For an overview of the 'new' political economy see Mueller (1989) and Inman (1987). Mitchell and Simmons (1994) provide a useful introduction to public choice.

4. Buchanan is probably best known for his joint work with Tullock (1962), and Tullock's influence must be recognized in any assessment of Buchanan. The tension between Buchanan's philosophical perspective and Tullock's economistic one led to a very productive collaboration.

5. This contribution, of course, has not been consistently recognized by establishment economists who worship the god of formalism. But, Buchanan's methodological statements throughout his career have warned about the costs of formalism for economic understanding, and they provide inspiration to those working outside the current formalistic fashions that real progress can be made in economic thought by persistently pursuing the elementary principles of the discipline. It would seem that one formalistic principle, that of Occam's Razor, actually would side with the anti-formalist.

6. Sen (1995) has recently attempted to address Buchanan's critique of the social choice literature.

7. Steven Pressman has pointed out to me that Abba Lerner's theory of functional finance argued against the idea that governments had to balance their budgets on a cyclical basis. Instead, Lerner's idea was that governments could run deficits indefinitely as long as citizens were willing to lend the government money. This aspect of the doctrine did not become part of the Keynesian orthodoxy as reflected in the thought of Paul Samuelson, Robert Solow, James Tobin and Lawrence Klein, who argued for cyclically balanced budgets. But implicit in the Buchanan critique is the idea that balancing the budget over the business cycle collapses into the Lerner position of indefinite deficits because of political behaviour.

8. Vaughn (1980) has pointed out the dilemma involved in this situation. To calculate the appropriate corrective tax, the policy-maker must know the equilibrium price; yet the situation demanding correction implies a disequilibrium situation.

9. In the classroom, for example, one of the most challenging and interesting questions asked of students was to write about the basic question: 'Who is the individual in economics?'. Buchanan's teaching method (at least by the time I had him as a formal instructor in the mid-1980s) was to assign no text, but to put on reserve about a dozen books that were to be read throughout the semester, and to grade students based on a series of short papers due about every two weeks throughout the semester. In one class I had with him, the writing assignments revolved around manipulating Adam Smith's deer–beaver model. Ironically, during that semester I also had the privilege of studying Great Books in Political Economy with Kenneth Boulding, who also spent most of the semester discussing Smith's basic model. I asked Boulding about this one afternoon, and he explained to me that Frank Knight (who taught both Buchanan and Boulding) spent his classes either discussing world religion or Adam Smith's deer–beaver model; so I should not fret, as I was simply being exposed to a long line of teaching methodology.

10. The veil of uncertainty was introduced by Buchanan and Tullock (1962) before the veil of ignorance that was made famous by John Rawls.

11. I say myopically, because Hayek's thought was much more than just a warning against constructivism (but this is not the place to discuss Hayek's contributions in any detail). It is the myopic reading of Hayek's critique of rational constructivism that moves Buchanan into opposition with Hayek.

12. Though I should point out immediately that Buchanan never considered himself (or economics) as a saviour. In fact, the economist as saviour is to Buchanan the highest form of moral conceit. (See the quote from Knight in Buchanan 1975, p. 166.)

13. Please excuse the obvious violation of methodological individualism implied in this sentence.

REFERENCES

Atkinson, A. (1987), 'James M. Buchanan's contributions to economics', *Scandavian Journal of Economics*, **89** (1), 5–15.

Boettke, P. (1987), 'Virginia political economy: a view from Vienna', in P.J. Boettke and D.L. Prychitko (eds), *The Market Process: Essays in Contemporary Austrian Economics*, Aldershot: Edward Elgar, 1994, pp. 244–60.

Boulding, K. (1948), 'Samuelson's *Foundations*: the role of mathematics in economics', *Journal of Political Economy*, **56**, June, 187–99.

Brennan, G. and J.M. Buchanan (1980), *The Power to Tax*, New York: Cambridge University Press.

Brennan, G. and J.M. Buchanan (1985), *The Reason of Rules*, New York: Cambridge University Press.

Buchanan, J. M. (1958), *Public Principles of Public Debt*, Homewood, IL: Irwin.

Buchanan, J.M. (1960), *Fiscal Theory and Political Economy*, Chapel Hill: University of North Carolina Press.

Buchanan, J.M. (1969), *Cost and Choice*, Chicago: University of Chicago Press.

Buchanan, J.M. (1975), *The Limits of Liberty*, Chicago: University of Chicago Press.

Buchanan, J.M. (1977), *Freedom in Constitutional Contract*, College Station: Texas A&M University Press.

Buchanan, J.M. (1979), *What Should Economists Do?*, Indianapolis: Liberty Press.

Buchanan, J.M. (1986), *Liberty, Market and State*, New York: New York University Press.

Buchanan, J.M. (1991), *The Economics and Ethics of Constitutional Order*, Ann Arbor: University of Michigan Press.

Buchanan, J.M. (1992), *Better than Plowing*, Chicago: University of Chicago Press.

Buchanan, J.M. and G.F. Thirlby (eds.) (1973), *L.S.E. Essays on Cost*, London: London School of Economics.

Buchanan, J.M., R.D. Tollison and G. Tullock (eds.) (1980), *Towards a Theory of the Rent-Seeking Society*, College Station: Texas A&M University Press.

Buchanan, J.M. and G. Tullock (1962), *The Calculus of Consent*, Ann Arbor: University of Michigan Press.

Buchanan, J.M. and J.Y. Yoon (eds.) (1994), *The Return of Increasing Returns*, Ann Arbor: University of Michigan Press.

Cushman, R. (1994), 'Rational fears', *Lingua Franca*, November/December, 42–54.

Inman, R. (1987), 'Markets, governments, and the "new" political economy', in A. Auerbach and M. Feldstein (eds), *The Handbook of Public Economics*, Vol. 2, Amsterdam: North-Holland, pp. 647–777.

Kuhn, T.S. (1959), 'The essential tension: tradition and innovation in scientific research', in C.W. Taylor (ed.), *The Third University of Utah Research Conference on the Identification of Scientific Talent*, Salt Lake City: University of Utah Press, pp. 162–74.

Leijonhufvud, A. (1981), 'Life among the econ', in *Information and Coordination*, New York: Oxford University Press, pp. 347–59.

McCloskey, D.N. (1995), 'Kelley Green golf shoes and the intellectual range from M to N', *Eastern Economic Journal*, 21 (3), Summer, 411–14.

Mitchell, W.C., and R.T. Simmons (1994), *Beyond Politics: Markets, Welfare, and the Failure of Bureaucracy*, Boulder: Westview.

Mueller, D. (1989), *Public Choice II*, New York: Cambridge University Press.

Nelson, R. (1991), *Reaching for Heaven on Earth*, New Jersey: Rowman & Littlefield.

Romer, T. (1988), 'On James Buchanan's contributions to public economics', *Journal of Economic Perspectives*, **2** (1), Fall, 165–79.

Sandmo, A. (1990) 'Buchanan on political economy: a review article', *Journal of Economic Literature*, **28** (1), March, 50–65.

Sen, A. (1995) 'Rationality and social choice', *American Economic Review*, **85** (1), March, 1–24.

Vaughn, K.I. (1980), 'Does it matter that costs are subjective?', *Southern Economic Journal*, **46** (1), January, 702–15.

3. John R. Commons and the compatibility of neoclassical and institutional economics

Jeff E. Biddle and Warren J. Samuels

INTRODUCTION

Historians wishing to work with the concept 'dissenting economist' quickly realize that it is a problematic concept. 'Dissent' must be defined in terms of some orthodox body of theory or practice, thus necessitating a definition of 'orthodoxy'. Undoubtedly, there are many views of what constitutes orthodoxy in economics at any point in time. Moreover, orthodoxy in one particular period may not correspond to orthodoxy in the future. Thus, an economist may be viewed as dissenting not only from the orthodoxy of his or her own day, but also from a later orthodoxy. For example, John Maynard Keynes can be viewed as dissenting both from the orthodox theory that prevailed when he was writing and from the Keynesian economics that developed in the years following his death.

While many economists have proclaimed their dissent from orthodoxy, historians can agree or disagree with these self-assessments. W.S. Jevons believed that his work represented a sharp break from the Ricardo–Mill tradition in economics; but Hollander (1985, p. 931) has claimed there is a fundamental continuity running from classical to marginalist, and then to neoclassical economics. History also presents examples of economists who identify themselves as part of some dominant tradition, while exercising their right to differ with that tradition along certain dimensions. Some may view these differences as trivial, others as crucial. For example, Frank Fetter (1915) proposed new psychological foundations for value theory, but Wesley Mitchell (1969, Vol. II, Ch. 12) and others have held that Fetter made a distinction where none existed.

In short, dissent must be thought of as a relative notion; it is to some extent in the eye of the beholder, dependent in part on the time and place in which the beholder lives.

The career of John Commons spanned a period in which economics was more open, diverse and catholic than it would become in the decades after World War II. Neoclassicism then was neither so hegemonic nor so crystallized, and neoclassical economists were not so exclusive in their conception of economics. In the late 1910s and the 1920s, institutionalist research strategies and topics were, for the most part, recognized as a legitimate part of economics; and those who pursued them were accepted as colleagues by many (though not all) neoclassical economists.

Unlike Thorstein Veblen, another important Institutionalist, Commons viewed himself as a member of the economics profession in good standing. His work on labour history and his advocacy of policy reform led to his election as President of the American Economic Association in 1917.

Commons also did not see himself as an opponent of economic theory *qua* theory. He accepted the need for theory, and he engaged in theorizing with regard to the legal foundations of the economy and the emergence and operation of institutions. Yet his conception of economics was considerably wider than that of the abstract market price mechanism allocating resources, and he challenged the equation of theory with price theory. Commons, however, did not question the value of theorizing about the price mechanism. Indeed, he was quite explicit that he considered institutional economics to be a supplement to, rather than a replacement for, neoclassical price theory.

Whatever the status of Commons during his life, and whatever his own interpretation of the relationship between his work and orthodox economics, today the contributions of Commons appear as a literature of dissent – dissent against certain tendencies in economic thought which, since his death, have become thoroughly ingrained in economics.

In what follows we explore some aspects of Commons as a dissenter. We first set forth the position of Commons that his work was compatible with, or supplementary to, neoclassical economics. But is the view correct? Ramstad (1992) has argued, contra Commons, that institutionalism and neoclassicism are mutually exclusive. We next address this question. The last part of this chapter addresses the question of why Commons has not been absorbed into the neoclassical mainstream.

COMMONS ON HIS DISSENT[1]

A first clue to the self-image of Commons as a dissenter can be found in the title of his most important theoretical work – *Institutional Economics: Its Place in Political Economy*. The clue is developed more fully in the first chapter, which Commons opens by stating that he has derived 'a theory of the part played by collective action in control of individual action'. He then begins a brief autobiographical sketch, designed to convey to the reader the origins of his institutional approach to economics. Discussing his research leading to the *Legal Foundations of Capitalism*, Commons (1934, p. 3) remarks 'I found that few of the economists had taken the point of view here developed, or had made contributions that would make it possible to fit legal institutions into economics'. A few pages later, he notes that his institutional economics:

> consists in going back through the writings of economists from John Locke to the Twentieth Century, to discover wherein they have or have not introduced collective action. Collective action, as well as individual action, has always been there; but from Smith to the Twentieth Century it has been excluded or ignored, except as attacks on trade unions or as postscripts on ethics or public policy. The problem now is not to create a different kind of economics – 'institutional economics' – divorced from preceding schools, but how to give collective action, in all its varieties, its due place throughout economic theory.
>
> In my judgement this collective control of individual transactions is the contribution of institutional economics to the whole of a rounded-out theory of Political Economy, which shall include and give a proper place to all economic theories since John Locke. (Commons 1934, pp. 5–6)

Commons then briefly discusses his main ideas and their relationship to the work of other economists. He concludes the discussion with a reference to 'older schools and their modern strict conformists' who 'select a single principle of causation', although 'modern theories are certainly theories of multiple causation'. He continues:

> I do not think that institutional causation excludes other causations. ... Institutional economics takes its place as the proprietary economics of rights, duties, liberties, and exposures, which, as I shall endeavor to show throughout, give to collective action its due place in economic theorizing.
>
> I do not see that there is anything new in this analysis. Everything herein can be found in the work of outstanding economists for two hundred years. It is only a somewhat different point of view. The things that have changed are the interpretations, the emphasis, the weights assigned to different ones of the thousands of factors which make up the world-wide economic process. All of these are traceable to the dominant political and economic problems by which economists were faced at the time and place in which they wrote, and to their different social philosophies in the changing conflicts of interest of two centuries. (Commons 1934, p. 8)

The language here is conciliatory rather than confrontational. Like Marshall, Commons emphasizes the continuity between his work and that of his predecessors. Commons (1934, p. 680) also sees complementarities between the institutional approach and the equilibrium approach of neoclassical economics:

But is it necessary to abandon the older individualistic, molecular, and equilibrium theories in despair and disgust when they can readily be adapted to the newer collective theories of Wieser's *Macht*, Pareto's *Social Utility*, or Fetter's *Masquerade*? The waves of the water seek their equilibrium just as naturally when the water is raised ten feet by a dam or sunk ten feet by a drainage canal, as when the lake remains at its 'natural' level. The difficulty with the older theory was in ascertaining how high up or low down the 'marginal utility' was located. Wherever it may be located, the 'equilibrium' and the 'marginal utility' occur at that level. If a labor organization raises the wage 100 per cent, then the capitalists, employers, and laborers adjust their individual competitions at that higher level. ... Always there is a tendency towards equilibrium amongst the individual molecules, though collective action ... depress(es) or raise(s) the level of social utility .... It is not needful to repudiate the older theories of individual economics when all that is needed is to adjust them to the newer theories of collective economics.

Should all this be taken at face value, or was it an attempt by Commons to make his ideas more palatable to fellow economists? We believe these remarks reflect Commons's view of the relationship between his approach to economics and that of other schools of economic thought because they are consistent with his views on methodology and epistemology.

Commons espoused a pragmatic epistemology centring on the 'active mind', a mind that created knowledge by interacting with the outside world. Knowledge creation was a goal-driven, problem-solving process. It involved selecting particular impressions from the external environment and combing them with pre-existing memories to create ideas or plans for action. Commons emphasized the unique ability of the human mind to seek out a few elements of complex situations that could help resolve the situation. Because selectively perceived reality was processed with the help of pre-existing memories, and because selective perception was partly the product of socialization, individual reality was very much a product of past experiences. Selective perception of reality, and the subsequent creation of knowledge, led to a situation like that portrayed in the fable of the blind men and the elephant – people examining a situation from different angles could come up with different assessments of the situation, each partially correct but none wholly correct.

From this it followed that a more complete, richer or more useful, account of any situation could be constructed out of the differing viewpoints of numerous observers. The eleven-volume *Documentary History of American Industrial Society* (Commons et al. 1910–11) reflects this approach. This massive compilation of primary sources contained different perspectives of various participants from numerous episodes in American economic history. Through the study and synthesis of these different perspectives, Commons and his students then constructed *The History of Labor in the United States* (Commons et al., 1918, 1935).

Commons came to see the scientific method as an institutionalized process, designed to work out differences in perception between individual investigators and to achieve consensus regarding the nature of reality. He claimed that this view of science came from Charles Sanders Peirce, who defined truth as the opinion 'fated to be agreed upon by all those who investigate'. Individual perceptions, even those of scientists, were unavoidably subjective, meaning that individual perception was always biased. But discussion and experiment served to reveal or eliminate individual bias, and helped establish a consensus regarding truth. Consensual truth was relative rather than absolute; it was relative to the shared preconceptions and purposes that formed the basis of the consensus. It was also an instrumental truth because it was a truth that the scientific community could accept and use as a basis for action.

This characterization of scientific activity is consistent with the respectful, though not uncritical, treatment that Commons gives to the work of other economists and other schools of economic thought. Disagreements among economists arise from the fact that they make different choices regarding which factors to emphasize in their theories and which to ignore. Also, this conciliatory approach arises from the desire of Commons to advance social science by achieving a consensus that recognizes the elements of reality reflected in the approaches of other individual investigators as well as his own institutional economics.

Commons's conception of the relationship between his own work and that of others also squares with his 'methodological holism' (see Ramstad 1986). As a holist, Commons conceived of social systems as complexes of interrelated parts. The meaning and significance of each part was determined by the totality of its possible relationships with other parts of the system and with the system as a whole. Any part of a system could be further understood as a whole which was itself made up of interrelated parts. The attempt to comprehend any aspect of the system necessarily focused on a subset of all the part-whole relationships relevant to that aspect of the system. Other attempts to comprehend the same aspect of the system, which focused on other part–whole relationships, provided alternative but overlapping explanations of that aspect of the system.

From this point of view, social scientists were attempting to understand a complex, evolving system. Collective action entered one way or another into almost all aspects of the economic system; yet other economists and schools of thought failed to recognize the true nature or significance of collective action. Commons, on the other hand, focused on collective action, and in doing so offered an alternative picture of economic activity. As Commons tells it, his thinking about the working of the economic system, which began by realizing the importance of collective action, was modified by pictures of the economy presented by other schools. Similarly, as the part–whole relationships associated with collective action were factored into the incomplete pictures of the various aspects of the economy presented by members of other schools of economic thought, their theories would acquire altered meaning. In the process a new, richer, more accurate theory would emerge – a new political economy, in which collective action had been given its proper place.

THE QUESTION OF MUTUAL EXCLUSIVITY

Commons believed that institutional economics supplemented mainstream economics and would round it out. But, Ramstad (1987) has suggested that Commons was wrong in considering institutional economics as supplementary, and not mutually exclusive, to mainstream microeconomics. He argues that in many, if not all, the places where Commons dissented from mainstream views, his ideas contradicted neoclassical economics and therefore the two could not coexist.

Ramstad identifies several fundamental differences between the economics described and practised by Commons, and the conception of economics embraced by modern neoclassical economists. For the most part, these differences do not involve neoclassical tools and techniques, but the status claimed for and ascribed to them. Consider the following model: $X = f(a, b)$. X is the object to be explained, and a and b are the explanatory variables. One can pursue an explanation of X in terms solely of a, and someone else can explain X in terms solely of b. Assuming that X is in fact a function of a and b, each leaves out what the other provides. It is a matter of selective perception and division of labour that the devotee of each sees their respective explanatory variable, a or b, as decisive and the other as irrelevant. The problem is not the mutually exclusive nature of a and b as theories of X, but the quest for social space by the devotees or practitioners of each theory.

Now, let a represent pure market relations, and b represent the operation of institutions, power structure and working rules. There is no reason why economics cannot include both factors. To identify economics only with a, or only with b, is myopic. Both provide an explanation for X, understood as the allocation of resources. Just because the devotees of a and the devotees of b have not combined their work does not mean that the two theories are mutually inconsistent.

One does not have to take antinomian positions with regard to rival or conflicting variables (explanations), even though the purist version of each is mutually exclusive of the other. This we think is the case with

Commons's dissenting views in relation to neoclassical orthodoxy. His work supplements microeconomics. Only by introducing ideological or disciplinary exclusivism can one reject one of the two explanations.

Commons assumed that neoclassical economics did not have to take an exclusivist, hardcore form; it could also take an ecumenical, soft form. In his day this was not an unreasonable assumption. But he failed to give adequate weight to factors such as ideological social control, 'scientific' disciplinary identity, and the contest for status. That neoclassical economics in the late twentieth century has excluded Common's institutional variables is due to such factors as: (1) the desire for exclusive social space and status; (2) fundamental ontological, epistemological and rhetorical differences; (3) the desire of professional economists to undergird the status of economics as an intellectual discipline; and (4) the desire of economists to maintain the imagery of non-interventionism and *laissez-faire*. Running through all these is a belief in the substantive and analytical autonomy of the economy. In short, Commons's status as a dissenter is due as much to the exclusivity of late twentieth century neoclassical economics as to his own ideas.

THE CONFLICT BETWEEN INSTITUTIONALISM AND NEOCLASSICISM

We have argued that Commons was correct in believing that his work could supplement neoclassicism, that neoclassical and institutional economics are not methodologically incompatible, and that the critical disagreements are on social, ontological, linguistic, ideological and psychological grounds. This section elaborates on these disagreements.

Commons and Capitalism

Commons had a particular view of the economic role of government, grounded in his holism and evolutionism. This set him apart from his orthodox peers. He was interested in the institutions which formed and operated through the economic system. He was especially interested in the evolution of these institutions, particularly the legal–economic nexus in which they arose. He therefore included both institutions and the legal–economic nexus (the economic role of government) within the ambit of institutional economics. Markets required institutions to exist and these institutions were increasingly governmental or legal in character. Moreover, these institutions were always changing, and government (or law) was a principal mode of their change. The heart of his analysis was changing legal working rules, as new cases, new values and new problems emerged. Government was important, as was legal change or interventionism.

This mindset conflicted with the neoclassical emphasis on non-interventionism. From a neoclassical perspective, institutions were not important; hence government as an institution, and as a mode of changing capitalism, was unimportant. Economics dealt with pure markets, and government was largely anathema. Economic policies, incongruent with the preconceptions of business, were both unsound and unsafe.

Commons recognized the role played by classical economics, and the emerging neoclassical economics, in reifying and reinforcing the status quo. He rejected this aspect of orthodox theory as part of his larger protest against capitalism as it had evolved and become institutionalized. In doing so he took a fundamental dissenting position – that capitalism is an artifact. It is not an abstract category, a 'natural' pattern of behaviours, or a flawed realization of a Platonic ideal. Rather, it is a product of legal and non-legal choices among conflicting parties in an infinitude of cases and instances. These choices help form the working rules and institutions that make capitalism what it is. Changing these choices has meant changes in working rules and institutions, and thereby changes in capitalism.

The capitalism resulting from this process was profoundly influenced by hierarchic vestiges from feudalism and by hierarchic forces within it. Specifically, capitalism emerged as a form of market economy in which capitalist domination – the predominant protection (through the control and use of government and public opinion) of capitalist interests over other interests – was the most characteristic feature. Commons felt that the market economy neither implied nor required capitalist domination. He sought an expansion of the interests effectively represented in the market economy. Hitherto the middle class had its interests protected along with the feudal and post-feudal landowners; Commons called for protecting the interests of the masses, especially the working class.

Commons did not wish to abandon capitalism. Compared to other economic systems, capitalism was relatively open; this openness and its productivity were the reasons he supported it. But capitalism must evolve. It must accommodate reforms to protect the interests of all individuals, as consumers and as workers, as well as the interests of investors. Unions and the apparatus of the welfare state were critical to protecting these interests. Such arrangements were the functional equivalent of property rights that protect capitalist interests. The view of many that Commons favoured regulation misinterprets one of his fundamental arguments. Government inevitably regulates by determining and redetermining rights; the only question is whose interests the government will protect through its definition and enforcement of rights.

The possibility of a more pluralistic capitalism, with rights redefined in such a way to protect previously unprotected interests, spurred Commons to design and promote reform legislation. Commons was a key player in the nationwide movement towards workers' compensation legislation in the 1910s. He publicized the problem of industrial accidents and the need for reform; and he helped draft a workers' compensation law for Wisconsin that became a model for legislation nationwide. The legislation shifted liability for industrial accidents from employees to employers while defining and limiting the extent of that liability, a shift that both ensured protection for the injured employees and used the profit motive to spur employers to increase workplace safety. A similar logic was behind proposals to provide relief for unemployed workers. Elements of this plan were integrated into state and federal unemployment insurance programmes set up in the United States in the 1930s, which established the right of unemployed workers to monetary payments. The payments came from an employer-financed fund, with payments into the fund depending on the number of workers an employer had laid off. Employers thus had incentives to minimize layoffs.

Commons realized that a legislative redefinition of rights would lead to new disputes between affected parties; and as disputes were resolved through the interpretation of statutory language, definitions of rights and duties would be further altered and refined. A more pluralistic capitalism required meaningful participation by a broader range of interests in this evolving process. The administrative features that Commons built into his reform proposals – creating new commissions, assigning new responsibilities to existing commissions, and developing procedural rules governing the adoption of new regulations – were designed to achieve that goal.

Language and the Social Construction of Reality

A refusal to support status quo institutions or idealized conceptions of competitive markets is consistent with other themes in the work of Commons, themes involving the role of language and the process of mythmaking in the social construction of reality. His willingness to deal with these matters, no less than the content of his views, marks a significant departure from the dominant ideology and practice of economics.

Legal Foundations of Capitalism (Commons 1924) contains an important analysis of legal, or legal–economic, discourse. It considers how words, as artifacts, encapsulate changing interpretations of experience and values, and how they have done so as part of the transformation from feudal to capitalist society.

Commons adopted a social constructivist (rather than a representational) conception of language. 'Words, prices and numbers', he wrote, 'are nominal and not real. They are signs and symbols needed for the operation of the working rules. Yet each is the only effective means by which human beings can deal with each other securely and accurately with regard to the things that are real. But each may be insecure and inaccurate' (Commons 1924, p. 9). Certain words embody and give effect to theories (for example, of property, liberty and value), which are sometimes erected into metaphysical and onto-logical absolutes, but (however held) serve as the basis for formulating and reformulating rights, duties, and so on. It is out of these processes that the economic system known as capitalism, and the lexicon used in comprehend-ing and describing it, emerged and evolved.

Commons focuses on the reinterpretation of legal and constitutional terms by the courts, especially the Supreme Court. As a result of this, concepts such as 'property' and 'liberty' get redefined and new theories arise, often inadver-tently. Changes in legal semantics thus incorporate subtle, but important, changes in law and therefore in relative rights, opportunities, exposures and immunities. Certain concepts like 'private property' become privileged and are regarded as natural, and therefore independent of government.

Commons (1924, pp. 124–5) rejects the 'illusion of certainty' provided by natural law and natural rights doctrines, giving 'rise to metaphysical "enti-ties" and "substances" conceived as existing apart from and independent of the behavior of officials and citizens. ... These illusions naturally arise', he says, 'from the hopes and fears of mankind which substitute wishes for behavior. We conceive that what we wish is the reality, the real thing. Thus rights and duties also, like the state, are given the illusion of a reality exist-ing apart from the conduct of officials'. His point is that 'The state is what its officials do' (Commons 1924, p. 122). 'Legal rights and duties are none other than the probability that officials will act in a certain way respecting the claims that citizens make against each other ' (Commons 1924, p. 125).

Commons is aware that such ideas are used for legitimation purposes. He emphasizes that preconceived absolutes have been revised through changing the definitions of terms. Changing definitions revise the mode of discourse, and therefore perception. They permit adjustment to, and revision of, the socially constructed reality. They also provide psychic balm, a sense of the predetermined to accompany the reality of change.

A change in definitions is such a simple and natural way of changing the con-stitution from what it is to what it ought to be, and the method is so universal and usually so gradual in all walks of life, that the will of God, or the will of the People, or the Corporate will, scarcely realizes what has happened. The method is, indeed, that common-sense device whereby man can go on believing in unchanging entities, and yet be practical. (Commons 1924, p. 373)

The idea that language has been used to disguise or mask ongoing changes in the socioeconomic system, and that this function of language arises, in part, from a psychological need for constancy and certainty, also appears in Commons's later work. The importance of this for our purposes is that, in so far as orthodox economists take for granted the metaphors that constitute the discourse of modern economics, they fail to address the meaning of words and the roles of mystification and myth-making within mainstream economics. As such, economics becomes part of the process of maintaining the status quo and gives it the patina of scientific approval. What purports to be 'the truth' serves as social control and psychic balm. What purports to be 'the economy' or 'the market' is a matter of systemic myth.

J.R. Commons: Pragmatist, Empiricist and Existentialist

Commons felt no need to follow a deterministic conception of science. Pursuit of unique determinate optimal equilibrium solutions (the hallmark of neoclassical theory) was incongruent with his conception of how serious research should be done and his identification of the problems to be studied. For the same reasons, Commons felt no need to pursue a technique-driven mathematical formalism. He did not deny others the opportunity to pursue such strategies; they simply were not for him. Nor was Commons interested in philosophical or scientific realism; he had a commonsense empiricism as epistemology and a commonsense attitude towards his objects of research. Things important to his interests were worthy of study; one could go far wrong by attributing universal status to transitory institutions and phenomena. Commons combined pragmatism and existentialism (see Ramstad 1987).

For Commons the economy was made, not found; but since individuals must operate in the system they find themselves, some individuals will change the system more than others. The economy was a product of individual and collective choice. Economic actors were continually engaged, through both individual and collective action, in the social reconstruction of the economy. People have the opportunity to, and the burden of, creating the economic system under which they live. This is achieved through both non-deliberative (habitual and customary) and deliberative (cognitive) action. This view does not take any particular status quo as given but rather as something continuing to evolve. The practices of reification and belief in determinism serve rationalizing, comforting and legitimizing functions, however much they may also point to substantive matters.

This approach extended to the practice of economists. Individual economists were responsible for their own choice of theory. Theory was not something one took as given; each individual made his or her own theoretical bed. If an individual chose to adopt some theoretical corpus that was his or her choice and burden; it was a fundamental fact of existence for the economist. Commons also emphasized personal experience rather than *a priori* generalizations and blind acceptance of received theory as the appropriate, sanctioned definition of reality. This was not a matter of mutual exclusiveness. Commons was prepared to use economic, social and legal theory, and discursive systems; but he used them *not* as *a priori* propositions available for further armchair theorizing, but in combination with his own blend of perceived experience and theorizing. On the one hand, each individual had to do this alone; on the other hand, each individual undertook professional work within the context of the academy in general and the economics profession in particular. In other words, the blend of individualist and collectivist reasoning that Commons brought to his substantive economic studies also characterized his understanding of being an economist and of doing economics.

It is worth noting that some people are comfortable with ambiguity and openendedness, while others require closure and determinacy. Commons's existentialism runs counter to the latter type of mentality. Most people are psychologically and intellectually uncomfortable with social constructionism. They prefer to believe that society and the economy were not human social reconstructions; they prefer a non-politicized existence where fundamental choices do not have to be made (see Ramstad 1987, p. 669). Politics is disreputable, a blemish on that which is given. Commons argued differently. Neoclassical economics, because it reaches unique determinate optimal equilibrium solutions, provides closure and determinacy as well as a sense of the reality of the non-political. It would seem that Commons's status as a dissenting economist rests in part on his existentialism and its correlative social constructivism – as well as his insistence that individuals are responsible for their own choices, including that of the use of theory (Ramstad 1987, p. 662 and *passim*). This existential view of the world sits on the periphery of economics because it 'is simply incompatible with the psychological predisposition of modern man' (Ramstad 1987, p. 670). Whether a different outcome was possible we shall never know. But this existentialist factor may be Commons's most subtle characteristic as a dissenter.

Why and How Institutions Matter

Commons insisted that institutions matter a great deal and devoted much effort to showing how and why they matter. Neoclassical economics was deficient because an ahistorical and non-institutional price mechanism constitutes the principal economic story. The theory takes existing institutions as given and independent, and it arrives at the mistaken policy of *laissez-faire* under the aegis of abstract individualism and the accompanying denigration of collective action of all kinds, including, and especially, government. Commons (1924, 1934) identifies several ways in which institutions matter.

1. Institutions are defined as collective action. They both control and liberate individual action. Institutions are moral, customary and legal as well as organizational (corporations, unions, and so on). Institutions may also be comprehended as commonly held belief systems (the Veblenian view), inasmuch as the thought-systems underlying and constituting working rules (for example, common law rules and constitutional clauses) are precisely that, elements of belief given form by the use of language.
2. Institutions exist within, and to a large degree, define the general interdependent system formed by individual volition (will) and action. This perspective is neither methodological individualism nor methodological collectivism, but the two together, perhaps in the form of institutional individualism.[2] Individuals choose and act, but individuals are what they are because of the institutions that form them as economically significant actors. In addition, institutions structure the economy of individual and organizational decision-makers, governing whose interests and decisions count.
3. The economy is a function of institutions. The economic system in any nation or group of nations at any time (and over time) is a function of the institutions defining and structuring individual and group relationships.
4. Markets are a function of institutions. Real-world markets are what they are because of the way institutions form and operate through them. Pure markets do not exist; only institutionally formed markets exist, and these are highly variable.
5. Resource allocation is a function of institutions. The level of aggregate income and the distribution of income and wealth depend on the institutions that shape and structure individual choice.
6. Institutions arise because of general interdependence, within both the economy as a whole and particular organizations. Scarcity requires choice among alternatives. This implies the necessity of structuring decision-making, which implies conflict, which implies the necessity of conflict resolution processes.
7. Choices must be made about how to work out the details of economic organization and structure. Underlying all institutional arrangements

are judgements about what reasonably serves the purposes of society; such judgements are required to resolve conflicts between interests and rights' claimants.

8. Decision-making processes are neither given nor operate in a mechanistic way; rather, they are modes of collective action and they exhibit evolution and cumulative causation in regard to their structure, their operation and their results (working rules).

9. If methodological individualism and methodological collectivism are to be combined, so must deliberative and non-deliberative (customary and non-cognitive) decision-making.

10. Government constitutes the principal form of collective action in the form of court, statute and administrative law. The economic system, markets and resource allocation, are all a function of law.

11. Law is the process through which working rules emerge that govern rights, powers, duties, exposures and immunities among people. It structures the distribution of participation, decision-making and opportunity. Policy and economy interact and jointly arise from the legal–economic nexus in which individual and group actions have both economic and political–legal significance.

12. The meaning and significance of economic phenomena is derived from legal–political and market interactions. These phenomena have evolved from an emphasis on physical property to incorporeal property, and from an emphasis on use value to exchange value.

13. The central unit of analysis is the transaction, which is not merely an exchange between two economic actors, but the presence of alternative actors and conflict resolution agencies such as the courts.

14. In the US, the authoritative body that determines which of various competing interests will prevail is the Supreme Court. In adjudicating between rival claims, the courts make law; they thereby help form and structure the future organization of the economy.

15. Working rules are formed through custom, court decisions (which often embody the choice between rival customs) and statute, but also through organizations adopting formal and informal by-laws.

16. Decisions about working rules (and thereby relative rights, immunities, and so on) resolve conflicts. They also structure access to power and use of power among individuals, groups, classes and organizations. Individuals, groups, classes and organizations are, in turn, themselves influenced by the working rules and decision-making structures.

17. Institutions not only control and liberate individual action, they also permit and structure joint action. Most economic activity involves collective action (for example, corporations), and this collective action is governed by other collective action.

18. There are numerous origins of institutions and many causes of institutional change, including deliberative and non-deliberative decision-making; the operation of the legal–economic nexus; changing working rules through resolving conflicts; changing perceptions of what is workable and reasonable in the resolution of nominally private conflicts; and the interplay between the practices of individuals and the working rules and the latter's enforcement (and interpretation) agencies. Institutions 'are constraints on individual and group action, and yet can be altered and used as instruments by individuals and groups' (Rutherford 1983, p. 722).

If all this seems to emphasize collective action, then it must be remembered that Commons intended to supplement the neoclassical theory of individual action with a theory of collective action and to bring out the implicit collective elements buried in individualist theory.

THE POSITION OF COMMONS

Economists have always been a heterogeneous and fractious group. Differing visions of economics are offered; adherents to each view attempt to portray their vision as the most scientific, the most useful, and the most worthy of a claim on society's resources. It is not hyperbole to characterize these activities as part of a struggle for social status and material resources. What gets labelled 'economics' as well as what constitutes 'dissenting economics' is a function of who wins and who loses.

When Commons was writing, this ongoing struggle involved those who identified themselves as institutionalists and those who identified themselves with neoclassical or orthodox economics. Commons entered the fray with his own version of institutional economics. He did not believe the orthodox approach to economics had no value, and he offered constructive criticism and a cautionary message for his colleagues – all approaches to economics were limited and those limits should be explicitly recognized; reliance on any one approach is misleading, and different approaches to economics could and should be combined. It is regrettable that his audience was attracted to exclusionary rhetoric and inflated claims for the validity and utility of particular models, tools and techniques. In the end, pursuit of an exclusionary strategy appears to have accompanied the dominance of neoclassicism in the struggle with institutionalism.

NOTES

1. The following five paragraphs are based on material in Biddle (1991), which provides references to support this interpretation of Commons.
2. Commons 'emphasizes the role that institutions play in shaping individuals ... [however his position] is quite consistent with the individualistic view that institutions emerge and change only through the actions of individual decision makers. Individuals, not autonomous social forces, determine the nature and evolution of institutions' (Rutherford 1990, pp. xx-xxi).

REFERENCES

Biddle, J.E. (1991), 'The ideas of the past as tools for the present: the instrumental presentism of John R. Commons', in J. Brown and D. van Keuren (eds), *The Estate of Social Knowledge*, Baltimore: Johns Hopkins University Press, pp. 84–105.

Commons, J.R. (1924), *Legal Foundations of Capitalism*, New York: Macmillan.

Commons, J.R. (1934), *Institutional Economics: Its Place in Political Economy*, New York: Macmillan.

Commons, J.R., Ulrich Bonnell Phillips, Eugene Allan Gilmore, Helen L. Sumner and John B.A. Andrews (eds) (1910–11), *A Documentary History of American Industrial Society*, 11 vols, Cleveland: Arthur C. Clark.

Commons J.R., David J. Saposs, Helen L. Sumner, Edward Becher Mittelman, Henry E. Hoagland, John B. Andrews and Selig Perlman (1918, 1935), *The History of Labor in the United States*, 4 vols, New York: Macmillan.

Fetter, F. (1915), *Economic Principles*, New York: Century Co.

Hollander, S. (1985), *The Economics of John Stuart Mill*, Oxford: Blackwell.

Mitchell, W. (1969), *Types of Economic Theory*, ed. J. Dorfman, New York: Augustus M. Kelley.

Ramstad, Y. (1986), 'A pragmatist's quest for holistic knowledge: the scientific methodology of John R. Commons', *Journal of Economic Issues*, **20**, December, 1067–106.

Ramstad, Y. (1987), 'Institutional existentialism: more on why John R. Commons has so few followers', *Journal of Economic Issues,* **21** (2), June, 661–71.

Ramstad, Y. (1992), 'A wolf in sheep's clothing: John R. Commons and the question of economic order', presented to the Association for Evolutionary Economics, 1992.

Rutherford, M. (1983), 'J.R. Commons's institutional economics', *Journal of Economic Issues*, **17** (3), September, 721–44.

Rutherford, M. (1990), 'Introduction', in J.R. Commons, *Institutional Economics: Its Place in Political Economy*, New Brunswick, NJ: Transaction Books.

4. The tenacious dissent of Milton Friedman

David Colander

Including Milton Friedman in a book on dissenting economists may seem strange to some. Many would not regard Friedman as a dissident; they would argue that he is, if anything, one of the consummate insiders of economics. While I agree that Friedman is an insider, over the entirety of one's career there is nothing inconsistent about being both an insider and a dissident. Many insiders are successful dissidents. In fact, being a successful dissident is one path to becoming an insider. Considering Friedman as a dissenting economist, I believe, can shed light both on the nature of dissent in the economics profession and on the economics profession itself.

I begin the chapter with a brief biographical sketch of Friedman, considering his publications and his many substantive contributions to economics. Then I turn to the concepts of dissent and orthodoxy in economics. Finally, I return to discuss Friedman's economic views and why he belongs in any book of important dissenting economists.

A BRIEF BIOGRAPHICAL SKETCH

Milton Friedman was born in New York City in 1912 into a family of relatively poor Jewish immigrants. He went to Rutgers University for undergraduate work; to the University of Chicago, where he received an MA at the age of 21; and to Columbia University, where he received a PhD at the age of 24. His movement from Chicago to Columbia concerned money: Columbia gave him a generous fellowship, Chicago did not. Like many graduate students in the Depression years, Friedman progressed slowly to his PhD. He took his time in part because there was a shortage of jobs in the 1930s, and it made little sense to complete graduate school in order to become unemployed. Also, his studies were interrupted by work and by World War II.

While working on his PhD, Friedman taught intermittently at Columbia. In 1935 he briefly took time off from the academic world and worked for the Industrial Section of the National Resources Committee, and in 1937 he worked with Simon Kuznets at the National Bureau of Economic Research. This research project eventually became his PhD thesis. During the war Friedman worked for the division of Tax Research at the US Treasury, where he wrote a book with Carl Shoup and Ruth Mack, *Taxing to Prevent Inflation* (Friedman, Shoup and Mack 1943).

Early in his career Friedman had numerous and diverse mentors, many of them part of the economic establishment. These included Arthur Burns, Frank Knight, Jacob Viner, Aaron Director (Friedman married Director's sister, Rose), Henry Simons, Henry Schultz and Wesley Mitchell.

After World War II, Friedman taught briefly at the University of Wisconsin and the University of Minnesota. In 1948 he moved to the University of Chicago. It is with this school that Friedman is most closely associated. He remained at the University of Chicago until his retirement in 1979 at the age of 67. He then became a Senior Research Fellow at the Hoover Institute at Stanford, where he is still working.

Throughout his career he has won a plethora of honours including the John Bates Clark Medal in 1951, given to the most promising economist under 40 that year. He was elected President of the American Economic Association in 1967 and won a Nobel Prize in 1976.

FRIEDMAN'S PUBLICATIONS AND CONTRIBUTIONS TO ECONOMICS

Milton Friedman is a prolific writer. His curriculum vitae includes an average of four or five academic publications each year, as well as a variety of popular articles and commentaries. He also is a copious letter writer, and he corresponds with a variety of economists. If the Federal Reserve undertakes some, according to Friedman, wrongheaded policies, they can expect to hear from Friedman.

Friedman's early publications included work in statistics, policy and theory. A reworking of his doctoral dissertation (Friedman and Kuznets 1945), was his first well-known book. His early work also contained a popular monograph. This book (Friedman and Stigler 1946), intended for the lay person, received many negative comments from the academic community because it took a strong stand against price controls in the housing market. At the time, such strong policy stands were considered non-academic.

Notable early articles included reviews of Robert Triffin's *Monopolistic Competition and General Equilibrium Theory* (Friedman 1941) and Abba Lerner's *Economics of Control* (Friedman 1947). In 1953 he published the influential book *Essays in Positive Economics*, which was a compilation of his articles on methodology and microeconomic issues. This book contained his well-known article in support of positive economics.

Friedman was especially prolific during the late 1950s and 1960s. It was in this period that most of his cutting-edge academic work was written: *Studies in the Quantity Theory of Money* (Friedman 1956b), a book that set out the tenets of monetarism; *A Theory of the Consumption Function* (Friedman 1957), a book that challenged the Keynesian notion that consumption was a function of current income; *Capitalism and Freedom* (Friedman 1962), a set of essays that translated economic reasoning into policy proposals understandable by the lay public; and (with Anna Schwartz 1963) *A Monetary History of the United States, 1867–1960*, which set out the empirical evidence for his views on monetary policy.

By the mid-1960s Friedman was considered a leader in the economics profession, which meant that by the late 1960s and 1970s many of his important articles were appearing as distinguished lectures. Two of the most famous of these are his American Economic Association Presidential address (Friedman 1968b) and his Nobel Lecture (Friedman 1977).

During the 1970s Friedman spent considerable time translating his academic ideas for the lay public. He was a regular columnist for *Newsweek* (many of his columns are reprinted in Friedman 1983), and *Free to Choose* (Friedman and R. Friedman 1980) influenced how economics was taught.

During the 1980s and 1990s his academic output of published papers decreased. But Friedman continues to influence policy significantly, both in his letter writing and in his discussions with other economists. He still keeps up a research agenda that would do a candidate for tenure proud. Two notable works include a continuation of his monetary study (Friedman and Schwartz 1982), and an article defending his approach to statistical work against the criticisms made by David Hendry (Friedman 1991).

This summary of Friedman's publications gives us a starting-point to consider Friedman's substantive contributions to economics. What is most impressive about these contributions are their breadth. They cover almost all aspects of economics – both microeconomics and macroeconomics as well as methodology, policy and theory. Because of that breadth, it is not possible to detail many aspects of those contributions in anything short of a book. Below I briefly summarize his contributions in the following areas: methodology, empirical work, micro theory, macro theory, monetary theory, macro policy and micro policy.

Methodology

Perhaps the one defining feature of Friedman's work is his methodology; that has influenced all other aspects of his economics. Early in his career Friedman played a major role in making economics be seen as a 'positive' science. That meant, for Friedman, focusing on the empirical support and testing of theories; although, as I shall discuss below, testing a theory then was not the same as it is now usually considered. He summed up his methodology in *Essays in Positive Economics* (Friedman 1953), a work that has been considered a classic in economic methodology. However, as Hirsch and de Marchi (1990) point out, Friedman's methodology is best seen through his actions, not through his writing on methodology. As they nicely document, the Friedman methodological approach is to concentrate on real problems, continually test one's theory against the empirical evidence, and not to bother with highly abstract theory except as a backdrop for developing a testable theory.

Empirical Work

Friedman's methodological work was closely tied to his empirical work. This, in turn, reflects his training as a student of Wesley Mitchell. As Hirsch and de Marchi (1990, p. 45) point out, economics for Friedman involved a constant 'interplay of fact-gathering with hypothesis formation at every step'. Friedman urged economists to consider theory in reference to the data, and to continually test theories against the data. That meant quickly moving away from abstract specification of theories, for which no empirical measures were available, and reducing abstract theories to simple testable equations and propositions. Friedman emphasized the interplay between facts and theory, and he rejected plausibility as a criterion for judging a theory. He also saw little use for case studies; facts for Friedman were numerical.

Consistent with his view of the importance of the empirical/theoretical interplay, many of Friedman's major contributions involved empirical work. His early microeconomic work involved collecting data about occupational pay, and his early monetary work involved empirical studies of the demand for money (Friedman and Meiselman 1963) and of the role of money in the economy (Friedman and Schwartz 1963).

These empirical views also significantly influenced his arguments against other approaches. Thus, when he criticized Lerner's *Economics of Control*, Friedman (1947) objected not to the logic of Lerner's arguments, but to the impossibility of empirically implementing it.

Micro Theory

Together with George Stigler, Friedman played a major role in making the
geometric presentation of microeconomic issues a mainstay of what undergraduate students are taught. *The Theory of Price* (Stigler 1966) carefully
spelled out many of the geometric conundrums of Marshallian micro
analysis. As is clear from that text, Friedman was, and is, an unabashed
Marshallian, and he popularized the price ceiling/price floor geometric
analysis that is standard in microeconomics texts, an analysis that makes it
look as though any type of price controls is bad. Friedman (and Savage
1952) extended utility analysis, and in his price theory text he clarified
many of the supply and demand tools. He also recognized the problems
which arise from attempting to extend a partial equilibrium analysis to a
general equilibrium framework in tax analysis (Friedman 1952).

Macro Theory

Almost from the beginning of his career Friedman was a strong critic of
Keynesian economics, and in that role as critic he made important contributions to macroeconomic theory. One important contribution was the
argument that consumption depended on permanent income, not yearly
income as in the simple Keynesian model. *A Theory of the Consumption
Function* (Friedman 1957) made that argument and developed it empirically. Friedman's views were subsequently integrated into mainstream
macroeconomics and, as a result, the simplicity of the earlier Keynesian
views was undermined.

In his AEA Presidential address Friedman (1968b) challenged the
Phillips curve analysis that was then prevalent, and introduced the concept of the natural rate of unemployment. The combination of the
natural rate and rational expectations formed the basis for the New
Classical Revolution of the 1980s. As such, Friedman's dissent played an
important role in changing economic orthodoxy.

Monetary Theory

The above contributions would be a superb career for most theoretical
economists, but for Friedman those contributions were sidelines. His
main theoretical contribution was reserved for monetary theory.
'Quantity theory of money – a restatement' (Friedman 1956a) almost
single-handedly revived, or created, the monetarist school of economics
(depending on which interpretation one accepts).

As is true in much of his theoretical work, the amount of explicit theory in this article is minimal. Friedman moved quickly from theory to applications of theory, making whatever assumptions were necessary to 'empirically test' the theory. At the time, his work of empirically testing the quantity theory (done with David Meiselman and Anna Schwartz) was well received, and it made monetarism the major alternative approach to the then-orthodox Keynesianism.

Macro Policy

Friedman's views on macroeconomic policy followed closely from his work on monetary theory and macroeconomic theory. In short, those views were a statement that *laissez-faire* was the appropriate policy, and that the government should be concerned with establishing a set of rules within which markets could function and individuals would be free to undertake activities, rather than being concerned with discretionary policy implemented in reaction to individual actions. In Friedman's view, the macro economy needed no driver, whereas in the orthodox Keynesian view, the economy needed the government to steer it.

In terms of specific macro policy, Friedman argued that a monetary rule was desired that set the money supply growth rate. After that was done, the government should leave the economy alone. Only such a rule would stop inflation which, according to Friedman, was everywhere and always a monetary phenomenon.

Micro Policy

Much of Friedman's popular writing was directed at microeconomic policy, and he consistently argued for keeping government out of the market. His microeconomic policy views are best seen as a reiteration of classical liberal views. Monopoly is bad, government intervention is bad, and the market is good – in the sense that people as a whole will benefit most from relying on the market. Friedman (1962, pp. 109–10) has put the argument as follows: 'The great danger to the consumer is monopoly – whether private or governmental. His most effective protection is free competition at home and free trade throughout the world'.

His arguments for the market relied not so much on pure theory as on the problems of government. For Friedman, government was a type of monopoly, necessary to a certain degree, but thereafter simply something that should be contained. He argued:

> The widespread use of the market reduces the strain on the social fabric by rendering conformity unnecessary with respect to any activities it encompasses.

The wider the range of activities covered by the market, the fewer are the issues on which explicitly political decisions are required and hence on which it is necessary to achieve agreement. (Friedman 1962, p. 24)

This political element supporting *laissez-faire* was emphasized more in his later writings (Friedman and R. Friedman 1980) and his *Newsweek* columns (see Friedman 1983).

THE NATURE OF DISSENT AND THE NATURE OF THE ECONOMICS PROFESSION

For all his orthodox achievements, in my view Friedman is a dissenting economist. To understand why, one must understand my view of the nature of the profession, and the nature of dissent in the profession. The first point to note is that what constitutes orthodoxy is often ambiguous and not clearly defined. It is not a Gertrude Stein profession; there is an orthodoxy there. But orthodoxy, like love, is something you have to feel – you cannot precisely define it. Should you violate that orthodoxy, you, and everyone, will know that you have, but the violation can only be understood contextually. The same views in different contexts could be categorized as orthodox or not orthodox. The second point to make is that orthodoxy changes; it is not a fixed point. The profession's views change over time, partly in response to dissenters.

Often, when Friedman first expressed his views, they were seen as radically unorthodox and completely foolish. Thus, while many of Friedman's views have become the profession's views, they were not always the profession's views. These include his negative assessment of Keynesianism, his advocacy of the quantity theory, his view of the political problem of governmental action to correct problems in the market, his view on the desirability of flexible exchange rates, and his view of the appropriate type of empirical work, which reflects his institutional roots.

Just how radical and unorthodox Friedman was considered cannot be completely garnered from reading his writings, even if one reads them in comparison with the literature of the time. In economists' writings, views are toned down and controversies smoothed over. While preparing a book (Colander and Landreth 1996), I had discussions with people who were Friedman's contemporaries and colleagues in his days as a graduate student. From these interviews I got a sense of how much of a dissident Friedman was. I was consistently told that (Keynesian) graduate students considered him outrageous and a dissenter by all measures. He operated in an entirely different framework. An example of this would be his well-known arguments with Abba Lerner about the relevance of fiscal policy. When most writers were thinking about what the design of fiscal policy should be, Friedman was arguing that fiscal policy could not be implemented.

Let me give an example of how hard it is to keep Friedman's earlier dissidence in perspective. In the 1950s and 1960s, Friedman was a strong advocate of flexible exchange rates. In the 1990s such advocacy among economists is not unusual and might be considered the norm. But in the 1950s and 1960s, it was a strongly dissenting position. The standard view at the time was that fixed exchange rates were a necessary foundation for international trade. If the gold standard was unachievable, an institutional arrangement which created some of the fixity of the gold standard was needed. Friedman disagreed entirely, and argued that exchange rates should be set in the market. Describing the reaction he received to his views, Friedman (1968a, p. 209) writes:

> I have for many years been in favor of setting free the prices of both gold and the dollar and letting them be determined by private trading in open markets. Time and again when I have made these proposals, I have been told that, however much sense they might make on economic grounds, they were not politically feasible. I have been, in effect, advised to stop wasting my time on idle dreams of a fundamental solution.

A dissident does not necessarily remain a dissident. Successful dissenters change the profession. One of the best ways to make a name in the profession is to dissent, to show the profession why its current views are misguided, and then to change the profession's views to one's own. Successful dissenters are temporary dissenters. A dissenter who is successful in changing the profession will not remain a dissenter.

In considering the nature of Friedman's dissent it is also important to note that the profession is multi-dimensional. By that I mean that it is not a single inquiry – it has a theoretical dimension, a policy dimension, and a methodological dimension of orthodoxy. At any time there is at least one (and possibly more) of each of these orthodoxies. This multi-dimensionality allows many avenues for dissent. An economist can, for example, be quite orthodox in policy, but quite unorthodox in methodology. Moreover, each of these dimensions is itself multi-dimensional. What the average economist believes is often quite different from what the textbooks present as orthodoxy which, in turn, is quite different from what the average person who teaches at a graduate school believes. And all these views can differ significantly from what the cutting-edge theorists believe. Because of this multi-dimensionality no economist is ever going to fit precisely into the classification 'orthodox economist', and if one is not careful to specify which orthodoxy one is referring to, the term 'orthodoxy', and likewise the idea of dissent from that orthodoxy, will be empty.

JUDGING DISSENT RELATIVE TO CUTTING-EDGE ORTHODOXY

In thinking about dissent I use as my reference point cutting-edge orthodoxy. You do not generally see cutting-edge orthodoxy in today's textbooks because the textbooks normally display a much slower-moving set of beliefs, beliefs that reflect an amalgam of the orthodoxies over the past 40 years, the period of time during which the current professors (who select the textbooks) were trained. (In my view, textbook orthodoxy is not a useful concept since it is such an amalgam.)

Why focus on cutting-edge orthodoxy rather than on standard orthodoxy? Because the interesting debates, the ones that determine the future direction of the profession, are on the cutting edge. Cutting-edge orthodoxy is to textbook and the average economists' orthodoxy what marginal costs are to average costs. As we teach our students, the action is at the margin.

Cutting-edge orthodoxy is the set of views held by the leading figures in the profession. These views, if expressed in the appropriate language and form, will be: (1) accepted as reasonable by other orthodox economists even though those views differ from their own, and (2) considered sufficiently noteworthy so that a person who comes along and expresses those views in the appropriate form would be seen as a desirable hire by a top graduate department. Another way to define cutting-edge orthodoxy is: *the conventional wisdom of economists who are held in highest regard by the leaders of the profession.* Even with these two definitions, the concept is still vague. So let me relate it to modern economists. On the one hand, Kenneth Arrow, Herbert Scarf, George Ackerlof, Edward Leamer, Paul Krugman and Nathaniel Rosenberg all hold views that are in some way unorthodox. None the less, if they had a student that they said was superb, and who was technically skilled, even if that student held unconventional views similar to theirs, that student would be highly sought after by graduate schools. Thus, their work belongs in cutting-edge orthodoxy even though it is unconventional. On the other hand, Paul Davidson, Leland Yeager, or Deirdre McCloskey would be seen as non-orthodox, even though, in many ways, they are as orthodox as the above-mentioned economists.

Let me give an example of how cutting-edge orthodoxy differs from a more standard view of orthodoxy: the analysis of production costs. Most textbooks generally treat cost analysis as marginal cost analysis. Some economists who are considered non-orthodox by many in the profession disagree with that treatment; they see the analysis of costs as far more complicated than can be presented in a marginal cost analysis. They favour an analysis that considers issues of non-linearities and increasing returns to scale. Cutting-edge orthodox economists now agree. For example, Scarf (1994, p. 127) writes:

> If economists are to study economies of scale, and the division of labor in the large firm, the first step is to take our trusty derivatives, pack them up carefully in mothballs and put them away respectfully; they have served us well for many a year. But derivatives are prices, and in the presence of indivisibilities in production, prices simply don't do the jobs that they are meant to.

There remains a difference, however, between this cutting-edge cost orthodoxy and the approach to costs that dissidents take. That difference lies in the way the issue is approached. Cutting-edge orthodox economists approach it in a highly abstract and mathematical manner; dissidents often approach the issue from a more historical perspective than the current mainstream finds unacceptable.

THE NATURE OF MODERN ORTHODOXY

For clarity's sake let me spell out what I regard as the movement of cutting-edge orthodoxy over the last 50 years. Although in the period from 1936 to the mid-1950s most textbooks were reflections of *laissez-faire* policy in macroeconomics, Keynesian economics was sweeping the top graduate schools despite political opposition both within and outside the profession. Thus, by the late 1930s Keynesian economics was cutting-edge orthodoxy.

The Keynesian orthodoxy was short lived, however. By the mid-1950s it was old hat. Because of Friedman, cutting-edge orthodoxy was amended by integrating money into the Keynesian model along IS/LM lines. By the mid-1960s monetarism was appended to Keynesianism and became the neoclassical synthesis orthodoxy. In the early 1970s the cutting-edge macro orthodoxy became a microfoundations, formalist approach to macroeconomic issues. In the late 1970s that evolved into the New Classical, rational expectations approach and, in the 1980s, into a New Keynesian approach emphasizing microeconomic explanations for wage and price rigidity. By the 1990s there was so much chaos in macroeconomics that it was practically impossible to define any theoretical orthodoxy – all that could be identified were approaches that were not orthodox.

In microeconomics, the cutting-edge orthodoxy in the 1930s was Pigovian economics, in which the role of government in correcting market flaws was acknowledged and the general equilibrium conditions

for efficiency were being explored in formal models. That Pigovian orthodoxy remained through the 1960s, moving, however, from a focus on pure
efficiency to issues of tradeoffs between equity and efficiency. Since the
1960s, microeconomic orthodoxy has become more diffused, so that by
the late 1990s, in terms of beliefs, it is difficult to capture any unique
orthodoxy. Orthodoxy is instead defined along methodological lines – as
long as it is put in a highly technical model one can come to almost any
conclusion and still be cutting-edge orthodox.

THE NATURE OF FRIEDMAN'S DISSENT

Having defined 'orthodoxy' and 'dissent', it should be clear that according
to my definition many of the profession's stars have at points in their life
been dissenters. In my view, dissent is a natural part of orthodoxy; it is the
way the profession develops. When dissenters are successful, their views
become cutting-edge economics. The profession's accolades will be much
higher for a successful dissenter than for a successful orthodox economist,
and the deeper one's successful dissent, the greater the accolades.

What will be lost in those accolades is the strength of character it took
to maintain that initial dissent because, after one is successful, history will
be selectively interpreted. Those holding opposite positions will see their
past opposition through a generous interpretative prism, and will emphasize in their writings how they really believed the new orthodoxy all along.
The totality of the writing and the vituperation given to dissenting views
in informal, unpublished, conversations will be lost. From discussions
with some of Friedman's fellow students it is clear that Friedman was considered a major dissenter during his graduate school days, and I can only
admire the strength of character it took for him to maintain his views.

With the above explanation it should be clear why I believe Friedman
can still be considered a dissenter even though he has received so many
accolades from the profession. The accolades came not because of his
orthodoxy, *but because of his dissent*.

Ironically, as I shall discuss below, he remains a dissident today.
Friedman's theoretical and methodological orthodoxies are no longer the
profession's orthodoxies. What happened was that during his lifetime the
orthodoxy in the profession has experienced wide swings, sometimes
coming close to Friedman's position on some points, but simultaneously
moving away from him on other points. Throughout these swings
Friedman remained steadfast in his approach, translating his ideas into
the current orthodoxy when necessary to transmit those ideas, but never
giving up his vision of the economy.

As I stated above, the profession is multi-dimensional and it includes, at a minimum, a theoretical, a methodological and a policy dimension. Friedman has dissented in all these, and it is precisely the multi-dimensionality of his dissent that has made him such a pivotal figure in twentieth century economics.

Friedman's Theoretical Dissent

Friedman's theoretical dissent has been both in microeconomics and in macroeconomics. Let us consider macro first. To understand his macro dissent, one must consider the policy position of the average graduate student in the mid and late 1930s when Friedman was a graduate student.

While it was true that many of the older professors were conservative and *laissez-faire*, cutting-edge macroeconomics in the late 1930s and 1940s was liberal, and even radical. In the 1930s the cutting-edge macroeconomic theory radically shifted away from *laissez-faire* economics. By the 1950s it had shifted towards Keynesian economics as interpreted by Paul Samuelson and the neoclassical synthesis. Friedman stood fast against this Keynesian liberal tide, and sided with what many of the young Turks considered the old fogies who were regarded as laggards and lacking modern theoretical understanding.

Friedman stood firm, and not only developed his ideas in his quantity theory framework, but simultaneously developed his ideas in the mainstream framework. His ability to translate from his framework to the standard framework is fundamentally important for understanding the success of Friedman's dissent and the failure of many other dissenting economists to get their ideas seriously considered. If one is not able to translate one's ideas to the mainstream framework, then one's ideas will remain tangential to mainstream economic inquiry.

In my view, Friedman never accepted the Keynesian Cross, IS/LM framework, but in order to convey his ideas to the orthodoxy he worked within that framework. Had Friedman insisted on only expressing his ideas in the quantity theory framework, he would have been far less influential. But he went beyond his framework and worked within the Keynesian framework. He showed how his views modified the consumption function and made it far more complicated with his idea of the permanent income hypothesis. If consumption depended on expected income, as it indeed would if people are globally rational (as is assumed in microeconomic theory), then the stability of the Keynesian consumption function, which depended on current income, was lost. Likewise, the stability of the Keynesian multiplier, upon which policy depended, was lost. Friedman then went on to test his permanent income hypothesis empirically against the current income hypothesis, and found that it better fit the facts.

Friedman further developed his monetary theory so that it fit the IS/LM framework, even though it was far too complicated to fit such a simplistic model. Then, when he had explained his view within the standard Keynesian framework of the time, he jumped up a step and said how that view does not capture his views at all. This explains the confusion and debate over the shape of the LM curve that occurred during the 1960s when, much to James Tobin's consternation, Friedman argued that none of his views depended on the shape of the LM curve as long as the LM curve was not perfectly elastic (Gordon 1974).

Friedman's micro theoretical dissent is more complicated and more closely related to methodology than are his macro views. As already noted, the cutting-edge orthodoxy of the 1940s was a liberal orthodoxy that centred around Pigovian taxes and government adjustments for externalities. Issues were discussed within a Walrasian equilibrium framework, and the goal of policy-oriented economists was to find formal general equilibrium solutions to problems. Lerner's economics of control was the early epitome of that approach, and Peter Diamond and James Mirrlees' work on optimal pricing was the 1970s epitome. The entire framework was, for the most part, liberal and was concerned with integrating equality with the efficiency of the market. Within this framework the market was seen as a machine to be tinkered with by governments in order to achieve the ideal mix of equity and efficiency.

Friedman accepted none of that, and instead proposed a political economy view of microeconomics, one that pointed out serious political problems with any assumption that government would work for the good of society. At the time, this was an enormous dissent from an orthodoxy that assumed that government generally was out to do good. This view was seldom explicitly stated or discussed; it was implicit in the models and framework of analysis. By setting up the problem as one of choosing polices to maximize a social welfare function, one implicitly assumes that someone wants to maximize that function. The implicit nature of these assumptions about government made it impossible for anyone to object to it without seeming an enormous dissenter. Friedman strongly opposed that view of government, and as such, anticipated the work of Anthony Downs, James Buchanan and Gordon Tullock.

Friedman was never a Walrasian and rejected much of the attempt to build such a theoretical general equilibrium model that was so far removed from reality. He saw microeconomic theory as Alfred Marshall saw it – an engine of analysis to further the study of specific problems, not to give one a grand understanding of the workings of the entire economy. That grand understanding was beyond analytic formalization. Friedman's view of the economy was biological rather than mechanistic.

Friedman's Methodological Dissent

To understand Friedman's methodological dissent and his empirical approach to economics one must understand his institutionalist training and beliefs. He was a student of Wesley Mitchell, and his views reflect many of the same institutional views that Mitchell held. These include the heavy reliance on statistical empirical work to determine one's positions, and a strong rejection of formal modelling as the means to understanding. The reason for rejecting formal models, especially general equilibrium models, is that they are too simple; institutions complicate the situation immensely. All we can see are reduced-form relationships that have too many complications to warrant extensive 'theoretical underpinnings'. This was an enormous dissent from the formalist orthodoxy which concentrated on precise formal models. Macroeconometric modelling was all the rage in the 1960s and Friedman, from the start, argued that the approach was inappropriate.

Similarly with formal testing. From his early work, Friedman never approached empirical testing from a classical statistical framework, where theory was specified independently of the data and then tested with data that were gathered with no knowledge of the theory in mind. Friedman's approach to economics was empirical in the sense that its only test of our understanding was its empirical validity. But that empirical validity was an interpretative empirical validity. Empirical data has meaning only to someone who understands history and institutions, and knows how to interpret events.

Friedman did not make this as clear as he should have, but his work focuses on an interplay of fact-gathering with hypothesis formation. This meant that Friedman had to translate his general theories quickly into empirically testable theories – making whatever assumptions were necessary to do so. This is an enormous dissent since the orthodox approach was to develop the logic of the theory completely, and only when that was done (if it ever was), to test the theory.

Friedman's view of empirical work never became generally held. I think one of the reasons why it did not is that Friedman claimed far more objectivity for such empirical work than it can deliver. But the fact that it has problems being objective does not make it wrong, and the fact that econometric models often look more objective than what might be called 'expert empirical statistical analysis with institutional understanding' does not make econometrics any more objective. The econometric approach simply does a better job of hiding the subjectivity. The reality is that empirical work necessarily has a subjective element to it.

Friedman's fundamental dissent is this methodological dissent; it underlies many of his theoretical objections to the formalist macroeconomic models. He wanted far more focus on empirical regularities that reflect the history and institutions than deductive reasoning. Given how far this was from orthodoxy, throughout his career Friedman had to modify his arguments and place them in a more formalistic model than I believe he would have wanted.

Friedman's Policy Dissent

Friedman also dissented in policy, and it is in policy that Friedman has had his greatest influence. His policy views have become the cutting-edge policy views of economists of many persuasions. Ironically, Friedman's policy dissent was not based on economic theory as much as it was based on a political economy vision. That vision combines economic understanding and a sense of politics, but this vision was lost in the 1930s as the ideas of the Classical economists were interpreted into formal models through the work of Pigou and others. Friedman remained almost a lone voice of classical liberalism through much of the 1950s and 1960s.

In macroeconomics, Friedman's famous debate with Lerner on the steering-wheel metaphor shows the strength of his views. Friedman argued against fine tuning when fine tuning was all the rage. In microeconomics he advocated an all-volunteer army, and *laissez-faire* when Pigovian externalities were all the rage. Also, and he continues to argue, I think correctly, for legalization of marijuana and other drugs, not because he favours their use, but because of what the laws prohibiting their use do to our society.

All these views, when they were first presented, constituted significant dissent. They involve either an extension of the market into areas where previously the market was not involved, or a reduction in government involvement in the economy. The orthodox 1950s view was that economic scientists had conquered the business cycle, and had the scientific knowledge to design institutions and policies to make the world wonderful. It was simply a matter of developing sufficient policy instruments to match the goals. The orthodox view was that government could, and would, maximize society's social welfare function by implementing taxes to offset the externalities that were pervasive in the economy.

CONCLUSION: FOREVER THE DISSENTER

Friedman continues to be a dissenting economist. Despite receiving many accolades, Friedman's methodological and theoretical views have not been generally accepted by the profession. In fact, the profession has gone the other way – it has gone full force into abstract models and formal econometric testing. Friedman's theoretical monetarism suffered the same fate as Keynesianism; it was discarded in the 1980s and replaced by New Classical economics that fit the general equilibrium mould, and the higher level econometric testing, in ways that Friedman's Marshallian approach never could. Thus, in the 1990s, on the methodological and theoretical front Friedman is more a dissenter than ever.

Despite one's views of Friedman's policies and approach to theory, one can only have the greatest respect for his tenacity and ability to stand up for what he believes. He is no wishy-washy academic, swaying to the latest fads; he is on a fixed path, and that steadfastness is the most important characteristic of a dissident. Thus Friedman will forever be a dissident, and because he is, the profession will be much better than it otherwise would have been.

REFERENCES

Butler, E. (1985), *Milton Friedman: A Guide to His Economic Thought*, New York: Universe Books.

Colander, D. and H. Landreth (1996), *The Coming of Keynesianism to America*, Cheltenham, UK, and Brookfield, U.S.: Edward Elgar.

Friedman, M. (1941), 'Review of Robert Triffin's *Monopolistic Competition and General Equilibrium Theory*', *Journal of Farm Economics*, **23**, March, 389–91.

Friedman, M. (1947), 'Lerner on the economics of control', *Journal of Political Economy*, **55**, October, 405–16.

Friedman, M. (1952), 'The "Welfare" effects of an income tax and an excise tax', *Journal of Political Economy*, **60**, February, 25–33.

Friedman, M. (1953), *Essays in Positive Economics*, Chicago: University of Chicago Press.

Friedman, M. (1956a), 'Quantity theory of money – a restatement' in Friedman (ed.), *Studies in the Quantity Theory of Money*, Chicago: University of Chicago Press, pp. 3–21.

Friedman, M. (ed.) (1956b), *Studies in the Quantity Theory of Money*, Chicago: University of Chicago Press.

Friedman, M. (1957), *A Theory of the Consumption Function*, Princeton: Princeton University Press.

Friedman, M. (1962), *Capitalism and Freedom*, Chicago: University of Chicago Press.

Friedman, M. (1968a), *Dollars and Deficits: Inflation, Monetary Policy and the Balance of Payments*, Englewood Cliffs, NJ: Prentice-Hall.

Friedman, M. (1968b) 'The role of monetary policy', *American Economic Review*, **58**, March, 1–17.

Friedman, M. (1977), 'Inflation and Unemployment', *Journal of Political Economy*, June, 451–72.

Friedman, M. (1983), *Bright Promises, Dismal Performance: An Economist's Protest*, Sun Lakes, AZ: Thomas Horton & Daughters.

Friedman, M. (1991), 'Old wine in new bottles', *Economic Journal*, **101** (404), January, 33–40.

Friedman, M. and R. Friedman (1980), *Free to Choose*, New York: Harcourt Brace Jovanovich.

Friedman, M. and S. Kuznets (1945), *Income From Independent Professional Practice*, New York: National Bureau of Economic Research.

Friedman, M. and D. Meiselman (1963), 'The relative stability of monetary velocity and the investment multiplier in the United States, 1897–1958' in *Stabilization Policies*, Englewood Cliffs, NJ: Prentice-Hall, pp. 165–268.

Friedman, M. and L.J. Savage (1952), 'The expected utility hypothesis and the measurability of utility', *Journal of Political Economy*, **60**, December, 463–74.

Friedman, M. and A. Schwartz (1963), *A Monetary History of the United States, 1867–1960*, Princeton: Princeton University Press.

Friedman, M. and A Schwartz (1982), *Monetary Trends in the United States and the United Kingdom: Their Relation to Income, Prices, and Interest Rates, 1867–1975*, Chicago: University of Chicago Press.

Friedman, M., C. Shoup and R.P. Mack (1943), *Taxing to Prevent Inflation*, New York: National Bureau of Economic Research.

Friedman, M. and G. Stigler (1946), *Roofs or Ceilings? The Current Housing Problem*, Irvington-on-Hudson, NY: Foundation for Economic Education.

Gordon, R. (ed.) (1974), *Milton Friedman's Monetary Framework: A Debate with His Critics*, Chicago: University of Chicago Press.

Hirsch, A. and N. de Marchi (1990), *Milton Friedman: Economics in Theory and Practice*, Ann Arbor: University of Michigan Press.

Rayack, E. (1987), *Not So Free to Choose: The Political Economy of Milton Friedman and Ronald Reagan*, New York: Praeger.

Scarf, H. (1994), 'The allocation of resources in the presence of indivisibilities', *Journal of Economic Perspectives*, **8**, Fall, 111–128.

Stigler, G.J. (1966), *The Theory of Price*, third edn, New York: Macmillan.

5. Friedrich A. Hayek: super-dissenter

Laurence S. Moss

INTRODUCTION

A Biographical Dictionary of Dissenting Economists contains entries on more than 85 dissenting economists, but no entry on Hayek. According to Arestis and Sawyer (1992), the people picked for the book include members of several dissenting sects – institutionalist, post-Keynesian, Marxian, and Sraffian. For the most part their contributions were unrecognized and unwelcomed by the gatekeepers of neoclassical economic journals. Hayek's links with Carl Menger, Eugen von Böhm-Bawerk, Ludwig von Mises, and the Austrian School no doubt excluded him from the Arestis and Sawyer volume. Hayek is perhaps seen as a bothersome naysayer in the flock of the neoclassical orthodox economists rather than as a genuine heretic.

John King (1998, pp. 89–105) contrasts a dissenting economist with other economists, who are referred to as 'orthodox', 'mainstream', and 'neoclassical'. Non-dissenting economists (1) subscribe to methodological individualism, (2) adhere to a strict dichotomy between normative and positive economics, (3) are favourably disposed to capitalism. By these criteria, Hayek would not be a dissenting economist. He adhered to methodological individualism throughout most of his life, and believed in the possibility of a value-free economics that would illuminate the coordinative features of markets. Hayek (1960) readily admitted that markets contain many blemishes, some unsightly enough to require active government intervention; and although Hayek (1963b) did not insist that market outcomes are the 'best of all conceivable outcomes', he was favourably disposed towards market economies and felt that they were preferable to central planning and totalitarian concepts of 'national unity'. So, if we are to name Hayek a dissenter, it cannot be because he rejected methodological individualism as a research strategy, accepted the possibility of an economic discipline separate and distinct from ethics, or had serious concerns about capitalism. Rather, Hayek's rupture with orthodoxy was more fundamental. He came to adopt certain radical and original conceptions about what economists studied. For Hayek, the economy came to represent something far different from what generations of economists took it to be.

The purpose of this chapter is to demonstrate that there is in Hayek at least one core conception that is both central to his teachings, and also a radical break with neoclassical thought and most other dissenting sects. By harking back to the eighteenth century cosmopolitan roots of economics, Hayek moved ahead towards global economics, an economics free of geographical location and material characteristics of production. Such a discipline would be filled with subjectivist images, speech acts of shared meaning and understanding, and individual actions coordinated by the adoption of norms, customs, and ethical rules, but not by government agencies or central banks. This economics would be transnational and fuelled by the development of communications technology. Hayek called this new coordinating arrangement 'the extended order'.

The extended order rejects one central tenet of modern economic orthodoxy. Most economists speak of 'the' economic system. The economic system is a subsystem of society that has boundaries largely coextensive with the political–geographical borders of the nation-state. Such national economies are characterized by certain macroeconomic measurements. The problem with this familiar approach is that each time a particular region of the world forms a successful common market or, at the other extreme, balkanizes into distinct nation-states, a decision must be made as to whether the system is now larger or smaller. It is cumbersome, and sometimes without theoretical justification, to link the image of the economic system to the vicissitudes of modern political life. Yet this problem has yet to be addressed by the profession. Economists of all stripes speak of the development of *nation-states*, the rise of productivity *within a nation*, the rate of inflation within a *national currency area* and the number of unemployed workers seeking jobs in particular *national jurisdictions*.

There is, however, some dissent among the orthodox. The distinction between gross domestic product and gross national product distinguishes the *geographical* origin of value added from the *national* origin of the people credited with producing it. Paul Krugman (1991, pp. 1, 87) addressed this point when he suggested reviving economic geography, a return to 'the location of production in space' and the dethronement of 'countries (that is, nation-states) as natural units of analysis'. Krugman reminds us that the geographical region including Buffalo, New York, and Toronto has a greater claim to be called 'an economy' than the political entity called 'Canada' that includes Toronto and Vancouver! Dethroning nation-states as the main focus of economic analysis has long been of interest to members of the modern Austrian School of economics.

The Austrian School takes a distinctively cosmopolitan view of economic integration. It is credited with demonstrating that the source of one region's success is available to other regions, and that rising living standards have more to do with institutions and incentives than with race, genetics or national political culture (Mises 1978). Of course, nations are important because their coercive interventions at geographical borders (and sometimes within regions) can distort economic activity and interfere with capturing the gains from trade. Menger (1950), the founder of the Austrian School, searched for general laws of economic development that applied to all regions regardless of language, and to some extent regardless of geography. Similarly, von Mises (1949) envisioned a general science of human action that isolated the principal forms that human action may take from particular historical and political contexts.

Hayek belonged to this Austrian tradition. During the 1920s he was influenced by his teacher, Friedrich von Wieser, as well as von Mises. But nearly seven decades later, Hayek preferred a radically distinctive concept, the extended order, which is the fruit of his long struggle to escape from habitual modes of thinking. The extended order – cosmopolitan in spirit – was intended to replace a more primitive and ancient notion of economic activity, what I shall call the 'household management model'. The 'household management model' was used by neoclassicals, Austrians and myriad other schools and sects. While pioneering his extra-national approach to economic integration, Hayek broke with habitual modes of thought in economics and dissented from both the orthodox schools of thought as well as from dissenting sects. Hayek's thoroughgoing dissent from neoclassical economics, Austrian economics and other deviant sects over the household management model has yet to be adequately recognized even by modern Austrian writers.

My thesis can be stated in a nutshell: Hayek dissented from the most basic paradigm of economics, the household management model of everyday economic life. Early in his career, he accepted this model, and did not abandon it completely until his last book (Hayek 1988).[1] I offer an original account of this remarkable transition. When all is said and done, the extended order moves beyond Paul Krugman's treatment of the location of production and towards a notion of global economic integration where location may become economically insignificant – at least for certain types of economic problems.

The next section explains the household management model and its relevance for understanding allocative efficiency. Then I explain Hayek's move away from this model and towards the notion of the extended order. These sections demonstrate how committed Hayek was to denationalizing economic reasoning. The last two sections discuss some implications of his global vision.

THE HOUSEHOLD MANAGEMENT MODEL AND ITS RELEVANCE

Consider a large patriarchal household from the Roman Empire – a wife, children, and an army of servants reside on the landed estate of our patriarch. It is reasonable to suppose that the patriarch can order the disparate preferences of the entire household according to a single scale of values from 'most urgent' down to 'less urgent'. The patriarch has the ability and authority to decide at what rate his older daughter's desired goods can be 'traded off' for his wife's, and so on. The patriarch may make interpersonal utility comparisons and try to increase total household utility, or he may selfishly arrange matters for his own betterment. Thus, the patriarch can choose how to allocate scarce resources among alternative ends and thereby solve the economic problem faced by his household-society. The economic problem can be solved because when a single mind evaluates the alternatives, economic organization is largely a matter of technological choice.

The first Western writer to equate the household with its property, and its management with the undivided authority of the household head, was the Greek writer Xenophon (1992). He coined the word 'economicus' to mean estate management. But it was the Roman Columella (1968, 1993) who, in the first century AD, wrote the most systematic of all treatises about the art of managing an agricultural estate. Columella (1968, p. 321) prided himself on providing a 'complete account of the science of gaining knowledge of the land and all that was required for the business of raising cattle'. Columella did not explain how the wine output, meat produce, and so on would be transformed to meet the specific practical needs of his wife, daughters, sons and servants; but there is little doubt that market exchange played an important part in the transformation of household production into final consumption goods. The focus was on technology and production and not market exchange or what the Greeks termed 'catallactics'.

Lionel Robbins first explained that economics studied an aspect of human behaviour that guided decision-makers. Although more than 1800 years separate Columella from Robbins, Columella would have understood Robbins (1962, p. 16) when he defined economics as the science that deals with 'human behavior as a relationship between ends and scarce means which have alternative uses'. Whether we choose to read Xenophon or Columella, there is little doubt that household economies required something extra that had not been accounted for fully in the household management recipes. Producing households need some deliberate exchange arrangements to transform their surplus stocks into other more useful goods and materials (Austin and Vidal-Naquet 1977, pp. 8–10). The notion that these exchange arrangements do not need to be set up by specific persons, and can arise spontaneously, was virtually overlooked until the emergence of liberal economic ideas from the sixteenth to the eighteenth centuries (see Chalk 1951; Hayek 1973).

Extending the approach of Robbins to an entire economy seems to have created some difficulties and debates. As early as the fourth century BC, Aristotle noted that Plato had committed a serious error when he conflated the management of a household with the management of an entire polity. Plato's assertion in *The Statesman* that 'the state is like the family, only larger' led Aristotle to an alternative view of the state as 'a community of equals, aiming at the best life possible' (Sabine 1959, p. 92). The tension between these two possibly irreconcilable views dominates much political philosophy in the West, but scarcely occupies the attention of economists, who are content to generalize from the household management model to the entire nation-state, and to take maximization of production as the criterion for evaluating economic arrangements.

Instead, suppose we think of a nation or polity as a collection of households under the direction of a charismatic leader. In the twelfth and thirteenth centuries, Chingis Khan and his heirs had the allegiance of entire family groups that came to his camp and pledged their loyalty (Kahn 1984, pp. xx–xxii). Mongolian armies claimed a large territory, including parts of Asia Minor and Eastern Europe, so Khan had to delegate tasks to ministers. His third son, Ogodei, was responsible for consolidating the administrative structure of the Mongolian empire from Northern China to the steppe region of Russia, the Middle East and most of Eastern Europe.

Tribal organization has been particularly effective in times of war, when the need to respond to a common enemy can unite families in a successful military organization. Customs and rituals such as the 'anda bond', a sacred pledge of mutual aid between the leaders, were especially important to the early success of the Mongol empire (Kahn 1984, p. xxiv). Tribal feuds, raids and wars were driven by a single leader able to organize and channel the efforts of family groups towards a single (military) objective. Hayek (1967, p. 75) named this kind of society a '*taxis*', because the knowledge and goals of the leader largely determined the structure of society and the sequence of economic events. The leader received information from his subordinates, established the priorities of member households, and determined the appropriate rates by which trade-offs can be made among these households.

For a large commercial–industrial society (such as emerged in Western Europe during the seventeenth and eighteenth centuries), such tribal organization is unwieldy if not impossible. There are many diverse house-holds whose needs extend beyond food and shelter. People in commercial–industrial societies also have a taste for independence and liberty. If they are to live together and prosper, the spontaneously gener-ated order of the market systems must arise with force and effect. This type of order is the result of human action, but not the result of any leader's plans. Neither patriarch nor chieftain will consciously mould the general shape of things. Hayek (1967, p. 76) termed this kind of society a *'cosmos'* and contrasted it with the tribal taxis. Where knowledge is dis-persed among thousands or millions of separate individuals, a spontaneous order is required for each individual to utilize his or her knowledge in ways that unintentionally increase the chances that others will be successful in achieving their plans.

People tacitly agree to rely on spontaneous ordering forces when they 'agree only [to abide by] abstract rules'. Most significantly, there is no need for people to 'agree or be made to submit to a common hierarchy of ends' (Hayek 1967, p. 76). Hayek's distinction between *cosmos* and *taxis* seriously limits the relevance of the household management model to economics, although Hayek did not originally see things this way, as I now demonstrate.

HAYEK'S BREAK WITH THE OLDER AUSTRIAN SCHOOL

Until the 1930s, Hayek distinguished himself as practitioner of the 'new' economics located in Cambridge, Lausanne, and Vienna. When he moved to London in 1931 he shared the latest Continental developments in eco-nomics with an enthusiastic English audience (Caldwell 1995). A perfect example of this 'team spirit' occurred in 1935, during the course of the famous economic calculation controversy. Hayek (1963a) patiently restated the position of the early Austrian School writers for the benefit of socialist writers. According to Hayek (1952, p. 121), economists are trained to detect 'big economic problems' in society, especially the ones involving the allocation of resources among different uses. This same big economic problem remains to be solved in a socialist world, where means of production (factories and other capital goods) have been nationalized and all market trading of capital goods has been prohibited. In a market economy, the problem of resource allocation is not solved 'deliberately by anybody in the sense in which the economic problems of a household reach solution' (Hayek 1952, p. 121). The problem is solved silently and invisibly by the competitive market mechanism. But what mechanisms exist under socialism that have any chance of solving the resource allocation problem? This was Hayek's challenge to socialist intellectuals (Vaughn 1980).

Let us engage (in classic Austrian fashion) in a thought experiment. Suppose we invite a dictatorial tribal leader to solve the basic problems of economic organization. He would have to decide what is to be produced, when it is to be produced, and to whom it will be distributed. He could not solve these problems without first determining 'the order of importance of the different needs of the community [and to assume that they] were fixed in such a definite and absolute way that provision for one could always be made irrespective of cost' (Hayek 1952, p. 122). Only if he were able to abstract from the 'multiplicity of individuals following their personal [value] scales' could a benevolent tribal dictator manage the entire economy as if he were the patriarch of a single household. Only under these fantastic circumstances could our dictator achieve any degree of management success.

Hayek explained that this hypothetical model of a benevolent dictator managing the economy as if it were a single household was an expository device only; it was not to be taken literally (Moss 1994). But the experiment served an important pedagogic purpose (Hayek 1962, p. 27). The household management model was invoked to show that a benevolent dictator allocating resources among alternative uses would still have to confront 'essentially the same value phenomena' (that is, rent and interest rates) that are the hallmark of a competitive market system (Hayek 1952, p. 137). The presence of rent and interest rates along with wages in a market system was not due to the particular institutional organization of that society – that is, private ownership and exchange of the means of production – but rather to the nature of human valuation itself when resources are scarce.

It courts disaster to move from thought experiments to installing a real dictator, as was done by the Bolsheviks in Russia in 1917 and the National Socialists in Germany in 1936, because there is no way that any common scale of values could be drawn up to guide the dictator, no matter how benevolent his or her intentions. The household management model is an expository device only. It was developed for a limited but important pedagogic purpose. It allows us to appreciate the valuation problem that competitive markets try to solve. But to suggest that the model is a blueprint to be followed by any political party is irresponsible (Hayek 1952, p. 137). Again, in modern society it is impossible to come up with a common scale of values so long as individuals possess the liberty to debate and disagree.

Hayek responded to socialist writers who thought otherwise. Dickinson (1939) had casually admitted the necessity for socialist deception, and this more than anything else drew Hayek's fire. Apparently, Dickinson agreed with Hayek that a socialist commonwealth required constructing a common scale of values. He explained that the 'powerful engine of propaganda and advertisement employed by public organs of education and the enlightenment' could 'divert demand into socially desirable directions'. This Socialist Ministry of Propaganda could overcome the problem of household diversity and decentralized knowledge by simple manipulation. The Ministry of Propaganda would at the same time preserve 'the subjective impression ... of free choice' (cited in Hayek 1952, p. 205).

Dickinson tried to defend these deceptions by pointing out that competitive market systems contain privately funded institutions (such as Madison Avenue advertising agencies) which generate propaganda in support of private business; as a result, the Ministry of Propaganda would hardly be breaking new ground. Perhaps in response to Dickinson, Hayek developed an argument to demonstrate why enforcing a common scale of values among members of a modern society would have to be achieved by propaganda, violence and terror. Any attempt to put the mental experiment of a benevolent dictator into practice would result in the demise of the liberal order. *The Road to Serfdom* (Hayek 1963b) argued that leaders wishing to establish a common scale of values would have to appeal to the most deep-seated prejudices, fears, instincts and jealousies animating the majority of people in the community. Appealing to their intelligence or diverse tastes would result in a plethora of bickering factions. In twentieth century Europe, the outcome of totalitarian efforts has often been racism and scapegoating a minority population, as seen, for example, in Hitler's wars of exclusion against the genetically unfit and 'racially unclean' (Proctor 1988; Goldhagen 1996). According to Hayek, a liberal order based on central planning is a chimera. With central planning, totalitarian political organization is inevitable.

From the beginning of his career, Hayek emphasized that what distinguished the competitive market order from a patriarchal estate or a Mongolian tribal empire was that it could *operate without any need to establish a single hierarchical scale of values for the larger community*. The head of a large Roman household or a tribal leader might manage the affairs of his domain according to his own values, but no common scale of values exists for a diverse community of many households that participate in what Hayek (1988, p. 6) termed the 'extended order'.

THE CONSEQUENCES OF EMBRACING THE EXTENDED ORDER

During the last part of his career Hayek came to realize that the household management model was inherently flawed and misleading. Seeing the economy as a household disguised important evolutionary and organizational features of modern society. As a metaphor, its defects and blemishes outweighed its considerable pedagogical benefits. In his last book, *The Fatal Conceit*, Hayek (1988) blamed Aristotle for shunting the train of economics onto the wrong tracks. Aristotle condemned communities with excessively large populations because he thought them to be disorderly, and he failed to understand the process of adaptation to unforeseen change by the observation of abstract rules which, when successful, could lead to an increase in population (Hayek 1988, pp. 88–105). Aristotle's ignorance led to an anti-commercial idea of morality that eventually made its way into Western culture, especially the official teachings of the Roman Catholic Church. The attacks on usury and mercantile profit-making that occupy the attention of so much of Western culture and civilization have their roots in Aristotle's ethical writings. These attacks seem to have blinded generations of scholars to the importance of the market system.[2]

Aristotle did not know that nature contains 'self-organizing structures' that can contribute to enhanced specialization and the division of labour. Self-organization makes possible an 'extended order of human cooperation' (Hayek 1988, p. 6) characterized by a cumulative expansion of economic activity leading to greater population growth and higher living standards (see Arthur 1996). Had Aristotle seen this, Hayek speculated, his moral theories would have been more conducive to business activity and the subsequent Christian philosophers would have been less critical of these integrative features of business life.

The extended order does not operate by the actions of individuals allocating known means among given ends to achieve a common scale of values. Indeed, household management plays a relatively minor role in the dynamic market process. Modern society does not really resemble a household. The problem of valuation that characterizes household allocation is different from what takes place in large societies. What makes modern economic life possible is that individuals adopt abstract rules of conduct. The great achievement of the market system is its capability of satisfying the diverse, privately held plans of individuals residing in densely populated regions. It does this because individuals are willing to guide their conduct by 'end-independent abstract rules' (Hayek 1988, p. 31).

These end-independent abstract rules deal with questions such as property, honesty, contract, exchange, trade, competition, gain and privacy (Hayek 1988, p. 12). They are by nature abstract. Although Hayek does not analyse the structure of these rules, my own suspicion is that they have the following form: 'Do not steal the property of another', 'Always try to keep a promise you have solemnly made to another' and so on. I would characterize Hayek's rules as general, abstract and universal rhetorical maxims of the type a parent sometimes says to a young child but which the child comes to fully understand only by observing and participating in situations that test the limits of these maxims. Hence the child learns that it might be necessary to violate someone's property rights in a lightning storm by taking shelter in someone's barn, and that the maxim 'do not trespass on to the property of another' is subject to some important exceptions (see also Hayek 1978, p. 89).

Rules, *and the exceptions* to them, are handed down by tradition, custom, habit and, perhaps, children's bedtime stories and fairy tales. They are embedded in the subtleties of film, song, cultures and popular prejudice, and they function to coordinate and integrate separate individuals. In some cases the coercive power of government forces agents to follow these rules (or special versions of the rules), but in many cases it is a matter of will as to whether individuals will blindly follow their elders and teachers or pioneer an original set of rules for themselves. Hayek's point is that those who blindly follow the rules without fully knowing how they work or why they are important are in many cases more likely to be successful in life. Communities populated with rule-following agents tend to flourish, whereas communities where individuals all follow different rules (or no rules) tend to sink into poverty and despair. The rules that guide the market order operate in roundabout ways to produce spontaneously coordinated orders that make civilized life both possible and commodious. Such rules are needed because knowledge is dispersed and not located in any central place, and attempts to centralize bits and pieces of information by crushing it into aggregate categories will destroy its relevant and unique content (Hayek 1945). Decentralized information is best utilized by a global division of knowledge coordinated in part through the pricing system. This division of knowledge is as profound as the productivity-enhancing features of the division of labour first emphasized by eighteenth century writers such as Adam Smith and Bernard Mandeville.

Hayek's notion of the extended order is the key to appreciating his arguments against central planning. The household management model is misleading because 'there is not, and never could be, a single directing mind at work; there will always be some council ... designing a plan of action for some enterprise' (Hayek 1988, p. 87). Even with the Khan as dictator, the leading families of the Mongolian tribes met at council and debated before the Great Khan took action. The separate members of any council were called upon to use their own knowledge. Each contribution or intervention sparked replies by others, who also drew on private opinions or local information. The process of council deliberation remains one of 'making use of dispersed knowledge' (Hayek 1988, p. 87). By centralizing decision-making, the council forgoes the rigorous checks and balances of competition and accountability that Hayek associates with the market economy. Highly centralized planning mechanisms produce inferior results, especially compared with outcomes that the system has produced in the past and is capable of producing well into the future.

The extended order is not a static description of allocations made by the market system but a vision of economic relationships among strangers over time and extending across vast regions. It makes a successful division of labour and regional specialization possible by drawing upon knowledge dispersed among large numbers of individuals. The number of people, and the density of the population, expands in particular regions without any apparent limit. *Fatal Conceit* presents the reader with a vision of economic life where growth seems endless. Since replicating rules and customs is inexpensive, there is no limiting resource other than the time spent communicating and copying. Hayek's vision of the future is one where fixed factors of production play no significant role whatsoever, making his approach unusual in the history of economics (Black 1995, p. 113). Unfortunately, Hayek's final statement about these matters was all too brief and resembled more an outline of research topics then a polished treatment. He left his students the arduous task of reconciling the several positions he held over his long career (Vanberg 1994). However, the Hayek of *Fatal Conceit* had become a genuine dissenter from economics in both its orthodox and heretical forms.

HAYEK AS THE SUPER-DISSENTER

Mainstream economics is committed to the notion of economic efficiency. The goals of macroeconomic policy are to keep resources fully employed and to employ them in uses with the greatest market value. In particular regions, in nation-states, and increasingly in economic unions (such as common markets), it is customary to seek the appropriate combination of laws, customs and institutional practices that make some index of regional output or production as large as possible. The steady rise of productivity in particular regions remains the surest prediction of what is important in life, including culture and even decency. Hayek was not averse to thinking of the economy in these practical terms, but he thought of productivity less in terms of indexes of physical output (such as steel per capita) and more in terms of subjective attitudes held by the agents residing.in a region (or seeking to move to this region), which would determine whether or not they would be successful in achieving their privately held plans (Hayek 1967, p. 163).

Curiously, Hayek devoted several pages in his 1988 book to the causes and effects of population growth. He used population growth as an index of economic welfare. According to Hayek (1988, pp. 124–5), whose optimism seemed in places to defy limits, 'as long as an increase in population has been made possible by the growing productivity of the populations in the regions concerned, or by more effective utilization of their resources, and not by deliberate artificial support of this growth from outside, there is little cause for concern'. Thus, if a population is kept alive by international donations while its war-torn economy remains incapable of feeding it, the growth of that population will be a source of alarm to the entire international community. Otherwise, population growth is not a problem in an extended order.

Hayek drew on the work of Simon (1981), who also denied the existence of limiting resources. He confidently concluded that population grows in a 'chain reaction' and without tragic consequences, when groups move away from 'tribal organization' and adopt the abstract rules of the market system. Hayek's references to population growth as an index of social progress seem crude, perhaps enough so to brand the elder Hayek a vulgar Social Darwinist (compare Vanberg 1994).

Despite the interpretative problems that remain, there seems to be a welfare economics loosely attached to the extended order. Hayek celebrates the coordinative features of the extended order. But what happens if the coordinative customs and practices conflict with existing ideas about human rights and passions for liberty? What will the normative economics of the extended order be like? Hayek gives us no direction here.

The direction to Hayek's positive analysis is, however, much more easily discerned. It points away from the economics of households and tribes. Nation-states are neither households writ large nor isolated market systems with claims to be natural units of analysis. An economy is a delicate latticework of interlocking plans and shared images. The glue preventing chaos is the abstract rules and customs that much of orthodox economics seems to overlook. Dissolving this glue in favour of some socialist ideology may indeed 'condemn millions to starvation', as happened in Communist China, Russia, India, North Korea and the Ukraine in this century.

TOWARDS A GLOBALIZED NOTION OF THE ECONOMIC SYSTEM

Hayek adopted an enlightenment view of a world in which all people, united by trade and mutual understanding, may increase their living standards indefinitely and without limit. In its present form, Hayek's theory is incomplete because it does not specify criteria for deciding which rules belong to the extended order and which do not. We take it to be Hayek's position that at least *some* abstract rules resulting from human action, but not human design, contribute to rising living standards in ways not fully appreciated by inquiring minds. What follows is a different vision of the market system.

The macroeconomic features of the economy are no longer confined to territories understood as nation-states. All men and women can grab hold of the dynamics of rising living standards by adopting the rules, customs and habits of commercial society. Presumably these rules have evolved and continue to evolve. They develop in ways that integrate human activities first by regions, then across continents, and today, around the globe.

The steady evolution of Hayek's thinking away from the nation-state and towards a global economics is evident at many places in his writings. In the 1930s, Hayek (1937) opposed the shift towards monetary nationalism in which nation-states tried to immunize their respective monetary and credit structures from the imperatives of international trade and specialization. Hayek and Keynes clashed dramatically in the 1930s over monetary nationalism, with Hayek insisting on the cosmopolitan ideal of a world united by open trade and commerce. During the 1940s, Hayek advocated a state-supported commodity money system (a commodity reserve standard) to capture some of the valuable features of the lost gold standard.

In 1976, he went much further, calling for the denationalization of money. Privatization was a practical way to improve the quality of money itself. Hayek was finally willing to extend the principle of competition to the money commodity itself. As he put the matter, 'we have always had bad money ... private enterprise was not permitted to give us a better one' (Hayek 1976b, p. 100). In 1988, Hayek criticized both socialists and economists for failing to appreciate the dynamic character of abstract rules, customs and habits that have evolved to form our market institutions. The extended order produces dramatic rises in living standards by coordinating and aligning private incentives so that information is constantly discovered and put to more productive uses. Economics as a discipline should study this process. Hayek likened economics to a metatheory about the creative and dynamic processes by which the participants in the market system discover new and more valuable ways of achieving their diverse and incommensurable ends. Economics studies 'the theories people have developed to explain how most effectively to discover and use different means for diverse purposes' (Hayek 1988, p. 98). Indeed, economics is a discipline that we rename 'catallactics' because its focus is not the management of households but the steady and orderly coordination of households communicating with one another.

Earlier, this chapter highlighted the efforts of Krugman and others to shift the focus of economics from nation-states towards regional economics. Hayek wanted to shift the focus away from both the nation-state and geography. He urged us to recognize the existence of certain global norms and institutions that are available to all people regardless of location. Not only is the information dispersed that needs to be utilized, but so are the agents who will do the job of capturing and utilizing this information. The communication networks from which subsequent valuable discoveries can be made and sustained are no longer geographically determined. The advances in communication over the last 150 years, from telegraph to the Internet, are vast and still unfathomable in their dimensions and ramifications.

By freeing economic reasoning from an emphasis on allocative efficiency, which is more suitable to the management of patriarchal households than to the contemporary world, Hayek pioneered a strikingly new approach. At the same time he dissented quite dramatically from the prevailing orthodoxies. Both orthodox and heretical schools of thought place their emphasis on physical material resources and their allocation among well-defined ends. Although all sides agree that the signals established by the pricing system make adhering to a common scale of values unnecessary, the household management model still guides their understanding of the nature of the economic problem. Economics is not only about the production and distribution of scarce things. It is about communication and shared meanings across time and geographic distance. Hayek's extended order breaks new ground. It underlines the importance of information, knowledge, global communication and coordination through rules, rituals and customs that have evolved spontaneously from centuries of social life and practice. This contribution breaks with the economics of household management and the management of administrative geographical units (nation-states), and makes Hayek a super-dissenter.

NOTES

1. In his 1967 lecture 'The Confusion of Language in Political Thought', presented at the Walter Eucken Institute in Freiburg, Hayek confessed that 'I now find somewhat misleading the definition of the science as "the study of the disposal of scarce means towards the realisation of given ends", ... which I should long have defended. ... The reason why Robbins' widely accepted definition now seems to me to be misleading is that the ends which a *catallaxy* serve are not *given* in their totality to anyone, that is, are not known either to any individual participant in the process or to the scientist studying it' (in Hayek 1978, p. 90).

2. As my earlier remarks indicate, I think that when Aristotle faulted Plato for thinking of the state as 'just like' a large family he laid the cornerstone for a systematic attack on the household management model such as cleverly developed in Hayek's later notion of the extended order (compare Sabine 1959, p. 92). Thus, I find the intensity of Hayek's (1988) attack on Aristotle somewhat surprising (compare Hayek 1976a, p. 17n).

REFERENCES

Arestis, P. and M. Sawyer (1992), *A Biographical Dictionary of Dissenting Economists*, Aldershot: Edward Elgar.

Arthur, B. (1996), 'Increasing returns and the new world of business', *Harvard Business Review*, **74**, July–August, 100–109.

Austin, M.M. and P. Vidal-Naquet (1977), *Economic and Social History of Ancient Greece: An Introduction*, Los Angeles: University of California Press.

Black, F. (1995), *Exploring General Equilibrium*, Cambridge, MA: MIT Press.

Caldwell, B. (1995), 'Introduction', in F.A. Hayek, *Contra Keynes and Cambridge: Essays & Correspondence*, ed. B. Caldwell, Vol. 9, pp. 1–48, *The Collected Works of F.A. Hayek*, Chicago: University of Chicago Press.

Chalk, A.F. (1951), 'Natural law and the rise of economic individualism in England', *Journal of Political Economy*, **59**, August, 330–47.

Columella, L.J.M. (1968), *On Agriculture V–IX*, Cambridge, MA: Harvard University Press.

Columella, L.J.M. (1993), *On Agriculture I–IV*, Cambridge, MA: Harvard University Press.

Dickinson, H.D. (1939), *Economics of Socialism*, Oxford: Oxford University Press.

Goldhagen, D.J. (1996), *Hitler's Willing Executioners*, New York: Alfred A. Knopf.

Hayek, F.A. (1937), *Monetary Nationalism and International Stability*, New York: Augustus M. Kelley.

Hayek, F.A. (1945), 'The use of knowledge in society,' *American Economic Review*, **35**, September, 519–30.

Hayek, F.A. (1952), *Individualism and Economic Order*, London: Routledge & Kegan Paul.

Hayek, F.A. (1960), *The Constitution of Liberty*, Chicago: University of Chicago Press.

Hayek, F.A. (1962) [1941], *The Pure Theory of Capital*, London: Routledge & Kegan Paul.

Hayek, F.A. (1963a) [1935], *Collectivist Economic Planning*, London: Routledge & Kegan Paul.

Hayek, F.A. (1963b) [1944], *The Road to Serfdom*, Chicago: University of Chicago Press.

Hayek, F.A. (1967), *Studies in Philosophy, Politics and Economics*, New York: Simon & Schuster.

Hayek, F.A. (1973), *Law, Legislation and Liberty: Rules and Order*, Vol. 1, Chicago: University of Chicago Press.

Hayek, F.A. (1976a), *Law, Legislation and Liberty: The Mirage of Social Justice*, Vol. 2, Chicago: University of Chicago Press.

Hayek, F.A. (1976b), *Denationalisation of Money: An Analysis of the Theory and Practice of Concurrent Currencies*, London: Institute of Economic Affairs.

Hayek, F.A. (1978), *New Studies in Philosophy, Politics, Economics and the History of Ideas*, Chicago: University of Chicago Press.

Hayek, F.A. (1988), *The Fatal Conceit: The Errors of Socialism*, Vol. I, in *The Collected Works of F.A. Hayek*, ed. W.W. Bartley, Chicago: University of Chicago Press.

Kahn, P. (1984), *The Secret History of the Mongols: The Origins of Chinghis Khan*, San Francisco: North Point Press.

King, J.E. (1998), 'John Hobson: dissenting labour economists', in R. Holt and S. Pressman (eds) *Economics and its Discontents: 20th Century Dissenting Economists*, Cheltenham: Edward Elgar, pp. 89–105.

Krugman, P. (1991), *Geography and Trade*, Cambridge, MA: MIT Press.

Menger, C. (1950) [1871], *Principles of Economics*, trans. J. Dingwall and B.F. Hoselitz, Glencoe, Illinois: Free Press.

Mises, L. von. (1949), *Human Action: A Treatise on Economics*, New Haven: Yale University Press.

Mises, L. von. (1978), *Liberalism: A Socio-economic Exposition*, trans. R. Raico, Kansas City: Sheed Andrews & McMeel.

Moss, L. (1994) 'Hayek and the several faces of socialism,' in M. Colonna, H. Hagemann and O.F. Hamouda (eds), *The Economics of F.A. Hayek: Capitalism, Socialism and Knowledge*, Vol. 2, Aldershot: Edward Elgar, pp. 94–116.

Proctor, R.N. (1988), *Racial Hygiene: Medicine Under the Nazis*, Cambridge, MA: Harvard University Press.

Robbins, L. (1962) [1932], *An Essay on the Nature and Significance of Economic Science*, London: Macmillan.

Sabine, G.H. (1959), *A History of Political Thought*, London: George G. Harrap.

Simon, J. (1981), *The Ultimate Resource*, Princeton: Princeton University Press.

Vanberg, V. (1994), 'Hayek's legacy and the future of liberal thought: rational liberalism versus evolutionary agnosticism', *Cato Journal*, **14**, Fall, 179–99.

Vaughn, K. (1980), 'Economic calculation under socialism: the Austrian contribution', *Economic Inquiry*, **18**, October, 535–54.

Xenophon (1992), 'The Oeconomicus: a discussion on estate management,' in *Memorabilia, Oeconomicus, Symposium, and Apology*, trans. E.C. Marchat and O.J. Todd, Cambridge, MA: Harvard University Press.

6. John A. Hobson: dissenting labour economist

J.E. King*

THE NATURE OF ECONOMIC DISSENT

To explain what it means to be a dissenting economist is no easy matter. Such a task requires a definition of the mainstream, and orthodox economists have displayed great resiliency over the years. Almost anything said against orthodox economics becomes open to challenge on the grounds that the critic misunderstood or vulgarized mainstream analysis, or simply failed to realize that these objections were implied by or contained within mainstream analysis. Thus Karl Marx gets dismissed as a minor post-Ricardian, J.M. Keynes as an inept would-be Walrasian with a fixation on wage rigidity, and Piero Sraffa as an unimportant rediscoverer of the non-substitution theorem.[1] Such is the protean nature of establishment economics that it is often impossible to rescue dissenters from what Thompson (1968, p. 13) once referred to, in a very different context, as the enormous condescension of posterity'.

J.A. Hobson's ideas, nevertheless, are worth rescuing because they are so relevant to current issues. In what follows I distinguish mainstream economics and identify dissent along three lines – method, substantive analysis and policy conclusions.

One characteristic of dissident economists is a profound interest in methodology; in contrast, neoclassical theorists are more inclined to paraphrase Samuel Johnson on patriotism ('the last refuge of a scoundrel') or Josef Goebbels on culture ('when I hear that word I reach for my revolver'), picking up their metaphorical guns at the very mention of the term. Orthodox economic methodology is therefore something of a ragbag, even if we disregard such eccentricities as Milton Friedman's (1953) highly influential conventionalism.

What unites John Neville Keynes's (1890) *Scope and Method of Political Economy*, which was the canonical text at the beginning of Hobson's career; Lionel Robbins's (1932) *Nature and Significance of Economic*

Science, the most influential book on method to appear in the last decade of Hobson's life; and Mark Blaug's (1975) celebrated article on paradigms and research programmes, which introduced economists to the mysteries of Thomas Kuhn and Imre Lakatos half a century later? Methodological individualism for one thing. Insistence on disciplinary borders, and on the superiority of economics over the other social sciences, for another. The attempt to draw a sharp distinction between ends and means, and between 'positive' and 'normative' statements, for a third. Methodological intolerance, for a fourth.

The belief that all economic analysis must have microfoundations, that all propositions must be reducible to statements about the motives and behaviour of individuals, has been shared by every mainstream theorist since Adam Smith, virtually without exception. Although it has been challenged continuously by Marxists, institutionalists, systems theorists and other heretics, its appeal is so strong that Post Keynesians often feel obliged to search for microfoundations and even some Marxians have succumbed to its fatal charms.[2]

Methodological individualism contributes to the tenacity with which mainstream thinkers defend the boundaries of their subject against inferior disciplines such as history, sociology, political science and anthropology. Sometimes this intellectual xenophobia manifests itself in contemptuous dismissal, as in the aphorism attributed to George Stigler: 'a political scientist is someone who thinks the plural of "anecdote" is "data"'. More often, it takes the form of aggressive academic imperialism, such as the 'new institutional economics', or Gary Becker's economic models of social behaviour and personal life.

This poses problems for the third methodological principle of mainstream economics, the sanctity of the end–means and positive–normative dichotomies. If society is to be regarded as a case study in neoclassical consumer theory, how can the preferences of individual economic agents be treated as exogenous to the economy? But, if utility functions are endogenously determined, what criteria can there be, independent of market outcomes, for passing judgement on those market outcomes?

These dilemmas do not prevent any but the most scrupulous mainstream theorists from continuing to assert the value-neutral, and therefore 'scientific', status of their work. Nor, and this is the fourth methodological question on which orthodox economists agree, does it deter them from reacting with considerable intolerance to any demonstration of dissent. The belief that there is only one correct way to do economics, and that those who suggest alternatives are deluded or dishonest, is not confined to the neoclassical camp. But dissenting economists tend to be more tolerant, more open to criticism, more receptive to advocates of methodological pluralism, than their counterparts in the mainstream. There is no equivalent among the dissidents (at least since the death of Joseph Stalin) to the rigid orthodoxy revealed by Melvin Reder's (1982) account of the Chicago school and amplified by the proud publication of Harry Johnson's (1973, pp. 263–92) PhD examination papers, almost Orwellian in their requirement for the parroting of the neoclassical party line.

Dissenters, in contrast, tend to be sceptical of methodological individualism and of value-neutrality, more apt to stray (without hostile intent) into the foreign territory of other disciplines, and more open to methodological criticism and debate.

On questions of substantive theory, however, the differences between heretical and orthodox ideas are less easily identified. For the most part these differences follow from their respective positions on method. The instinctive reaction of mainstream theorists when faced with an economic problem is to set up a model of constrained maximization with a given objective function and a market-determined budget constraint. Collective behaviour makes sense, for an orthodox economist, only if it can be interpreted as rational in this individual, calculative, instrumental sense. And the properties of the economic system as a whole can only be understood as the outcome of individual maximizing decisions.

The orthodox approach to labour economics follows from these broad unifying principles. The focus is on the individual agent, be it a utility-maximizing worker–consumer or a profit-maximizing firm. The former allocates time to work, leisure and the formation of human capital through education and training, ensuring that the appropriate marginal equalities are satisfied. The latter employs labour up to the point where its marginal revenue product equals its marginal cost. Market supply and demand functions are derived from the sum of these individual decisions, and establish equilibrium wage and employment outcomes. Theories of wage differentials, the distribution of employment incomes, labour mobility, job search and equilibrium unemployment are readily generated from these individualistic underpinnings, or microfoundations.

Within this framework there is considerable flexibility, for labour economists and for neoclassical theorists more generally. The behaviour of small numbers of agents can be modelled (or so it is claimed) as easily as the decisions of large numbers. Risk can be analysed as readily as situations involving perfect (and perfectly symmetric) information; and the subject matter of economics is, in principle, infinitely expansible. The traditional focus on market activities has been augmented, in recent decades, by the application of economic modelling to apparently non-market behaviour within the firm, the government bureaucracy and the household. The 'social science imperialists', as Geoff Harcourt once described them, are on the march.

Dissident economists do not always, or even predominantly, reject mainstream theorizing out of hand. It is possible to agree that constrained maximization by individuals does explain some aspects of economic (and perhaps also social) behaviour, without being forced to conclude that this is the only form of economic analysis, or even the most fruitful and interesting variety. Thus there are many non-neoclassical approaches to studying economic institutions, comparing economic systems and modelling macroeconomic processes that make no pretence to reduce aggregative behaviour to individual decisions (and, indeed, point to the need for *macro*economic foundations for microeconomic theory). No individual dissenting economist would agree with all of this. He or she may well use mainstream techniques, and construct neoclassical models, from time to time. But these will not be the only, or the most important, part of his or her analytical endeavours.

If orthodox economics is hard to pin down on questions of substantive theory, it is even more slippery where policy issues are concerned. Indeed, many neoclassical theorists would claim that the positive–normative distinction prevents them from issuing any policy prescriptions whatsoever *as economists*: only in their role as citizens, with values and political beliefs which are independent of their scientific expertise, can economists make judgements on matters of current controversy. Moreover (and here we encounter a final methodological position), there is often a tendency towards formalism which verges on deliberate abstruseness. Many mainstream economists are reluctant to dirty their hands with policy questions, and for this they are often criticized by outsiders and occasionally are also self-critical.

And yet, to paraphrase Robert Solow, life as a neoclassical economist does tend to lead one to respect the market. Among the dissidents, this faith is shared by the Austrians, who often take it to absurdly Panglossian extremes. Most dissenting economists, however, are more sceptical of the virtues of unlimited competition, and much more inclined to accept the need for social regulation of market behaviour. This need not be the product of Marxist contamination. Monetary heresies, in particular, have been associated as often with the far right as with the left, as can be seen from the sad fate of C.H. Douglas's social credit ideas (King 1988, Ch. 7). Nor should the radicalism of the majority of dissenters be exaggerated. Mainstream economists, like everyone else, are social creatures subject to the influence of prevailing ideas and swings of the political pendulum. No conservative today could write a book like A.C. Pigou's (1939) *Socialism versus Capitalism*. Few social democrats, and even fewer liberals, would now agree with Oskar Lange and Joan Robinson that Walrasian general equilibrium analysis had solved the economic problems of market socialism. On balance, though, orthodox economists have always been more favourably disposed to capitalism than the large majority of the dissenters. This was certainly true in 1890. It remained so in 1940, despite the traumas of the Great Depression and the theoretical advances of the (aborted) Keynesian Revolution. It is scarcely necessary to affirm that it is still true today.

HOBSON AS A DISSENTING ECONOMIST

If to be a dissenting economist is to swim against the mainstream, then Hobson had to do battle with a constantly shifting current. Throughout his life he was opposed to majority opinion on questions of method, theory and policy. Hobson advocated a multidisciplinary approach to economic issues. He took a distinctive and often idiosyncratic position on the problems of value and distribution, and was a forceful critic of 'classical' macroeconomics several decades before Keynes. As a 'new liberal' (in effect a social democrat) Hobson urged more comprehensive and thoroughgoing state intervention than most mainstream economists were prepared to contemplate (Schneider 1996b).

Hobson wrote more than 40 books, which have generated a substantial scholarly literature of their own.[3] His writings on imperialism and on underconsumption are so familiar that in secondary work Hobson sometimes seems to assume importance only as a forerunner of Lenin or Keynes. I have chosen to concentrate here on labour economics, a relatively neglected aspect of Hobson's work. Thus underconsumption plays only a minor role in what follows, and imperialism none at all.

Hobson on Method

At first glance, Hobson's heterodoxy with respect to method is very limited. He was a strong defender of theoretical, deductive models of argument, supported the use of what he termed 'Crusoe economics', and opposed the institutionalist approach on the grounds that inductive reasoning from controlled experiments was impossible in economics (Hobson 1900, pp. 3–4). He defined the economic problem as the maximization of the sum of individual utilities, less the corresponding disutilities associated with work, and found no problem employing 'a modified utilitarianism' (Hobson 1926, p. 64n.). Both W.S. Jevons and Alfred Marshall won his endorsement (Hobson 1930, pp. xiii, xviii, 103). In contrast, a prominent Institutionalist complained bitterly that Hobson rejected the organic viewpoint in favour of 'a concept of social welfare ... saturated with individualistic notions' (Hamilton 1915, p. 570).

On further investigation, however, Hobson's methodological orthodoxy proves to be only skin-deep. On five crucial points he broke with
the method of mainstream economics. First, he repudiated methodological individualism. For Hobson society was an organic unity, and 'the
real underlying error of Mr [Herbert] Spencer and his legion of followers
is that they persist in regarding society as an aggregate of individuals'
(Hobson 1901, p. 146; compare Freeden 1978). It follows that no purely
individual theory of value could be substantiated. 'While value in use is
strictly personal', Hobson maintained, 'value in exchange is distinctively
social. A market, however crudely formed, is a social institution'
(Hobson 1901, p. 144).

Second, Hobson claimed that individual tastes and preferences could
not be regarded as exogenous to the economic system, and consequently
should not be privileged as the sole criterion for assessing changes in economic and social welfare. Consumer tastes depend on what is consumed,
and how it is consumed. More fundamentally, an individual's preferences,
character and personality are influenced by the nature of the work that
he or she performs. Even the best neoclassical theorists, Hobson argues,
neglected these truths, exaggerated the significance of consumption *vis-à-
vis* production, and emphasized quantity at the expense of quality
(Hobson 1930, pp. xix, 103, 108–9).

This led to a third criticism of the mainstream position – its reliance
on market valuations expressed in monetary terms. 'In order to transform
political economy into a science of human wealth', he wrote, one vital
step is 'the deposition of money and the substitution of social utility as
the standard of wealth' (Hobson 1901, p. 39). Like John Ruskin before
him, Hobson believed that market values were in principle incapable of
accounting for the social merit (or demerit) of the goods produced; for
the conditions of work that their production required; for their distribution among the different members of the community; or for their effect
on the moral and intellectual status of the people who consume them
(Hobson 1901, pp. 45–8). Thus Hobson took a rather heretical approach
to welfare economics (Liu 1934) and hence, as will be seen in the final section, to questions of economic policy.

This also lay behind his fourth objection to orthodox methodology.
Hobson had no patience with the distinction between 'is' and 'ought',
criticizing attempts by theorists such as A.C. Pigou to build a value-free
'positive' science of economics purified of any normative elements and
making a sharp demarcation between efficiency and equity. Such distinctions belonged, at best, to static theory:

So long as economists confine themselves to a purely descriptive analysis of actual economic structure and processes, this refusal of all ethical considera- tion is proper enough. But when they take an evolutionary view of the economic system, and concern themselves with the wills and desires of the par- ticipants in changing methods of production, discussing new relations between capital and labour, or between producer and consumer, or the functions of the state in industry, it is impossible to keep out 'normative science'. (Hobson 1927, p. 127)

Since productivity depended on 'the good will and effective cooperation of the participants of production', Hobson continued, considerations of distributive justice and fair treatment were central to the determination of wages and employment. On questions of dynamics, then, economics and ethics were inextricably connected.

Hobson's fifth point of methodological dissent is perhaps the most important of all, for it concerns the status of economics as an autonomous discipline. In *Wealth and Life* he asked whether it was possible for economics to survive as a separate science. His answer was, yes and no. While 'there will remain plenty of specifically economic work to be done, both descriptive and interpretative, in industry, finance and commerce', this would become less and less useful as economics is increasingly subordinated to ethics. 'This growing sense of unity in life and conduct is, therefore, bound to exercise a dissolvent influence upon economics as a separate science and art' (Hobson 1930, p. 136). Increasingly, Hobson concluded, economics would become a branch of social philosophy. Neoclassical economics has always seen it the other way round.

Hobson the Theorist

Much of Hobson's economic work was concerned with labour. Again, on the theoretical level, his status as a dissident is not always easy to estab- lish; many of his ideas appear rather orthodox and some (as will be seen below) have a distinctly modern ring. Correctly interpreted, however, Hobson's writings constitute a damaging critique of neoclassical labour economics. We now examine his arguments on four issues – the theory of distribution, the connection between productivity and wages, the disutil- ity of work and the economic appraisal of industrial relations.

Hobson's initial approach to the analysis of income distribution was consciously Ricardian, and therefore marginalistic. Indeed, along with Sidney Webb (1888) and J.B. Clark (1891), Hobson (1891) can be regarded as one of the pioneers of the marginal productivity theory of distribution. He attempted to generalize David Ricardo's theory of rent, making it applicable to all three factors of production, not solely to land. The implication of factor heterogeneity and inelastic factor supplies, Hobson argued, is that rent is paid on intramarginal units of labour and capital no less than on intramarginal land. These rents, which are payments in excess of the minimum payments required by the factor owners, constitute the economic surplus. In practice, rents accruing to manual workers are very small, while 'rents of ability' paid to 'inventors, organizers, overseers, officials, professional men, artists, skilled technicians of every sort' are much greater (Hobson 1911, p. 108). The rents obtained by owners of capital, because of entry barriers and restraints on competition, are the largest of all.

Surplus incomes were extremely important to Hobson for two reasons. First, the propensity to save out of rents is very high, contributing powerfully to the tendency towards oversaving, or underconsumption, which lay at the heart of his explanations of imperialism and the trade cycle. Second, the existence of huge intramarginal payments to capitalists introduces a major element of indeterminacy into the theory of wages, and offers considerable scope for the exercise of trade union bargaining power. This is true even under perfect competition, since competition only sets limits to price and wage formation; within these limits, the bargaining strengths of the parties determine the actual price (Hobson 1900, p. 19). This essentially empirical objection to the neoclassical theory of distribution foreshadows the semi-institutionalist criticisms of Kurt Rothschild (1954) and the US 'neorealists' (Kerr 1983).

Hobson also attacked orthodox analysis at a more fundamental level, arguing that it was in principle impossible to impute marginal productivity to any individual producer. This is true in the rather obvious sense that 'in a large proportion of industrial operations, the productive unit of direct labour is not an individual, but an organic complex of individuals, working in such union as forbids the exact calculation of individual piece-wages' (Hobson 1901, p. 159). There is also a more subtle reason why marginal productivity fails. Even if universal piecework were possible, the value of output depends '*to an unknown extent*, upon the economic forces embodied in the tools and machinery employed, the organisation of the business and the trade, and of the whole industrial and political society in, for, and with which they generally work' (Hobson 1901, p. 159, original emphasis).

Non-imputation destroys the marginal productivity theory in both its positive and normative guises. These aspects are for Hobson totally inseparable. The 'intellectual maker', he maintains, has no full and absolute right of property in his product, but only a right limited by the relative importance assigned to his individuality of effort. ... Who shall say how far the *Oedipus Tyrannus* was the product of Sophocles, how much of Athens, how much of the Hellenic genius, or how much belongs to humanity? (Hobson 1901, p. 148)

This conclusion is a general one, since 'no product or its value is rightly attributable as a whole to any merely individual effort', and is true of the incomes of capitalists and managers. Hobson draws from his non-imputation theorem the conclusion that marginal productivity theory is irredeemably circular:

To judge that one man is twice as 'productive' because he can earn an income twice as large exposes the circular argument which vitiates it; for if we ask, 'How do you know he is twice as productive?' no other answer is forthcoming than this: 'Because he receives an income twice as large'. (Hobson 1901, p. 160)

If neither effort nor productivity can explain or justify income differentials, what can? Hobson affirms a third principle, that of needs. In the case of managers and responsible officials it had long been recognized that neither effort nor production could be measured, and that the best guarantee of capable and energetic work was the payment of a generous salary, sufficient to meet all reasonable wants. Gradually, Hobson suggests,

this more enlightened doctrine is creeping down to the less skilled and less responsible grades of labour. ... This is, in fact, the *rationale* of the labour movement in its struggle for a 'living' or a 'minimum wage'. This claim is simply the first step towards the substitution of a rational wage-system, based upon needs, for the anarchic struggle of disordered competition, which only feigns to apportion pay according to individual productivity. (Hobson 1901, pp. 162–3)

The assertion that productivity is positively related to wages is what Hobson means by 'the economy of high wages' (Hobson 1901, p. 100). It has recently been rediscovered by dissenting labour economists and also by some more orthodox theorists, spawning a substantial literature on 'efficiency wages'. As Hobson knew, it is profoundly subversive of neoclassical theory, not least in dissolving the distinctions between efficiency and equity, and between positive and normative economics (compare Stiglitz 1987; Currie and Steedman 1993).

Hobson was at pains to deny that the economy of high wages promoted complete harmony of interests between worker and employer:

This harmony exists only in certain industries, and there only within certain limits. ... It is not necessarily to the employer's interest to pay wages sufficient to maintain properly the vital energies given out in work; still less to increase wages with the view of raising the standard of efficiency. Whether or how far he will do so depends upon a great variety of conditions. (Hobson 1901, pp. 100–101)

In fact, as will be seen in the next section, the economy of high wages supplies a powerful rationale for both trade union activity and government intervention in the labour market.

Hobson's reference to 'the vital energies given out in work' leads us to his third challenge to orthodox thinking. Jevons, he argued, placed excessive emphasis on consumption as the sole purpose of economic activity. In this error

> he has been followed by most of our neo-classical economists, who, taking consumption as the economic goal, treat the wants and desires of man exclusively from the standpoint of consumptive utility or satisfaction, ignoring the need of a corresponding recognition of human needs and desires conveyed in workmanship. (Hobson 1927, p. 128)

Acknowledging the priority of John Ruskin, Hobson called for the replacement of 'a coarse quantitative economy' by 'a more qualitative economy of adaptive variety and human art', in which work would be a source of enjoyment and personal development rather than irksome toil. In this way the very distinction between production and consumption could be eliminated, as was already the case for the practitioners of the fine arts (Hobson 1910, pp. 332–4; compare Hobson 1920, p. 90). As he wrote in *Work and Wealth*:

> Current economic science has not only treated each cost and each utility as a separate item or unit of economic power, it has treated each man as two men, producer and consumer. ... The standpoint of organic welfare reduces to its natural limits this useful distinction of producer and consumer, and enables us to trace the true interactions of the two processes. In a word, it obliges us to value every act of production or consumption with regard to its aggregate effect upon the life and character of the agent. (Hobson 1914, pp. 13–14)

Sixty years later, a similar case against the orthodox conception of labour would be made by E.F. Schumacher (1979) and Herbert Gintis (1972).

Thus, for Hobson, work was always a process of joint production, in which labour inputs gave rise to two distinct types of output – goods and services for sale on the market, and a changed (all too often a damaged) worker.[4] Hobson was a keen student of 'the human costs of labour'. Surveying contemporary literature on the physical and mental effects of repetitive manual work, he concluded that such efforts entailed not just high 'disutility' but, more importantly, a significant impairment of the worker's personality and character. The evidence on industrial fatigue revealed that its accumulative effect constitutes one of the heaviest of human costs, a lowering of mentality and of moral resistance closely corresponding to the decline of physical resistance. Drink and other sensational excesses are the normal reactions of this lowered morale. Thus fatigue ranks as a main determinant of the 'character' of the working-classes and has a social significance in its bearing upon order and progress not less important than its influence upon the individual organism. (Hobson 1914, p. 70)

These consequences, he insisted, transcended any narrow utilitarian calculus. They also exposed the liberal myth that unregulated markets protected individual freedom. On the contrary, Hobson maintained, the division of labour is itself a form of tyranny:

over-specialisation looms before us as one of the gravest and largest social dangers, the more insidious because it conceals its 'social nature', and masquerades as 'individual liberty'. In fact society – not, indeed, through the organisation of the State, but through the looser voluntary, but not the less effective and powerful, organisation of markets – coerces the individual, and narrows and distorts his individuality, by this enforced growing specialisation. (Hobson 1901, p. 226)

Consumer sovereignty means virtual slavery for the worker. 'This brings to light a paradox. "Free Competition", the force which is worshipped by those who style themselves Defenders of the Individual, is seen to be the very force which destroys individuality in work, and compels an absolute submission to the will of society' (Hobson 1901, p. 228).

This was the dark side of work in capitalist economies. But there was also a bright side. Modern technology had the potential to liberate the worker from a great deal of drudgery (Hobson 1914, pp. 76–8). In addition, the growing diversity and improving quality of consumer tastes, 'flowing from the educated individuality of consumers', would limit the extent to which the standardization of production could proceed. This, Hobson claimed, was

a most important influence in the lightening of the human costs of labour. ... It will do this in two ways. In the first place, it will cause a larger proportion of demand to be directed to the classes of products, such as intellectual, aesthetic, and personal services, which are by their nature less susceptible of mechanical production. In the second place, weakening the traditional and the imitative factors in taste and demand, it will cause consumption, even of the higher forms of material commodities, to be a more accurate expression of the changing needs and tastes of the individual, stamping upon the processes of production the same impress of individuality. (Hobson 1914, pp. 76–7; compare Thompson 1994)

Such repetitive, soul-destroying work as remains must be equally shared, to the benefit of all classes. As Ruskin and Leo Tolstoy had insisted, nature intended that all men should do some manual work. Those who managed to avoid this law were physically damaged (Hobson 1901, pp. 120–21).

Creative and rewarding work would then be undertaken for its own sake, not merely as a means to pecuniary ends. 'Must the worker necessarily', Hobson asked rhetorically, 'and in all cases, find his motive to labour in the desire to possess as his "property" the product of his labour, or may he find it in the satisfaction afforded by the process?' (Hobson 1901, p. 107). In a good society, Hobson believed, the answer would be self-evident.

These considerations led Hobson to a very personal perspective on industrial relations. He was no syndicalist, believing that people's interests as citizens and consumers should not be suppressed in favour of their rights as producers (Hobson 1914, pp. 257–71). Even the milder doctrines of the Guild Socialists held no appeal for him. He was often critical of what he regarded as the narrow, selfish, backward-looking attitudes of the trade unions, and the 'ill-devised lopsided Socialism' they tended to support (Hobson 1914, p. 259; compare Hobson 1922b, pp. 480–81).

Despite these reservations, Hobson was a strong defender of the labour movement. This followed from his theories of wages and income distribution. Union wage pressure would promote productivity improvements, and would help eliminate the rents appropriated by capital (Hobson 1900, pp. 336–9; 1910, pp. 207–9; 1911, pp. 213-16). But there was more to organized labour than higher wages and shorter working hours.

> The real demand of Labour is at once more radical and more human. It is a demand that Labour shall no longer be bought and sold as a dead commodity subject to the fluctuations of Demand and Supply in the market, but that its remuneration shall be regulated on the basis of the human needs of a family living in a civilised society. (Hobson 1914, p. 190)

Hobson doubted the capacity of the labour movement, unaided, to obtain for the workers either the humanization of their lives or an adequate share of the surplus wealth. Thus, as will be seen in the next section, he supported state intervention both in the labour market and on questions of social policy.

Hobson's socialism, however, was moderate and cautious. While he favoured the nationalization of the principal centres of economic power, it was as part of a mixed economy with substantial residues of private ownership. Social justice was a prerequisite for the viability of such a system, for only then could class conflict be expected to give way to harmony. But this was a necessary condition, not a sufficient one. For Hobson, some of the fundamental causes of industrial unrest were found at the workplace, where the discontents produced by the physical strains of labour were compounded by 'those related to a loss of liberty, or an encroachment upon personality' (Hobson 1914, p. 86). Unquestioned obedience was increasingly difficult for management to obtain. 'A new sense of personal dignity and value has now arisen in the better educated grades of workers which interferes with arbitrary modes of discipline' (Hobson 1914, pp. 86–7). Suspicion of industrial authority helped to explain the strength of working-class resistance to improvements in the techniques of production, on which the worker was rarely consulted and which seemed to benefit only the employer: 'So far, then, as initiative, interest, variation, experiment, and personal responsibility are factors of human value, qualifying the human costs of labour, it seems evident that Scientific Management involves a loss or injury to the workers' (Hobson 1914, p. 212), even if accompanied by higher wages. Once again, quality had succumbed to quantity.

A large part of the solution, Hobson was convinced, lay in reducing the hours of work and expanding the leisure time of workers. Another large part of the solution lay in establishing good industrial relations. Such changes required broad-ranging social reform, and could not be attained solely by tinkering at the workplace. Hobson was sceptical of the benefits of profit-sharing schemes and worker-managed cooperatives (Hobson 1914, pp. 254–7), and sometimes denied that the self-interest of enlightened employers could have any significant practical effects (Hobson 1901, p. 101). He became more optimistic after 1918, sensing a major change in the intellectual and moral climate. Joint consultative committees, co-partnership schemes, insurance and welfare plans, all testified to the emergence of a new spirit of cooperation between labour and capital, and pointed the way to a transformation of 'the older, grasping, domineering capitalism' (Hobson 1927, pp. 124–5). But this 'new ethical compromise' must be encouraged, and administered, by the state. Hence Hobson's concern with questions of economic policy.

Hobson on Policy

On some policy matters Hobson was remarkably orthodox. He was never a 'currency crank', and, fearing their inflationary consequences, opposed 'proposals which rely on the habitual, or periodic expansion of credit in advance of production' (Brailsford et al. 1926, pp. 15–16).[5] He believed strongly in free trade, and attacked protectionism. His argument here hinged on the hallowed doctrine of comparative costs, and he did not shrink from the full employment postulate that was, as he clearly recognized, required to sustain it (Hobson 1903, pp. 60–61). He objected also to the political consequences of protection, which pandered to special interests and engendered a 'general corruption and debasement of Government' (Hobson 1903, pp. 88–9).

Hobson claimed, however, that free trade with the rest of the world did not entail complete *laissez-faire* at home. Indeed, he began his discussion of domestic economic policy by asserting the axiom that labour should not be treated like a commodity, to be bought and sold in the market-place under conditions of unrestricted competition: 'to buy labour-power, like other commodities, at a price determined purely by relations of Supply and Demand, is a policy dangerous to the life and well-being of the individual whose labour-power is thus bought and sold, to those of his family and of society' (Hobson 1914, p. 192). This principle followed from Hobson's theory of the economic surplus, which provided a measure of the degree to which the economic and the human laws of distribution diverged. Without social control over the economy, neither justice nor efficiency could be ensured. Thus, for Hobson, public policy had to be underpinned by a concern for the equitable distribution of income and wealth: 'The absorption and utilisation of the surplus for the betterment of the working-class and the enrichment of public life are essential conditions for the humanisation of industry' (Hobson 1914, p. viii).

He was not a radical egalitarian, believing as he did that 'individuals may differ as widely in their needs as in their efforts or their productivity. ... It would be wanton folly to lavish arithmetical equality of opportunities either in the shape of material property or immaterial wealth, upon individuals not equally capable of making a good use of them' (Hobson 1914, pp. 165–6). But this did not justify existing income differentials, which were demonstrably excessive. The state should therefore intervene to increase labour's share in total output, not simply in the interests of justice, but also as a safeguard against underconsumption. Trade unionism should be encouraged, legal controls over hours of work strengthened and universalized by international agreement, emigration promoted and immigration restricted (compare Mummery and Hobson 1889, pp. 209–15; Hobson 1900, pp. 359–61).

Unlike the conservatives of his day, Hobson refused to blame the victims of economic malaise for their plight. He demanded social reform, not private charity, which degraded donor and recipient alike; parasitism was pernicious, however benevolent the parasites (Hobson 1901, pp. 113–17). And Hobson meant *social* reform, not well-intentioned but futile efforts to improve the morals or character of the working class. Thus he was an early advocate of the welfare state, calling for generous old-age pensions, unemployment benefits and (especially) family allowances (Brailsford et al. 1926, pp. 20–26). Hobson also advocated establishing a minimum socially-acceptable wage, which would be binding upon all government agencies and extended through collective bargaining to workers in the private sector. This 'living wage' should be set at a level adequate for 'the maintenance of all wholesome and pleasant elements of customary consumption', and also allow for 'a margin of energy, of leisure, of material means, [which are] the needful conditions of the growth of new physical, intellectual, and moral needs' (Hobson 1896, p. 129). Industries unable to pay such a minimum wage should be reorganized under state supervision (Brailsford et al. 1926, pp. 27–41).

It was a bold move to advocate higher wages in Britain just after the defeat of the General Strike, when unemployment was high and there were strong pressures, both economic and political, for money wage reductions in declining industries and depressed regions. Hobson sharply criticized such proposals in his *Economics of Unemployment*. Wage cuts would redistribute income from workers to capitalists, he argued, increasing profits and the propensity to save and strengthening the already powerful tendency towards underconsumption. Lower wages would also lead to reduced productivity, through their long-term effects on the morale and efficiency of the labour force, and by deterring mechanization and technical change (Hobson 1922a, Ch. 6). For Hobson there was nothing to be said for wage reductions, even as a response to a financial crisis as grave as that of 1931. The National Government's policy of wage cutting would merely reduce output and expenditure, and lower the price level. In contrast to government policy, the fundamental problem was to ensure that consumption rose at the same rate as productive potential (Hobson 1931, pp. 465–6). On this issue, Hobson was a dissenter to the very end.

NOTES

*I am grateful for constructive criticism from Steven Pressman and Michael Schneider; responsibility for errors and opinions is mine.

1. On Marx, see Brewer (1995); on Sraffa, see Hahn (1982).
2. See, respectively, Lavoie (1992) and Roemer (1988).
3. See, especially, Allett (1981), Freeden (1978, 1990), Nemmers (1956) and Pheby (1994); the latter has a very comprehensive bibliography.
4. There is a close parallel here with the von Neumann–Sraffa treatment of production processes which use fixed capital (Steedman 1977, Ch. 10).
5. Although this tract appeared under the names of three other authors, Hobson was almost certainly its principal inspiration.

REFERENCES

Allett, J. (1981), *The Political Economy of J.A. Hobson*, Toronto: Toronto University Press.

Blaug, M. (1975), 'Kuhn versus Lakatos, or paradigms versus research programmes in the history of economics', *History of Political Economy*, **7** (4), Winter, 399–433.

Brailsford, H., J. Hobson, A. Jones and E. Wise (1926), *The Living Wage*, London: Independent Labour Party.

Brewer, A. (1995), 'A minor post-Ricardian? Marx as an economist', *History of Political Economy*, **27** (1), Spring, 111–45.

Clark, J.B. (1891), 'Distribution as determined by a law of rent', *Quarterly Journal of Economics*, **5** (3), April, 289–318.

Currie, M. and I. Steedman (1993), 'Taking effort seriously', *Metroeconomica*, **44** (2), June, 134–45.

Freeden, M. (1978), *The New Liberalism: An Ideology of Social Reform*, Oxford: Clarendon Press.

Freeden, M. (ed.) (1990), *Reappraising J.A. Hobson: Humanism and Welfare*, London: Unwin Hyman.

Friedman, M. (1953), 'The methodology of positive economics', in Friedman, *Essays in Positive Economics*, Chicago: Chicago University Press, pp. 3–43.

Gintis, H. (1972), 'A radical analysis of welfare economics and individual development', *Quarterly Journal of Economics*, **86** (4), November, 572–99.

Hahn, F. (1982), 'The neo-Ricardians', *Cambridge Journal of Economics*, **6** (4), December, 353–72.

Hamilton, W. (1915), 'Economic theory and "social reform"', *Journal of Political Economy*, **23** (4), June, 562–84.

Hobson, J. (1891), 'The law of the three rents', *Quarterly Journal of Economics*, **5** (3), April, 263–88.

Hobson, J. (1896), 'A living wage', *Commonwealth*, **1**, 128–9.

Hobson, J. (1900), *The Economics of Distribution*, London: Macmillan.

Hobson, J. (1901), *The Social Problem: Life and Work*, London: Nisbet.

Hobson, J. (1903), 'Protection as a working-class policy', in H. Massingham (ed.), *Labour and Protection*, London: Unwin, pp. 38–92.

Hobson, J. 1910), *The Industrial System*, London: Longmans, Green.

Hobson, J. (1911), *The Science of Wealth*, London: Williams & Norgate.

Hobson, J. (1914), *Work and Wealth: A Human Valuation*, London: Macmillan.

Hobson, J. (1920), 'Ruskin as a political economist', in J. Whitehouse (ed.), *Ruskin the Prophet*, London: E.P. Dutton, pp. 81–98.

Hobson, J. (1922a), *The Economics of Unemployment*, London: Allen & Unwin.

Hobson, J. (1922b), 'Britain's economic outlook on Europe', *Journal of Political Economy*, **30** (4), August, 469–93.

Hobson, J. (1926), *Free-thought in the Social Sciences*, London: Allen & Unwin.

Hobson, J. (1927), 'Economics and ethics', in W. Ogburn and A. Goldenweiser (eds), *The Social Sciences and their Interrelations*, Boston: Houghton Mifflin, pp. 121–30.

Hobson, J. (1930), *Wealth and Life: A Study in Values*, London: Macmillan.

Hobson, J. (1931), 'Reactions of national policy on trade and employment', *Political Quarterly*, **2** (4), October, 463–6.

Hobson, J. (1932), 'The tariff victory in Britain', *The Nation*, **134** (6) April, 393–4.

Johnson, H. (1973), *The Theory of Income Distribution*, London: Gray-Mills.

Kerr, C. (1983), 'The intellectual role of neorealists in labor economics', *Industrial Relations*, **22** (2), Spring, 298–318.

Keynes, J.N. (1890), *The Scope and Method of Political Economy*, London: Macmillan.

King, J.E. (1988), *Economic Exiles*, London: Macmillan.

Lavoie, M. (1992), *Foundations of Post-Keynesian Economic Analysis*, Aldershot: Elgar.

Liu, W. (1934), *A Study of Hobson's Welfare Economics*, New York: Stechert.

Mummery, A. and J. Hobson (1889), *The Physiology of Industry: Being an Exposure of Certain Fallacies in Existing Theories of Economics*, London: J. Murray.

Nemmers, E. (1956), *Hobson and Underconsumption*, Amsterdam: North-Holland.

Pheby, J. (ed.) (1994), *J.A. Hobson after Fifty Years: Freethinker of the Social Sciences*, London: Macmillan.

Pigou, A.C. (1939), *Socialism versus Capitalism*, London: Macmillan.

Reder, M. (1982), 'Chicago economics: permanence and change', *Journal of Economic Literature*, **20** (1), March, 1–38.

Robbins, L. (1932), *An Essay on the Nature and Significance of Economic Science*, London: Macmillan.

Roemer, J. (1988), *Free to Lose*, Cambridge, MA: Harvard University Press.

Rothschild, K. (1954), *The Theory of Wages*, Oxford: Blackwell.

Schneider, M. (1996), *J.A. Hobson*, London: Macmillan.

Schumacher, E.F. (1979), *Good Work*, London: Cape.

Steedman, I. (1977), *Marx after Sraffa*, London: New Left Books.

Stiglitz, J. (1987), 'The causes and consequences of the dependence of quality on price', *Journal of Economic Literature*, **25** (1), March, 1–48.

Thompson, E.P. (1968), *The Making of the English Working Class*, Harmondsworth: Penguin.

Thompson, N. (1994), 'Hobson and the Fabians: two roads to socialism in the 1920s', *History of Political Economy*, **26** (2), Summer, 203–20.

Webb, S. (1888), 'The rate of interest and the laws of distribution', *Quarterly Journal of Economics*, **2** (2), January, 188–208.

7. The policy dissent of Nicholas Kaldor

Steven Pressman

WHAT IS A DISSENTING ECONOMIST?

In their introduction to the *Biographical Dictionary of Dissenting Economists*, Arestis and Sawyer (1992) identify four recurring themes that run through the work of dissenting economists. First, there is an emphasis on realism, or developing theories that accurately describe economic reality. Second, dissenting economists incorporate institutions and history into their analysis, and do not regard economics as distinct and separate from other social sciences. A third similarity among dissenting economists is their view that human beings are social animals rather than isolated, individual entities. Finally, dissenting economists analyse income distribution in terms of class conflict rather than as the result of individual productivities.

While the intent of Arestis and Sawyer was laudable in identifying these traits, and while they did succeed in pointing out some constructive aspects of non-neoclassical economics, this approach is ultimately unsatisfying.

Identifying a set of beliefs held by all dissenting economists makes it appear that dissenting economists comprise a single, unified school of economic thought. Yet, as Arestis and Sawyer readily admit, there are probably more differences than similarities among dissenting economists. In addition, defining dissidents based upon a set of shared doctrines runs the risk of excluding someone from the ranks of the heterodox because he or she fails to accept some of the positive heuristics. Similarly, important dissidents might be ignored because their major contributions were of a critical, rather than constructive, nature. Some dissenting economists, by opening the eyes of orthodox economists, can and do make important contributions to economic knowledge.

Many of these problems are particularly acute in the case of Nicholas Kaldor. With the exception of his famous class analysis of income distribution (Kaldor 1956), it is not clear that Kaldor adhered to the four definiens of dissenting economists identified by Arestis and Sawyer.

Kaldor (1972) was known to rely on 'stylized facts' rather than actual facts, a method that can hardly be construed as economic realism, and he claimed that empirical estimation was supposed to decorate a theory rather than support hypotheses.

The economic advice Kaldor gave to less-developed countries was remarkably insensitive to their customs, history and institutions. Regardless of national experiences with tax collection and tax compliance, and regardless of the national level of economic development, Kaldor invariably recommended that third world countries adopt an expenditure tax. Almost as invariably, this advice was ignored by third world politicians. Where Kaldor's advice was followed – in India and Sri Lanka during the late 1950s – adoption of an expenditure tax was followed by mass demonstrations in the streets, and the tax on expenditures was soon repealed (see Thirlwall 1987, Ch. 5; Pressman 1995).

Finally, it is not even clear that Kaldor saw individuals as social beings rather than as individual utility maximizers. To take one well-known example, Kaldor's (1939) classic *Economic Journal* paper 'Welfare propositions of economics and interpersonal comparisons' proposed the now famous Kaldor Compensation Test. This test was designed to determine whether redistributing income improved overall economic well-being. According to Kaldor, a redistribution satisfied the efficiency test if the winner was willing to compensate the loser for his or her utility loss due to the redistribution. Individual utility assessments thus provide the justification for income redistributions. To take yet another example, Kaldor (1955) proposed taxing expenditures rather than incomes because he thought that individuals would respond to the incentives of such a tax system by spending less and saving more.

Because of the general problems defining a dissenting economist in terms of his or her positive beliefs, and because of the specific difficulties in the case of Kaldor, it may be preferable to define dissenting economists by stressing *the adjective* rather than the noun. With this emphasis, dissenting economists can be identified by their refusal to accept the neoclassical economic paradigm. Put most simply, this paradigm consists of three elements – a set of beliefs about how individuals behave, a tool of economic analysis and a policy conclusion which purportedly follows from the assumptions and the mode of analysis.

Several people have pointed out (Hausman 1992; Hollis and Nell 1975) that neoclassical economics rests upon a belief in rational economic man. Economists hold that individual agents have knowledge of all possible alternatives available to them. Agents are also assumed to know the utility they would receive from choosing each of these alternatives. These preferences among alternatives, or the utility that an individual receives from selecting different alternatives, are taken as given. Moreover, as Stigler and Becker (1977) argued, tastes are not subject to dispute or further analysis; any attempt to assess individual utilities (besides judgements about the joint consistency of an individual's preference set) is outside the purview of economics.

The assumption of rational economic man also has an action-oriented side to it. Based upon the alternatives open to them, and their own personal preferences, it is expected that individuals will select the alternative that provides them with the greatest utility. Individuals are thus, in practice, subjective utility maximizers.

The second leg of the neoclassical stool is a reliance on equilibrium analysis to study economic relationships. This method involves showing that economies will move towards a stable, market-clearing position barring any rigidities or market imperfections. Given individual endowments and preferences, economic analysis attempts to prove the existence of an equilibrium in every market, and also that the set of market equilibria are jointly stable.

Finally, *laissez-faire* constitutes the neoclassical policy conclusion. Given the utilities of individual agents comprising the national economy, and given the resulting equilibrium outcome, the neoclassical argument demonstrates that deviations from this *laissez-faire* outcome are suboptimal.

This trilogy of assumptions, method and policy conclusion brings out the different ways that heterodox economists can dissent from the neoclassical paradigm. First, the assumptions about rational economic man can be denied. Institutionalists probably provide the best example of this line of dissent. Second, the neoclassical mode of analysis can be rejected. The Austrian School perhaps provides the best example of an attempt to critique the neoclassical mode of analysis. Finally, the *laissez-faire* policy conclusions of neoclassical economics can be repudiated. Here the Post Keynesians have focused their attention and made their largest contribution.

NICHOLAS KALDOR AS A DISSENTING ECONOMIST

Although he dissented from all three elements of the neoclassical paradigm, Kaldor can best be characterized as a dissenter from the *laissez-faire* policy conclusions of neoclassical economics. The two ideas that Kaldor is probably most famous for are his proposals for an industrial policy and for an expenditure tax. A third key idea set forth by Kaldor was that incomes policies rather than tight monetary policy should be used to battle inflation. All three policy proposals reject the neoclassical policy conclusion of *laissez-faire*.

However, this is not the only way Kaldor dissented from neoclassical orthodoxy. He vigorously opposed equilibrium analysis (Kaldor 1972, 1985). In arguing for his economic policies, Kaldor employed a non-equilibrium model of cumulative causation, whereby economic growth and economic decline were self-perpetuating. Starting virtuous cycles and remedying vicious cycles were therefore critically important. Kaldor advanced his economic policy proposals as a means of spurring a positive growth cycle. He thought that his three economic policies would all start a cumulative growth process, especially compared to the results of following neoclassical policy advice.

Finally, the arguments that Kaldor made for industrial policies, for expenditure taxation and for incomes policies rest on a contradiction between short-run individual utility maximization and long-run economic outcomes. While this conflict does not entail an outright rejection of the neoclassical assumptions about rational economic man, the conflict serves to explain why individual utility maximization does not result in optimal economic outcomes and why economic policies are necessary to improve macroeconomic performance. It also points to the limitations of beginning economic analysis with strong assumptions about short-run utility maximization, and thus represents a quasi-dissent from neoclassical economics.

Moreover, at times Kaldor did go so far as to reject the assumptions that lie behind the neoclassical vision of rational economic man. In a 1984 interview, Kaldor discussed the struggle in Cambridge against neoclassical economics during the 1930s, especially the struggle against the assumptions of methodological individualism and rationality in individual action.

> Some of us, Joan [Robinson] ... and I in another way, were struggling against what you call mainstream economics in America, which is neoclassical economics. This whole excessive emphasis on methodological individualism, the rationality of individuals and the maximization of profits ... and a tremendous emphasis, which was never openly admitted, on this principle of limited substitution, being the substitutability at the margin ... and the whole marginal economics, the marginal product, the marginal this, the marginal that. ... Substitutability has a place no doubt ... but there is also complementarity, which is the opposite of substitutability. (Turner 1993, pp. 113f.)

The following sections flesh out how Kaldor's advocacy of an industrial policy, of an expenditure tax, and of an incomes policy can be seen as a dissent from the three elements of neoclassical economics.

INDUSTRIAL POLICY

In *Strategic Factors in Economic Development* Kaldor (1967) argued for a government industrial policy to encourage the growth of the national manufacturing sector. His argument was based upon three empirical regularities. (For a good summary of Kaldor's growth laws, see Thirlwall 1983.) First, Kaldor found a high correlation between the growth of GDP and the rate of growth of manufacturing output for 12 industrial countries during the 1950s and 1960s. He argued that aggregate growth rates were dependent upon manufacturing growth rates rather than vice versa, and that this could be explained by increasing returns to scale in industrial activities.

Second, Kaldor found a high correlation between productivity growth in the manufacturing sector and the growth of manufacturing output. Here he argued that productivity growth was dependent on the growth of manufacturing output. This relationship, sometimes known as Verdoon's Law, has been explained by appeals to economies of scale in manufacturing. (On Verdoon's Law, see Chatterji and Wickens 1983.)

Third, Kaldor found that the growth of manufacturing sector output was correlated with the growth of productivity in other economic sectors. This comes about because of the absorption of surplus agricultural labour by manufacturing, and because 'industrialization tends to accelerate the rate of change of technology, not just one sector, but in the economy as a whole' (Kaldor 1967, p. 23).

One conclusion that Kaldor drew from his study of the stylized empirical facts about economic growth, productivity growth, and sectoral growth is that economic growth depends first and foremost on the growth of an industrial sector. Manufacturing for Kaldor thus constitutes the engine of economic and income growth. The policy implication stemming from this analysis is that national governments must support domestic manufacturing industries. Governments can do this through the direct purchase of manufactured goods, or by supporting manufacturing industries with tax breaks, regulatory relief or other incentives or assistance. Such support may also lead to an 'export-led increase in demand' (Kaldor 1967, p. 42) for manufactured goods and a virtuous cycle of rapid productivity and income growth.

Another interesting policy proposal that followed from this analysis was the *selective employment tax*. The idea behind this proposal was to encourage employment in manufacturing industries experiencing increasing returns to scale. Kaldor (1966, Ch. 7) proposed that firms in the service sector be taxed based upon the number of workers they employed. The money collected by the government would then be used to provide tax breaks to manufacturing firms, again based on the number of workers they employed. This tax and subsidy scheme would provide incentives for the development of national manufacturing industries and disincentives for the development of service industries.

Both the policy proposals and the analysis here clearly lie outside the neoclassical mainstream. Government support for manufacturing rejects the policy of *laissez-faire* in favour of targeting specific industries or economic sectors.

The argument for this conclusion rests upon the theory of cumulative causation. Cumulative causation rejects the neoclassical contention that there is a stationary state towards which the economy is headed, and presents a dynamic approach to economic analysis. Cumulative causation involves a positive or negative feedback mechanism involving two or more variables. Since changes in any one variable lead to similar changes in other variables, the entire system moves along in one direction. The principle of cumulative causation was first applied in economic analysis by Knut Wicksell, when he examined what happens when real and natural interest rates diverge. It was Gunnar Myrdal, however, who first described this principle and recognized its importance.

A cumulative economic process contrasts sharply with a simple, unidirectional causal schema, where A causes changes in B, but the possibility of B having further effects on A is excluded. With unidirectional causation, changes in A lead to changes in B and things end there; the system reaches a new steady state with higher (or lower) values for the variables A and B.

With cumulative causation, the variables A and B will impact upon each other. Changes in A will affect B, which will further affect A, again impact B, and so on. When A and B both increase, we have a virtuous cycle or positive feedback loop; and when A and B both decline, we have a vicious cycle or negative feedback loop.

Kaldor applied this conception of cumulative causation to study economy growth and development. Those nations that develop their manufacturing sector, according to Kaldor, will embark on a virtuous cycle of productivity and income growth; while nations that specialize in agriculture or services will experience stagnating productivity and incomes, and a vicious cycle of decline.

Finally, Kaldor's case for an industrial policy rests on the fact that if the citizens of a nation prefer services and agricultural goods to manufactured goods, and prefer producing primary and tertiary sector goods, they should *not* be allowed to satisfy these preferences. Allowing these preferences to be satisfied will result in economic decline, and individuals do not want to be part of a vicious cycle of economic decline.

Individuals living in a nation where everyone prefers to produce and consume primary and tertiary goods are thus caught in a prisoner's dilemma. If everyone satisfied his or her preferences, the national economy would decline, which is an undesired macroeconomic outcome.

Anyone voluntarily altering his or her behaviour by producing or consuming manufactured goods will suffer the greatest utility loss, while those who do not make the switch become free riders. Thus no incentives exist for individuals to ignore their own preferences, or to not act based upon them. Yet the result of allowing everyone to satisfy his or her individual preferences is not the most desired outcome. The problem encountered here can only be solved by some national authority that supports the manufacturing sector of the economy and prevents the prisoner's dilemma game from being played out.

Like the famous paradox of thrift set forth by Keynes (1971), the microeconomic case for an industrial policy must be that individuals focus only on short-run utilities and do not notice that short-run utility maximization contradicts long-run preferences. And as Keynes also showed, government economic policy is the only means to prevent this undesirable macroeconomic result.

THE EXPENDITURE TAX

The expenditure tax has had a long and distinguished economic history. It has been advanced by John Stuart Mill, by Alfred Marshall, by Irving Fisher and by A.C. Pigou. More recently, expenditure taxation has been embraced by a number of economists with good mainstream, neoclassical credentials (Seidman 1980, 1990; Meade Report 1978; Pechman 1989). In the 1950s, Kaldor (1955) pushed expenditure taxation on both developed countries and less-developed countries, arguing that how much an individual spends, rather than how much money an individual makes, should determine the tax base.

Kaldor set forth three different arguments against the income tax – a philosophical objection against the income tax base, a complaint about the distributional consequences of income taxation, and a warning about the economic consequences of the income tax.

His philosophical objection was that all attempts to measure income for the purposes of taxation would be inadequate. Income falls short as a national tax base because income does not adequately measure the ability of an individual to pay taxes. To cite just one glaring problem, unrealized capital gains remain untaxed. Even when realized, manipulations of the amount of the gain usually take place; thus the income tax treats capital income too lightly.

This all works to the benefit of property owners, Kaldor argues. Since income from property escapes taxation, the income tax treats wealthy individuals too leniently. In addition, the very wealthy have inherited most of their wealth and do not earn much additional income. Consequently, taxing income allows these individuals to virtually escape taxation.

The income tax also has serious economic defects, according to Kaldor. It reduces the propensity to save and assume risks; thus it retards capital formation. It also encourages speculative activities at the expense of enterprise.

Finally, Kaldor argues that the income tax is a poor vehicle for controlling the macroeconomy. Stabilization policy, which depends on temporary changes in income tax rates, does not work very efficiently when people base their spending on longer-term income horizons.

Conceptually, one should think of the expenditure tax as an income tax system which allows all annual savings to be deducted from the tax base. To keep tax revenues from falling it will, of course, be necessary to impose higher tax rates on expenditures than currently exist on income.

The notion of taxing expenditures rather than consumption has, unfortunately, made Post Keynesian economists, who regard Kaldor as one of their own, very uncomfortable. The simple idea behind the expenditure tax seems to contradict the theory of effective demand, which has been cited as one of the few doctrines holding together the Post Keynesian paradigm (Arestis 1996; Hamouda and Harcourt 1989). If the problem facing capitalist economies is a lack of spending, then an expenditure tax, by rewarding saving and penalizing, would only make matters worse. Post Keynesians also seem to feel uncomfortable with the distributional consequences of an expenditure tax. Exempting savings from taxation seems *prima facie* to have negative distributional consequences.

In practice, though, it is easy to design an expenditure tax that is as progressive as one wishes. All that is necessary is that we manipulate marginal tax rates in order to yield the desired distributional outcome. For example, the poor can be given substantial tax rebates, as in the current US income tax system, through something like an earned income tax credit (see Hoffman and Seidman 1990). Alternatively, the poor can pay negative taxes, as in several proposed negative income tax plans (see Friedman 1962, pp. 177–95; Tobin et al. 1967), if we subject the first $X of consumption to negative consumption tax rates. By increasing the marginal tax rates on higher and higher levels of consumption we can thereby achieve any desired degree of tax progressivity in the expenditure tax system.

Not only are fears about negative distributional consequences unfounded, but the expenditure tax itself should be seen as a dissent from neoclassical orthodoxy because Kaldor expected that it would make the distribution of income more equal rather than less equal (Turner 1993, p. 45). Neoclassical theory takes the distribution of income as the natural result of different marginal productivities. Given this perspective, redistributions cannot be justified on economic grounds both because interpersonal utility comparisons are impossible, and because any redistribution would distort work incentives and lead to greater inefficiencies overall.

Heterodox economists, however, have advocated progressive tax policy for years. In the *General Theory*, Keynes (1973, p. 95) argued that fiscal policy would be more effective if the tax system were made more progressive. Kaldor (1955, p. 99) similarly viewed the expenditure tax as a means of equalizing disposable incomes: 'A progressive expenditure tax would do far more than the present system of income taxation to equalize the standard of living of the different classes and thereby bring us nearer to social and economic equality'. It would do this by imposing extremely high tax rates on high levels of consumption. Kaldor, in fact (1955, p. 241), suggested that the highest marginal tax rate on expenditures be set above 199 per cent, and possibly as high as 300 per cent. An expenditure tax would also tend to redistribute income by taxing inheritances whenever they were spent. In contrast, accumulated wealth passed down from generation to generation pretty much escapes taxation today (see Cooper 1979).

The expenditure tax can also be regarded as a dissenting economic policy because it advocates government activism to improve economic performance. Unfortunately, Kaldor at times spoke of the expenditure tax as a means of reducing the incentives that the income tax provided for consumption. This makes it appear as though he favoured the expenditure tax as a means of reducing the distortions caused by taxation, and thereby allowing individual preferences to determine economic outcomes. However, at other times Kaldor makes arguments that indicate his goal is to *change preferences* towards greater savings rather than letting given preferences run freely and rule the economy. This latter thrust is clearest in Chapter VII of *An Expenditure Tax* ('Taxation and economic progress') which argues that economic growth requires savings, and that this, in turn, would set in motion a virtuous cycle of income growth, additional savings and investment, technological improvements and productivity growth. An expenditure tax would explicitly contribute to this virtuous cycle of growth by changing individual preferences. Thus an expenditure tax can also be regarded as a dissent from neoclassical orthodoxy because it does not accept individual preferences as fixed and beyond dispute. When individual decisions lead to suboptimal results, government economic policy is needed to change those decisions and improve economic outcomes.

Finally, while the argument for an expenditure tax rejects the analysis and policy conclusion of neoclassical analysis, the argument also rejects a key neoclassical assumption. This assumption is the same one that

Kaldor rejected when he advanced an industrial policy – namely that short-run utility maximization leads to optimal long-run outcomes. In the case of industrial policy, Kaldor's argument was that a short-run focus on spending for services would lead to a long-run economic decline, which would reduce incomes and the ability to consume both services and manufactured goods. In the case of the expenditure tax, it is spending in the short run that leads to less investment, and therefore to lower productivity growth and smaller incomes in the future. Short-run utility maximization, given existing endowments, again leads to an undesirable long-run outcome.

INCOMES POLICY AND THE REJECTION OF MONETARISM

During the 1970s, as inflation became the main economic problem in the world economy, Kaldor changed the focus of his attention and his policy efforts. But first he had to contend with the rising tide of monetarism.

Modern monetarism holds that changes in the supply of money are the cause of higher prices for goods. The way to control inflation was to make sure that the money supply grows at a constant and slow rate, 3–5 per cent per year, which monetarists take to be the rate at which real economic output normally grows from year to year.

Kaldor felt that slow money growth would create too much unemployment. He also felt that there were better ways to deal with inflation than throwing people out of work. For these reasons he developed (Kaldor 1982) a critique of the monetarist position and then proposed an alternative anti-inflation policy.

Kaldor raised several objections against monetarism. First, he noted that according to the *equation of exchange*, $MV = PQ$, more money (M) leads to greater inflation (a rising P) only if the velocity of money (V) was stable. Kaldor denied that the velocity of money was constant, and produced substantial empirical evidence to show how the velocity of money changed over time and differed from country to country.

Second, Kaldor held that the direction of causation was actually the reverse of that claimed by the monetarists. For Kaldor, a rise in economic activity or a rise in prices causes a rise in the money supply. In modern economies, money is created when banks make loans. When economic activity expands, firms and individuals want to borrow money. Banks make money by lending, and so they will find ways to meet the needs of their customers for loans. In contrast, when economic activity slows down, no one wants to borrow money. As banks stop making new loans, the money supply stops growing.

Within this framework, a central or national bank can only enable banks to make more loans; it cannot get people to borrow. Central banks, therefore, cannot control the money supply. Rather, money was endogenous for Kaldor; the quantity of money existing was determined by the economic system itself rather than by the central bank.

Finally, Kaldor objected to the monetarists' constant harping about inflation. He noted that even the monetarists themselves admitted there were relatively few costs to inflation, since inflation was by definition a *general* rise in the price level. When all prices and all incomes go up by roughly the same proportion, there are only trivial costs to the economy, essentially the time and expense of firms physically having to increase the prices of the goods and services they charge (hence, these costs are sometimes called 'menu change costs'). Creating unemployment, on the other hand, creates severe hardship for those thrown out of work. Advocating joblessness in order to avoid the trivial costs of inflation, as monetarists did, was clearly a bad policy prescription.

Rejecting tight monetary policy to control inflation, Kaldor (1982, pp. 61–5) argued for an incomes policy to replace the current wage bargaining system. For Kaldor, inflation was not caused by too much money, but rather was caused by costs and prices pushing each other up in an endless spiral. Workers would demand pay increases to keep their wages up in the face of higher prices. But higher wages means higher costs for businesses, which get passed on to consumers in the form of higher prices, starting another cycle.

Individually, we all want to maintain our standard of living. Thus, as prices rise, we seek higher wages; similarly, as business costs rise, firms increase prices in order to maintain (real) profits. But with a fixed level of output, greater claims on this output can only lead to inflation, which no one wants. Thus, again, individual preferences lead to an undesirable outcome.

Kaldor suggested that government get into the wage-bargaining process in order to stop the spiral. They could do this either by freezing all wages and prices, or they could get labour and business to sit down together and cooperate on keeping inflation under control. Labour, for example, would agree to keep its wage increases in line with productivity gains; business, in turn, would agree not to raise prices.

Again, this policy proposal rejects not only *laissez-faire* policy proposals, but also neoclassical assumptions about equilibrium and individual preferences. With the wage–price spiral, we get no price equilibrium, but rather a vicious cycle of rising prices. And although individuals prefer to keep up with inflation over losing real income, when everyone behaves in ways that try to maintain their real income, the result is that prices go up and nominal income gains do not become real income gains.

CONCLUSION

We have seen that Kaldor rejected two of the three pillars of neoclassical orthodoxy. He shunned *laissez-faire* by favouring macroeconomic policies that would improve economic performance.

Kaldor (1972, 1985) also rejected equilibrium analysis as a means of doing economics, contending that these models 'created a serious break on the development of economic thought' (Kaldor 1985, p. 57). He favoured, instead, models of cumulative causation. In these models, government support for manufacturing industries would lead to a self-reinforcing process of economic growth; tax breaks for savings would result in greater investment and a virtuous cycle of income and productivity growth; and incomes policies would break a vicious cycle of wage and price increases feeding off one another.

Finally, while Kaldor did not reject the neoclassical vision of rational economic man outright, the problem he saw with this vision was that short-run utility maximization might not be in the long-term best interests of the individual or the nation. In such cases, maximizing short-run utility would not result in the most desirable economic outcome.

The failure of individual rationality was due to the fact that cumulative causation described economic activity better than equilibrium analysis, and that cumulative processes might generate lower future output. The consequence of this failure in rationality was that proactive economic policies were required. It is for these reasons that Nicholas Kaldor was a dissenting economist.

REFERENCES

Arestis, P. (1996), 'Post-Keynesian economics: towards coherence', *Cambridge Journal of Economics*, **20**, 111–35.

Arestis, P. and M. Sawyer (eds) (1992), *A Biographical Dictionary of Dissenting Economists*, Aldershot, Edward Elgar.

Chatterji, M. and M.P. Wickens (1983), 'Verdoon's Law and Kaldor's Law: a revisionist interpretation', *Journal of Post Keynesian Economics*, **5** (3), Spring, 397–413.

Cooper, G. (1979), *A Voluntary Tax?*, Washington, DC: Brookings Institution.

Friedman, M. (1962), *Capitalism and Freedom*, Chicago: University of Chicago Press.

Hamouda, O. and G. Harcourt (1989), 'Post-Keynesianism: from criticism to coherence?', in J. Pheby (ed.), *New Directions in Post-Keynesian Economics*, Aldershot: Edward Elgar, pp. 1–34.

Hausman, D. (1992), *The Inexact and Separate Science of Economics*, New York: Cambridge University Press.

Hoffman, S.D. and L.S. Seidman (1990), *The Earned Income Tax Credit: Antipoverty Effectiveness and Labor Market Effects*, Kalamazoo, Mich.: W.E. Upjohn Institute.

Hollis, M. and E.J. Nell (1975), *Rational Economic Man*, New York: Cambridge University Press.

Kaldor, N. (1939), 'Welfare propositions of economics and interpersonal comparisons', *Economic Journal*, **49**, September, 549–52.

Kaldor, N. (1955), *An Expenditure Tax*, London: Allen & Unwin.

Kaldor, N. (1956), 'Alternative theories of distribution', *Review of Economic Studies*, **22** (2), 209–36.

Kaldor, N. (1966), *Causes of the Slow Rate of Economic Growth in the United Kingdom*, Cambridge: Cambridge University Press.

Kaldor, N. (1967), *Strategic Factors in Economic Development*, Ithaca: New York State School of Industrial and Labor Relations.

Kaldor, N. (1972), 'The irrelevance of equilibrium economics', *Economic Journal*, **82**, December, 1237–55.

Kaldor, N. (1982), *The Scourge of Monetarism*, Oxford: Oxford University Press.

Kaldor, N. (1985), *Economics without Equilibrium*, Armonk, NY: M.E. Sharpe.

Keynes, J.M. (1971), *The Collected Writings of John Maynard Keynes*, Vol. IV, *A Tract on Monetary Reform*, London: Macmillan.

Keynes, J.M. (1973), *The Collected Writings of John Maynard Keynes*, Vol. VII, *The General Theory of Employment, Interest and Money*, London: Macmillan.

[Meade Report] (1978), *The Structure and Reform of Direct Taxation: Report of a Committee Chaired by Professor J.E. Meade*, London: George Allen & Unwin.

Pechman, J.A. (ed.) (1989), *What Should Be Taxed: Income or Expenditure?*, Washington, DC: Brookings Institution.

Pressman, S. (1995), 'Is an expenditure tax feasible?', *International Journal of Social Economics*, **22** (8), August, 3–15.

Seidman, L.S. (1980), 'The personal consumption tax and social welfare', *Challenge*, **23** (3), September–October, 10–16.

Seidman, L.S. (1990), *Saving for America's Economic Future: Parables and Policies*, Armonk, N.Y.: M.E. Sharpe.

Stigler, G.J. and G.S. Becker (1977), 'De gustibus non est disputandum', *American Economic Review*, **67** (2), March, 76–90.

Thirlwall, A.P. (1983), 'A plain man's guide to Kaldor's growth laws', *Journal of Post Keynesian Economics*, **5** (3), Spring, 345–58.

Thirlwall, A.P. (1987), *Nicholas Kaldor*, New York: NYU Press.

Tobin, J., J.A. Pechman and P.M. Mieszkowski (1967) 'Is a negative income tax practical?', *Yale Law Journal*, **77**, November, 1–27.

Turner, M.S. (1993), *Nicholas Kaldor and the Real World*, Armonk: M.E. Sharpe.

8. The positive dissent of Michal Kalecki

Malcolm Sawyer*

DISSENT IN ECONOMICS

Dissent in economics signifies rejection from the prevailing neoclassical orthodoxy in Anglo-American economics. Dissent, of course, can have a variety of negative connotations; as when one objects to or departs from orthodoxy because it is the orthodoxy, or adopts particular modes of analysis because they are in some way at variance with that orthodoxy. There is little or no evidence that Kalecki was a dissenter in this sense. There are few direct criticisms of orthodox analysis in his writings.[1] Several times he even drew on orthodox work, particularly his analysis of pricing and the degree of monopoly (Kalecki 1940).

The orthodox position can be defined in various ways. Although precisely defining that approach is not unproblematic, the heart of the neoclassical approach would include: (1) the pursuit of self-interest by individuals subject to a set of constraints; (2) unbounded rationality; (3) the interaction of atomistic individuals through perfectly competitive markets, where individuals are price takers; and (4) the use of equilibrium analysis.

Neoclassical analysis focuses on the behaviour of the individual, who is viewed as a rational being with well-defined objectives which are ruthlessly pursued in an environment with good information. The interaction between individuals takes place through arm's-length market relationships; and questions of power, class and race are ignored. Society is viewed from the point of view of the individual, rather than the individual in relation to society. Economic actors, whether households or firms, are seen as subordinate to a market mechanism and seen as relating to one another through this mechanism.

This asocial element is not limited to exchange; it also covers production where factors are combined according to a technically determined relationship to produce the output (see Arestis 1992, Ch. 3, Section 2).

Little attention gets paid to social and political institutions, although markets can be seen as institutions. While neoclassical attempts (for example, Williamson 1979, 1986) to explain the emergence of institutions (such as the large corporation) in terms of economizing behaviour have softened the dominance of the market in economic analysis, they nevertheless retain methodological individualism.

The presumption of full employment flows from the other assumptions of neoclassical economics in a variety of ways. Competitive markets, and in particular labour markets, always clear, with the equality between demand and supply providing a full-employment outcome. The sum of individual budget constraints yields Say's Law, so that the economy is supply constrained rather than demand constrained. Income distribution follows from profit maximization and market clearing, with each factor paid the equivalent of its marginal product.[2]

Neoclassical economics can be amended and expanded in a variety of ways. Oligopolist elements can be recognized and analysed (but at the cost of losing the marginal productivity theory). Externalities can be introduced and used to provide a rationale for government intervention of a limited form. Transaction costs can help explain the existence of firms rather than ubiquitous markets. Each of these additions softens the dominance of the market.

KALECKI'S DISSENT

This is not the place to consider the full range of Kalecki's analysis, which has been done elsewhere (Sawyer 1985). The purpose here is to highlight how the approach of Kalecki can be contrasted with orthodoxy, and hence how Kalecki can be considered as a dissenter. Kalecki was a positive rather than a negative dissenter; that is, he sought to construct an alternative mode of economic analysis rather than to criticize the prevailing orthodoxy. In this discussion we must also note that in a number of areas his analysis evolved and changed in significant ways. The two areas where this is most notable are investment behaviour and pricing.[3]

Kalecki initially studied engineering. He was largely self-taught in economics, influenced by Karl Marx, Rosa Luxembourg and Mikhail Turan-Baranovski. His background in economics was rather different from most American and British economists[4] and from many Polish economists in the interwar period, who were influenced by Léon Walras and the general equilibrium approach. As a result Kalecki was not concerned with the same questions that preoccupied neoclassical economists, such as whether equilibrium with involuntary unemployment was a theoretical possibility or a contradiction in terms, since he did not think in terms of equilibrium positions and saw capitalism as involving substantial unemployment and contradictions. It could be said that Kalecki did not dissent because he did not study the orthodoxy from which he could dissent; rather, his ideas evolved from his Marxian background,[5] his involvement in the Polish socialist movement and his everyday experiences of unemployment.

Kalecki was the grand theorist seeking to provide universal analyses or solutions. While most of his work was theoretical, it was based on perceptions of the actual economy. For example, he assumed unit costs were approximately constant with respect to output, since this not only simplified his analysis, but also reflected the cost conditions under which enterprises typically operate.[6]

The following eight sections each discuss a specific aspect of Kalecki's economics and contrast it with the prevailing orthodoxy. The main point, however, is not that Kalecki differed in this or that way from the prevailing orthodoxy; rather, he presented a different theoretical framework. His approach is not based on methodological individualism and does not employ equilibrium analysis. Kalecki paid little attention to individual behaviour in terms of consumption or labour supply; rather, his analysis of firm decisions regarding prices and investment recognized the influence of society and history. His microeconomic analysis was also more class based than individual based, and he saw macroeconomic forces constraining individual decisions.

His broad macroeconomic approach can be described as follows. Most, though not all, of the relationship between price and unit cost is determined in each industry by the degree of monopoly in that industry. From the price–cost relationship, both the profit-to-sales ratio and the distribution of income can be calculated. There is a double-sided relationship between investment and profits: investment decisions are implemented with a lag and the resulting investment expenditure determines the volume of profits. Profits and profitability, in turn, influence investment decisions and hence future investment. Increases in investment expenditure, which cannot be financed from internal funds and other prior savings, require the creation of loans; and the banking system is viewed as accommodating. If banks do not provide loans, increased investment expenditure cannot take place. Because of increasing risk, the cost of loans for an enterprise may rise as it seeks to extend its borrowing. The interaction of investment and profits lies at the heart of the business cycles and the growth process. The degree of monopoly approach suggests that price changes will be strongly influenced by cost changes, and that real wages (the relationship between money wages and prices) will be influenced by product market factors (for example, the degree of monopoly) rather than labour market factors. The level of unemployment and the degree of excess capacity are byproducts of the level of aggregate demand, which in turn depend on the level of investment.

Unemployment as the norm

Perhaps the most significant assumption made by Kalecki was that capitalist economies generally experience significant unemployment and excess capacity.

> A considerable proportion of capital equipment lies idle in the slump. Even on average, the degree of utilisation throughout the business cycle will be substantially below the maximum reached during the boom. Fluctuations in the utilisation of available labour parallel those in the utilisation of equipment. Not only is there mass unemployment in the slump, but average employment throughout the cycle is considerably below the peak reached in the boom. The reserve of capital equipment and the reserve army of unemployed are typical features of capitalist economy, at least throughout a considerable part of the cycle. (Kalecki 1971a, p. 139)

Neoclassical economics holds that full employment is the normal state of affairs. This arises for (at least) two reasons. First, following Robbins (1932), economics is defined as a science of people using their limited or scarce means to choose among alternatives. Rationality is not only assumed, but plays a central role in neoclassical theory. The combination of scarcity and rationality leads inexorably to full employment because, in the face of scarcity, it would be irrational to leave resources (including labour) underutilized or unemployed.[7] Second, general equilibrium analysis suggests full employment, perhaps by definition, since the labour market should clear with a balance between labour demand and labour supply.

Kalecki rejected this approach on many grounds. The economy cannot be characterized as perfectly competitive, and equilibrium positions should not be confused with what actually happens. Further, Kalecki rejected rationality at the level of the economy (under capitalism), although not, I think, at the level of the individual.[8] While it may be rational for the individual entrepreneur to reduce wages (since it helps to increase profits), it does not follow that it is rational for entrepreneurs collectively to lower wages (since demand will be affected) . Similarly, it is collectively beneficial (in terms of profits) when investment is increased, but an individual entrepreneur increasing investment runs the risk of not being able to sell the extra output produced. Kalecki (1971a, p. 147) also argued that 'the capitalist system is not a "harmonious" regime, whose purpose is the satisfaction of the needs of its citizens but an "antagonistic" regime which is to secure profits for capitalists'. This contrasts sharply with the harmonious portrait of market economies in neoclassical theory. There is also a rejection of Say's Law, with the level of economic activity (under capitalism) seen as generally demand constrained.

Kalecki dismissed the neoclassical mechanism where changes in relative prices clear the labour market and maintain full employment. The ability of prices to clear markets was blocked in two ways. First, prices are set by firms based upon their degree of monopoly. Since unit costs and the mark-up were insensitive to the level of demand, prices did not respond to changes in demand. Second, real wages are the relationship between money wages and prices. Kalecki viewed the determination of prices, given the level of money wages and degree of monopoly, as effectively deciding (at least in the short period) real wages. Hence, real wages are set largely outside the labour market and in the output market. A reduction in money wages (or in their rate of increase) would be largely matched (given the level of aggregate demand) by a reduction in prices (of their rate of increase), leaving real wages unaffected. Thus a reduction in money wages would not stimulate employment, and through its negative impact on the level of demand may actually reduce employment.

Macroeconomic Analysis

Macroeconomics is often seen as no more than simplified general equilibrium theory, arising from the sum of choices made by individuals. Kalecki rejected the notion of macroeconomic analysis as built up from microeconomic foundations. He did not draw on choice-theoretic behaviour; nor did he cast his analysis in terms of general equilibrium theory with its assumption of price-taking along perfectly competitive lines. His macroeconomics always had microeconomic elements, but ones derived from observations about real-world firm behaviour. Further, his microeconomic analysis was more class based than individual based. He argued that there are aggregate or system-level relationships that have no micro-level counterparts.

There are two clear examples of this in the work of Kalecki. The first is the equation that profits equal investment expenditure plus capitalists' consumption (under a range of simplifying assumptions). This causal relationship (running from investment to profits) holds only at the aggregate level; at the enterprise level there is no equality between investment expenditure (plus capitalist consumption) and profits, and causation runs from investment to profits (Kalecki 1971a). The second is the determination of capacity utilization and unemployment levels. In neoclassical analysis, these are determined by the choices made by enterprises and workers. For Kalecki, they are determined by the level of aggregate demand, which enterprises respond to in their production decisions.

Analysis of business cycles[9]

The business cycle was central to Kalecki's analysis of capitalism, and his analysis of business cycles reflects many features of his work. The level of economic activity is strongly influenced by the level of aggregate demand; capitalism is demand constrained rather than supply constrained. Unemployment is a general characteristic of capitalism, and even at the top of the business cycle there is rarely full employment. Little use is made of equilibrium analysis, and aggregates play a key role. The key ingredient driving aggregate demand is investment rather than consumer expenditure. The generation of cycles is closely linked to investment, which itself is affected by a form of accelerator mechanism.

Kalecki did not link investment to changes in output *per se*, but rather to variables such as changes in the rate of profit, which tend to be correlated with output. Further, he argued that investment decisions were linked with both the level of economic activity and changes in economic activity. Indeed, Kalecki (1968, p. 263) viewed 'the determination of investment decisions by, broadly speaking, the level and the rate of change of economic activity' as the *pièce de résistance* of economics. Economic activity is relevant because of its impact on savings and profitability, and not because it creates the requirement for a larger capital stock to produce a higher level of output:

> it would appear to be more realistic to base the acceleration principle on the grounds suggested above ... than to deduce it from the necessity of expanding capacity in order to increase output. It is well known that large reserve capacities exist, at least throughout a considerable part of the cycle, and that output may therefore increase without an actual increase in existing capacities. But whatever the basis of the acceleration principle may be, it is inadequate not only because it does not take into consideration the other determinants of investment decisions examined above, but also because it does not agree with the facts. In the course of the business cycle, the highest rate of increase in output will be somewhere close to the medium position. This, however, is unrealistic. (Kalecki 1990–93, Vol. 2, p. 285)

Kalecki assumed that a passive monetary system would provide credit on demand, and that this would permit expansion to occur. But he did recognize that banks could choke off expansion by not lending enough or by raising interest rates in response to any increased demand for loans. 'If the banking system reacted so inflexibly to every increase in the demand for credit, then no boom would be possible on account of a new invention, nor any automatic upswing in the business cycle' (Kalecki, 1990–93, Vol. 1, p. 489). This analysis reflects the Polish economic situation in the interwar and earlypost war period, where brakes on expansion did arise because banks were unwilling to finance that expansion.

It could be said that Kalecki adopted a fix-price approach. He distinguished between cost-determined and demand-determined prices, with the former predominant in the industrial sector and the latter in the primary goods sectors. Prices are not rigid, but are cost determined; they move in response to cost changes, and are little affected by demand variations. Over the trade cycle, prices and wages may well vary in both absolute and relative terms; but Kalecki did not see those price movements as having any significant effect on the course of the trade cycle. In effect it is permissible to work in real terms.

However, in other work, Kalecki (1990–93, Vol. 1, p. 101) suggests that the price–cost margin and the degree of monopoly may vary counter-cyclically: 'there is a tendency for the degree of monopoly [and thereby the price–cost margin] to rise in the slump, a tendency which is reversed in the boom', though this is only a basic tendency and there can be price-cutting in the depression. Kalecki, though, argued that 'gross profitability is at each moment determined by the mechanism of the business cycle' and that 'fluctuations of the share of gross profits in aggregate output during the trade cycle are independent of the wage struggle'. Essentially, real gross profits are determined by prior real investment decisions and are not affected by changes in money wages. However, in an open economy 'wage reductions or increases will unquestionably cause a shift in the distribution of social income between capitalists and workers'.

The central feature of Kalecki's explanation for the business cycle is the influence of investment on economic activity, and the determinants of investment. Kalecki built into his analysis the equality between savings and investment (assuming foreign trade and the government budget being in balance) . Investment decisions are assumed to be implemented in full, though not immediately. This can be assumed because of a lag between the investment decisions and the actual investment expenditure, and because credit expansion permits investment decisions to be financed. He drew no distinction between desired and actual savings, or between *ex ante* and *ex post* savings. Hence savings are generated by the level of investment, but there is no effect if the actual savings deviate from desired savings (for the level of income, profits, and so on).

Growth and Trend

While Kalecki's versions of the business cycle dealt with a stationary economy, later versions incorporated the trend as well as the cycle. Consideration of a trend introduces two new elements.

The first new element concerns the determinants of the trend and its relationship with the growth of the labour force. In a simple neoclassical growth model, the rate of growth is set by the exogenous growth of the labour force plus the growth of technology. Kalecki saw technological change as an essential ingredient in the growth process. In the absence of technological change, net investment would eventually grind to a halt. Also productivity growth would end. Kalecki does not include any consideration of the labour market: real wages are set by the relationship of prices to wages through the degree of monopoly, and employment is determined by the level of economic activity and demand. Hence, there is no reason to think that the growth of employment will match the growth of the labour force, and so perpetually rising or falling unemployment may result.

The second new element concerns the determination of the trend. In a simple neoclassical model, the growth rate is set by the exogenous growth of the output and converges to that rate. For Kalecki, the rate of growth (of the capital stock and also, implicitly, of output) is determined within the model. In his last paper on cycles and growth, Kalecki (1968) discusses the underlying nature of his approach, which differs sharply from orthodoxy. He argues that the analysis of the short run and the long run has to be integrated, which to some extent, he suggests, is a criticism of his own earlier work where 'I started from developing a theory of the "pure business cycle" in a stationary economy, and at a later stage I modified the respective equations to get the trend into the picture' (Kalecki 1971a, p. 166). But it is also a criticism of neoclassical theory, which holds that demand factors determine short-run cyclical movements while supply-side factors set the long-run growth path.

Several features of capitalist growth as perceived by Kalecki stand out from the above discussion. Kalecki (1990–93, Vol. 2, p. 337) saw his own analysis as showing 'that long-run development is not inherent in the capitalist economy'. He viewed innovations as the 'most important promoter of development'. Echoing Steindl (1952) to some degree, Kalecki (1990–93, Vol. 2, p. 337) wrote in 1954 that 'a decline in the intensity of innovations in the later stages of capitalist development results in a retardation of the increase in capital and output'. He also saw that a rising degree of monopoly and rentier savings, through their adverse effects on consumer expenditure and investment, would slow down long run growth. Unemployment rises when the growth of output falls short of the growth of productivity plus the labour force, but no forces automatically tend to reduce unemployment. Kalecki (1971a, p. 183) also argued that the growth rate depends on

> past economic, social and technological developments rather than determined fully by the coefficients of our equations as is the case with the business cycle. This is, indeed, very different from the approach of purely 'mechanistic' theories ... but seems to me much closer to the realities of the process of development. To my mind future inquiry into the problems of growth should be directed ... towards treating ... the coefficients used in our equations ... as slowly changing variables rooted in past developments of the system.

These variables include the degree of monopoly and responsiveness of investment to profitability. This passage clearly indicates that Kalecki thought the growth rate would evolve over time in response to changes in the underlying parameters.

Kalecki's (1972; 1986; 1990–93, Vol. 3) writings on growth can be highlighted by using his equation for the rate of growth of output, $r = (1/m)(I/Y) - a + u$, where r is the rate of growth of output (labelled Y), m the productive effect of gross investment (labelled I), a the loss of production due to depreciation, and u the change in capacity utilization. This equation shows that the growth of output is affected by three factors – new investment, the loss of productive potential through depreciation and changes in capacity utilization. This equation is effectively an identity, and holds under both capitalism and socialism. Yet Kalecki sees three differences between these two systems. First, capitalist economies are demand constrained whereas socialist economies are supply constrained. Second, decisions about savings and investment are made in the private sector under capitalism, whereas under socialism these decisions are made by planners. Third, there may be more price flexibility under socialism than under capitalism, since in capitalism prices (relative to wages) are set by the relevant degree of monopoly, which may change with the industrial structure but is not flexible enough to restore balance between savings and investment at full employment.

Equilibrium Analysis

Kalecki made little use of equilibrium analysis (Asimakopulos 1977) , and could even be described as hostile to its use. In neoclassical economics, equilibrium is a situation of rest with no forces generating change, but where forces take the economy towards the equilibrium. The position of equilibrium is supposed to tell us something about what will happen in the real world, and any theory whose predictions are derived from an equilibrium position can only be tested if it is assumed that the real world is in or near equilibrium.

In contrast, Kalecki regarded equilibrium positions as hypothetical ones which would not usually be reached. Moreover, there was a danger of confusing possible equilibrium positions with what actually happens. Thus equilibrium analysis may be used, but it needs to be treated with care; it can investigate a possible golden age, but real life should not be confused with the Garden of Eden.

Sebastiani (1994, p. 39) contends that Kalecki had a greater interest in equilibrium analysis, and suggests that the purpose of Kalecki's early essays was 'to provide a theory of the business cycle; subordinate to this purpose is the explanation of the equilibrium level of income at a given moment'. Kalecki's early essays do employ equilibrium analysis, but of the thought experiment kind.[10] Sebastiani (1994, p. 30) also argues that Kalecki and Keynes employed the same notion of equilibrium.

Kalecki generally looked at the evolution of an economic system through time, without imposing any view that the system would reach some ultimate equilibrium position or that it would grow at some balanced equilibrium rate of growth. The titles of Kalecki's books are suggestive here; they contain words such as 'cycles', 'dynamic' and 'fluctuations'.

Another important ingredient of his approach is summarized in the oft-quoted statement that 'the long-run trend is but a slowly changing component of a chain of short-period situations; it has no independent entity' (Kalecki 1971a, p. 165). This laconic statement can be interpreted as undermining the equilibrium approach to economic analysis. There is the clear suggestion of a long-run equilibrium position 'out there' which pre-exists and towards which the economy (or at least the model of the economy) converges. The clearest example of this is in neoclassical growth models where the equilibrium growth rate is the 'natural' rate (that is, the exogenously given growth of the labour force) towards which the 'warranted' rate (equal to savings propensity divided by the capital–output ratio) tends through movements in the capital–output ratio. A further example would be the neo-Ricardian approach where prices of production, based on an equalized rate of profit, are centres of gravity for market prices.

Kalecki's statement could be read as saying that the economy cannot be modelled in terms of a long-run equilibrium without consideration of a short-run adjustment mechanism by which the economy moves towards the long-run equilibrium. The short-run situation and its evolution has to be examined, and from this the long run can be built up. The long-term trend is built up from a series of short-period situations, and as such does not have to be characterized by full employment or full capacity utilization. Kalecki (1941) conducts long-term analysis involving excess capacity utilization.[11] In the neoclassical approach, full employment and market clearing would be key elements of the long-run equilibrium, while in the neo-Ricardian approach full capacity utilization would be seen as essential in the long period. Third, there is some suggestion of path dependency, whereby the route that the economy travels influences the destination reached (or the places passed through, since there is no final destination). As noted above, Kalecki (1971a, p. 183) held that 'the rate of growth at a given time is a phenomenon rooted in the past economic, social and technological developments' and that 'future inquiry into the problems of growth should be directed ... towards treating the coefficients used in our equations ... as slowly changing variables rooted in past developments of the system'.

Class-based Analysis

The microeconomics of Kalecki is undertaken at the level of social class rather than at the level of the individual. The basic class division in a capitalist economy is between capitalists, who own and control the means of production and receive property income, and workers who do not own the means of production and receive labour income. For Kalecki the roles of these two classes are quite different.

Workers supply labour because it is their only means of income, and labour income is used mainly to finance consumption. Kalecki generally assumed that workers did not save, while a substantial proportion of profits were saved. These assumptions help him show that workers spend what they earn while capitalists earn what they spend (because in the aggregate profits are equal to investment expenditure plus capitalists' consumption).

The aims of capitalists are quite different. They hire labour to produce output at a profit; profits and survival are the key driving forces of capitalists. For Kalecki, the ownership of firms (and hence the means of production) is limited to the capitalist class. 'Many economists assume that ... anyone endowed with entrepreneurial ability can obtain capital for starting a business venture. This picture ... is, to put it mildly, unrealistic. The most important prerequisite for becoming an entrepreneur is the *ownership* of capital' (Kalecki 1971a, p. 109, original emphasis). The capitalist class can be divided into entrepreneurs and rentiers. The latter group, while having an ownership interest, does not actively participate in control. The terms on which rentiers are prepared to supply finance to entrepreneurs can limit the expansion of firms, and rentier savings may slow the economy through its depressing effect on investment (Kalecki 1954, p. 159). Entrepreneurs are controllers and part-owners of firms, and they make decisions about its operations.

Degree of Monopoly and Pricing

Kalecki's theory of pricing and the degree of monopoly has been contro-versial and misunderstood; it has also been accused of being neoclassical. The theory went through several versions,[12] but Kalecki always held that the relationship between price and unit costs depends on the market power of the firm involved, or its degree of monopoly. This theory should be seen as having two analytically separable elements. The first is the idea that the distribution of income between wages and profits depends primarily upon the market power of firms as expressed in the price–cost margin. (There are other factors involved, notably imported material prices.) Further, the volume of profits (as opposed to the share of profits in national income) depends upon the investment decisions of capitalists themselves.

Kalecki was the first to articulate the important macroeconomic impli-cations which flow from the simple observation that the relationship between price and cost is governed by the degree of market power. First, the distribution of income is governed by considerations of market power rather than marginal productivity. The share of profits in national income (or, alternatively, the real wage) depends on the degree of monopoly. Second, at the level of the enterprise the balance between price and costs sets the real product wage, and then by aggregation (which is not without its difficulties) pricing decisions by enterprises set the real wage (which is also influenced by prices of imports of consumption goods). Real wages are now seen as set in product markets through the pricing decisions of enterprises, rather than in the labour market through the interaction of demand and supply of labour. Third, real wages are not linked with any notion of subsistence, but depend instead on the degree of monopoly within the economy, where that degree of monopoly could be modified by trade union activity and collective bargaining (Kalecki 1971b).

The second element is an analysis of pricing behaviour. Some earlier versions did incorporate profit maximization; however, later versions were not so clearly based on profit maximization. Firms were seen as pri-marily interested in profits, but could not pursue profit maximization with any precision because of the uncertainty they faced.

Money, Savings and Investment

Post Keynesian economists largely subscribe to two basic tenets – money is credit money created within the private sector in response to the needs of trade, and causation runs from investment expenditure to savings rather than conversely. In each case, there are caveats and qualifications, and some Post Keynesians would not fully subscribe to both tenets. Yet, in both cases, the Post Keynesian position diverges substantially from the prevailing orthodoxy, which models money as exogenous[13] and calls for controlling the growth of the money supply. Further, although Keynesian economics retains the primacy of investment over savings (as seen in the simplest multiplier analysis), there is much acceptance of the idea that investment and growth are constrained by savings.

Kalecki was at the forefront of these two Post Keynesian tenets (see Arestis 1996). The following quotation provides a useful summary of his analysis:

> Let us assume that as a result of some important invention there is an increase in investment. ... [F]inancing of additional investment is effected by the so-called creation of purchasing power. The demand for bank credit increases and these are granted by the banks. The means used by the entrepreneurs for construction of new establishments reach the industries of investment goods. This additional demand makes for setting to work idle equipment and unemployed labour. The increased employment is a source of additional demand for consumer goods and thus results in turn in higher employment in the respective industries. Finally, the additional investment outlay finds its way directly and through the workers' spending into the pockets of capitalists (we assume that workers do not save). The additional profits flow back as deposits to the banks. Bank credits increase by the amount additionally invested and deposits by the amount of additional profits. The entrepreneurs who engage in additional investment are 'propelling' profits into the pockets of other capitalists profits which are equal to their investment, and they are becoming indebted to those capitalists to the same extent *via* banks. ... The increase in output will result in an increased demand for money in circulation, and thus will case for a rise in the credits of the Central Bank. Should the Bank respond to it by raising the rate of interest to a level at which total investment would decline by an amount equal to the additional investment caused by the new invention, no increase in investment would ensue and the economic situation would not improve. (Kalecki 1971a, pp. 28f.)

Kalecki assumes here that banks can meet any increased demand for loans. Kalecki (1944) also argued that the Pigou (1943) or real balance effect would be ineffective in a world of credit money. Falling prices would increase the real value of money only if the money were backed by gold. Also, falling prices and wages would mean that the real value of outstanding debts would increase. Firms unable to repay those debts would face bankruptcy and the economy would face a crisis of confidence. Rather than restoring full employment, this would increase unemployment further.

Money creation through loans permits investment to proceed ahead of the corresponding savings being generated. Kalecki's work contains two differing views on the links between investment and savings.[14]

The first, which is contained in the long quotation given above, is that causal link runs from investment to savings. However, as can be seen from that quotation, the causal link is based on a thought experiment where planned investment expenditure rises. Kalecki never examined what happened when savings rose. From that it could be inferred that he saw increased intended investment as leading to increased savings but that increased intended savings would not lead to increased investment.

The second is contained in Kalecki's analysis of the trade cycle. Since the trade cycle is seen as a continuous process with no beginning and no end, it is impossible to talk of an initial cause. There is a two-way relationship between profits and investment. At the level of the enterprise, profits influence investment decisions, while at the aggregate level investment expenditure generates profits. Since profits and savings are closely linked in Kalecki's work, it could be said that savings and investment affect each other. In some versions of his trade cycle analysis, Kalecki included a reinvestment factor, reflecting the degree to which savings in one period influence investment in a subsequent period (at the level of enterprise). A firm's financial resources are based on its current savings, although there is 'incomplete reinvestment' additional savings generate some additional investment but on a less than one-for-one basis. 'The inflow of new gross savings ... push forward the barriers set to investment plans by the limited accessibility of the capital market and "increasing risk"' (Kalecki 1990–93, Vol. 2, p. 164). However, as noted above, Kalecki (1954, p. 159) did suggest that rentier savings (and by extension worker savings) would depress (rather than stimulate) investment expenditure.

The simple circular flow of income suggests a separation between those who make savings decisions and those who make investment decisions. It is thus possible to ask causal questions about the relationship between savings and investment, and about the mechanisms for bringing them into equality. When much savings is undertaken by the same individuals who make investment decisions, answering the causal question is much more difficult, especially when mutual influences are at work.

CONCLUSIONS

This chapter has focused on how Kalecki was a positive dissenter from neoclassical orthodoxy. It has argued that he largely dispensed with equilibrium analysis and with the presumption of full employment under market capitalism. But Kalecki dissented in other positive ways. He developed a mark-up theory of pricing, which also served as a theory of income distribution between capital and labour; and he argued that investment drives savings, rather than vice versa. Finally, Kalecki sought to develop a true macroeconomics, one which was not built upon microfoundations.

NOTES

*I am grateful to Philip Arestis, Geoff Harcourt, Ric Holt, Steve Pressman and Jan Toporowski for helpful comments on a first draft. The usual caveats apply.

1. One example was when Kalecki (1971a, p. 158) dismissed perfect competition 'as a most unrealistic assumption'.
2. It is well known that this theory has difficulties unless there are constant returns to scale, and also when it is used as an aggregate theory of income distribution.
3. In the area of investment (and business cycles) Steindl (1981) identifies three versions, which I have discussed in Sawyer (1996). In the area of pricing, see Kriesler (1987, 1988), Basile and Salvadori (1984/85, 1990/91).
4. Many figures included in the *Biographical Dictionary of Dissenting Economists* (Arestis and Sawyer 1992) came to economics via mathematics or physics, and were influenced by political events in the 1930s or the 1960s.
5. On the relationship between the work of Kalecki and Marx, see Sawyer (1985, Ch. 8) and Sebastiani (1994, Ch. 5).
6. Kalecki sometimes made assumptions to simplify his analysis, for example his assumption of a close economy.
7. For further discussion, see Sawyer (1995, Ch. 2).
8. As far as I know, Kalecki never discussed individual rationality. However, at times his approach can be read as one of 'bounded rationality'. Kalecki (1954) argued that enterprise decision-makers could only vaguely know demand and cost conditions because of the uncertainties faced by the firm.
9. For further discussion on Kalecki and cycles, see Sawyer (1996).
10. Kalecki (1990–93, Vol. 1, pp. 201–20) uses 'equilibrium' to refer to a situation of full employment.
11. Keynes rejected this paper for the *Economic Journal* because he was reluctant to accept a long-term analysis that included excess capacity. Part of the correspondence is reproduced in Keynes (1983).
12. See Kriesler (1987, 1988) and Basile and Salvadori (1984/85, 1990/91) on whether there was continuity in these versions.
13. Goodhart (1994, p. 1424) also argues that 'virtually every monetary economist believes that the CB [Central Bank] *can* control the monetary base, and, subject to errors in predicting the monetary multiplier, the broader monetary aggregates as well' (original emphasis). However, 'Almost all those who have worked in a CB believe that this view is totally mistaken'.
14. For discussion on the causal links between investment and savings, see Asimakopulos (1983), Harcourt (1995) and Kregel (1995).

REFERENCES

Arestis, P. (1992), *The Post-Keynesian Approach to Economics*, Aldershot: Edward Elgar.
Arestis, P. (1996), 'Kalecki's role in post Keynesian economics: an overview', in J. King (ed.), *An Alternative Macroeconomic Theory: The Kaleckian Model and Post Keynesian Economics*, New York: Kluwer.
Arestis, P. and M. Sawyer (eds) (1992), *A Biographical Dictionary of Dissenting Economists*, Aldershot: Edward Elgar.
Asimakopulos, A. (1977), 'Profits and investment: a Kaleckian approach', in G. C. Harcourt (ed.), *The Microeconomic Foundations of Macroeconomics*, London: Macmillan.
Asimakopulos, A. (1983), 'Kalecki and Keynes on finance, investment and savings', *Cambridge Journal of Economics*, 7 (3/4), September/December, 221–33.
Basile, L. and N. Salvadori (1984/85), 'Kalecki's pricing theory', *Journal of Post Keynesian Economics*, 7 (2), Winter, 249–62.

Basile, L. and N. Salvador (1990/91), 'Kalecki's pricing theory revisited: a comment', *Journal of Post Keynesian Economics*, **13** (2), Winter, 293–7.
Goodhart, C.A.E. (1994), 'What should central banks do? What should be their macroeconomic objectives and operations?', *Economic Journal*, **104** (427), November, 1424–36.
Harcourt, G.C. (1995), 'The structure of Tom Asimakopulos's later writings', in G.C. Harcourt, A. Roncaglia and R. Rowley (eds) *Income and Employment in Theory and Practice*, London: Macmillan and New York: St. Martin's Press.
Kalecki, M. (1940), 'The supply curve of an industry under imperfect competition', *Review of Economic Studies*, **7**, 91–112.
Kalecki, M. (1941), 'A theorem on technical progress', *Review of Economic Studies*, **8**, 178–84
Kalecki, M. (1944), 'Professor Pigou on "The classical stationary state": a comment', *Economic Journal*, **54**, 131–2.
Kalecki, M. (1954), *Theory of Economic Dynamics*, London: Allen & Unwin.
Kalecki, M. (1968), 'Trend and the business cycle', *Economic Journal*, **78**, 165–83.
Kalecki, M. (1971a), *Selected Essays on the Dynamics of the Capitalist Economy*, Cambridge: Cambridge University Press.
Kalecki, M. (1971b) 'The class struggle and the distribution of national income', *Kyklos*, **24**, 1–9.
Kalecki, M. (1972), *Selected Essays on the Economic Growth of the Socialist and the Mixed Economy*, Cambridge: Cambridge University Press.
Kalecki, M. (1986), *Selected Essays on Economic Planning*, Cambridge: Cambridge University Press.
Kalecki, M. (1990–93), *Collected Works of Michal Kalecki*, 4 vols, ed. J. Osiatynski, Oxford: Clarendon Press.
Keynes, J.M. (1983), *Economic Articles and Correspondence: Investment and Editorial, Collected Works, Vol. 12*, London: Macmillan.
Kregel, J. (1995), 'Causality and real time in Asimakopulos's approach to saving and investment in the theory of distribution', in G. Harcourt, A. Roncaglia and R. Rowley (eds) *Income and Employment in Theory and Practice*, London: Macmillan and New York: St. Martin's Press, pp. 67–82.
Kriesler, P. (1987), *Kalecki's Microanalysis*, Cambridge: Cambridge University Press.
Kriesler, P. (1988), 'Kalecki's pricing theory revisited', *Journal of Post Keynesian Economics*, **11** (1), Fall, 108–30.
Osiatynski, J. (1986), *Michal Kalecki on a Socialist Economy*, London: Macmillan.
Pigou, A.C. (1943), 'The classical stationary state', *Economic Journal*, **53**, 343–51.
Robbins, L. (1932), *An Essay on the Nature and Significance of Economic Science*, London: Macmillan.
Sawyer, M. (1985), *The Economics of Michal Kalecki*, London: Macmillan.
Sawyer, M. (1995), *Unemployment, Imperfect Competition and Macro-economics*, Aldershot: Edward Elgar.
Sawyer, M. (1996), 'Kalecki on the trade cycle and economic growth' in J. King (ed.), *An Alternative Macroeconomic Theory: The Kaleckian Model and Post Keynesian Economics*, New York: Kluwer, pp. 93–114.
Sebastiani, M. (ed.) (1989), *Kalecki's Relevance Today*, London: Macmillan.
Sebastiani, M. (1994), *Kalecki and Unemployment Equilibrium*, London: Macmillan.
Steindl, J. (1952), *Maturity and Stagnation in American Capitalism*, Oxford: Blackwell.
Steindl, J. (1981), 'Some comments on the three versions of Kalecki's theory of the trade cycle' in J. Los et al. (eds) *Studies in Economic Theory and Practice. Essays in Honour of Edward Lipinski*, Amsterdam: North-Holland.
Williamson, O.E. (1979), 'Transaction cost economics: the governance of contractual relations', *Journal of Law and Economics*, **22** (2), October, 233–62.
Williamson, O.E. (1986), *Economic Organisation: Firms, Markets and Policy Controls*, Brighton: Wheatsheaf.

9. Dissent and continuity: John Maynard Keynes

Victoria Chick

DISSENT AS AN APPLIED SUBJECT

The *Oxford Universal Dictionary* defines dissent as follows: '1. Not to assent; to disagree with or object to an action .... 2. to think differently, disagree, differ *from*' (original emphasis). This definition makes clear the contextual nature of dissent as objection. In the history of an intellectual discipline, dissent is a difference with the majority, where that majority can be defined in any number of ways. Constituencies change with the subject at hand, and 'majority' may indicate the locus of power, as well as number. Being context specific, dissent is not a suitable subject for abstract theorizing; it is an applied subject, where defining the context is an important element. In this introduction I shall delineate some of the areas in which Keynes was a dissenter. The brush is necessarily broad; in later sections I shall trace more finely how his dissent changed with his own development and the context.

John Maynard Keynes is the greatest economist of the twentieth century, and it is perhaps a measure of his dissent (or our conformity) that he is still the most controversial. His masterwork, *The General Theory of Employment, Interest and Money* (Keynes 1973–89, Vol. 7), forms the basis for what is known as the 'Keynesian Revolution', and revolution is undeniably dissent; it is the overthrow of an existing order and has no meaning without that order. Yet Keynes was also a preserver of continuity; and the tension between tradition and novelty is everywhere evident in his work. Thus in the case of Keynes, dissent is a subtle and complex matter. It is a mode of thought and a way of life which is ahead of its time and yet expresses, as Skidelsky (1996, p. 1070) puts it, 'a 20th century revolution in consciousness – in ways of thinking about ourselves and our relationship with the world'. Keynes's dissent from nineteenth century norms is manifest in his economics, his values and his personal life. All are bound up together and develop over time.

Keynes's dissent, even within economics, can be viewed at many different levels; and it becomes more radical the deeper one goes – through policy, theory, methodology, mode of thought and philosophy. Working backwards, we start with the policy conclusion identified by many with his name – that in a slump the government should stimulate the economy by deficit spending. This policy conclusion was widely advocated in the 1920s; the difficulty was that there was no theoretical support for it. Coexisting with those who supported public works to cure unemployment was the so-called Treasury view that such an action would result only in inflation and could be of no genuine assistance. This follows directly from the conventional theory of the time, which held that the economy had an automatic tendency to full employment. *The General Theory* produced the revolutionary conclusion that underemployment equilibrium was a possibility. This conclusion dissented from the economics of both his day and ours. It offends the most common definition of equilibrium, in which all markets clear, and the assumed dynamic stability of that position. Unemployment equilibrium is possible because those who have the power to change a position which does not suit them (namely firms) are satisfied, and although workers might not like the outcome, they have no power to change it. The equilibrium is stable, no matter whether it is at full employment or less than full employment, because costs rise faster than demand.

The theory of unemployment equilibrium is, in turn, based on an assumption most uncommon in economics yet familiar in everyday life – that the future is unknown, yet we must act in the face of that ignorance. Thus firms, even small ones, cannot take prices (a proxy for the strength of demand) as given; they produce for an unknown level of demand on the basis of their best guess (more elegantly, their expectation). Entrepreneurs who contemplate adding to their capital stock face an even greater problem, for the profit from expanding capacity lies even further in the future; the uncertainty is thus greater. Furthermore, the wisdom of their decision, as revealed over the life of the capital, can never serve as a guide to further action, for the world will change over time.

Action in the face of uncertainty is to Keynes more than a practical problem: its meaning and solution is at the root of his philosophy. Here, too, he dissents from mainstream English-language philosophy, moving 'both backwards and forwards in intellectual time' (Fitzgibbons 1988, p. 10) to forge a unique system of thought. Keynes rejected the view, dominant then and now, that only logically demonstrable arguments have validity; in contrast, probabilistic epistemology informs his philosophy, economics and ethics.

Economics, and even philosophy, were servants, not masters. The aim was to live a life of truth, beauty and friendship. Philosophy can guide us in discovering truth; economics is a means of affording it. Economics was still classified as a Moral Science in Keynes's time, but the influence of science, and the Humean belief that ethics were not logical but only opinion, had weakened the Moral and exalted the Science, a process which continues to this day. In the tradition of natural law, and against the prevailing view that ethics were non-rational, Keynes held that rational action was possible and was a virtue. Just and fair consequences were, of course, desirable; but the full consequences of an action could not be known, so could not guide action. Keynes was, in any event, opposed to concentration on ends, especially the end of accumulating money. Motives, rather than ends, were at the centre of his ethics; the moral quality of the act could be directly apprehended by intuition.

In politics Keynes also dissented. It is a surprise that he found inspiration in Edmund Burke (Helburn 1991), but Keynes took only part of Burke's political philosophy, his doctrine of expediency, and discarded both his support for conservative institutions and his appeal to conventions as the basis for political action (Keynes also rejected G.E. Moore's support of convention as the basis of private social life). Rather, truth and justice were the ideals, to be expressed according to circumstances rather than through conventions. Reason, based on appreciation of circumstances, mediated between the ideal and practical action.

Rational action was a good in itself, but if knowledge was imperfect and uncertain, how was rational action to be achieved? From the days of the Greek philosophers, there was a dualistic conception: stable laws of causality were thought to underlie the appearances of experience, and rationality involved the apprehension of those laws (Vercelli 1991, Ch. 4). To Keynes, however, knowledge was at best probabilistic. Probability, rather than strict (deterministic) causality connects propositions about (some) events, and between some other events one can make no logical connection. One of the tasks of rationality is to distinguish between these. It is in this area that Keynes made a substantial explicit contribution, and we shall have more to say about it below.

Although I have illustrated Keynes's dissent with applications from many different fields, there does seem to be a unifying factor. Fitzgibbons (1988) emphasizes the pre-modern wellsprings of Keynes's thought; O'Donnell (1989) and Skidelsky (1994) point to Keynes's instinct to find a middle way between apparent opposites. Perhaps they both have their roots in an instinctive rejection of the many dualities that constitute logical positivism: logic versus intuition, knowledge versus uncertainty, truth versus experience, art versus science. These dualities all become integrated in Keynes's thought.

In this introduction I have portrayed Keynes as more of an idealist than he eventually became. The foundations of his dissent remained stable, but the focus of his dissent changes with new experiences. He began at the idealist end of the spectrum of belief about human nature and later became less optimistic, just as most of those who begin by thinking that man is all evil find some good in him/her in the end. Since the development of Keynes's thought is closely integrated with his life, we shall discuss the first in the context of the second.

BEGINNINGS

Keynes was born in Cambridge, England, the eldest of three children. His father, John Neville Keynes, was a don and later Registrar of the University. He lectured in Logic and Political Economy. His *The Scope and Method of Political Economy* (J.N. Keynes 1890) remains a classic. Maynard's instruction in economics, along with the other essential subjects, began at home; his father closely supervised his studies. Maynard was perceived as being exceptionally intelligent and was pushed rather hard, but he revelled in the work and excelled.

His mother, Florence Ada Keynes (née Brown), was unusual for her time. She was educated at Newnham College, Cambridge in the pioneering days of women's education at Cambridge. She engaged in progressive social projects and became the first woman mayor of Cambridge. The family was Congregationalist – dissenters from the established religion.

Maynard won a scholarship to Eton, where he developed his knowledge of philosophy and began to cultivate a collector's interest in rare books. He went from there to King's College, Cambridge, where philosophy and ethics claimed his attention more than mathematics, the subject he was supposed to be reading. As an undergraduate his dissent, at least from the life outside his circle in Cambridge, was most evident in his homosexuality and the philosophical stance he developed.

KEYNES DEVELOPS HIS PHILOSOPHY

Keynes's early education, at home and at Eton, was very broad. Eton encouraged his interest in philosophy and he developed it further at Cambridge, where he and his circle, especially the members of the exclusive Apostles, were influenced by the philosophy of G.E. Moore. For Moore, the contemplation of beauty and the enjoyment of friendship were the true purpose of life. This view was deeply subversive of

Victorian values. It came to characterize the philosophy of that disparate and hugely talented group now known as Bloomsbury. They showed their dissent in their way of life as well as in their art. Truth-telling was a rule with them. Their conversation was uninhibited (shockingly so to the outside world); their sex lives and living arrangements were a radical departure from the norm; their literature and painting broke new ground. Conventional society showed firm disapproval. They lived Moore's 'religion' (his ethical principles) while rejecting his 'morality' – the acceptance of convention ('My Early Beliefs', Keynes 1973–89, Vol. 10.).

Keynes balanced his Moorean goals with a Victorian virtue – the acceptance of a duty to contribute to public life, which he did in abundance.

Keynes obtained his First Class degree in Mathematics in 1905. Alfred Marshall got him interested in economics. He stayed on in Cambridge to study for the Economics examinations but elected to sit for the Civil Service examinations instead. He came second and joined the India Office.

Keynes spent just two years in the India Office. While there, he transformed an early critique of Moore into a pioneering work on the philosophy of probability, which he submitted to King's College as a Fellowship Dissertation in 1908. He was not elected until the following year, after the thesis had been revised. It was published in 1921 as *A Treatise on Probability* (Keynes 1973–89, Vol. 8).

The purpose of the *Treatise* is to derive principles of rational action when there is true uncertainty. True uncertainty is to be distinguished from the type of uncertainty where appropriate behaviour can be properly called 'risk', derived by means of the classical probability calculus. Classical probability pertains to regularities revealed when events are repeated under the same set of circumstances, as in controlled experiment. But life is not a controlled experiment, and the rules of classical probability offer no insight into true uncertainty.

The outcomes of the experiment must be independent of time, both the time at which the experiment is conducted (context) and the sequence of the events within the experiment. The problem of decision-making in the face of an uncertain future is qualitatively different from the controlled experiment for two reasons: history does not repeat itself, and decisions may change the environment itself. However, Keynes argued, there are many circumstances amenable to systematic analysis even in these conditions. We need not be paralysed by inaction or resort to irrational behaviour. Clues exist to guide rational action in some (but not all) cases, and repeated evidence from these clues, while not definitive, adds to what Keynes called the 'degree of rational belief' in the connection between an action and the outcome which the agent expects.

Behaviour under irreducible uncertainty came to play a central role in *The General Theory*, though whether the *Treatise* has a direct bearing on *The General Theory* is a matter of considerable debate: Carabelli (1988) and O'Donnell (1989) argue that it had, while Bateman (1987) and Davis (1994) maintain that Keynes's sensitivity to his own wide-ranging experience of the economic world and changes in the world of thought were the important influences. It is surely correct to say that the emphasis on convention represents a change from the *Treatise*, but it is equally true that the willingness to face true uncertainty without being nihilistic was prepared by the *Treatise*.

Once the *Treatise* was published, philosophy and political theory cease to find explicit expression in Keynes's work. Economics comes to the fore. The path to *The General Theory* was long and far from straight, and Keynes's dissent took many forms; in the realm of politics, it was spectacular.

EARLY ECONOMICS

While at the India Office Keynes examined India's monetary system. He published *Indian Currency and Finance* (Keynes 1973–89, Vol. 1) in 1913. Although the analysis of this book is traditional, it shows two characteristic features of Keynes's work – a thorough knowledge of economic institutions and a pragmatic approach to policy, which involved making practical recommendations to improve those institutions. (Here, again, Keynes was less out of tune with his contemporaries than with present-day economists, the majority of whom have accepted the idea that economics should concern itself with discovering immutable laws and be 'institution-free'.)

His pragmatism shows in his support of discretionary policy over rule-following in monetary matters. Thus he is sceptical of the gold standard. Keynes understood that success of the gold standard in the latter part of the nineteenth century was not due to the standard itself, but was contingent on the existence of a single, strong financial centre – at the time, London. This understanding of the institutional and historical context was not part of the conventional wisdom of the time, which regarded the gold standard as the self-evident source of monetary order. Indeed, Britain would have to undergo her unfortunate interwar experience of the gold standard before majority opinion would change.

From 1908 until the outbreak of the 1914–18 war Keynes was back in Cambridge, lecturing in Economics and revising his Fellowship Dissertation.

THE GREAT WAR

During the war Keynes entered the Treasury. His activities there are over-shadowed by what happened at the Paris Peace Conference, where he was the Treasury's chief representative. Keynes bitterly opposed the settlement France wished to impose on Germany. His stance was both practical and moral: France was being greedy and so also ignoring the delicate balance of an interrelated European economy. Germany could not pay what France was asking; the attempt would first bankrupt, and then embitter, Germany and that was dangerous (so it proved!).

When his view did not prevail, Keynes resigned in protest and published *The Economic Consequences of the Peace* (Keynes 1973–89, Vol. 2). The book caused a sensation for its deep analysis of the economic causes of the war and the consequences of the proposed peace, its vivid depiction of the strong political forces at the Conference, and its devastating characterization of the chief participants. Keynes was now famous, not as an academic, but in the world of affairs.

This was dissent of the highest order. In official circles the book was (understandably) deeply offensive. The Treasury sent Keynes into outer darkness – until they needed him again.

THE 1920s

After the war, Keynes returned to a life of lecturing at Cambridge (unpaid, in order to leave time for writing), journalism, financial dealings (now his main source of income), academic writing and the enjoyment of friendship and of beauty. He spent part of each week at King's College and the other part at Gordon Square in London. Eventually he also took a lease on a country house, Tilton, in Sussex. The academic was balanced by the man of affairs, the manager by the aesthete (the latter contrast is made by Skidelsky 1983). He courted, and in 1925, to the amazement (and some disapproval) of his friends, married Lydia Lopokova of the Ballets Russes.

The *Treatise on Probability* was revised and published (in 1921) while Keynes the political economist, with virtually the sole support of Reginald McKenna, applied his persuasive powers to opposing Britain's return to the gold standard. Keynes the academic put together several of his monetary writings in the *Tract on Monetary Reform* (Keynes 1973–89, Vol. 4).

Keynes's position on the gold standard began where *Indian Currency and Finance* left off. The international context had changed. London's position as the single, well-developed, strong financial centre was now challenged by New York. To Keynes, this would have been sufficient cause for dissent from the majority view. In addition, the debate was entirely about going back to the gold standard at the prewar parity, despite the fact that prices in Britain had risen far higher than in the countries which constituted the competition – most notably America. Thus Britain would have to deflate, which she duly did. To those who understood monetary factors as creators of only temporary disruption this was perhaps not a daunting prospect, but to Keynes the personal tragedy and the social waste of the unemployment which would (and did) follow far outweighed any potential benefits from the gold standard.

Keynes lost the argument; Britain returned to gold in 1925. The gold standard was almost universally perceived as the only right arrangement, and the return to prewar parity as the only honourable course, because to establish a lower parity would be to default in part to one's creditors. Britain, of course, went heavily into debt to fight the war, and a substantial portion of the debt was held abroad.

In the first two years after the war, Britain experienced one of the sharpest price fluctuations of her modern peacetime history. The retail price index rose 16 per cent in 1920, then fell by 28 per cent over the next two years. This fall was still not enough to achieve parity, but it had had the effects Keynes feared: unemployment rose above 10 per cent in 1922 and worse was to come. Unemployment remained at or above (sometimes well above) that figure until Britain began to rearm for World War II. The deflation, which had been undertaken in preparation for the return to gold, was continued after the return in order to support parity. Wage income was eroded even more savagely. Workers rebelled in 1926 with the General Strike; but it took the slide into world depression provoked by the Wall Street crash, and the collapse of world trade, to make the gold standard finally untenable. Britain left the gold standard in 1931.

The gold standard experience also must be at the heart of Keynes's dislike of the rentier, whose 'euthanasia' he recommends in *The General Theory*. In 1917, the Treasury had issued a large War Loan at 5 per cent, even though the market rate at the time was 6 per cent. The Treasury was relatively lucky: as it was, payments of interest on this one item came to 12 per cent of the budget. Allowing for deflation, the real rate of return to creditors on this loan was prodigious, and the loan could not be converted on terms more favourable to the Treasury until after the gold standard was abandoned.

In the face of all this upheaval, one can understand the impatience Keynes felt with the traditional methodology of the long run determined by real factors, disturbed by transitory monetary factors. The famous statement, often taken out of context, comes from the *Tract on Monetary Reform:*

But the *long run* is a misleading guide to current affairs. *In the long run* we are all dead. Economists set themselves too easy, too useless a task if in tempestuous seasons they can only tell us that when the storm is long past the ocean is flat again. (Keynes 1971–89, Vol. 4, p. 65, original emphasis)

In the tempestuous season associated with the return to gold, Keynes also displayed a distinct preference for avoiding unemployment, at the expense of profits if necessary. In the *Tract* he argued for high interest rates to engineer a deflation of profits rather than a demand deflation, which would cause incomes to fall and layoffs to rise.

The contribution of the *Tract* to the Keynesian Revolution lies in its rejection of the long run as the foundation of economic analysis – the equivalent in economics of rejecting the duality of observed change and stable universal laws. This rejection of the long run formed the basis of the transition from the *Treatise on Money* to the *General Theory*. But first the *Treatise* had to be written.

FROM THE *TREATISE ON MONEY* TO *THE GENERAL THEORY*

Postwar events had emphasized the influence of banking and monetary policy on the economy. It is a mystery that even today most economists conduct their analysis in real terms, believing that money is neutral and affects only nominal variables. Certainly Keynes, who was always prepared to accept the evidence of his own eyes, could not sustain such a belief.

Trusting one's own perceptions of the world, and questioning whether received theory explains them, is itself a manifestation of dissent, though in Keynes's time it was not yet quite the case that the style of doing economics deductively from self-evident axioms had become the standard it is today. There was still a tension between those who believed in the efficacy of pure logic in building economic knowledge, and those who took a more inductive, policy-orientated approach. Keynes was too engaged in the affairs of the day, too confident of his own perceptions, and too practical, for the purely deductive approach.

He decided to write a treatise on money to consolidate his accumulated knowledge of the working of money markets and the role of money in the economy. Its two volumes reflect, ironically, the traditional separation of pure theory from applied theory.

The *Treatise on Money* (Keynes 1973–89, Vols 5 and 6) is important both for the wealth of institutional and historical detail it contains and for its development of an approach towards the 'deviations from the long run' in which monetary and real factors are integrated. The *Treatise* takes up the challenge of the *Tract*: what adjustment processes are provoked by variations in demand, which result in unexpected ('windfall') profits and losses? Windfalls are defined as deviations from the 'flat sea' of a long-period equilibrium. This long-period equilibrium is completely traditional: normal profits and normal real wages, with equilibrium prices determined by the quantity of money. Departures from long-period full employment are attributed to a lack of entrepreneurial nerve (if they would produce more they would discover they could sell it) and assumed to be temporary. It is a conclusion of the theory that wages must fall to cure unemployment.

These are thoroughly classical conclusions, but the *Treatise* contained an important step towards *The General Theory*: the rate of interest (the price of securities), instead of being determined by flows of saving and demands for funds to finance investment, was set by the activities of optimistic and pessimistic speculators ('bulls' and 'bears'). These activities involved the deployment of the stock of financial wealth, not just flows. In modern terms, Keynes took a portfolio approach. By concentrating on the activities of bulls and bears, Keynes broke the traditional link between the rate of interest and the rate of profit and thus the link to 'fundamentals'; speculators are not interested in fundamentals but in a quick profit on their financial dealings. (Keynes would know: he earned his living that way.)

When Keynes published the *Treatise* in 1930, the British economy had been depressed since 1922 and the slide to the bottom of the depression, caused by the collapse first of American economic activity and then of world trade, had begun. After eight years of unemployment exceeding 10 per cent, Keynes was not one to argue that the problem was transitory monetary factors. The development of Keynes's thinking towards *The General Theory* began immediately the *Treatise* was published, as he explained his views to the Macmillan Committee on the Finance of Industry (Clarke 1988).

Another impetus for a change in theory was the 'Circus', a group of brilliant younger colleagues in Cambridge who met to discuss the *Treatise*. They provided criticism, particularly of the inability of the *Treatise* to explain variations in output and employment except as random variation. That was not an acceptable explanation, and explanation was urgent. *The General Theory* provided that explanation, and in the course of doing so, provided a radically altered structure of economic theory. In mid-1931, Keynes began to revise the *Treatise*; the result was the Keynesian Revolution of *The General Theory of Employment, Interest and Money*.

THE KEYNESIAN REVOLUTION

The General Theory is the great achievement of Keynes the dissenting economist. It also integrates, as none of his other work did completely, his philosophy, ethics and practical politics.

The Keynesian Revolution is popularly understood to be the policy conclusion associated with *The General Theory* – governments should run deficits to counteract a slump. But others had advocated this policy long before Keynes. The problem was that this policy recommendation could not be supported by existing theory. It was something of a revolution to provide the theory which justifies that policy and outlines the circumstances in which it should be pursued. But the story does not end there. As the previous paragraph indicates, properly understood, *The General Theory* is a revolution in the method and mode of thought in economics. The world is in flux, but sufficient sense can be made of it to refute orthodoxy and prescribe a practical remedy.

The key concept in *The General Theory* is the Principle of Effective Demand. This Principle states that employment is determined by aggregate demand, given prevailing wages and technical conditions of supply. Demand determines the level of output it is profitable for firms to supply, as well as appropriate prices. This is true even for small firms, which in traditional theory are said to take prices as given. Thus the aggregate takes precedence over decisions taken at the level of the firm: there is no way that firms, even those too small to influence the market by their actions, can determine appropriate output and hiring policy without forming expectations about aggregate demand. This is necessary because, in contrast to the framework of the *Treatise*, aggregate demand can vary, perhaps suddenly and unexpectedly but not randomly.

If demand is not adequate to justify full employment, there is *involuntary unemployment*. Moreover, there is no mechanism by which an adequate level of demand can be brought about by the actions of workers. If producer expectations are met at a level of production that does not absorb all the labour willing to work at the going wage, unemployment can continue indefinitely. Equilibrium will be a position of full employment only by accident; unemployment equilibrium is just as likely.

The General Theory concerns precisely the area ignored by the *Treatise on Money*. Where the *Treatise* has a long period with only one level of output (normal output) supplemented by random fluctuations, *The General Theory* explores the determination of output in the context where it actually takes place: when the capital stock is given and output can only be expanded by hiring more labour; that is, in the short period.[1] The classical anchor of the long run has finally been abandoned and with it the 'classical dichotomy', whereby the quantity of money determined prices and real variables were determined by real factors. Aggregate demand is a monetary variable; there are no elements determined by purely real forces. Monetary factors are neither neutral nor transitory.

Keynes divided aggregate demand into two categories – consumption and investment. Consumption responds when aggregate income rises, but it typically does initiate such a rise. Investment, on the other hand, is free of current income, for two reasons: the purpose of investment is to expand capacity to meet *future*, not current, demand; and at least some investment is financed by bank loans rather than by current cash flows. Since the banking system can make loans even if there is no prior saving, this source of lending makes possible an excess of investment over current saving, in contrast to the classical story where investment is constrained by the amount of saving. Saving now adjusted to investment and not the other way round.

Both by reason of the potential volatility of expectations of future demand and the lack of any financial constraint other than bankers' opinion, investment is the unpredictable element of demand. This is not all bad, for investment can lift the economy out of recession in the short run and provide capacity and improved competitiveness for the future. The endogeneity of consumption implies that investment not only provides additional income equal to itself, but also initiates further rounds of expenditure. This is, of course, the multiplier, an idea first expressed by Keynes and Hubert Henderson (*Can Lloyd George Do It?* in Keynes 1973–89, Vol 9, pp. 86–125) and developed by Richard Kahn (1931).

The rate of interest is the price paid for borrowing to finance investment. It is determined, Keynes argued, by the same forces described in the *Treatise*: the speculative expectations and activities of bulls, bears and the government broker. If the speculators, and bankers in their role as lenders, share the same ups and downs of optimism as the investing producers, investment will be still more volatile.

It had been believed that if employers as a whole simply decide to produce more, they would sell the increased output, since employment and income would have risen (Say's Law). This is where the 'fundamental psychological law' that the marginal propensity to consume is less than one is of crucial importance, for it settles the question of the stability of equilibrium determined by the equality of aggregate demand and supply. If the equilibrium is stable, the economy is not self-righting; it may stop short of full employment. The slope of aggregate supply under the competitive conditions Keynes assumed cannot be less than one; the slope of aggregate demand is less than one. In other words, costs rise faster than potential revenues as output increases, and the equilibrium is stable.

Once equilibrium is reached, and assuming the consumption function is stable, there is a gap to be filled if income is to rise further. If new investment will not fill that gap, there are two possibilities – give encouragement to investment or increase some other form of exogenous expenditure.

Investment depends on interest rates and expectations of the future. It is difficult to 'talk up' future prospects of an economy in order to affect expectations (though some governments have tried this), and in time of recession it is extremely difficult to push interest rates down. This leaves government expenditure to fill a gap left by depressed investment in a time of high unemployment. The resulting improvement in economic activity would go a long way towards financing the policy through lower unemployment benefits and higher tax yields.

The alternative 'cure' for unemployment, proposed at the time (and by many now), is to lower wages. *The General Theory* shows that this proposition assumes that wages are only a cost, whereas they are both a cost and a source of demand. It is therefore impossible to argue that a cut in wages would leave demand unaffected. It is difficult to predict what would actually happen, but one certainly cannot assert an unambiguous improvement. Keynes held that employment would increase little, if at all.

WORLD WAR II AND AFTER

Keynes's 'long struggle to escape', which began with his dissatisfaction with long-period analysis in the *Tract on Monetary Reform*, was achieved in *The General Theory*. In 1936, its message was urgent, for there were alternative systems claiming to have the answer to unemployment and poverty – communism and fascism. In the ten years between the General Strike and the publication of *The General Theory* the plight of the worker had worsened. But it was rearmament, not *The General Theory*, that came to the rescue; unemployment turned around in 1937.

In the same year, Keynes suffered his first heart attack. Despite the limitations this imposed, he maintained a staggering pace of work. He applied the analysis of *The General Theory* to inflation in *How to Pay for the War* (Keynes 1973–89, Vol. 9). He then joined the Chancellor of the Exchequer's Consultative Council, where he concerned himself not only with the financing of the war but also with preparing to shape postwar trade and payments.

The *Treatise on Money* ended with a plan for a supranational bank, an idea which Keynes had mooted in his first book, *Indian Currency and*

Finance. His proposal for an International Clearing Union, which became known as the Keynes Plan, formed the British starting-point at the negotiations culminating at Bretton Woods, where the framework for the international monetary system was put together.

The Clearing Union represented a complete break with any automaticity in international monetary mechanisms in favour of discretionary monetary management, albeit with a limited brief on this international scale. Keynes's concern was to prevent creditor countries from building up idle balances. This is a direct generalization to the international sphere of the concern in *The General Theory* that, especially in a recession, people would prefer liquidity, with the result that the rate of interest would remain high and exert a deflationary influence.

The Americans could not be persuaded to go as far as the Keynes Plan, not least because they knew that they were already a chief creditor and they feared a further outpouring of dollar loans. Keynes was in a weak bargaining position: he would soon have to negotiate an American loan to Britain. He dared not walk out, as he had in Paris. Consequently, the International Monetary Fund (IMF) corresponded more closely to the plan of American representative, Harry Dexter White.

The terms of the loan were quite onerous but the best Keynes could do. Despite his reservations, he argued passionately for its acceptance, most notably in a moving speech in the House of Lords, to which he had been elevated in 1942. The Loan Agreement was signed just in time for Parliament to ratify the Bretton Woods Articles of Agreement. Three months later Keynes went to the inaugural meeting of the Bretton Woods institutions (the IMF and World Bank) at Savannah, Georgia in March 1946. It was not, as Keynes expected, a pleasant party; there was an agenda of final details, but in these, all the old conflicts surfaced.

On the train back to New York, Keynes suffered another heart attack. The next one, at Tilton on Easter Sunday a few weeks later, killed him.

CONCLUSION

Keynes's contribution, and the nature of his dissent as an economist, can be evaluated at two levels: the contribution of his entire career as an economist and the contribution of the source-book of the Keynesian Revolution. This chapter has stressed the continuous evolution of his thought and the application of his theoretical framework, as it evolved, to social and political questions at the highest level.

Keynes's masterwork, *The General Theory*, was perhaps too radical for its time, or even for ours. The book comes to some very uncomfortable conclusions:

1. When there is widespread unemployment, workers cannot improve their employment prospects because employment is determined by what employers expect demand to be, and the main element altering demand from one period to the next is investment, also a decision of capital.
2. Workers can bargain for a money wage, but the price level, and hence the real wage, is determined by aggregate demand.
3. Producers determine investment independently of saving, and households have no control over that element of aggregate demand through their decisions to save.
4. Finance is in the hands of bankers, who can create credit with the stroke of the pen. These bankers are subject to waves of optimism and pessimism as are entrepreneurs, and these expectations make investment volatile.
5. The price of borrowing (the rate of interest) is determined in the market for securities, where speculators care little for the economic fundamentals (the profit of productive firms), but only aim to make money by outwitting each other and the government broker.
6. Lending by bankers results in changes in the money supply over which the public at large has no control. Yet the willingness of bankers to lend determines, through investment, the level of employment, output and even future competitiveness.

These things are true because production is organized along capitalist lines, where ownership of the means of production is in the hands of a few. Firms must commit themselves to hiring labour, at contractual wages, to produce for market sale in the future. By definition, the future, and thus the market for output, is uncertain. Firms therefore take the risk that their decisions will not be profitable, or not as profitable as they had expected.

Workers, on the other hand, face uncertain employment and have no bargaining power over their real wage; the demand for output determines prices and thus the real wage.

Society reacts to this uncertainty by developing monetary and financial instruments. Thus the monetary side of Keynes's story also pertains to a specific stage of institutional development, though that stage was arrived at by gradual evolution. Unlike the classical theory of the rate of interest, which depends on flows of saving and investment, this theory recognizes the importance of markets for secondhand financial assets. Markets in secondhand financial claims invest securities with liquidity for the individual (though of course they are not liquid for their holders collectively); banking spreads and redistributes risk. Securities allow the individual to hold a claim on the profits of business without the risks that the entrepreneurs run of being locked in to their investments, having to run them, and finding profits disappointing – in the limit, the risk of bankruptcy. The advantage to the individual is balanced by the divorce this market creates between long-term profits expected from running the business and the rate of return to the financial players. This may cause funds to be misallocated.

The theory also recognizes, albeit implicitly, that bankers have the power to create money, though Keynes assumed that the monetary authorities were strong enough to counteract any movement of the money supply caused by banks: thus the money supply is taken as given.

The General Theory, in other words, examines the world as it is, even if some of its power relations are unpleasant to behold. It is in fundamental dissent with the kind of theory which develops propositions about how the world would look if everyone were in possession of full knowledge, not only of him or herself and the present world, but also of the future, and where all are able to pursue their interests with equality of power.

The roots of Keynes's dissent go very deep: to his very mode of thought. Where most builders of theoretical systems want certainty, Keynes not only accepts, but actively defends, ambiguity. Where eighteenth century rationalism had calcified into logical positivism, Keynes thinks both logically and intuitively, deductively and inductively, rejecting dualism. Although he felt it necessary to ally himself with that rationalism in his essay on Newton (Keynes 1973–89, Vol. 10, pp. 310–23), his thinking was more like Newton's own, which he characterized as Babylonian – a method of approaching a complex problem from many different angles to get an impression of the truth, recognizing that the complete truth was not obtainable (see Dow 1985, 1996). He rejected both pure individualism and collectivism – methodologically, politically and in his personal life. He accepted fundamental uncertainty but found a way to avoid the subjectivism, irrationalism or nihilism which for others logically follows.

Finally, he trusted his own perceptions and thought processes, even when these were not fully conscious. This to my mind is the deepest dissent of all, and the sense in which I believe Skidelsky's assessment, quoted in the second paragraph, above, is correct. It is, I think, not an accident that Sigmund Freud was first published by Keynes's friends Leonard and Virginia Woolf, that Virginia created the stream-of-consciousness technique, and that Lytton Strachey's *Eminent Victorians* (1918) debunked authority figures. Keynes trusted his perceptions and his subconscious. This is a profoundly anti-authoritarian act. By contrast, to trust in only the demonstrable, whether carefully measured fact or theory derived from axioms by impeccable logic, is an act of distrust of the full range of human potential, distrust of the senses, reliance on the authority of a useful but restrictive method. From this world-view Keynes dissented, in his philosophy, his economics and his life.

NOTE

1. The short period was a Marshallian construction; it should be carefully distinguished from the short run. The latter is a length of actual time, but the short period can last a long or a short length of actual time, depending on how fast new capital comes on stream and begins to contribute to production.

REFERENCES

Bateman, B. (1987), 'Keynes's changing conception of probability', *Economics and Philosophy*, 3, 97–120.

Carabelli, A. (1988), *On Keynes's Method*, New York: St. Martin's Press.

Clarke, P. (1988), *The Keynesian Revolution in the Making 1924–1936*, Oxford: The Clarendon Press.

Davis, J.B. (1994), *Keynes's Philosophical Development*, New York: Cambridge University Press.

Dow, S.C. (1985), *Macroeconomic Thought: A Methodological Approach*, Oxford: Basil Blackwell.

Dow, S.C. (1996), *The Methodology of Macroeconomic Thought: A Conceptual Analysis of Schools of Thought in Economics*, Cheltenham, UK: Edward Elgar.

Fitzgibbons, A. (1988), *Keynes's Vision: A New Political Economy*, Oxford: Basil Blackwell.

Helburn, S. (1991), 'Burke and Keynes', in B.W. Bateman and J.B. Davis (eds), *Keynes and Philosophy: Essays on the Origins of Keynes's Thought*, Aldershot, Hants: Edward Elgar, pp. 30–54.

Kahn, R.F. (1931), 'The relation of home investment to unemployment', *Economic Journal*, **41**, June, 173–98.

Keynes, J.M. (1973–89), *The Collected Writings of J.M. Keynes*, 30 volumes, London: Macmillan.

Keynes, J.N. [1890] (1963), *The Scope and Method of Political Economy*, New York: A. Kelley.

O'Donnell, R.M. (1989), *Keynes's Philosophy, Economics and Politics: The Philosophical Foundations of Keynes's Thought and Their Influence on his Economics and Politics*, London: Macmillan.

Skidelsky, R. (1983), *John Maynard Keynes: Hopes Betrayed, 1883–1920*, London: Macmillan.

Skidelsky, R. (1994), *John Maynard Keynes: The Economist as Saviour*, London: Macmillan.

Skidelsky, R. (1996), 'Review of J.B. Davis, *Keynes's Philosophical Development*', Economic Journal, **106**, 1070–72.

Strachey, L. (1918), *Eminent Victorians*, London: G.P. Putnam.

Vercelli, A. (1991), *Methodological Foundations of Macroeconomics: Keynes and Lucas*, Cambridge: Cambridge University Press.

10. Frank Knight's dissent from progressive social science

Ross B. Emmett

DISSENT IS MORE THAN DISAGREEMENT

Does dissent mean anything other than disagreement with a dominant paradigm of scientific discourse? Including Frank Knight in the roster of dissenting economists must assume that it does. To see why, consider the following.

Knight wrote at a time (the interwar period) when American economic thought was not dominated by one paradigm. Instead, it was characterized by the conflux of several methods and theories. Marginalism occupied an important position, but not until the end of the interwar period did neoclassical economics begin to dominate in America.

Second, the rise of neoclassical economics during the interwar period is, in no small part, directly attributable to Knight. In fact, many consider Knight the quintessential American twentieth century neoclassical economist. His early book *Risk, Uncertainty, and Profit* (1921b; hereafter *Risk*) defined neoclassical economics and ensured its acceptance. His subsequent articles clarified some of the most difficult problem areas in economics, especially cost theory (1921a), the notion of social cost in welfare theory (1924b), and capital theory (1933a, 1934, 1935c and 1936b). For these contributions, Knight was awarded the Francis A. Walker medal by the American Economic Association in 1957.

But perhaps more important, as a professor at the University of Chicago from 1928 until the 1950s, Knight occupied a unique position among American economists. As 'the dominant intellectual influence' (American Economic Association 1973, p. 1048; also see Patinkin 1981) in the Economics Department at Chicago, which was 'the intellectual center of American academic life, especially in the ... social sciences' (Purcell 1973, p. 3; also see Bulmer 1984, pp. 211–14), Knight defined what graduate schools in economics taught. The Chicago School, which emerged during Knight's tenure at the University of Chicago, has played an important role in North American economics ever since (Reder 1982; Samuels 1976).

Third, Knight was an economist who wrote extensively about philosophical issues – especially the relation between economics and ethics (Knight 1922 and 1923), economic methodology (Knight 1924a and 1940), and the dilemmas of liberalism (Knight 1947a, 1947b, 1948, 1951 and 1960). Contemporary economists often consider this work ancillary to his scientific contributions. LeRoy and Singell (1987, p. 402) complain about having to wade through 'extended Austrian-style disquisitions on the foundations of human knowledge and conduct and the like' in *Risk*, but Knight regarded this as part of his work as a social scientist. At the root of his work lies the question of what it means to be a social scientist.

For Knight, social inquiry was not science, but an art involving the application of critical judgement. He confronted an ideology giving unique authority to science and appointing social scientists as the guardians of public discourse about social problems. In dissenting from this ideology, Knight challenged the authority of science within social inquiry and the public role of the social scientist. To understand his dissent, therefore, we have to approach it from the standpoint of his disaffection with giving social science a special social status. If we focus only on his agreement or disagreement with economic theory we shall miss Knight's dissent.

Drawing together the observations, we can say that dissent needs to be located, not in the context of economic discourse, but rather in the general intellectual framework where social science discourse is set. In that context, dissent emerges from disaffection with the underlying social and political ideology. The dissenter searches for an intellectual strategy that can successfully confront an ideology which legitimates certain social institutions, circumscribes the boundaries of social discourse, and elevates certain groups to the status of guardians of that social discourse. The social and political power of the dominant ideology, I shall argue, comes from widespread acceptance of its response to what society perceives as the fundamental social question.[1]

Knight's dissent therefore, must be located within an ideological context. He sought to break the boundaries of acceptable social discourse, and he attacked the social and political status certain institutions and groups had achieved because of that ideology. Underlying our analysis of Knight's dissent will be recognition of the fact that the power of the dissenter's voice as *dissent*, and not just disagreement, lies in the extent to which the dissenter engages the dominant ideology at its deepest level. Only when dissent challenges the widely accepted solutions to the most fundamental problems of society will the dissenter's voice be understood as a significant threat to dominant social and political power.

THE ORTHODOXY OF PROGRESSIVE SOCIAL SCIENCE

To understand Knight as a dissenter is to see him disaffected by the social and political ideology of Progressive social science, an orthodoxy that increasingly came to depend upon science to help it address society's most fundamental problems. The ideological power of Progressivism evaporated at the end of World War I under the onslaught of social pluralism through immigration, the ongoing naturalistic attack on religion, and the failure of President Woodrow Wilson's foreign policy. But the dream remained of solving the 'social question' (a common Progressive era term for the set of dilemmas posed by the intersection of scarcity and inequality) in a manner that allowed Americans to recognize their interdependence and exercise their collective responsibility for society. To replace the religious moralism that motivated previous generations to action, American intellectuals turned to the one certainty that weathered the storms of the late nineteenth and early twentieth centuries – science. Combining the notions of social cohesion, interdependence and social responsibility, with the 'noble dream' of scientific objectivity, social scientists in the interwar years created a powerful new progressive framework for social discourse. At the centre of that framework stood a new solution to America's 'social question': scarcity and economic inequality would be requited by economic progress guided by social control. Social scientists, claiming the authority of science, offered their expertise to assist in directing that process.

The new Progressive ideological framework, which we shall call 'the language of social control' (following Rodgers 1982, p. 126), emphasized the need to apply scientific intelligence to the problems of social action. Despite a lingering debate over exactly what science was, and what a science of society was (see Ross 1991; Smith 1994), for most Americans there was little doubt about what science could do. New advances in the control of nature had emerged from the scientific study of the natural order; social scientists argued that similar advances in the control of society could be expected from a scientific study of the social order. The demise of American Protestantism as the prominent language of social discourse left the ship of democracy adrift in a sea of uncertainty. Who better to control the ship and lead it to safe harbour than the masters of the scientific method (imagery adapted from Lippmann 1914)?

The new language of social control did not immediately dominate social discourse; revolutions in social ideology are not the gestalt switches Thomas Kuhn described scientific revolutions to be. The old ideological frameworks of American Protestantism and classical liberalism lost their prominence slowly, and continued to shape social discourse long after they had lost their dominant position. Nevertheless, it is fair to say that the interwar period marked the crucial transition period. Before the end of the Great War, despite the inroads made by the social reformers, the place of prominence still belonged to the older ideologies. By the time the Great Depression began in the early 1930s, the new language of social control gained prominence, as well as the social sciences and the professions (management, social work, psychiatry) that depended upon them.

FRANK KNIGHT'S DISSENT

Knight dissented from the emerging orthodoxy of scientific social control. He viewed this belief in progress through science as dangerous. Also, the language of social control legitimized social science in ways that circumscribed public discourse. To attack the rising ideology, Knight needed to simultaneously undermine the authority of science and broaden the boundaries of public discourse. The strategy he adopted incorporated both of these elements. First, he attacked the quest to make social inquiry more scientific in order to weaken the authoritative position science held within the social sciences. Second, Knight attacked the role of the social sciences within American society in order to weaken their position as authorities. We next examine these two strategies.

Science and its Limits in Social Inquiry

Knight's (1940) virulent response to positivist methodology in economics is well known, and has previously been the focus of methodological commentary on his work (see Hammond 1991). Less well known is that Knight's infamous review of T.W. Hutchison's book in 1940 came after two decades of debate with other social scientists regarding the role of science in social inquiry.

The debate began for Knight in *Risk*, where he argued that economic theory was a necessary part of social inquiry because it used the scientific method of abstraction and analysis, but that the presence of uncertainty, which frustrated analysis, severely limited the applicability of scientific economics to the real problems of society. The latter half of *Risk* is an argument for a more institutional and historical approach to the problems of economic life. After publishing *Risk*, Knight moved the debate over science in social inquiry along two different lines.

First, he extended the argument of *Risk*. In subsequent articles and book reviews, Knight put forward several alternative formulations of the argument that economic theory was scientific, but partial, in its treatment of social and economic life; and therefore economics had a limited range of applicability. One place where he struggled to express the tension between the power of scientific theorizing and its limitations was his capital theory debate with the Austrians, especially Hayek (Emmett forthcoming). While we usually characterize the debate in terms of the conception of capital as a permanent fund or a non-permanent collection of temporal goods, the debate also involved competing conceptions of the scientific nature and role of equilibrium theory. Hayek's (1936) intertemporal equilibrium model was developed to demonstrate the pure logic of choice (independent of past historical events, and achievable by a dictator with the scientific expertise of an economist). Equilibrium was always possible because all contingencies were known. Because the logic of decision-making was a theoretical construct, Hayek simultaneously severed the world of theory from the real world and provided a theory accounting for future changes. However, in the context of the real world, with all its partially-known contingencies, Hayek's theoretical construct could only point out that market participants would more readily respond to change than central planners, and therefore markets had a tendency to move towards equilibrium.

Knight refused to sever the world of theory from reality. He insisted that capital decisions were historical events (Knight 1930b, 1933a, 1935b, 1936b). Explaining those events required understanding static equilibrium theory (which would illuminate the essential characteristics of choice), and understanding the historical and cultural evolution of the values, tastes, resources and technology (the givens of economic theory) that decision-makers have available at the moment of choice. Because the effects of changes after the moment of choice were uncertain, and evolution of the 'givens' of economic theory was a historical process, economic theory had little to say outside the context of the moment of choice. Therefore, Knight (1936a, 1936b) dismissed dynamic equilibrium theory in favour of historical or institutional analysis for explaining economic change. Furthermore, Knight (1936b, p. 463) argued that the uncertainty of potential changes, and the dependence of capital decisions on their institutional context, provided powerful reasons to reject the notion that there was any necessary movement towards equilibrium in a market or collectivist system.

Similar arguments regarding the role of scientific economics appear in Knight's writings on economics and economic methodology. A proper understanding of neoclassical value theory is essential to explaining human conduct because it illuminates important choices facing the decision-maker. But it cannot predict choice in a scientific sense, both because of uncertainty and because the theory ignores the historical evolution of the institutional context within which a decision-maker operates. The theorist articulates the theoretical core of economics as carefully as possible, and the historian interprets the evolution of the institutional context. The applied economist has a responsibility to assist the decision-maker in judging the relevance of history and theory to particular decisions (Knight 1924a, p. 143; 1930a, pp. 8–11; 1951b). Decision-making (that is, life itself) was ultimately an art, not a science.

The second line of argument Knight used to develop his dissent from the ideology of scientific social control takes us closer to the heart of our concerns here. In several places (most importantly in Knight 1922) he argued that if one considered human action to be a scientific problem, economics was the only science of society; but since human action was ultimately not a scientific problem, scientific economics had little place in social inquiry. Economics had to be supplemented by an ethical theory of value. In order to understand the import of this line of argument, we need to backtrack slightly and look more closely at the assumed relationship between science and value in the new ideology of social control.

Social scientists operating within the language of social control wanted to create a scientific basis for social inquiry that would provide society with the means to realize the traditional values of American democracy. This implied that the social sciences were primarily concerned with the relation between a set of possible means (alternative forms of social organization, as well as potential modifications to the existing social arrangements) and a given set of ends (traditional American liberal values).

Wolfe (1924, pp. 473–82) placed this means–end relation at the centre of his argument for an economics modelled after the natural sciences. He argued that, because the economic system was a set of means organized around given ends, scientific analysis of the available means was only possible within the context of social agreement on what ends the system would seek to achieve. Wolfe rejected appeals to an absolute system of ethics as the foundation upon which agreement on social values could be built. Instead, he argued that because human conduct was socially determined, scientific analysis could uncover human values in the same way that it could discover the correct means to fulfil those values (Wolfe 1924, pp. 473–82). Like other social scientists of his time, Wolfe assumed that the scientific study of values would affirm America's traditional democratic values.

Knight took up the argument about the means–end relation that Wolfe and others used to defend the role of social science in achieving America's common values. If the scientific point of view assumes that the central problem of life is using available means to given ends, Knight argued, then economics is the science of life, because economics studies the social consequences of the effort by members of society to satisfy their given preferences efficiently. The realm of economics, therefore, covered every aspect of human activity – from individuals economizing within budget constraints, to the organizing activities of firms (which Knight explored in *Risk*) and to the institutions of liberal democracy.

> In so far as the means are viewed as given, as data, then all activity is economic. The question of the effectiveness of the adaptation of means is the only question to be asked regarding conduct, and economics is the one and all-inclusive science of conduct. ... The assumption that wants or ends are data reduces life to economics. (Knight 1922, p. 34)

Despite the imperialistic tone of this passage, Knight did not argue that economics was the science of society in order to assert the supremacy of economics over the other social sciences. Rather, his argument was designed to emphasize the tension between the need for a science of society (economics) and its inherent limitations. The scientific view makes choice an economic problem. But *human* choices, he argued, are more than economic problems. They are also moral, and possibly even spiritual, problems.

> The problem of life is to utilize resources 'economically,' to make them go as far as possible in the production of desired results. The general theory of economics is therefore simply the rationale of life.... how far life is rational, how far its problems reduce to the form of using given means to achieve given ends. Now this, we shall contend, is not very far; the scientific view of life is a limited and partial view; *life is at bottom an exploration in the field of values, an attempt to discover values, rather than on the basis of knowledge of them to produce and enjoy them to the greatest possible extent.* We strive to 'know ourselves,' to find out our real wants, more than to get what we want. This fact sets a first and most sweeping limitation to the conception of economics as a science. (Knight 1924a, p. 105; emphasis added)

Reducing life to economics was merely a prelude to asking: 'Is life all economics or does this view require supplementing by an ethical view of value?' (Knight 1922, p. 35). Knight answered that an ethical theory of value was needed in addition to an economic theory of value.

Before we consider the realm of values, we might examine the impact that Knight's attempts to limit the range of scientific economics had upon economics. Ironically, the argument that economics was scientific, but its applicability was limited and it needed supplementing with an ethical theory of value, laid the groundwork for two developments in American economics that Knight resisted. On the one hand, Knight's isolation of the scientific core of economic theory from economic policy, or institutional and historical study, became dominant as mathematical formalism took over economics after World War II. Jettisoning the last vestiges of progressive interest in social reform, many economists sought to analyse the structure of the economy through abstract mathematics (echoing Knight's description of economics in the first chapter of *Risk*). Knight assisted this process by severing theoretical considerations from historical or policy considerations; yet he resisted the effort to circumscribe the economist's role as social scientist by the formal boundaries of economic theory (Knight 1947b, 1956, 1960). On the other hand, it took only one small (and fundamental) change in assumptions to reject Knight's call for an ethical theory of value to supplement the universal presence of economics in human life (and thereby lead to the Chicago School of Economics). That change was due to Stigler and Becker (1977), who argued that, as scientists, economists had to take values and preferences as given. If values could not be criticized, all life becomes economic, and economics could emerge as the only science of human conduct and society. In an ironic twist, Knight's dissent from the use of science to undergird the ideology of his day prepared the way for a social science that depends even more heavily on the authority of science for ideological power.

Value and the Role of Social Science in a Liberal Democracy

The second strand of Knight's dissent from the ideology of scientific social control was his attack on the role that ideology assigned to social scientists as the guardians of public discourse on social problems. In order to understand this argument, we need to look first at his understanding of the nature of a democratic society.

For Knight, the essence of democracy was a social conversation (he used the word 'discussion') among all members of society about what wants and values we should have, or the kind of people we want to become. Coordinating our wants and values with the resources available was a technical problem best solved by the price system. Just as scientific economics does not encompass all of life, so too the market does not encompass all human conduct.

For Knight, the actual practice of democracy was only distantly related to its ideal. During the early 1930s, he argued that the ideal of government by discussion was debased by the lack of any real desire for intelligent judgement among the general public. But when discussion was trivialized, the door was open for groups with powerful voices and agendas, like some social scientists, to manipulate the discussion to their own advantage.

For democracy as discussion to work, Knight argued, people had to talk about their wants and values, and do so in a manner that was cooperative rather than conflictual or competitive. They had to decide it was more important to work together to discover the truth, than to insist upon the correctness of their own ideas and beliefs. Discussion, Knight (1933b, p. xxxiii) said, 'is a co-operative quest of an impersonally, "objectively" right (or best) solution of an impersonal problem. It cannot be an attempt to "sell" a solution already reached, or it is not discussion'. Two things prevented modern democracy from being a true discussion.

The first is aptly summarized in Knight's (1991 [1933], p. 64) 'First Law of Talk: cheaper talk drives out of circulation that which is less cheap'. In a free society, as in a free market, there is no guarantee that people will actually *want* to improve the quality of their wants and values. Rather, it is likely that exactly the opposite will occur; freedom to pursue our own interests and form our own opinions will reduce our conversation to the lowest common denominator, the basest interests and the cheapest talk. Thus, paradoxically, the freedom democracy allows as part of the search for the best values handicaps that search by allowing the propagation of cheap tastes.

The second thing that Knight thought hindered democracy as discussion was a tendency to turn discussion into debate. In actual practice, social discussion became 'a contest for personal aggrandizement' (Knight 1933b, p. xxxv). Here Knight blamed those whom he believed ought to know better – economists and other social scientists. In their enthusiasm to apply the scientific method to the practical problems of social life, they failed to recognize that the method of science was inappropriate to social discussion. The difference between these two types of activity, Knight argued, could not be greater – where social discussion required the generation of new ideas, the scientific method tested ideas that were already held; where social discussion drew people into a cooperative quest for better values, the scientific method focused attention on the conflict between competing theories; where social discussion required *conversation*, the scientific method encouraged *debate*. Knight's 'Second Law of Talk' made the point in a characteristic fashion:

> The more intelligent people are, the more certain they are to disagree on matters of social principle and policy, and the more acute will be the disagreement. The more intelligent they are, the more finely they discriminate and the more importance they attach to fine discriminations, and the more completely their entire mental activity runs into the borderland region of doubt. (Knight 1991 [1933], p. 68)

By carrying the scientific method over into social discussion, social scientists reduced the latter to debate and competition. The inevitable result would be social 'conflict, and finally chaos and tyranny' (Knight 1933b, p. xxxiv). The irony, of course, was that the tyranny would be exercised by the 'protectors' of American values and 'objective' observers of American life – social scientists and professionals.

CONCLUSION

Knight's dissent during the interwar period, involved a twofold strategy. On the one side, he tried to isolate economic theory from criticism by describing it as scientific. On the other side, he wanted social discourse to be an open discussion in which members of society explored together what the true, the good, and beautiful could mean in the modern world. The desire to keep social discourse open-ended led Knight to protest the emerging dominance of the language of social control, which granted social scientists special privileges in public discussion. Because the privileged position of economists and other social scientists depends on their scientific authority, Knight sought to de-legitimize that authority, both within the realm of social inquiry and in social discourse. In the realm of social inquiry, Knight argued that the scientific part of economics was limited in its range of applicability, or that, despite the relevance of economic analysis to every aspect of life, social inquiry must be supplemented by an ethical analysis of values. Either way, Knight claimed, economists had no special status in social discourse. Unfortunately, Knight was not optimistic about the ability of society to resist the language of social control, and he despaired about the prospects for a post-liberal society dominated by the tyranny of expertise. In the end (that is, after the interwar period) his dissent was soured by his cynicism.

NOTE

1. The notion of dissent used here stems from English Dissent during the eighteenth century. These Dissenters found themselves walled in by a social and political ideology, grounded in the authority of Christianity, which legitimated the dominant institutions of public life (Church, King and Parliament), and circumscribed the boundaries of acceptable public discourse. To create space for themselves in the realm of public discourse. The Dissenters had to break down the hegemonic position that held in English social thought (see Clark 1985, pp. 258–77).

REFERENCES

American Economic Association (1973), 'In memoriam: Frank H. Knight, 1885–1972', *American Economic Review*, **63**, December, 1047–8.

Bulmer, M. (1984), *The Chicago School of Sociology: Institutionalization, Diversity, and the Rise of Sociological Research*, Chicago: University of Chicago Press.

Clark, J.C.D. (1985), *English Society 1688–1832: Ideology, Social Structure and Political Practice during the Ancien Regime*, Cambridge: Cambridge University Press.

Emmett, R.B. (forthcoming), '"What is truth" in capital theory? Five stories relevant to the evaluation of Frank H. Knight's Contributions to the capital controversy', in John Davis (ed.), *Writing the New Economics*, annual supplement to *History of Political Economy*.

Hammond, J.D. (1991), 'Frank Knight's antipositivism', *History of Political Economy*, **23**, Fall, 359–81.

Hayek, F.A. von (1936), 'The mythology of capital', *Quarterly Journal of Economics*, **50**, February, 199–228.

Knight, F.H. (1921a), 'Cost of production over long and short periods', reprinted in Knight 1935b, pp. 186–216.

Knight, F.H. (1921b), *Risk, Uncertainty, and Profit*, Chicago: University of Chicago Press.

Knight, F.H. (1922), 'Ethics and the economic interpretation', in Knight 1935b, pp. 19–41.

Knight, F.H. (1923), 'The ethics of competition', in Knight 1935b, pp. 41–75.

Knight, F.H. (1924a), 'The limitations of scientific method in economics', in Knight 1935b, pp. 105–47.

Knight, F.H. (1924b), 'Some fallacies in the interpretation of social cost', in Knight 1935b, pp. 217–36.

Knight, F.H. (1930a), 'Fact and interpretation in economics', *Special Lectures on Economics*, Washington, DC: US Department of Agriculture, Graduate School, February–March.

Knight, F.H. (1930b), 'Statics and dynamics: some queries regarding the mechanical analogy in economics', in Knight 1935b, pp. 161–85.

Knight, F.H. (1933a), 'Capitalistic production, time and the rate of return', in *Economic Essays in Honour of Gustav Cassel*, London: George Allen & Unwin, pp. 327–42.

Knight, F.H. (1933b), 'Preface to the re-issue', in *Risk, Uncertainty, and Profit*, London: London School of Economics and Political Science, pp. xi–xxxvi.

Knight, F.H. (1934), 'Capital, time, and the interest rate', *Economica*, n.s. 1, August, 257–86.

Knight, F.H. (1935a), 'Economic theory and nationalism', in Knight 1935b, pp. 277–359.

Knight, F.H. (1935b), *The Ethics of Competition and Other Essays*, New York: Harper & Bros.

Knight, F.H. (1935c), 'Professor Hayek and the theory of investment', *Economic Journal*, **45**, March, 77–94.

Knight, F.H. (1936a), 'The place of marginal economics in a collectivist system,' *American Economic Review*, **26**, March, 255–66.

Knight, F.H. (1936b), 'The quantity of capital and the rate of interest, I-II', *Journal of Political Economy*, **44**, August and October, 433–63, 612–42.

Knight, F.H. (1940), '"What is truth" in economics?', in Knight 1956, pp. 151–78.

Knight, F.H. (1947a), 'Salvation by science: the gospel according to Professor Lundberg', in Knight 1956, pp. 227–47.

Knight, F.H. (1947b), *Freedom and Reform: Essays in Economics and Social Philosophy*, New York: Harper & Bros.

Knight, F.H. (1948), 'Free society: its basic nature and problem', in Knight 1956, pp. 282–99.

Knight, F.H. (1951), 'The role of principles in economics and politics', in Knight 1956, pp. 251–81.

Knight, F.H. (1956), *On the History and Method of Economics: Selected Essays*, Chicago: University of Chicago Press.

Knight, F.H. (1960), *Intelligence and Democratic Action*, Cambridge, MA: Harvard University Press.

Knight, F.H. (1991) [1933], 'The case for communism: from the standpoint of an ex-liberal', in Warren J. Samuels (ed.), *Research in the History of Economic Thought and Methodology*, Greenwich, CT: JAI Press, pp. 57–108.

LeRoy, S.F. and L.D. Singell, Jr. (1987), 'Knight on risk and uncertainty', *Journal of Political Economy*, **95**, April, 394–406.

Lippmann, W. (1914), *Drift and Mastery: An Attempt to Diagnose the Current Unrest*, New York: Mitchell Kinnerley.

Patinkin, D. (1981), 'Frank Knight as teacher', in *Essays On and In the Chicago Tradition*, Durham: Duke University Press, pp. 23–51.

Purcell, E.A., Jr. (1973), *The Crisis of Democratic Theory: Scientific Naturalism and the Problem of Value*, Lexington: University Press of Kentucky.

Reder, M. (1982), 'Chicago economics: permanence and change', *Journal of Economic Literature*, **20** (1), March, 1–38.

Rodgers, D.T. (1982), 'In search of Progressivism', *Reviews in American History*, **10**, December, 113–32.

Ross, D. (1991), *The Origins of American Social Science*, Cambridge: Cambridge University Press.

Samuels, W.J. (ed.) (1976), *The Chicago School of Political Economy*, East Lansing: Michigan State University.

Smith, M.C. (1994), *Social Science in the Crucible: The American Debate Over Objectivity and Purpose, 1918-1941*, Durham, NC: Duke University Press.

Stigler, G.J. and G.S. Becker (1977), 'De gustibus non est disputandum', *American Economic Review*, **67**, March, 76–90.

Wolfe, A.B. (1924), 'Functional economics', in R. Tugwell (ed.), *The Trend of Economics*, New York: F.S. Crofts, pp. 445–81.

11. Oskar Lange's dissent from market capitalism and state socialism

Christine Rider*

THE MEANING OF DISSENT

Dissent is often defined in terms of differing from or rejecting the doctrines of an established church. Arestis and Sawyer (1992) refer to the mainstream tradition in economics in distinctly religious terms: using phrases such as 'a strong belief', 'the high priests of the economics profession' and 'the prevailing orthodoxy'. To them, a dissenting economist is one who does not work within that prevailing orthodoxy, one who has not received the 'blessing' of the high economic priests, and one who does not get published in the profession's sanctified journals. Arestis and Sawyer use the religious analogy to underscore the fact that economics is not a neutral, value-free science. In contrast to the followers of the orthodox tradition, dissenters recognize that economic thought and practice have social and political effects, but their lack of influence in professional and political circles limits their impact on real-life outcomes.

Whether or not one accepts this religious characterization of dissent, the important message is that dissenters are different. This sense of difference is important in economics, and one can identify and classify various ways in which an economist can be different. First, there is the person who is an outsider by choice, and who is also perceived by others as an outsider. This makes it easy for the majority to ignore the dissenter, even when their views are compatible with orthodox views. Thorstein Veblen is the obvious example of such an outsider-by-choice. Second, there is the economist who shares the goals of the majority but advocates a different approach. Such an economist will usually be considered irrelevant by the majority of the profession. A modern example of this type of dissenter could be Paul Davidson. Finally, it is possible to identify dissenters who work with mainstream tools, but aim them at a different goal. Examples here could include Marxian economists who use standard econometric techniques to demonstrate Marxist conclusions.

165

These categories may overlap, and they may also change over time. Thus, work which does not meet the approval of orthodox economists at one time may become acceptable at a different time or, more likely, what was once acceptable ceases to be so later.

The appearance of dissenting work is particularly common in times of dramatic change or upheaval, when there is fertile ground for an upsurge in reformist or revolutionary tendencies. The twentieth century has witnessed several major upheavals, all of which have had an impact on economic organizations, economic behaviour and the way economists think about economics. In the socio-political arena, the main challenge to the Western capitalist ideology came from socialism, and some countries briefly flirted with alternative (non-market) methods of organizing economic activity. But in economic analysis the neoclassical paradigm remains dominant and has survived repeated attempts to dislodge it. This is not the place for a discussion of the merits, or relevance, of these alternatives; suffice it to say that this paradigm represents the prevailing orthodoxy and hence the main target of dissent.

In general, there are certain common features that characterize dissenters, both in economics and in other fields. Dissenters are idealistic and dissatisfied with the status quo. Dissenters are willing to look beyond the conventional and consider alternatives. In economics, this is perhaps best exemplified by a willingness to use a dynamic or a non-equilibrium methodology, in contrast to a static equilibrium approach, or to reject the neoclassical model entirely, with its implicit idealization of private enterprise capitalism.

Dissenters are usually regarded with suspicion by prominent members of the orthodox tradition. Non-neoclassical economists experience this in a variety of ways. At worst, they are ignored; at best, they are trivialized by not having their work taken seriously. They find it difficult to get published in the leading mainstream journals; consequently they have a low citation count because they do not publish in those journals from which this count is made. As a result, their work is not as widely disseminated within the mainstream tradition, further reinforcing the trivialization.

To what extent is Oskar Lange a dissenting economist? Can our criteria (lack of acceptance and publications, having a different goal, using a different method) help provide an answer?

The case will be made here that Lange was a dissenting economist who achieved the remarkable distinction of dissenting from the two dominant ideologies of his time – free market capitalism and state socialism. He was a life-long socialist, and his desire to create a democratic, humane society that would maximize human well-being led him to develop the market socialist model, a model that uses mainstream tools to accomplish non-mainstream goals. Yet oddly enough, after the collapse of centrally planned communist regimes, when the feasibility of this model relative to what many saw as a flawed capitalist model would seem to be most appropriate, it has not been subject to serious consideration. Lange was an idealist; he could have remained a well-respected and successful academic in the United States. Yet, in a move that put his own personal safety at risk, he unselfishly subordinated his personal advancement (and probably also wrecked his intellectual career) by returning to serve his native Poland (Fisher 1966, p. 735). His most distinctive work, on market socialism, is now considered incidental to the main trends of economic development in the West, although not in China (see note 6). His work to further the acceptance of Keynesian ideas in the United States, while radical in the 1930s, became conventional after World War II, but marginal following the fall from favour of Keynesian theory after the 1970s.

During his lifetime, Lange had the odd distinction of being on the cutting edge both of what would subsequently become orthodox (welfare economics, and econometrics to a lesser extent) and potentially subversive (the market socialism model and his analysis of the failings of capitalism). His work was published in many of the top journals, including *American Economic Review*, *Econometrica*, *Economica* and *Review of Economic Studies*, and he took over the editorship of *Econometrica* during World War II while Ragnar Frisch was imprisoned by the Nazis. He was neither ignored nor trivialized by his contemporaries, and unlike most of them, even achieved establishment status outside the profession as a statesman.

How is it possible to explain this curious duality of acceptance and dissent? While Lange is generally marginalized by establishment economists today, this is most likely because there is now a more clearly defined mainstream tradition from which it is easier to identify those working in alternative traditions. The economics profession was not as well established when Lange was writing. At that time, economics was undergoing a 'paradigm shift', so an establishment orthodoxy and a tradition of dissent did not really exist when Lange did his most productive work, even though they did eventually coalesce into such a reality. Lange would probably have preferred to be classified as a *political* dissenter rather than as an *economic* dissenter. His devotion to socialist ideals would today set him apart from the American mainstream (in the 1930s there was a greater acceptance of the non-Communist left than there is now), while his commitment to democratic values was not in accordance with the views of postwar Soviet rulers. By harmonizing socialist and bourgeois elements in his work on the socialist market economy, Lange dissented from both of these orthodox positions. In true dissenting fashion, his

Economics and its discontents

work reflects an awareness that economics is not a value-free discipline and that people do matter. If one accepts that the mainstream orthodoxy centres around the operation of free market forces in a capitalist economic system, then Oskar Lange was no mainstream economist. He was a dissenter because he had a different ideal from the two competing ideologies of his day; he used mainstream analytical tools to demonstrate the validity of his alternative model; and he continues to be a thorn in the side of those supporting *laissez-faire* policies.

BIOGRAPHICAL

Oskar Lange was the rare economist whose life and work seem to be reflections of each other. The times he lived through and the places he lived in gave a breadth to his personal experiences that few others can equal. His intimate knowledge, both theoretical and personal, of the two major competing economic systems of the twentieth century, of their advantages and disadvantages, and of their impact on 'peripheral' and developing economies, encouraged his efforts to develop a third alternative – the socialist market model.

Lange was born on 27 July 1904 in Tomaszow Mazowieki, near the textile centre of Lodz, in Western Poland. His father was a textile manufacturer who produced for export, a situation common to many dual-economy, peripheral capitalist economies. The family's prosperity was abruptly reduced as export markets were cut off during World War I.

The end of the war, the regaining of Poland's independence, and Poland's success in its 1920 war with Russia must have had an impact on the young Lange in opening up new possibilities for social development. In addition, the successful Russian Revolution, and his own interest in Marxist writings, seemed to indicate that a radical change – the overthrow of capitalism and its replacement by socialism – would improve not only Poland's situation but also human conditions in general. After an early interest in biology, mathematics and the social sciences, Lange studied law and economics in Poznan and Cracow. He published his doctoral thesis on business cycles in 1928 and began his teaching career.

However, his active involvement in the socialist movement antagonized the (conservative) university authorities, and Lange was prevented from teaching in his preferred field of political economy. Instead, he was forced to accept positions in the politically neutral field of statistics from 1931–34.

In 1933, Lange applied for, and was granted, a Rockefeller Foundation Fellowship to study in the United States. The next several years were the most productive phase of his life. During this time Lange analysed the inner workings of the capitalist system from within the largest capitalist economy. Apparently his leftist leanings were no barrier as far as any of his university contacts were concerned: one after another, in their reports to the Rockefeller Foundation, they comment on his expertise in economic analytics. Frank Taussig (Harvard) thought Lange 'an unusually able man, [who] has complete command of all modern methodological apparatus'; Carl Landauer (Berkeley) said that 'He is especially equipped for research in field of economic theory because he has an excellent mathematical background and at the same time is conscious of limitations of mathematical methods in social sciences' [sic]. Other comments along the same lines can be found in Lange's file at the Rockefeller Foundation archives.

Lange's time in the US (both as a visiting fellow and as a teacher) coincided with F.D. Roosevelt's New Deal and the spread of Keynesian analysis. These revitalized the study of economics and moved it away from the orthodox concerns with a self-regulating mechanism, a balanced budget and a sound currency. Lange, in fact, was instrumental in the dissemination of Keynesian macroeconomics in the United States during this period. It is probably true, therefore, to say that during this time of tremendous socioeconomic upheaval and intellectual excitement, political views which would have prevented his arrival in the United States at a different time (say, the McCarthy 1950s) were viewed with greater tolerance in the 1930s. In addition, Lange's amiable personality deflected the hostility of many who otherwise would have objected to him on account of his views. According to Melvin Reder, he 'knew how to disagree without giving personal offense. The net effect was that everyone loved him'. Abba Lerner (1977, p. 238), one of Lange's closest collaborators, recalled that 'it seems to me that no disagreement between Lange and myself on economic theory ever survived an hour's discussion'. Fisher (1966, p. 735) has also made the point that Lange was a great teacher and expositor, a point agreed on by all who met him, regardless of background or ideology.

Lange's fellowship was renewed at the end of the year, specifically to permit him to study problems of intertemporal equilibrium of production and the theory of interest. In the spring of 1935, he returned to Cracow to lecture (he retained his lectureship until 1937), before returning to the United States. This pattern continued until 1938. He took a temporary appointment as a lecturer at the University of Michigan in 1936; returned to Poland in the summer; resumed his fellowship in England (where economists at the London School of Economics, and Oxford and Cambridge Universities had the same reactions to him as their American colleagues); and returned to the United States in 1937.

He accepted a one-year visiting lectureship at the University of California, and then a teaching position at the University of Chicago in 1938. His plan to accept an appointment at the Polish Free University was blocked by Hitler's invasion of Poland, and he remained at Chicago for the duration of the war.

Lange was extremely active in political circles throughout this period, and in the years leading up to the war he worked energetically to promote progressive policies. He worked with the New America group to pressure for what would now be seen as a socialist influence within the Democratic Party, developing *A Democratic Program for Full Employment* for this group. He considered himself a left-wing New Dealer, recommending public expenditures to increase employment, a progressive income tax, the socialization of investment, support for labour and US intervention in World War II to fight fascism. Lange's support of US intervention on the side of the Allies is indicative of his independence from the Communist Party, which opposed such a move until Germany violated the agreement made between Hitler and Stalin, and invaded the Soviet Union in 1941. Hyman Minsky recalls Lange justifying the war as 'Not a war for socialism but a war for the possibility of socialism'. Reder believes that by 1941, Lange may have concluded that socialism was a politically unrealistic option for the United States, and unnecessary with the correct use of Keynesian policies. By that time, of course, US entry into the war and the stimulus to the economy given by wartime demands, solved any unemployment problems remaining from the depression years.

However, Lange retained his hope of seeing socialism flourish in Poland once the war was over. He was involved with the efforts of wartime Polish expatriates to prepare for a new government in Poland after the war. During this time his views on the structure of a socialist economy changed. He broke with the London-based Polish government-in-exile and became associated with the Soviet-sponsored Lublin Committee, which eventually evolved into the first postwar government in Warsaw.

This move, and his subsequent support for the Soviet-dominated Polish government, has puzzled many people. Lange's views on the model of a socialist economy had evolved in such a way that he now favoured reduced intervention in the economy. He proposed a plurality of ownership forms, a greater role for free price-setting by the market, and as large an extension of democracy as possible.[1] Why, and how, could he then throw his support behind a government wanting to restructure society in a way that, personally and theoretically, he opposed?

A possible answer, suggested by Reder, is that although Lange was an anti-Stalinist left-wing social democrat, he felt that the Stalinists could ultimately be a force for progress (especially in their fight against fascism), unlike the reactionary wartime government-in-exile based in London. A similar view is voiced by Wassily Leontief, who believed that Lange returned to Poland in spite of his distaste for its political situation, because he felt that he would be in a better position to help Poland than if he remained in the United States. According to Kowalik (1991, p. 92), Lange believed that the pressures of fighting a foreign war against imperialism and a domestic war against economic backwardness encouraged the development of a coercive administrative structure in the Soviet Union. Once these wars were over, the Soviet Union and the satellite countries under its domination (like Poland) would begin moving towards democracy and socialism. Kowalik thinks this optimistic faith in the potential for good that the new Polish government could have thus justified Lange's support for it, and his association with it after 1945.

If the early part of Lange's life in Poland was characterized by the emergence and development of his socialist ideals, and the years in the United States to the maturing of his intellectual gifts, the third part of his life can be characterized as an attempt to put these ideals and insights into practice. Undoubtedly, Lange's international reputation was valuable to the new Polish government; it often 'used' him to add respectability to Soviet communist schemes. Lange held both official appointments and elective ones, and combined these with various academic positions. Immediately following World War II Lange remained in the United States, first as the new Polish Ambassador to Washington (1945–46), and then as the first Polish delegate to the UN Security Council (1946–47).

After his return to Poland in 1947, Lange made only brief visits abroad. In spite of the various political upheavals (including the worsening of the Cold War), which periodically threatened his activities,[2] he refused to remain inactive. His work reflects an increased involvement with practical problems of both the Polish economy and developing economies. In one sense, this reflects a rounding out of his intellectual ideas: Lange previously analysed how a capitalist market economy works, and how a socialist market economy should be structured, so it seemed appropriate that he should turn to the problems of development plaguing so large a proportion of the world's population.

After the death of Stalin in 1953, and the change of government in Poland in 1956, Lange took a more active role in the reform movement. At this time, he felt the main task was to find the correct balance between centralization and decentralization. But instead of returning to the idea of market socialism, he favoured taking account of actual historical movements in a country; what was more important was to remove bureaucratic elements. To this end 'market mechanisms ought to be a tool

Economics and its discontents

in the hands of central planners and ... their operation should be subordinated to the need to determine consciously the direction of economic
development' (Kowalik 1991, p. 93). Therefore, the problem was how to
advise central planners and make sure they made correct decisions. Part
of the answer was in providing the most modern mathematical tools for
analysis, forecasting and planning.

Lange's political and academic positions in Poland gave him considerable influence, although with the qualifications noted previously. He was
involved in discussions of the problems of socialist planning both before
and after the events of 1956 in Poland. However, some of his teaching
and administrative functions were directly in the service of the Soviet
propaganda machine. For example, in 1952 Lange organized an
International Conference on Economic Cooperation in Moscow and
published an apologia about Stalin ('On the economic problems of
socialism in the USSR'), which some think Lange wrote as a guarantee
for his own survival (Kowalik 1991, p. 93).[3]

LANGE'S WRITINGS

Lange was a remarkably prolific writer, knowledgeable in many different
areas. His mastery of orthodox economic tools was widely acknowledged. He made contributions to the fields of Keynesian macroeconomic
analysis, the theory of interest, business cycles, welfare economics, utility
analysis, econometrics and development planning. The unifying theme in
all this work is a concern with the problem of how to make economic systems work so that human well-being can be maximized. Lange analysed
market capitalism and state socialism, and found them both falling short
of this requirement; he believed that a socialist system was superior
because it could be structured to prevent monopolization and bureaucratization while encouraging the development of democracy.

This is what makes Lange a dissenting economist. He was not satisfied
with the status quo, he did not like mature capitalism or Soviet-style planning, and he did not believe that either model provided a useful guide for
developing economies. His view of what the world should look like, and
of what economics should be about, was radically different from the
orthodoxies of both East and West. He also resisted the trend to treat the
practice of economics in terms of maximizing, or as a 'means–end'
schema. This he believed was too restrictive, and removed economics
from the social sciences (Fisher 1966, p. 734). However, Lange did accept
marginalist and neoclassical theory as a valid part of political economy
from which socialism could learn. In other words, he was a dissenter who

continually reminds us of the values that should influence the economist's task and who, as a master technician, worked to refine the tools of economic analysis in order to improve the human condition.

Lange has been chiefly identified as the architect of the socialist market model. This has attracted much attention and has been severely criticized, especially by von Mises, Hayek and their followers; and it gave rise to the famous von Mises–Lange debate on the rationality of a socialist system (see Hayek 1935). Although highly respected during his lifetime, in the last years of the twentieth century Lange rates only a brief mention in most history of thought texts – an illustration of the difference that time makes to the determination of who is a major economist and who is merely a 'dissenting' economist. To the extent that he *does* get more extensive coverage, it is usually in connection with the von Mises–Lange debate. While capitalist market structures have been the preferred ones since Lange's time, the fact that this debate has been subject to frequent reinterpretation, criticism, and demonstrations that Lange was wrong (or right) in maintaining that a socialist system could achieve the same optimum position as a competitive model and was feasible, simply reminds us that we are dealing with an important unresolved question here.

Lange's work displays an interesting duality. His writings on welfare economics, his work on econometrics and his mathematical elaborations of economics published in *Econometrica*, *Economica* and the *Review of Economic Studies* are the kind of work one would expect from a highly regarded mathematical economist.[4] Then there are the writings that set out the basis for what became known as the socialist market economy. Here Lange combines socialist thought with welfare economics. This adds a scientific element in keeping with Tinbergen's (1965) requirement that, if socialism is to be scientific, it must be interested in the scientific treatment of economic and social policy. But, as noted previously, the underlying theme of all Lange's work is related to his basic idealism regarding the effective working of a humane economic system. So, if capitalism is an inadequate mode of organization because of its instability, it is important to measure and analyse these movements. This leads to his work on business cycles and econometrics.

There is a rough progression in Lange's writings. It begins with the stability problems of capitalism; moves on to the economics of socialism, interest rate theory and other macroeconomic issues, to welfare economics, then econometrics and finally economic development issues and cybernetics. In what follows, I focus mainly on the development, evolution and criticism of his model of the socialist market economy. Although this area is the most relevant for discussing Lange as a dissenting economist, it should not be forgotten that all his work can be regarded in this same light.

THE SOCIALIST MARKET MODEL

Lange is best remembered as a major proponent of the socialist market economy. His model is usually considered to be the definitive version of market socialism, even if it has been criticized as unworkable, idealistic and too static (Keizer 1989; Murrell 1983; Richter 1992). It has, however, been an important influence on non-mainstream thinking, such as social economics, precisely because it offers a positive and democratic alternative to *laissez-faire* capitalism. The origin of the famous Lange–von Mises debate in fact goes back to the turn of the century, and can be seen in the context of two different strands of thinking, both of which Lange mastered. One strand was microeconomic, and dealt with the formation of prices in a market economy. The second was the question of how a socialist society, in the absence of private property and markets to coordinate economic activity, would organize economic behaviour. This question became relevant once European social democratic parties gained sufficient strength in the late nineteenth century to make them capable of forming a government and exerting effective control over economic activity.

These two issues were linked through welfare economics, whose focus was the maximization of utility or well-being. Lange's contribution was to show, as others had before him, that the institutional structure of society was irrelevant to this maximization. Von Mises and Hayek disagreed (in Hayek, ed., 1935). They maintained that the institution of private property was essential both to the functioning of an economy and to the maximization of welfare because without it there could be no markets for capital and hence no efficient allocation of resources.

The common root lies in the Walrasian system of equations describing how an exchange economy reaches equilibrium. The problem is that the Walrasian model cannot, without specific constraints, establish determinate and meaningful results under general conditions – multiple equilibria are possible, there may be no solution (that is, quantities supplied and demanded may not be equal at any price), the solutions may be meaningless (there may be zero or negative values), or the solutions may be unstable. Hence it became necessary to consider the nature of the demand and supply functions, and to raise questions about their existence, stability and the process by which equilibrium was reached. (See Spiegel 1983, pp. 554–5 for a discussion of these problems.)

Although F.Y. Edgeworth had criticized the Walrasian *tâtonnement* procedure as a way of approaching equilibrium, it played a role in Enrico Barone's theory of the socialist market economy, and was subsequently incorporated into the Lange model for the establishment of prices (Richter 1992; Spiegel 1983, p. 554). Both Barone and Vilfredo Pareto, who was certainly no friend to socialism, had shown that private property was not essential to the determination of market-clearing prices; competitive conditions were all that were necessary.

To reproduce these competitive conditions in a socialist society was Lange's contribution, with input from Abba Lerner. He identified two simple rules that operating units must follow – they must produce the level of output where the average cost of production is minimized and where price (each manager can assume all other prices are constant) equals marginal cost (Lange 1936, 1937, 1938). This corresponds to the position reached by the textbook model of long-run equilibrium in perfect competition. If shortages or surpluses appeared, planners were required to make the necessary adjustments, just as in a capitalist market economy. Thus, the planners effectively take over the functions of the Walrasian auctioneer. While both systems could produce an efficient allocation of resources (at least in the static sense), Lange preferred the socialist model because of its greater suitability for the exercise of democratic control. Throughout his life he fought against the growth of bureaucratic tendencies in economic life, believing that it was more important to retain openness than to achieve efficient resource allocation. The advantage of his model was that officials were subject to democratic control, unlike the executives of private corporations (Lange 1938, p. 109).

Obviously, his discussion of the operating procedures of a socialist market economy has much in common with the interests of welfare economics, which is 'concerned with the conditions which determine the total economic welfare of a community' (Lange 1942, p. 215). Lange's own work in welfare economics, however, went beyond simply finding the static equilibrium conditions associated with efficient resource allocation. He established that an 'efficient outcome' was compatible with any income distribution. To find a social optimum, it became necessary to incorporate some type of social valuation which assigns weights to the utilities of individuals so as to permit a more accurate balancing of relative losses and gains in utility in relation to the professed ideal of an economic society. This, Lange (1942, p. 221) points out, is similar to the principles underlying income tax legislation. What is important is that the propositions of welfare economics can be divided into two groups. One set of propositions are those most closely related to the traditional concerns of welfare economics and Pareto-optimality: finding the conditions which ensure the efficient allocation of resources. The second group is concerned with the optimum distribution of income, and involves maximizing a social value function.

This concern clearly overlaps with his continuing, and evolving, interest in the socialist economy; a major difference is the explicit focus on
improving democratic outcomes. However, there is no such thing as 'the'
Lange market socialism model because his ideas about market socialism
changed over his lifetime, partly in response to actual experience. Three
versions can be identified: the Lange–Breit model, the Lange–Lerner
model or what Kowalik (1987, p. 126) calls 'the classical model', and a
later mixed-economy version.

The first version is the outcome of a collaboration with Marek Breit, a
brilliant young Polish economist who was murdered by the Nazis in 1942.
Lange had been influenced by English guild socialism, and early in his
career supported the idea of industrial self-government with limited
political intervention in the economy. As a young man, he was a member
of a group wanting to build a socialist society in Poland that would be
different from the Soviet model. The group published a collective work in
1934 containing one chapter, written by Lange and Breit, setting out the
early market socialist model. Production facilities would be socialized by
transferring ownership to a public bank (the main central planning institution). All enterprises would be grouped into trusts, organized by
industrial branches. The bank plays a central role. It determines the economy's rate of growth and the allocation of investment resources, and it
controls access to finance capital. Although trusts nominally have considerable monopoly power, they have only limited ability to raise wages and
prices, as they would be required to employ all those who apply for work.
Workers' councils would have influence over trust policies, and were
expected to prevent bureaucratization. In both the labour and commodities markets, prices would be determined by market forces, and so the
composition of output would reflect consumer needs.

Lange and Breit believed an economy structured along these lines,
with most productive assets publicly owned but using the market mechanism to communicate and coordinate decisions, would be superior to
both   the (depressed) capitalist model of that time and the Soviet
model. Although they conceded that the Soviet model did work, it did so
only because of the enthusiasm of the people; its long-run effectiveness
was not guaranteed. Indeed, they noted, 'in the long run, socialism will
take root only if it manages to transcend its moral achievements to show
that its economy functions better than capitalism' (Lange 1934; quoted
by Kowalik 1991, p. 88).

Not long after arriving in the United States, Lange (1936, 1937, 1938)
published a second version of his model. While more sophisticated than
the earlier one, its major drawback is its static nature. Given that Lange
was pessimistic about the future of capitalism at this time it seems curi-

ous that he did not specifically consider long-run dynamics.[5] In this version, organization of the economy is similar to the earlier model, except that a central planning board replaces the public bank. This board takes over some price-setting functions; it is responsible for determining prices of capital goods, and must also make sure that the operating units follow the two basic rules for economic efficiency. By requiring that resources be combined to minimize the average costs of production and that output be at the level where price equals marginal cost, the rules would substitute for both the profit maximization and easy entry principles of a capitalist economy. Lange believed that with democratic control exercised over officials an outcome superior to market capitalism could be obtained; however, the problem of democracy continued to concern him. Lange subsequently spent considerable time grappling with the question of the extent of democratic freedoms. In fact, his dissatisfaction with the democratic elements of the 1936–38 model led him to turn down the opportunity to update and republish it (Kowalik 1991, p. 90).

What subsequently emerged as the third version has to be distilled from several different published works (Kowalik 1987, p. 127). The major differences include practically eliminating the planning board as a price-setter, extending the role of the private sector (especially for small and medium-sized enterprises), and putting emphasis on Poland as the location for this experiment (Lange 1987). Only key industries, such as banking and transport, would be publicly owned; while the extension of private enterprise was intended to be a foundation for democracy and an element encouraging greater economic flexibility. In other words, this version is much more like a mixed market economy. It is possible that the evolution of Lange's ideas reflects both idealistic hope for economic justice and a realistic recognition that perhaps capitalism was not doomed to self-destruction. That is, Lange was hopeful that continuing industrialization and economic development would create an informed population in which democratic institutions and practices could take root and flourish. Centralization might be necessary to get the process of development started, but it would become less necessary as the economy became more developed and sophisticated.

Much criticism leveled against Lange's market socialism seems directed at the earlier version of the model, which has been misinterpreted. Many proponents of an unregulated market capitalism (see Roberts 1971) seem to assume that a socialist model, by definition, must be a model of centralized planning. Therefore, they argue, to the extent that Lange does allow a role for markets, his model is not a socialist one, which proves the critics' point that socialism is unworkable.

This criticism trivializes Lange's work and rests on faulty logic. Furthermore, the critics fail to look at the development of the model, or to put it in the context of Lange's theoretical work. In particular, by including his policy-orientated studies (Lange 1944a,b and 1987) and his considerable work on Keynesian macroeconomics (which has not been discussed here), it is possible to see how much more complex his vision of an operational economic system really was.

Lange himself did not complete a definitive, comprehensive model of a market socialist society, so it is not very useful to speculate on what it would have looked like if he did. His critics, mainly the Austrian variant of mainstream theory, believe they have shown that his model does not demonstrate the ability of a socialist economy to function. This conclusion arises because, they claim, he does not deal with the problems of change, incentives or the formation of new firms. These are clearly important aspects of a functioning capitalist economy. However, a more complete reading of Lange's works shows that he was concerned with the questions of imbalances and uncertainties, and has an advantage over the Austrians by incorporating the equally important issues of income distribution, social justice and democracy into his model.

Even if some questions remain unanswered, and even if one can demonstrate logical flaws in Lange's model, why is there still an interest in proving that the market socialist model does not and cannot work? It is possible to identify other flaws, such as the absence of a financial system and institutions. But the basic issue that the critics cannot counter, and which informs Lange's work and makes it perennially interesting, is his vision of an alternative to capitalism. To Lange, market socialism is preferable to capitalism because of its greater democratic control, its more equitable income distribution and its improved stability. This concern with goals and ideals, rather than just means, is explicit in Lange's work on the socialist market economy and implicit in his macroeconomics and welfare economics. This is what makes him both a dissenting economist and one whose work cannot be ignored, even when the orthodox tradition would prefer that economics deal only with means, and not with ends or values.

CONCLUSION

The preceding section has given a brief account of some aspects of Lange's intellectual work. It has focused mainly on the evolution of his ideas for an alternative model for the economy because this is most relevant to his classification as a dissenting economist. Even what could be called his mainstream work (on welfare economics and econometrics) is orientated to improving the design and functioning of an alternative to capitalist reality. In the preface to his econometrics textbook, written as a guide to socialist planners, Lange (1959, p. 7) states that 'econometric methods can be applied in the socialist economy ... they constitute a necessary instrument for efficient planning and management of the socialist economy'. And furthermore, 'I have devoted particular attention to dynamic programming and to efficiency of investment'. As Fisher noted, Lange, especially in his later years, was concerned with the practical application of economic insights, particularly to Poland. Thus, the task of socialists was not to discuss utopian schemes, but to 'deal with such earthly problems as avoidance of "disproportionalities", provision of adequate incentives to managers, and determination of the proper balance between centralization and decentralization' (Fisher 1966, p. 735).

Lange's skills as an analyst were respected; his publications and interactions with other leading economists attest to that, and his own life experiences gave him insight into the practical economic problems of the twentieth century. Yet Lange has become marginalized by the economics profession. Probably the reason so little attention is now paid to Lange has to do with real-world events. Throughout his life, two monolithic competing economic systems, capitalism and state socialism, were in competition with one another. Lange believed that monopolization tendencies and the lack of democratic outcomes in capitalism made it undesirable (although he later modified his position on the possibility of reforming capitalism). He also opposed the undemocratic and coercive nature of the Soviet system. Hence his third way is an alternative to both systems. The collapse of Communism in the late 1980s has not led to a reconsideration of Langean market socialism, however. Instead, the post-Communist societies of Europe have embraced an unregenerated *laissez-faire* capitalism,[6] perhaps because 'the communists have destroyed the noncommunist socialist and social-democratic left' (Kowalik 1991, p. 95) so that there are no credible advocates of an alternative approach. Although an extensive literature on alternatives exists, it is not considered relevant – a good example of marginalization.

The idea of the dissenter advocating a different goal from the majority is another aspect that clearly distinguishes Lange. In his emphasis on assuring democratic outcomes, and his concern with human well-being from both economic and non-economic angles, Lange goes beyond the limits of economic analysis as narrowly defined. Many economists try to separate their own (non-economic) values and preferences from the implications of their economic analysis. Lange did not. He was always conscious of the importance of democratic elements, hence his continuing search for the 'best' social structure. He incorporated purely analytical principles into a larger political vision. As he put it, 'The formal principles of the theory of economic equilibrium are the same for any type of exchange economy' (Lange 1935, p. 197). He goes on to say that the ownership of productive services has no importance for the formal aspects of theory, but is an important issue when considering the future of the system. Thus, the exchange and pricing process is important for equilibrium analysis, but has nothing to do with the evolution of the system; this depends on the institutional arrangements (Lange 1935, p. 200).

Lange's focus on these institutional arrangements, and his preference for democratic socialism, make his work distinctive. He was not satisfied working within a given framework, but wanted to push beyond it. Again, using his work on welfare economics as an example, Lange was not satisfied just to determine the conditions necessary for equilibrium; rather, he wanted to find the optimum. This requires searching for the 'best' social valuation so that welfare really will be maximized. This, in turn, requires a consideration of the 'best' social system.

Interestingly enough, if one sees the economist as attempting to maximize human well-being, then Lange can be seen as a dissenter in yet another light – one who shares the goals of the majority but advocates a different approach. Lange's preferred approach is clearly different – adoption of a democratic socialist mechanism.

It is tempting to speculate what Lange would have thought and written had he not died when he did (2 October 1965). Considering the changes that have occurred since the mid-1960s – an end to the Cold War, the collapse of Communism, immense political and economic changes in Poland – it is easy to say that he would not have been silent. Given his broad-ranging expertise, and his commitment to developing mechanisms to improve social well-being, it is likely that he would recommend the most democratic alternative. His considerable skills as an economist, when combined with an idealist's vision of improving society, make him important in the late twentieth century, when economics has become a sterile and technocratic discipline concerned with building elegant mathematical models that have little practical relevance.

NOTES

*I am deeply grateful for the generous input of Lawrence Klein, Wassily Leontief, Hyman Minsky and Melvin Reder, who kindly shared their personal recollections of Oskar Lange with me. I am also grateful to the Rockefeller Archive Center, which provided me with information relating to Lange's Rockefeller Foundation Fellowship and his contacts in the United States; and to the History Project at the London School of Economics. Many thanks must also go to Cathy Rizzo, who typed the first draft of this chapter. Finally, I wish to acknowledge the continuing encouragement of Gary Mongiovi, my most critical and supportive reader.

1. This reworking was so extensive that he dropped his previous proposal to revise and republish his original model of market socialism as set out in *On the Economic Theory of Socialism* (Lange 1936, 1937).
2. A note dated 11/29/49 in the Rockefeller Archive Center on Lange reads, in part: 'L. is reported to have been forced into virtual retirement in Warsaw. ... His war-time acquaintance with Prime Minister Stalin alone is preserving him from something worse, is the information reaching David Nichol, Chicago Daily News Correspondent in Berlin'.
3. Oddly enough, publication of Stalin's book permitted an open discussion of the problems of economic management, and helped undermine the theoretical basis for the policy of forced industrialization which had created so many social tensions in Poland. Ultimately, therefore, it contributed to a climate much more favourable to the types of reforms Lange had earlier advocated.
4. Lange was anxious to maintain rigorous standards of mathematical analysis in economics. Hyman Minsky, as a young mathematically-inclined student at Chicago, recalls being advised by Lange to study economics, where his quantitative skills could be put to good use.
5. It is not true, as some critics have maintained, that he was not concerned with the long run. As a Keynesian macroeconomist, Lange (1937, 1938, pp. 110ff.) clearly understood the connection between the short-run problem of unemployment and the long-run problems of capital accumulation and investment. He can more easily be faulted for his omission of financial considerations.
6. The exception is China, which since 1992, has announced its intent to develop a socialist market economy (Shan 1993).

REFERENCES

Arestis, P. and M. Sawyer (1992), *Dictionary of Dissenting Economists*, Aldershot: Edward Elgar.

Fisher, W.D. (1966), 'Oskar Ryszard Lange: Obituary', *Econometrica*, **34** (4), October, 733–8.

Hayek, F. (ed.) (1935), *Collective Economic Planning*, London: Routledge & Sons.

Keizer, W. (1989), 'Recent reinterpretations of the socialist calculation debate', *Journal of Economic Studies*, **16** (2), 63–83.

Kowalik, T. (1987), 'Oskar Ryszard Lange', in *The New Palgrave Dictionary of Economics*, London: Macmillan, pp. 123–8.

Kowalik, T. (1991), 'Oskar Lange's market socialism', *Dissent*, **38** (1), Winter, 86–95.

Lange, O. (1935), 'Marxian economics and modern economic theory', *Review of Economic Studies*, **2** (3), June, 189–201.

Lange, O. (1936), 'On the economic theory of socialism, part 1', *Review of Economic Studies*, **4** (1), October, 53–71.

Lange, O. (1937), 'On the economic theory of socialism, part 2', *Review of Economic Studies*, **4** (2), February, 123–42.

Lange, O. (1938), with Fred M. Taylor, *On the Economic Theory of Socialism*, *Minneapolis*: University of Minnesota Press.

Lange, O. (1942), 'The foundations of welfare economics', *Econometrica*, **10** (3–4), July–October, 215–28.

Lange, O. (1944a), *The Stability of Economic Equilibrium*, Chicago: Cowles Commission Papers, No. 8.

Lange, O. (1944b), *Price Flexibility and Employment*, Bloomington: Principia Press.

Lange, O. (1959), *Introduction to Econometrics*, translated by Eugene Lepa, Oxford and London: Pergamon Press.

Lange, O. (1987) [1942], 'The economic operations of a socialist society', in *Contributions to Political Economy*, **6**, 3–24. (Originally lectures 6 and 7 in the series on Capitalism and Socialism, held at the University of Chicago, May 1942.)

Lange, O. and M. Breit (1934) 'The road to the socialist planned economy', in *The Economics, Politics, Tactics and Organization of Socialism*. In Gospodarka – polityka – taktyka – organizacja socjalizma. Warsaw. In Polish.

Lerner, A. (1977), 'Marginal cost pricing in the 1930s', *American Economic Review*, **67** (1), February, 235–9.

Murrell, P. (1983), 'Did the theory of market socialism answer the challenge of Ludwig von Mises?', *History of Political Economy*, **15**, Spring, 92–105.

Richter, R. (1992), 'A socialist market economy – can it work?', *Kyklos*, **45** (2), 185–207.

Roberts, P.C. (1971) 'Oskar Lange's theory of socialist planning', *Journal of Political Economy*, **79** (3), May/June, 562–77.

Shan, P. (1993) 'The prospect of Chinese socialist market economy', unpublished paper presented in Osaka.

Spiegel, H.W. (1983), *The Growth of Economic Thought*, Durham: Duke University Press.

Tinbergen, J. (1965), 'The significance of welfare economics for socialism', in *On Political Economy and Econometrics: Essays in Honour of Oskar Lange*, Oxford: Pergamon Press, pp. 591–9.

12. Imagining the possibilities: the dissent of Adolph Lowe

Mathew Forstater

INTRODUCTION

Adolph Lowe's work is the fruit of a great mind and a generous spirit grappling with complex social problems. His analyses of modern social life extend beyond the narrow confines of contemporary economics to encompass the sociological, historical, political and philosophical questions that arise when seeking to understand and transform society.

Lowe's dissents are complex. He questioned conventional economics at its very roots – its definition, its scope and relation to the other social sciences, the relation of history and theory, and the nature of economic policy in a modern capitalist economy. Taken as a whole, his work is nothing less than a wholesale rejection of conventional economics.

In what follows, it is argued that the notion of dissent must be understood in relation to some referent, and that in the case of twentieth century economics, the neoclassical approach is the proper referent. After an overview of the main characteristics of neoclassical economics, Lowe's work is examined to determine how it departs from the mainstream. It will be seen that Lowe dissents from the orthodoxy in virtually every respect. Instances where Lowe deviates from other positions of dissent will also be pointed out; differences among those who dissent from the dominant paradigm should not be viewed as unusual.

THE NATURE OF DISSENT

Dissent is difference. All difference is relational; it depends on some referent. But it is not *disinterested* difference. Dissent implies an *active engagement* with the referent, a shared history, and not mere random dissimilarity.

Since dissent depends on a referent, the content of dissent may change over time as the referent changes. In addition, there are multiple possible positions of dissent, and thus concurrent and oppositional forms of dissent. Dissent is therefore context dependent and historically relative; it emerges relative to what is dominant in a particular time and place.

In the twentieth century, neoclassical economics is the dominant paradigm. There are many different aspects of neoclassical economics and, of course, there has been diversity within this school. Nevertheless, the broadly accepted characteristics of neoclassical economics help us to identify dissent in twentieth century economics.

The first issue concerns the object and scope of economic inquiry. Neoclassical economics focuses on constrained decision-making. This narrows the discipline, which has become more and more alienated from the other social sciences; it also abandons socio-political considerations as a central part of the analysis. On the other hand, such a conception broadens the discipline's traditional area of application, so that we now have an economics of everything from marriage and suicide to politics and law.

Not unrelated to this shift in the object and scope of economic inquiry is the neoclassical claim that its laws are universally valid. All decisions are seen as subject to marginal analysis, and rationality is seen as a fixed aspect of human nature. The laws of supply and demand, diminishing marginal utility, and so on, are seen as having no spatial or temporal restrictions on their applicability. As a result, we get laboratory rats 'minimizing expenditure' and 'revealing preferences' for one soft drink over another.

Reducing economics to an optimization problem has led to a number of other developments. One is an almost religious adherence to mathematical formalism and the 'scientific' (deductive) method. Following this method is regarded as positive science; everything else is viewed as unscientific and, unlike positive economics, value laden.

A focus on the logic of choice also leads to a subjective (utility) theory of value. Social structure and economic classes are thus ignored in favour of a methodological individualism that takes the atomistic agent as the fundamental unit of analysis.

Another characteristic of neoclassical economics is the ideal of perfect competition, which includes assumptions such as perfect knowledge, perfect foresight and perfect mobility of factors of production. Even where imperfect information is acknowledged, it is usually treated as a case of risk rather than radical uncertainty. Elasticity of supply and factor substitutability make for rapid equilibration in response to changing market circumstances, while ignoring the lags in economic processes that occur in real historical time.

Neoclassical economics also emphasizes the primacy of exchange, with production treated as indirect exchange. The market is viewed primarily as an allocative mechanism, with dynamic aspects of growth and structural change generally underexamined. Technology is taken as exogenous, rather than rooted in the system. The production process itself is viewed as linear – leading from factors of production to consumer outputs – ignoring the crucial circularities associated with produced means of production.

Finally, neoclassical economics assumes full employment, or a systematic tendency to the full employment of all resources, including labour. The neoclassical equilibrium framework depicts the market system as orderly, predictable and satisfactory. Policies should thus counter market imperfections, so that the self-adjusting market mechanism can lead the economy to its optimal state.

This overview is in no way comprehensive, but it does set out the main characteristics of twentieth century economics. Approaches that reject these positions and offer alternative views may be described as dissent. There are thus many possible strands of this dissent. Dissenting views can stress evolutionary processes and sociological variables, focus on production rather than exchange, emphasize circularities in the production process, view material provisioning as the object of economic inquiry, endogenize technological change, reject positivism and formalism as tools of social inquiry, embrace structuralism or holism over methodological individualism, emphasize the dynamic features of capitalism, emphasize changing historical and institutional contexts rather than universal laws, reject rational economic man, or conclude that problems such as persistent unemployment, maldistribution of income and poverty are normal and systematic tendencies of modern capitalism.

This list is not exhaustive. Likewise, it is not necessary that dissenters subscribe to all of these positions. Nor does this deny the possibility that work which is in, or comes out of, the neoclassical tradition might take some of these views. In the case of Lowe, however, these fine lines are not a problem. This is because his work departs strikingly from the neoclassical school in many ways. What makes Lowe particularly interesting is that his dissent differs not only from the neoclassical mainstream, but also from the most prominent dissenters. Lowe has often played down this aspect of his work. Moreover, Lowe has consistently stressed the importance of moving beyond negative criticism to offering positive alternatives.

THE NATURE OF ECONOMICS

For Lowe (1965, pp. 6–18) economics is concerned with providing *material means*, or harnessing society's material resources to provide for the needs and wants of its members. Such a view was attacked by Robbins (1962, p. 16), who defined economics as 'the science which studies human behaviour as a relationship between ends and scarce means which have alternative uses'.

Lowe (1965, pp. 9f., 13) rejected the 'grandiose expansion of economics into a general "logic of choice"', de-emphasized the central place of the concepts of 'scarcity' and 'unlimited wants', and exposed their supposed universality as historically, culturally, and institutionally constituted. He argues that the neoclassical notion of scarcity is a *relative* notion, relative to unlimited wants. In fact, however,

> the wants which require material means for their satisfaction are by no means intrinsically limitless ... [because] we can certainly conceive of many states of material provision, above the threshold of mere subsistence, in which the prevailing cultural value system would limit the scale of wants requiring material means. (Lowe 1965, p. 10f.)

Thus, the size and distribution of material output relative to requirements for human subsistence and cultural values determine the importance of scarcity. As a result, the 'scarcity of resources cannot be made the criterion for economic activity' (Lowe 1965, p. 12).

Lowe uses two heuristic devices to highlight the fundamental technological and material basis of economic activity. The first is a Robinson Crusoe story, which might seem surprising given Lowe's vision of the economy as embedded in social life. He is aware of the misuses to which this fiction has been put in the history of economics; Lowe (1965, pp. 6f.) engages in the Crusoe exercise because he recognizes that the sociality of economic activity is so overwhelming that it threatens to blind the observer to the material-technological core of any economic system.

The primary task for Crusoe is to transform material inputs into outputs adequate for reproduction. The traditional emphasis on maximizing through time is a trivial, obfuscatory non-issue; whatever allocation between consumption today and consumption tomorrow Crusoe selects will be optimal by virtue of the fact that he chose it over any possible alternative. Likewise, meeting material requirements for biological subsistence is a necessary precondition for experiencing 'utility'.

Lowe argues that the determinant of Crusoe's decisions concerning resource allocation is *technological*; that is, his commonsense knowledge of the feasible methods of transforming available resources into outputs that replace the reproducible inputs used up in production, including the replenishment of his own labour power. Such knowledge pertains to '*engineering rules* in the widest sense of the term' (1965, p. 18, original emphasis). Material provisioning is thus likely to be inconsistent with independent economic laws regarding human motivations and/or behaviours. Crusoe's behaviour *must be* suitable for the adequate application of such rules to the production of the prescribed outputs; there is no necessary reason why an independent behavioural law will result in suitable behaviour.

Lowe's view of technology as the core of economic activity is revealed though another heuristic device – a fully automated system of production and distribution. Under such conditions, once computers are programmed, 'the structure of the path and the operation of the active "forces" suitable for goal attainment ... can be derived from the knowledge of engineering rules alone' (Lowe 1969a, p. 24). In this case, the active forces are 'subhuman', but the system leads to several important insights: 'it stands to reason that the behavior of the human agents must follow a path identical with that pursued by the automated system. Under no circumstances must it be ruled by laws of its own' (Lowe 1965, p. 333).

Lowe (1969a, p. 21) emphatically denies his position is 'that economics is nothing but technology', but once a particular end state has been stipulated 'the search for the suitable means is first of all a study of the suitable materials, devices, and processes – in a word, a technological problem' . Behaviour suitable to activate the system must be free to conform to the requirements imposed by such goals and rules, and thus will likely be inconsistent with 'extraneous' laws of economic behaviour (Lowe 1965, p. 333).

This view of production contrasts sharply with the neoclassical focus on exchange, choice and utility maximization. Rather, it follows along the lines of F. Quesnay's *Tableaux* and Karl Marx's reproduction schemes, which deal with physical flows, technical conditions of production, minimum and maximum (physical) conditions, and sectoral proportionality and balance.

In fact, during the 1920s Lowe and his colleagues at Kiel University used Quesnay–Marx reproduction models to analyse accumulation, cycles, employment, and structural and technological change. Lowe expanded Marx's Department 1 into two sectors, producing means of production for the capital goods and the consumption goods sectors, respectively. He was then able to demonstrate the fruitfulness of isolating the machine tools sector when studying structural change in industrial systems. This entailed a critique of E. von Böhm-Bawerk's 'linear imperialism', but led ultimately to what Gehrke and Hagemann (1990, p. 24) have called 'a unique synthesis of Austrian sequentiality and classical (or Sraffian) circularity'. Thus, while dismissing the linear view of production and reviving the view of production as a circular process, Lowe (1976, p. 34 n. 6) also rejected as 'an extreme position' Sraffa's 'eliminat[ion of] linear processes of production altogether'.

Lowe begins with a technical sequence of production depicting working capital moving through a series of successive stages *en route* to becoming final output. We can follow working capital through a series of transformations, such as cotton–yarn–cloth–dress in dress production or wheat–flour–bread in the production of bread. At each stage, labor (N_i), natural resources (R_i), and fixed capital (F_i), combine to produce the working capital (W_i) as output:

$$N_1 \; \cup \; R_1 \; \cup \; F_1 \qquad\qquad \rightarrow w_1 \; (= \text{cotton})$$
$$N_2 \; \cup \; R_2 \; \cup \; F_2 \; \cup \; w_1 \; \rightarrow w_2 \; (= \text{yarn})$$
$$N_3 \; \cup \; R_3 \; \cup \; F_3 \; \cup \; w_2 \; \rightarrow w_3 \; (= \text{cloth})$$
$$N_4 \; \cup \; R_4 \; \cup \; F_4 \; \cup \; w_3 \; \rightarrow w_4 \; (= \text{dress})$$

Except for the first stage, working capital from the previous period, w_{i-1}, is also an input. This follows along the lines of the Austrian linear view: the process can be traced back from the final output through each intermediate stage to an initial stage in which no working capital had been taken over from a previous stage. The picture, however, as thus far presented, does not explain the origin of fixed capital. In addition, accounting for the origin of fixed capital would only guarantee temporary provision; continuity of production requires the ongoing replenishment of stocks undergoing wear and tear in the production process and thus a second sector in which fixed capital equipment is produced and reproduced.

Thus if F_1 to F_4 are gin, spindle, loom and sewing machine, a technical sequence of production of several stages may be derived for each, similar in structure to that of dress production, but with inputs appropriate for production of the equipment good as final output. The weakness of this solution is immediately clear – another production flow will be required to account for the production of the fixed capital used to produce the gin, spindle, loom and sewing machine. The analysis appears mired in an infinite regress. Lowe rejected the possibility that industrial production could be accurately described by such an infinite regress.

The Austrian solution was to posit some original stage where only labour and natural resources were used. Lowe rejected this on historical, theoretical, empirical and commonsense grounds. His solution to the infinite regress came from a clue in the bread production example given above. When specifying the input requirements for bread production, one in particular stands out:

> We can imagine dispensing with plows and, perhaps, even human labor, and yet raising wheat, but we cannot imagine dispensing with another input so far not mentioned: seed-wheat. But what is seed-wheat, and how is it obtained? It so happens that it is physically identical with the semi-finished output bread-wheat, and it is a moot question whether it can really be called a natural resource. But whatever the correct classification may be, seed-wheat not only is indispensable but it possesses an outstanding quality which is absent from

flour and bread, from plows and mills and ovens: the power of self-reproduction. Differently stated, seed-wheat as an input is capable of producing two types of outputs: bread wheat as a potential consumer good and seed-wheat as its own replacement good. (Lowe 1965, pp. 269f.)

The technological condition for continuous production of wheat is the physical identity of the input and output – its capacity for self-reproduction. A similar condition might also explain the seeming paradox of infinite regress in the replacement of fixed capital. Lowe searched for a special equipment good that could produce other equipment goods as well as reproducing itself.

What we actually find is not one such mechanical instrument, but a comprehensive group which is defined as machine tools. In conjunction and combined with labor and working capital goods such as steel, machine tools are the progenitors of all other machinery *and also of themselves*. For the physical maintenance of an industrial regime of production they play the same strategic role as seed-wheat plays in agriculture, and the reproductive system plays in the maintenance of organic life. (Lowe 1965, p. 270, original emphasis)

Thus it is not necessary to add more sectors in order to depict industrial production. To focus on the crucial role of the machine tools sector, it is sufficient to divide the capital goods sector into Sectors 1 and 2, producing means of production utilized in capital goods production and consumption goods production, respectively.

One result of this analysis is that a primary obstacle to running an economy at full employment after unexpected changes in technology, or the supply of labour or natural resources, is the inadequate structure of the real capital stock. The problems are technological: 'Obstruction of resource shifts, bottlenecks in production, inelasticity of supply owing to the *longue durée* of capital formation and even more to the large costs of sunk capital' (Lowe 1976, p. 9). Recognizing these bottlenecks, rigidities, distortions, and time lags brings issues of the *'formation, application and liquidation of real capital'* (Lowe 1976, p. 10, original emphasis) to the centre of the production process.

This modified circular reproduction framework contrasts sharply with the static equilibrium models of neoclassical theory. As far back as the 1920s, Lowe (1926) rejected static equilibrium models as unsuitable for analysing systems exhibiting periodic fluctuations, and called for uncovering the endogenous determinants of business cycles. While others thought that monetary crises led to the business cycle, Lowe claimed that these explanations were insufficient, and put forward the view that technological change was the primary disturbing factor. In addition, Lowe felt that Keynes did not pay adequate attention to technological change and its labour-displacing effects.

LOWE'S DISSENT AGAINST SUPPLY AND DEMAND ANALYSIS

By the 1930s, Lowe came to reject the orthodox idea that universal economic laws exist. At that time he began to explore the notion that
economic theories are historically relative, their differences deriving
primarily from the selection of data depicting structural features repre-
senting alternative historical economic systems. Conventional market
generalizations described a very specific set of socio-historical circumstances; these generalizations were not applicable to modern industrial
capitalism.

Lowe focused on the law that traditionally performs the theoretical role
of providing stability in a liberal society using markets to organize its economic life – the law of supply and demand. In dissecting the law of supply
and demand Lowe begins by distinguishing between behaviour and motivation. The determinacy and stability of traditional theory, Lowe stressed,
depends on how buyers and sellers behave in response to price changes
and how they behave in the face of excess demand or supply.

This simple observation undermines the traditional association of
individual free choice with market order under *laissez-faire*. Individuals
are free to choose, yet they *must* choose to act in accord with the law of
supply and demand for markets to function. Truly free choice, however,
leaves behavioural outcomes indeterminate. Lowe (1935, pp. 51f.; 1951,
pp. 405, 413) thus dispenses with the neoclassical idea that utility (or any
subjective principle) can be the basis of economic theory. Assuming free
choice, behaviour guided by the utility principle cannot guarantee actions
in accord with the law of supply and demand.

Behavioural stipulations require some *objective* principle. 'Economic
man' performs this function for traditional theory. Citing historical
examples and drawing on the work of anthropologists, Lowe (1935, pp.
50f.; 1942, p. 436; 1951, p. 405) questioned whether economic man could
provide a universal depiction of human nature. Individual identity is
complicated, contradictory, multifaceted, and socially constructed for
Lowe. Individual decisions are the 'result of fragmentary experience and
information, of speculation and hunches, and ... of *communication with
others*' (1965, pp. 16f, emphasis added). Also, 'both buyers' preferences and
sellers' incentives ... give way to all sorts of personal, national, racial,
and other discriminations' (Lowe 1951, pp. 413). This contrasts sharply
with the traditional view of economic man, which presents the economic
subject as natural, universal, and coherent, and identity as fixed and
asocial (Milberg 1991, pp. 93, 96). Lowe (1951, pp. 424ff.) rejects method-

ological individualism because it takes the subjectivity of agents as given; rather, continuously changing social structure shapes and reshapes each participant's interpretation of market events.

Lowe (1951, p. 409) recognizes that traditional economics treats behaviour inconsistent with the economic man construct as a deviation from the normal case. But he points out that acceptability of the construct depends on demonstrating that the normal case guarantees a determinate outcome. This, Lowe argues, cannot in fact be demonstrated. Even if the profit motive is assumed, this does not assure conduct in accord with the law of supply and demand. It is simply not sufficient to describe motivations.

> Unfortunately, not even in a completely rational world – in the sense of one completely motivated by pecuniary considerations – would actions in accord with our law rise to the level of causal necessity. Rather it has to be admitted that calculation of pecuniary gains often suggests behavior that sharply contradicts its propositions. From all this we have to conclude that neither an understanding of human motives in general, nor the special criterion of the pecuniary motive, entitles us to predict any one course of action as the normal outcome of changes in demand or supply, or of variations in price. (Lowe 1942, p. 437)

For Lowe, then, the law of supply and demand has no claim to either causal necessity or statistical probability. Neither free choice nor rationality guarantee any determinate outcome, much less behaviour consistent with the law. Under such circumstances, the law can only be understood as a prescription or stability condition. In this sense it constitutes a general rule of conduct regarding market behaviour, and thus its usefulness for explanation or prediction depends on the concatenation of factors that determine the resilience of the rule and rule-following behaviour (Lowe 1942, pp. 433, 446, 451; 1951, pp. 415f.)

The order-bestowing properties of the law of supply and demand, however, are not unleashed when individual conduct conforms to the behavioural stipulations of economic man; rather they arise from the regular behavioural *patterns* that result from aggregating the individual behaviours of all market participants (Lowe 1935, pp. 60f.; 1951, pp. 411f.)

Each and every act of material provisioning entails a sequence of subactivities requiring a 'chain of interlocking decisions'. For decisions to interlock in this manner, market participants must be able to predict the response of other participants to their own decisions or behaviour (Lowe 1942, pp. 439ff.; 1951, p. 412). Otherwise, there will be no reason to expect that one's actions will lead to the intended outcome. There are, however, no logical or psychological reasons why an individual should be able to predict the decisions or behaviour of all other market participants (Lowe 1942, pp. 443f.) Moreover, while an objective social rule might play a role in decreasing the instability resulting from uncertainty, 'the radical subjectivism of the marginalist school has deprived modern theory of any criterion by which a *pattern of interlocking* choices can be distinguished from a *sum of random* choices' (Lowe 1942, p. 445, original emphasis).

Behaviour consistent with the law of supply and demand thus requires not only that individuals intend to behave in conformity with the law, but also that they expect others will do so (Lowe 1969b, pp. 180f.). Paying careful attention to the impact of (historically changing) socioeconomic structure on behaviour and motivation, and the changing limits upon and consequences of economic action under different structural and institutional conditions, leads to conclusions quite different from the neoclassical and the Austrian schools. Even assuming both a behavioural code in conformity with economic man and stabilizing expectations, these can only secure the *willingness* to respond in a manner conforming with the necessary conduct; if there is to be system stability, the law also requires assurance concerning the *ability* of market participants to respond as well. In the first instance, preconditions for this ability include certain rights (usually identified with private property) regarding access to, and utilization and disposal of, resources, the right to engage in contractual relations, and other political and legal conditions associated with a society of 'free exchange' (Lowe 1935, pp. 56f.). The ability to respond also implies a high degree of mobility. This is especially significant on the supply side, where producers must be able to increase supply when prices rise.

A technical structure enabling quick response to changing market conditions will also have a stabilizing effect on expectations, while a structure that makes response difficult will be destabilizing. 'The faster the required adjustment can be carried out, the nearer to the present are the relevant future dates, and the smaller the danger that uncalculable events will interfere' (Lowe 1951, p. 429). This highlights an essential feature of Lowe's analysis of expectations, and the main flaw in Keynesian and Austrian analyses of uncertainty – the importance of economic and technological structures in shaping and determining expectations.

We can thus begin to comprehend how the same motivating force (the profit principle) can express itself in diametrically opposed forms of conduct, or how the same conduct can induce different responses by other market participants. The key for Lowe (1942, p. 456; 1951, pp. 420, 429) is the socioeconomic structures and institutional contexts that prevail in a particular case.

Dependence of the law of supply and demand on such factors has implications for the extent and substance of any changes in economic structure that are possible without threatening breakdown of the conditions for its operation. Thus economic and social evolution not only must exhibit regularity, it must also exhibit regularity of a specific type – regularity conforming to the requirements for the existence and stability of the law (Lowe 1935, pp. 70–73, 92).

Lowe (1935, p. 73) uncovers the sociological assumptions of the law of supply and demand, thereby defining the institutional setting for its applicability. These data are broadly identified as the behavioural code of economic man and the institutional and technical environment implicit in the concept of 'free competition'. Thus, the probability of the law's operation depends on the probability that such structural conditions actually apply.

Such a concatenation of structural features is more appropriate for early capitalism than for modern industrial society (Lowe 1935, p. 59). This does not mean that human nature in that early period is properly depicted by the economic man construct. Rather, Lowe (1942, p. 452) identifies 'exogenous stabilizers' that have historically compensated for whatever deviations might threaten the stability of the system. Large portions of the population living at or near subsistence negate the need to either assign particular psychological characteristics to human nature or establish social pressures to behave in conformity with the credo of the economic man. In this case, a certain type of maximizing behaviour is rooted in the pressures for survival (Lowe 1951, p. 414).

At levels above subsistence greater discretion is possible, although the profit principle may still be valid by determining 'upper and lower levels of extravagance'. Interestingly, Lowe (1951, p. 415) points out that the range of individual deviation permitted under these circumstances has no necessary relation to the system's ability to tolerate those deviations, leading him to conclude that while 'occasional breaches may be tolerated ... the system will collapse before the exception becomes the rule'.

Lowe places even more emphasis on the different technological structures in early market society and modern capitalism. Small-scale, labour-intensive production, carried out by independent producers with low fixed costs and operating at low levels of mechanization, makes for greater mobility. It therefore results in a high degree of adaptability to price or quantity variations. Large-scale, modern industrial capitalism, with its huge fixed costs, capital-intensive methods and rapidly changing technologies, is characterized by great immobility, and thus an inability to make fast adjustments (Lowe 1935, pp. 57ff., 87f., 109). These differences in technical structure are at the root of a whole series of social and institutional transformations: 'It has transformed private property into monopoly, money into capital, money incentive into the acquisitive drive, and the utopian possibility of a moving equilibrium into the historical reality of the trade cycle' (Lowe 1935, p. 128).

Claims for the universal applicability of traditional theory must be rejected, in so far as determinacy is guaranteed only under 'one very definite and exceptional social order' (Lowe 1935, pp. 147f.) . Traditional economics obtains its exactness and determinacy not by abstracting from sociological and historical factors, but rather as a result of the narrow limits of its applicability that follow from its underlying sociological assumptions. The laws of traditional economics are not absent because of their purity, but rather because of their limited sociological, psychological and technical applicability (Lowe 1942, pp. 456f.) Thus Lowe's (1935) 'plea for cooperation in the social sciences'.

LOWE'S INSTRUMENTAL METHOD

Just as the law of supply and demand does not apply to the contemporary economy with a high degree of reliability, so too the structural characteristics of modern industrial capitalism are not adequately depicted by traditional theory. Lowe's view, however, was not simply that a different theory was necessary, one which more adequately represented the structure of modern capitalism; at this stage, he began to put forward the view that the nature of the modern industrial process is such that *the data itself is largely determined bv economic processes* (see, for example, Lowe 1935, pp. 97ff.)

From roughly the mid-1930s to the mid-1950s, Lowe (1935, p. 98) referred to the approach he was attempting to develop as 'modern realistic theory', an approach to the dynamics of capitalist accumulation that would adequately consider both economic structure and process. The central focus of this analysis is the business cycle. But any theory of cycles must be accompanied 'by a theory of the evolution of its social data', since 'essential variations of those data [are] effected by the course of the trade cycle itself' (Lowe 1935, pp. 93ff.) . In such circumstances, 'any deductive operation with invariable data is defective from the very outset' (Lowe 1935, pp. 138f.), and the structural conditions themselves must become the object of theoretical inquiry (Lowe 1936, pp. 23f.)

Lowe was committed to the idea that regularities exist and could be uncovered, even though they were different regularities than those described by traditional theory. These were the 'strange regularit[ies] of the real dis-equilibrium' (Lowe 1935, p. 90). Although Lowe (1936, p. 25) did not feel that the exactness and determinacy of traditional market generalizations would be obtainable, he felt this loss was necessary in order to regain realism. But Lowe (1951, p. 403) held steadfast to the view that the traditional method, if refined, could help analyse the modern system.

By the late 1950s, Lowe began to see that historical changes in the structure of capitalist society altered economic inquiry in such a way that the traditional methodological approach had to be abandoned. Analysis henceforth had to be conducted within an alternative, instrumental framework.

Lowe's critique does not focus on flaws of the deductive method. In fact, he believes that social and technological conditions rendered it appropriate for the period of Classical analysis (Lowe 1959b, p. 163; 1969a, pp. 3, 11, 12, 28, 32; 1976, p. 7; 1977, pp. 46, 68ff.). However, with the historical structural–technological transformation of capitalism and associated feedback effects resulting in environmental, institutional, behavioural and socio-psychological changes, these conditions no longer hold (Lowe 1937, pp. 163–6; 1965, p. 325; 1969a, pp. 3, 11, 32; 1969b, pp. 169–71, 180; 1987a, p. 236). Such factors include the increasing concentration and centralization of capital; the rapid pace of technological change; the emerging middle classes in industrialized nations; the increasing role of the state in the economy; and the environmental impact of economic growth.

From the end of the 1950s, Lowe rejected the argument that the historical changes from early industrialization to modern industrial capitalism merely indicate a shift from one kind of stable system to another. Rather, the traditional 'deductive method [is] inapplicable ... [because] neither the macro-movements of modern markets nor the underlying micro-patterns of behavior exhibit the degree of orderliness that is essential for scientific generalization' (Lowe 1969b, p. 180). The ability to make abstract generalizations serve as high-level hypotheses from which deduction can proceed requires that the research object exhibit some minimum degree of orderliness. Without such minimum order, the generalizations necessary to employ the traditional deductive method cannot be made.

Discussion of Lowe's methodological work has focused on his thesis that the regular behavioural and motivational patterns, upon which scientific generalizations depend, can no longer be trusted. In Lowe's (1969a, p. 15) 'inclusive concept of order', the ability to identify reliable phenomena is a necessary but not sufficient condition for the appropriate applicability of the traditional deductive method. It is also required that the macro outcomes of such behavioural and motivational patterns be consistent with society's macro goals (Lowe 1969a, pp. 6f.). Order must thus be understood in the double-sense of underlying regularity of the research object and socially satisfactory macro outcomes.

This position is certainly foreign to the traditional method and contrary to the usual view that theorizing about an economic system is separable from whether or not that system produces an outcome which is consistent with society's goals. In such a view, if society does not like the economic outcomes, then economic policy is undertaken. In contrast, Lowe (1969a, p. 7) emphatically rejects any approach that neglects consideration of macro outcomes at the ground level of theoretical analysis. Furthermore, he believes that primary interventions are no longer adequate to address the inability of the market system to result in goal-adequate outcomes (Lowe 1969b, pp. 169, 188f.). The separation of positive and normative 'can no longer be justified ... recent developments demand the conscious integration of the analytical and normative aspects' (Lowe 1967, p. 180).

Rather than taking initial conditions as given and attempting to predict outcomes, Lowe proposed starting with a predetermined end state. The task then becomes to derive, or discover, the technical and social path(s) by which those outcomes might be achieved, the behavioural and motivational patterns capable of setting the system on to a suitable path, the environmental contexts capable of encouraging these patterns, and the policies shaping or creating the environmental contexts. Economic theory must not determine the ends (macro goals) but devise the means for their attainment.

The Instrumental Method is thus a *regressive* procedure. It begins from where we want to go, and works backwards to the present state or a state within our reach (Lowe 1977, pp. 143f.). Analysis moves from our goals to the conditions for their attainment. This is the realm of structural analysis, which investigates the technical consistency of goals without any reference to assumptions concerning behaviour or motivation. In other words, the procedure is independent of any behavioural assumptions (Lowe 1969a, pp. 23f.; 1969b, p. 182).

Such independence from behavioural assumptions broadens the range of economic theory. Lowe believed that the deductive method was appropriate for the special case in which motivational and behavioural patterns exhibited in the system provided a particular and sufficient orderliness. Historically, these conditions were satisfied during early industrial capitalism, when external natural and social pressures emanating from a specific constellation of structural features enforced such motivational and behavioural conditions. Instrumentalism encompasses this special case, as well as other cases where motivational and behavioural patterns do not satisfy these conditions (Lowe 1969a, p. 32). In this sense, Political Economics may be seen as a general theory of economic structure and behaviour.

Since the traditional deductive method is no longer possible, it might be thought that deduction itself is rendered obsolete. But through the conscious recreation of the conditions appropriate for its application, the possibility for powerful economic reasoning of this type is recaptured.

Lowe's (1992, pp. 326f.) analysis thus provides a foundation for 'the restoration of deductive theory'. Since the conditions are established by design and control, replacing the deductive method with the instrumental–deductive method becomes 'the core of Political Economics' (Lowe 1969b, p. 179).

Far from endorsing rational planning, Lowe explores the possibilities of instrumental inference as a policy-discovery procedure. Drawing on the work of Michael Polanyi, Charles Peirce and Norwood Hanson, he investigates aspects of the policy formulation process that employ tacit knowledge, retroduction and other heuristic problem-solving techniques. Instrumental inference is characterized as a 'search procedure' and a 'mental technique of problem solving'. Solutions are discovered 'through what Polanyi calls a logical "leap". ... But they are not leaps in the dark. ... [O]ur search is guided by past experience, analogies, and other clues. Yet it remains true that our ultimate insight springs from a non-rational act of "imagination"' (Lowe 1969b, p. 183).

In this sense, instrumentalism is not new. The implicit procedures and tactics of problem-solving, taken for granted in the scientific community, for the most part remain behind the scenes. Lowe calls for making these procedures conscious, and for recognizing their potential contribution to successful policy-making.

Lowe's work, and his original dissent, stem from his daring to imagine what might be. Lowe dared to imagine the possibility for greater cooperation in the social sciences, dared to imagine the possibility for a more realistic theory, dared to imagine the possibility of a healthier economy and a better society. It is this challenge – imagining the possibilities – that instrumentalism brings to economic theory, methodology, and public policy.

REFERENCES

Gehrke, C. and H. Hagemann (1990), 'Efficient traverses and bottlenecks: a structural approach', *Research Memorandum Nr. 9003*, Department of Economics, University of Graz.

Lowe, A. (1926), 'Wie ist Konjunkturtheorie Überhaupt Möglich?', *Weltwirtschaftliches Archiv*, **24**, October, 165–97.

Lowe, A. (1935), *Economics and Sociology: A Plea for Cooperation in the Social Sciences*, London: George Allen & Unwin.

Lowe, A. (1936), 'Economic analysis and social structure', *The Manchester School*, **7** (2), 18–37.

Lowe, A. (1937), *The Price of Liberty*, London: Hogarth.

Lowe, A. (1942), 'A reconsideration of the law of supply and demand', *Social Research*, **9** (3), 431–57.

Lowe, A. (1951), 'On the mechanistic approach in economics', *Social Research*, **18** (4), 403–34.

Lowe, A. (1959a), 'F.A. Burchardt, Part I: recollections of his work in Germany', *Bulletin of the Institute of Statistics*, **21**, May, 59–65.

Lowe, A. (1959b), 'The practical uses of theory: comment', *Social Research*, **26** (2), 161–6.

Lowe, A. (1965), *On Economic Knowledge: Toward a Science of Political Economics*, Armonk: M.E. Sharpe.

Lowe, A. (1967), 'The normative roots of economic value' in S. Hook (ed.) *Human Values and Economic Policy*, New York: NYU Press, pp. 170–80.

Lowe, A. (1969a), 'Toward a science of political economics' in R.L. Heilbroner (ed.), *Economic Means and Social Ends: Essays in Political Economics*, Englewood Cliffs: Prentice-Hall, pp. 1–36.

Lowe, A. (1969b), 'Economic means and social ends: a rejoinder' in R.L. Heilbroner (ed.) *Economic Means and Social Ends: Essays in Political Economics*, Englewood Cliffs: Prentice-Hall, pp. 167–99.

Lowe, A. (1976), *The Path of Economic Growth*, Cambridge: Cambridge University Press.

Lowe, A. (1977), 'Political economics in the late twentieth century', in *On Economic Knowledge: Toward a Science of Political Economics*, enlarged ed, Armonk: M.E. Sharpe.

Lowe, A. (1982), 'Is the glass half full or half empty?: a self-critique', *Social Research*, **49** (4), 927–49, reprinted in A. Oakley (ed.), *Essays in Political Economics: Public Control in a Democratic Society*, Brighton: Wheatsheaf Press, 1987, pp. 234–50.

Lowe, A. (1988), *Has Freedom a Future?*, New York: Praeger.

Lowe, A. (1992), 'A self-portrait', in P. Arestis and M. Sawyer (eds) *A Biographical Dictionary of Dissenting Economists*, Aldershot: Edward Elgar, pp. 323–8.

Milberg, W. (1991), 'Marxism, poststructuralism, and the discourse of economists', *Rethinking Marxism*, **4** (2), 93–104.

Robbins, L. (1962), *An Essay on the Nature and Significance of Economic Science*, second edn., London: Macmillan

13. Gardiner Means and the dissent of administered prices

Frederic Lee

THE NATURE OF DISSENT

A survey taken at the Royal Economic Society or the American Economic Association meetings would probably reveal that economists view themselves as dissenters. But following these economists to their sessions and listening to their papers, one would most likely see rows of mathematical formulae, and hear about unstable Nash multi-equilibria and rational economic agents maximizing their net present value. Were economists lying when they claimed to be dissenters? The answer is 'no', since the term 'dissenting economist' does not have an unambiguous meaning.

Accepting for the moment that economics is dominated by neoclassical economics, it is clear that there exists a high degree of functional and strategic dependence[1] among its practitioners. This is due to the customary methods of analysis and commonly accepted topics for investigation. These are emphasized in textbooks, and used to train economists at both the undergraduate and graduate levels. Within this context, an economist can accept the defining features of neoclassical economics (such as relative scarcity, maximization, rationality and mathematics *qua* equilibrium) and still be a dissenter if they utilize a new accepted mathematical technique to examine some 'strange' hypothesis. Thus, many economists see themselves as dissenters because of the unusual methods they use, the questions they ask, or the topics they investigate (Whitley 1984, 1986, 1991; Coats 1984).[2]

That neoclassical economics should have in-house dissenters is not surprising, since such individuals have shaped its evolution over time. In-house dissenters generally have the support of well-established reputable economists. They deliver papers at the annual conferences of the Royal Economic Society and American Economic Association; they are not discriminated against by the top journals; and they are openly accepted at the best PhD-awarding economic departments. In short, most in-house dissenters are viewed as good economists by their colleagues; they freely partake in activities which define and maintain the neoclassical paradigm, and also actively support and reinforce such activities.

However, there is a second kind of in-house dissenter that is out of favour and thus marginalized. Although exhibiting a high degree of functional and strategic dependence with their neoclassical colleagues, they arrive at unacceptable political conclusions when examining acceptable topics. Since neoclassical economists generally accept the conventional political wisdom of the day, there will always exist 'political' economists who are not quite acceptable. However, it is important to note that while extreme *laissez-faire* economists had a difficult time in the 1950s and 1960s, they did get drawn back into the mainstream as the political views of neoclassical economists shifted rightwards. On the other hand, progressive neoclassical economists[3] have never been accepted by the majority of the profession, and as such are somewhat of an anomaly among the in-house dissenters.

Because progressive neoclassical economists have been unable to participate fully in the activities of the mainstream, they perceive themselves to have much in common with those who reject neoclassical economics. The commonality between these two groups lies solely within the realm of politics, since many who reject neoclassical economics also hold progressive political views. Despite this point in common, sharp differences remain between the two groups. The manner in which progressive neoclassical economists examine the activities of a capitalist economy is fundamentally conservative; the ideological content of neoclassical economics overwhelms their progressive political views, if not while in graduate school then by middle age when the desire to be seen as successful becomes overpowering. As the need to be seen as successful becomes overwhelming, they start asserting the superiority of neoclassical theory over dissident theories, and begin transforming the ideological content of their dissident theories. In this regard they begin engaging in activities that define and maintain the neoclassical paradigm. Because of this, progressive neoclassical economists are unable to cross the great divide into the nether world of non-neoclassical economics, where the chance of their becoming a successful economist (or even being recognized as an economist at all) drops rapidly towards zero.

Non-neoclassical economists can dissent on a number of different levels. Most obviously, non-neoclassical economists are theoretical dissenters from neoclassical economics. As a result their access to core economic journals, their participation at conferences and their ability to get research funding is blocked.

The continuous process of convention-building with regard to methods of analysis and topics for investigation makes it possible for dissenting in-school economists to exist at different levels within the field of non-neoclassical economics.[4] For example, changing political winds with regard to socialism, central planning, markets and large business corporations have, over the last half-century, altered the acceptable research topics and political opinions for non-neoclassical economists. Post Keynesian defenders of big business have found their more radical colleagues adopting their benign view of the competitive dynamics of large corporate enterprises.[5] As a result, glorifying big business has become a more acceptable topic for research, while the small-is-beautiful research agenda has moved to the dissenting fringe. The change came about, in turn, because Post Keynesians accepted the ascendancy of American corporatist culture (see Lee 1997). So, changing political winds continually make and un-make dissenting economists within the various schools of non-neoclassical economics.

With regard to methods of analysis, the situation is different; customary methods differ among Post Keynesians, Sraffians, Marxists and Institutionalists. Each school has conservative theoretical practitioners who are concerned solely with in-school puzzles and theoretical developments, and radical theoretical practitioners who attempt to introduce new methods of analysis into their school. The former deliberately take the non-dissenting narrow-church view of developing their school into a theoretical alternative to neoclassical economics, while the latter take the dissenting position of attempting to develop a broad-church theoretical alternative to it.[6] This last group of dissenting practitioners is of particular interest because their activities can potentially create a high degree of functional and strategic dependence among non-neoclassical economists.

Non-neoclassical dissenters take the view that the theoretical narrowness of any one school prevents it from developing into a truly comprehensive alternative to neoclassical economics; they believe it is necessary to draw from all the alternative schools. The process of synthesizing has produced two competing methods of analysis. One approaches economic analysis in the customary terms of abstract and mathematically tractable models, comparative statics, and ahistorical and asocial theorizing; explanation takes the form of equilibrium solutions. The second approaches economic analysis in terms of historically and realistically grounded models, complex open-ended models, and historical and social theorizing in the form of stories serving as explanations. Because most Post Keynesian, Marxist, Institutionalist and Sraffian economists have been educated to accept the customary approach to economic analysis, non-neoclassical economists who have adopted the historical approach to theory have become dissenters. They are, in fact, the ultimate dissenters because they reject both neoclassical economics and neoclassical method. As such, they run the risk of being classified as non-economists and accused of theoretical nihilism.

MEANS AS A DISSENTER

As delineated above, there are various degrees to which one can be a dissenting economist. In this chapter, a dissenting economist will be denoted rather starkly as one who rejects neoclassical economics, who attempts to develop a broad alternative to neoclassical theory, and who rejects the customary approach to economic analysis.

Gardiner Means rejected much of neoclassical economics. Those aspects of neoclassical orthodoxy that he explicitly or implicitly accepted formed a minor part of his doctrine of administered prices. As he argued in *The Modern Corporation and Private Property* (Berle and Means 1932), the large modern corporation rendered much of neoclassical economics obsolete. Hence, new concepts had to be forged and a new picture of economic relationships created. Below, three characteristics of Means's dissent are discussed – his methodological dissent, his theoretical dissent concerning market coordination and his theoretical dissent concerning the nature of the firm.

Theoretical Realism

Means thought that economic theory was supposed to provide an understanding and explanation of how the actual economy operated. Consequently, the primary parts of a theory had to accurately (albeit abstractly) represent their real-world counterparts. As long as this was the case, the synthetic concepts derived from the primary parts could be accepted as valid, and the simplified picture of how the economy operated could be accepted as an accurate representation of how the economy worked (Berle and Means 1932; Means 1939; Lee and Samuels 1992).

This unsophisticated methodology had many supporters in America prior to the Great Depression, primarily because it was thought that the primary parts of the theory were empirically accurate. Like many of his colleagues, Means believed that neoclassical theory accurately depicted and explained the operations of the American economy prior to 1840. However, his experiences in Turkey, and his research on the modern corporation, convinced Means that significant changes had occurred in the American economy since 1840. As a result, many fundamental concepts in neoclassical economics ceased to be empirically grounded, and the theory ceased to provide an accurate picture of how the economy operated. Means unequivocally accepted this conclusion and its corollary – that a new alternative economics had to be developed. Consequently, the fundamental basis of Means's break with neoclassical economics was that economic theory had to be empirically grounded to be accurate and that it had to be grounded in the presently existing economy.

Economic Coordination

The object of Means's theorizing was the current American economy. Drawing upon his instruction in Walrasian general equilibrium theory, Means conceived the economy in terms of an interdependent system where the physical flow of produced goods consisted of both one-way and circular flows. These physical flows were matched by a flow of money transactions between producers and consumers and between producers (reflecting interindustry transactions), as well as a quasi-circular flow between producers and consumers with respect to savings and the return on savings. Consequently, the economy was characterized by continuous and repeated economic transactions. At the micro level this involved consumers buying various goods on a regular and systematic basis, while business enterprises produced the same goods repeatedly in response to the consumer demand.

This model of the economy broke with neoclassical economics on three points. By viewing all economic transactions as only monetary transactions, Means rejected the real versus monetary dichotomy that underlies neoclassical theorizing. By placing his model in historical time, Means rejected the static nature of neoclassical theory. Finally, by arguing that the resources used in production were given neither in amount nor in specification, he rejected the neoclassical assumption of given resources, and with it the assumption of relative scarcity.

In breaking with neoclassical economics over the degree to which its model corresponded to the actual empirical features of the American corporate economy, Means felt it was necessary to break with other aspects of neoclassical economics. Two important breaks concerned the nature of consumer wants and the coordination of economic transactions.

As Director of the Industrial Section of the National Resources Committee, Means instituted a study of American consumption patterns. Hildegarde Kneeland collected data on the distribution of income, on the pattern of consumer expenditures and savings by income class, and on the distribution of total consumer expenditure by product groups. Drawing upon this data, Means argued that consumers ranked their wants according to biological and social need – with food first, followed by housing, clothing, and medical and personal care, and ending with the least necessary wants, such as tobacco, recreation and reading. He realized that this lexicographic ranking of wants violated the notion of substitution underpinning neoclassical consumer demand theory.

As for economic transactions, Means argued that they were coordinated by four different mechanisms – canalizing rules, common goals, administrative coordination and the market mechanism. In the case of the corporate enterprise, the internal coordination and direction of its economic activity were established in its articles of incorporation, especially with respect to the powers possessed by the board of directors and senior officers regarding the distribution of profits and the lines of activity the corporation was allowed to pursue. In addition, informal rules and customs, such as the use of double-entry bookkeeping or the pace of work on the job-floor, helped facilitate and coordinate production and commercial activities. Accepting profit-making as the primary goal of the enterprise, directing members of the enterprise would pursue a common end without the intervention of specific instructions.

Means placed most of his emphasis on the market mechanism and administrative coordination. He referred to the former as the organization and coordination of the economic activities of many separate producers and consumers through price and through buying and selling. Administrative coordination referred to situations where a common authority, such as an owner or manager of a business enterprise or government bureau, organized economic resources under its control and coordinated the resulting economic activity. For Means, the clearest examples of administrative coordination were found in the internal operations of the large modern corporation and in its administration of market prices.

As social constructs and social conventions, the coordination of economic activity by rules and goals rejects the asocial automated coordination mechanism of neoclassical theory encapsulated in the term 'the invisible hand'. Further, the social coordination was enhanced by the visible hand of administrative coordination carried out by social institutions such as large business enterprises and government. Thus, not only did Means break with the neoclassical paradigm over the broad framing of economic theory, he also broke with their view of consumer behaviour and most importantly with their view of how economic transactions are coordinated. Means then went on to develop a clear alternative to the neoclassical conception of economic coordination. This produced a very different picture of how American corporate capitalism worked and operated (Means 1939; National Resources Committee 1938, 1939; Lee and Samuels 1992).

Pricing Behaviour

The next aspects of neoclassical economics from which Means broke concerned the pricing behaviour of the business enterprise. Means divided the corporate economy into two sectors – the market sector and the corporate section. In the former, the market mechanism was the dominant coordinating mechanism; in the corporate sector, administration was dominant. Neoclassical economics applied to the market sector. The neoclassical competitive enterprise attempted to maximize profits by equating its marginal cost to market price; and market price and output could be explained by supply and demand.

On the other hand, Means felt that the corporate sector was entirely outside the realm of neoclassical economics. The representative firm in the corporate sector was a large, multiplant enterprise; ownership and control were separate, while control and management were closely linked.[7] Further, there were no constraints to the size of the large corporate enterprise; and size brings an ability to affect the competitive environment. In this context, Means argued, corporate leaders did not try to maximize profits; rather, they adopted a policy of making profits which would not induce entry or otherwise inhibit the growth of corporate profits or the corporation itself. To carry out this policy, corporate leaders set prices and administered them to the market. Price was thus determined in the offices of corporate leaders, and not in the marketplace as classical economics claimed.[8] Neoclassical economics could not explain the pricing behaviour of large corporate enterprises or the stable prices that ruled markets in the corporate sector (Means 1939, 1962; Lee and Samuels 1992).

In breaking with neoclassical economics over the determination of market prices, Means clearly had a non-neoclassical view of the economy. All prices were not determined in their respective markets; instead, some were determined by the market mechanism and some were determined by corporate administration. When demand was deficient, prices in the market sector would fall, and output levels would be maintained. In contrast, prices in the corporate sector would remain relatively stable while output fell. Since the American corporate economy contained both sectors, deficient demand would lower prices in the market sector and reduce production (leading to unemployment) in the corporate sector. Thus, for Means, the stability of administered prices was the primary reason for breakdowns in the coordination of economic activities. This turned business fluctuations from being the dance-of-prices to being a production and employment phenomenon (Lee and Samuels 1992).

This particular theoretical argument did not really differentiate Means from his neoclassical colleagues in the 1930s and 1940s; nor did advocating national economic planning in the 1930s or stimulative monetary policy in the 1940s. What differentiated Means from neoclassical economists was his insistence that the US economy did not operate as a cybernetic mechanism that tended to eliminate underutilization of economic resources. Administered prices were not an aberration in the economy, but were one of its fundamental and defining features. If administered prices were done away with, you would not return to pre-1840 competitive capitalism. Rather, Means argued, you would get economic chaos and a return to the horrible living standards of workers in Manchester's dark satanic textile mills. Government involvement in the economy in one form or another was necessary if full employment was to be maintained. Government, and not the market mechanism, was needed to ensure adequate coordination of economic activities and the full employment of labour. The position that the market mechanism is replaced by government as the guarantee of full employment in the American economy separates Means both theoretically and ideologically from neoclassical economists (Means 1939, 1962; Lee and Samuels 1992; Samuels and Medema 1990).

THE CONSEQUENCES OF DISSENT

In breaking with the neoclassical paradigm, Means encountered many problems common to dissenters. In the 1930s he had easy access to mainstream journals; after 1940 a change in his publication pattern emerged. More of his work was found in government publications, chapters in books, non-mainstream economic journals and non-economic journals. The change was initially prompted by the rise of neoclassical Keynesianism between 1937 and 1940.

Means attacked Keynesian analysis by questioning the assumption that economic activity was always smoothly coordinated through the market mechanism. American Keynesians argued that the Great Depression was due to the saturation of investment opportunities and called for a policy of compensatory fiscal spending by the government. They ignored Means's argument that the cause of the depression was a coordination problem due to the existence of administered prices. Means, on the other hand, argued that the Keynesian investment argument was incomplete, that the compensatory fiscal policy was inadequate, and that neoclassical price theory presented a false picture of the coordination of economic activity. American Keynesians rejected Means's explanation of the Great Depression as a way to protect their neoclassical theory of prices; and when they became dominant in the National Resources Committee, they made Means so unwelcome that he eventually resigned (Lee 1990; Means 1994).

This initial push into the wilderness accelerated during the 1950s, when the *American Economic Review* rejected all the papers submitted by Means. Means, thus, could no longer be found in the main journal that neoclassical economists read. Such marginalization led Means to have greater contact with other dissident economists and their organizations, such as the Association for Evolutionary Economics. This, in turn, made it easier for mainstream economists to dismiss his work.

Publication of *The Behavior of Industrial Prices* by Stigler and Kindahl (1970) provides a clear example of this marginalization process. The book attacked the doctrine of administered prices, and argued that the data failed to provide empirical support for the theory. Means analysed the price data in the book and came to the opposite conclusion. His findings were published in the *American Economic Review* (Means 1972). Stigler and Kindahl (1973) then responded. Means submitted a rejoinder alleging no less than 17 errors of fact in the interpretation of his position. The editor of the *American Economic Review* refused to publish the paper. However, subsequent research (Carlton 1986) on the Stigler–Kindahl price data shows that Means was correct (see Lee and Samuels 1992).

Rejecting neoclassical economics put Means among the dissenting economists. But it is also important to note that Means's work makes him a dissenter even among the dissenting economists. His social democratic political leanings and his desire to promote economic policies to make corporate capitalism work better does not distance him from most dissenting economists, with the exception of Marxians.

However, it is Means's theoretical work which distances him from many, if not most, dissenting economists. The doctrine of administered prices is a broad-based alternative to neoclassical economics, which includes or is compatible with features of different dissident schools. The general interdependent economic system which Means used as the basis for his doctrine is, when closely examined, not very different from the circular production, multi-industry, surplus models associated with Piero Sraffa, Wassily Leontief and Karl Marx. Further, Means insisted that integral to the structure of the physical flow of produced goods of a corporate economy was a continuous flow of money and series of money transactions. Consequently, the various money flows, he argued, created a single integrated monetary economy that could not be decomposed into 'real' and 'monetary' sectors.[9] Such a position is clearly compatible with the views held by Keynes and the Post Keynesians on money. Finally, target rate of return pricing, the role of the modern corporation and customs in the coordinating of economic activity, and the need for government involvement in guiding economic activity if the quality of human life was to be enhanced under corporate capitalism, are components of Means's doctrine of administered prices that have been adopted by many Post Keynesians and Institutionalists.

Ironically, one result of being compatible with features of different dissident schools is that Means and his doctrine of administered prices have been ignored or depreciated. Because of his insistence on institutions and money, he is ignored by the Sraffians. His somewhat uncritical use of capitalist institutions results in Marxists ignoring his work. Further, the prominent role of institutions in his work and his disagreement with Keynes over the determination of aggregate demand and unemployment, has prompted many Post Keynesians to classify him as an Institutionalist, and irrelevant to their agenda of redeveloping 'the whole of economics along Keynes/Kalecki lines' (Chick 1995, p. 20). Finally, Institutionalists, who most welcomed Means and the doctrine of administered prices, have largely ignored his general theoretical framework and his microeconomic analysis of production, costs, demand and competition. Thus, as a result of his attempt to develop a broad alternative to neoclassical economics, Means became a non-neoclassical dissenting economist in the eyes of those conservative economists who are concerned solely with their in-school puzzles and theoretical developments.[10]

CONCLUSION

In 1932 Means acknowledged that the large modern corporation rendered neoclassical economics obsolete. New concepts, new theories and a new picture of economic relationships therefore had to be developed. For the next 50 years Means developed a novel economic theory for understanding corporate capitalism – his doctrine of administered prices. Because of his iconoclastic personality, Means developed his doctrine without regard to any particular dissident school of thought, to the prevailing political winds, to the ideas of respectable economists, or to traditional modes of economic thinking. Thus, in the last analysis, Means is the ultimate dissenting economist – one who dissents from neoclassical economics and who is seen as a dissenter by dissenting economists as well.

NOTES

1. Functional dependence is defined as the extent to which workers in any scientific field need to coordinate task outcomes and demonstrate adherence to common competence standards; strategic dependence is defined as the need to coordinate research strategies and convince colleagues of the centrality of particular concerns to collective goals.
2. In 1994 a questionnaire was sent to British academic economists regarding the effect of the research assessment exercise on the recruitment and selection of non-neoclassical economists. One interesting result of the questionnaire was that many neoclassical economists felt marginalized in relation to the dominant neoclassical core because of the methods they used, the questions they asked and the topics they investigated (Harley and Lee 1997).
3. A progressive neoclassical economist is defined here as one whose political views range from social democracy to socialism.
4. Within each school certain methods of analysis dominate, but alternative methods also exist. The process by which a particular method of analysis challenges and replaces the previous dominant method, and then defends itself against challengers, I am identifying as convention-building.
5. Post Keynesians such as Alfred Eichner and David Levine do not approach big business with a very critical eye, as, for example, Walter Adams does.
6. Piero Garegnani, Paul Davidson, Walter Neale and Anwar Shaikh may be identified as working solely for the advance of their schools – Sraffian, Post Keynesian, Institutional and Marxian respectively. The more broad-church dissenting economists include Alessandro Roncaglia, Randall Wray, Bill Dugger, Philip Arestis, Geoff Hodgson and others.
7. In the 1930s, this view of the business enterprise placed Means at odds with neoclassical economics; however, this difference grew smaller over time since, as Means has argued, this view does not constitute a significant break with neoclassical economics.
8. Means argued that corporate pricing power was responsible for much of the inflation in the American economy from the 1950s to the 1970s. As a result, neoclassical methods for dealing with inflation were inappropriate since they operated through a market mechanism which did not work in the administered sector. If administrative inflation was to be controlled, some sort of social intervention into the pricing process was necessary.
9. For Means, this meant that in a monetary economy a wide variety of monetary prices could coordinate market activity between producers and consumers.
10. In addition, because he did not use mathematical, equilibrium models inhabited by maximizing economic actors in an ahistorical context, some dissenting economists have ignored Means and his analysis of corporate capitalism.

REFERENCES

Berle, A.A. and G.C. Means (1932), *The Modern Corporation and Private Property*, New York: Macmillan.

Carlton, D. (1986), 'The rigidity of prices', *American Economic Review*, **76**, September, 637–58.

Chick, V. (1995), 'Is there a case for Post Keynesian economics?', *Scottish Journal of Political Economy*, **42**, February, 20–36.

Coats, A.W. (1984), 'The sociology of knowledge and the history of economics', in W.J. Samuels (ed.), *Research in the History of Economic Thought and Methodology*, Vol. 2, London: JAI Press, pp. 211–34.

Harley, S. and F. S. Lee (1997), 'The academic labour process and the research assessment exercise: academic diversity and the future of non-mainstream economics in UK universities', *Human Relations*, **50**, November, 1427–1460.

Lee, F.S. (1990), 'From multi-industry planning to Keynesian planning: Gardiner Means, the American Keynesians, and national economic planning at the National Resources Committee', *Journal of Policy History* **2** (2), 186–212.

Lee, F.S. (1991), *Tributes in Memory of Alfred S. Eichner*, Leicester: Leicester Polytechnic.

Lee, F.S. (1997), 'Philanthropic foundations and the rehabilitation of big business, 1934–1977: a case study of directed economic research', in W.S. Samuels and J.E. Biddle (eds), *Research in the History of Economic Thought and Methodology*, Vol. 15, London: JAI Press, pp. 51–90.

Lee, F.S. and Samuels, W.J. (1992), *The Heterodox Economics of Gardiner C. Means: A Collection*, Armonk: M.E. Sharpe.

Means, G.C. (1939), *The Structure of the American Economy, Part I: Basic Characteristics*, Washington, DC: Government Printing Office.

Means, G.C. (1962), *Pricing Power and the Public Interest*, New York: Harpers & Brothers.

Means, G.C. (1972), 'The administered-price thesis reconfirmed', *American Economic Review*, **62**, June, 292–306.

Means, G.C. (1994), *A Monetary Theory of Employment*, W.J. Samuels and F.S. Lee (eds), Armonk: M.E. Sharpe.

National Resources Committee (1938), *Consumer Incomes in the United States: Their Distribution in 1935–36*, Washington, DC: Government Printing Office.

National Resources Committee (1939), *Consumer Expenditures in the United States: Estimates for 1935–36*, Washington, DC: Government Printing Office.

Samuels, W.J. and S.G. Medema (1990), *Gardiner C. Means: Institutionalist and Post Keynesian*, Armonk: M.E. Sharpe.

Stigler, G.J. and J.K. Kindahl (1970), *The Behavior of Industrial Prices*, New York: National Bureau of Economic Research.

Stigler, G.J. and J.K. Kindahl (1973), 'Industrial prices, as administered by Dr. Means', *American Economic Review*, **63**, September, 717–21.

Whitley, R. (1984), *The Intellectual and Social Organization of the Sciences*, Oxford: Clarendon Press.

Whitley, R. (1986), 'The structure and context of economics as a scientific field', in W.J. Samuels (ed.), *Research in the History of Economic Thought and Methodology*, Vol. 4, London: JAI Press, pp. 179–209.

Whitley, R. (1991), 'The organization and role of journals in economics and other scientific fields', *Economic Notes*, **20** (1), 6–32.

14. The theoretical, methodological and pedagogical dissent of Joan Robinson

Zohreh Emami

INTRODUCTION

Most dissent in economics begins with the vision, values and conceptual reality held by some individual. For dissenters, these visions and values are different from those of other economists. Robinson's vision, values and the reality she saw, were the polar opposite of those inherent in orthodox economics and its *laissez-faire* policy prescriptions. It is this vision and these different values that led Robinson to dissent from orthodox economics. As Jensen (1991, p. 26) points out, 'she viewed human beings as both creators and beneficiaries of those improvements in human welfare that economic activities are supposed to foster'.

Robinson's vision was a society (and a world) that can overcome poverty and provide a decent standard of living for its citizens, and a science of economics that could contribute to this outcome. She argued that we must 'reassert the authority of morality over technology' and that social scientists must explain 'how necessary and how difficult that task is going to be' (Robinson 1970, p. 124). Contrary to the focus on individual self-interest in orthodox economics, Robinson emphasized the moral potential of individuals, a potential far beyond what is currently manifest in most societies. In this vision, human nature is not constant; rather, it is variable and context determined. Rejecting the definition of economics as the study of the allocation of scarce resources, Robinson defines economics in the tradition of Karl Marx, J.M. Keynes and Piero Sraffa as a moral science involving the study of the social relations of production, distribution and accumulation.

Because of this moral vision, Robinson viewed reality very differently from orthodox economists. For Robinson, modern capitalism faced problems such as unemployment, poverty, massive waste, recurring crises, maldistribution of income and human misery. This is a far cry from the orthodox conception of capitalism as a harmonious system of exchange, production and distribution. Orthodox economics 'never even pretended to discuss the use of resources. It fell back upon the old defense of *laissez-faire*: what is profitable is right' (Robinson 1976, p. 9).

The following sections identify several interrelated aspects of dissent in the work of Joan Robinson. First, her well-known theoretical dissent is set forth. Then, her methodological dissent is discussed. Finally, I look at what Robinson had to say about teaching economics, and argue that this, too, constituted dissent.

THEORETICAL DISSENT

The theoretical work of Robinson is extensive. Here I discuss the development of this theoretical dissent, beginning with *Imperfect Competition*, then moving to the Keynesian Revolution, and ending with the capital controversies and long-period economic analysis.

Robinson credits Sraffa (1926) with beginning the revolution in value theory. *Imperfect Competition* (Robinson 1933a) provided a considerable challenge to perfect competition and its assumption that the firm faced an elastic demand. Under perfect competition, producers can sell all their products without affecting the price of what they sell, and each firm is constrained by its internal conditions of production. Sraffa, however, pointed out that firms should be analysed as monopolies constrained by falling demand rather than by rising marginal costs.

Imperfect Competition integrated Sraffa's suggestion that value theory should be treated in terms of monopoly with the economic 'foundations built by Marshall and Pigou' (Robinson 1933a, p. v). This synthesis solved what Robinson saw as an important problem with economic theory. The theory of perfect competition predicted that less efficient firms would close down as a result of any sustained fall in demand. Under perfect competition, each firm faces a perfectly elastic demand curve and maximizes output where price equals marginal cost. The representative firm is so small relative to the market that it can sell all it produces at the prevailing price without affecting the price. During the economic slump of the 1930s Robinson found it harder and harder to accept this orthodoxy.

> Each firm continuously produces the amount of output of which the marginal cost is equal to price. There are internal economies of scale only up to a certain size, at which average cost (including normal profit) is at a minimum. When demand is such as to call forth output beyond this size from a particular firm, marginal cost, and therefore price, exceeds average costs. Super-normal profits call in fresh competition which brings down the market price and

pushes back the output of the firm. When price is below average cost, some firms are driven out of business, and those that remain expand. Thus the optimum size of firm, with minimum average costs, is always tending to be established. (Robinson 1933a, pp. v–vi)

The real world, in contrast, contained mostly imperfect markets with large firms and restricted entry. Moreover, most firms were operating below capacity rather than closing down. *Imperfect Competition* showed that large firms face downward-sloping demand curves (and thus falling marginal revenue curves), and that they maximize profits at the output level where marginal revenue equals marginal cost and at a price above marginal cost. This explained why firms operated below capacity during the depression, rather than closing down, as perfect competition theory predicted.

Although she quickly lost interest in the theory of imperfect competition, Robinson remained interested in the exploitation of labour under monopoly. In perfectly competitive markets, labour receives the value of its marginal product, which is its marginal physical product multiplied by the price of the commodity. Under monopoly conditions, however, price is higher than the marginal revenue accruing to the firm, and workers receive their marginal physical product multiplied by this lower marginal revenue. In this case, monopolistic exploitation arises. Moreover, the 'extent to which the factors are exploited will depend upon the elasticity of demand for the commodities', and 'the smaller the elasticity of demand for the separate commodities the greater will be the degree of exploitation'. Finally, 'the smaller the number of firms producing any commodity the smaller will be the elasticity of demand for the output of any one of them' (Robinson 1933a, pp. 311–13).

The economic depression that led Robinson to abandon imperfect competition also spurred her interest in the Keynesian Revolution. In the early 1930s she became a member of the Circus, a group of Cambridge economists that met to discuss the ideas of Keynes on slumps and unemployment. For Robinson, the heart of the Keynesian Revolution was an insight about the historical specificity of capitalism and a recognition that economic life in a capitalist system results from individual decisions based on convention and guesswork.

Keynes saw the modern capitalist economy as a monetary economy based on rules and institutions that required a holistic analysis of production and money. Money creates uncertainty

for interest earning assets would always be preferred to cash if there was no doubt about their future value. In this light, the nature of interest becomes unclear. Keynes was able to resolve a deep-seated confusion in traditional teaching by emphasizing the distinction between the rate of interest, as the price of finance, and the rate of profit expected on an investment. (Robinson 1951–79, Vol. 5, p. 171)

Keynes was concerned about unemployment. He showed that output depends on demand, which itself is both determined by and determines income since 'One man's expenditure provides other men's incomes and one man's income is derived from other men's expenditure' (Robinson 1937, p. 3). Individuals spend only part of their income because they save. If this saving went directly to demand capital goods, then savings would not result in unemployment. 'But the demand for capital goods comes, not from saving, but from business concerns who use them in production, and no entrepreneur is inclined to acquire capital goods unless he can see a profit by doing so'. Moreover, since 'the profitability of capital goods depends upon the demand for the consumption goods which they pro-duce', individual saving does not 'encourage entrepreneurs to expect a greater profit from capital' (Robinson 1937, p. 4). If individual saving is higher than the demand for capital by entrepreneurs, then the result will be unemployment.

While either increased investment or decreased savings can increase employment, a decline in money wages will not significantly change employment. A decrease in wages, while decreasing the cost of produc-tion, will also reduce demand, yielding an ambiguous effect on employment. Similarly, higher wages will increase demand; but the boost to employment from more spending will be offset by a rise in the cost of production. As a result, 'any change in money wages will set up a number of complicated repercussions, which may lead to a change in employ-ment, in one direction or the other, to some extent, but a change in money wages is not likely to lead to any great change in employment in either direction' (Robinson 1937, p. 41). Money wages determine the price level, and are themselves the result of the relative bargaining power between workers and employers. Robinson (1951–79, Vol. 5, pp. 173f.) called the role of money wages in governing the level of prices 'the other half of the Keynesian revolution', and argued that this 'was a great shock to notions of equilibrium even than the concept of effective demand gov-erned by volatile expectations' (see also Robinson 1973; Rima 1991).

With the postwar boom, Robinson began to examine the conditions necessary for accumulation and growth. During the 1950s, she became interested in the causes and consequences of long-period development. This was the period of her initiation of the capital controversy (Robinson 1953–54) and her careful reconsideration of Marx (Robinson 1962b).

The capital controversies were debates within value and distribution theory about the origin and size of profit capitalist economy. Robinson began the debate by asking how we could measure capital independently of value and distribution. More specifically, the neoclassical view of price as an index of scarcity implies that the rate of profit (the price of capital) will be high or low depending on the degree of scarcity of capital. Therefore, a measure of capital must exist before the rate of profit can be determined. Yet neoclassical theory does not have such a measure. The question of the measure and meaning of capital was a long-period question. In the short period there is a fixed set of capital equipment, so it is possible to talk of a specific quantity of capital and a specific rate of profit. But in the long period, capital equipment changes in quantity and in design. So you come up against the question: 'What is the quantity of capital?' (Robinson 1973, p. 261). For Robinson, the concept of the marginal productivity of capital (the relative share of profits in distribution) was incoherent if a meaningful quantity of capital could not be identified. What was also particularly confusing for Robinson was that the neoclassical production function failed to distinguish between capital as the means of production and capital as the command over finance.

Robinson herself defined capital as a heterogeneous stock of produced means of production measured in terms of labour time. On this definition, the marginal product of capital has no relationship to the rate of profit or the return to the capitalist. Thus, the distribution of income in capitalist economies (that is, income from work versus income from property) cannot be determined by the same supply and demand principles that determine the price of commodities. Instead, the rate of profit is determined by the rate of technical progress and the accumulation process; wages depend on the relative bargaining power of workers and capitalists, and thus on exogenous institutional factors. Contrary to economic orthodoxy, for Robinson wage and profit rates are the determinants of other prices rather than simply being two prices among many.

METHODOLOGICAL DISSENT

Economic Philosophy discusses the nature of economic knowledge and the relationship between science and ideology. Robinson (1962a, p. 2) starts by claiming that economics functions both as 'a vehicle for the ruling ideology' and as 'a method of scientific investigation'. Separating the ideological and scientific dimensions of economic knowledge is a difficult task, since ideology is inherent in the metaphysical propositions of scientific theories. Metaphysical propositions, unlike scientific ones, cannot be tested or disputed on logical grounds. Moreover, they often provide the foundations from which hypotheses are drawn.

This view of ideology versus science is quite different from that of neoclassical economists. In neoclassical theory, personal points of view and moral feelings (Robinson's metaphysical propositions) only come into play at the end of the process of analysis, when policies are proposed. For Robinson (1962a, p. 3), in contrast, they are part of the scientific process from the beginning, and they are necessary to the realm of science since without them 'we would not know what it is that we wanted to know'.

Although the hypotheses, concepts and the very process of scientific investigation are value laden, Robinson argues that it is still possible to describe the main principles of an economic system objectively. This objectivity arises 'because many individuals are continually testing each other's theories' (Robinson 1962a, p. 23). Testing is certainly easier in the natural sciences since these sciences have agreed upon standards for disproving hypotheses. For the social sciences, the impossibility of controlled experiments makes practitioners 'rely on interpretation of evidence, and interpretation involves judgement' (Robinson 1962a, p. 22). By arguing that it is not possible to have a value-free science of economics, Robinson (1962, p. 14) implies that our present capitalist economic system 'is not the only possible system; in describing it we compare it (openly or tacitly) with other actual or imagined systems. Differences imply choices, and choices imply judgement'. Economists must also be more comfortable with doubt and uncertainty than with certainty.

This description of scientific practice is quite ambitious; it includes the notion of change through the use of our objective capacities as well our moral reasoning, imagination and empathy. Our judgement draws upon all these. This understanding of the nature of economic knowledge contrasts sharply with economic orthodoxy. It consciously and explicitly questions our disciplinary knowledge, and it is contrary to the mainstream practice of taking the nature of this knowledge for granted. Robinson did not accept the neoclassical optimism about doing objective economic science. At the same time she remained optimistic that substantive analytic work in economics could reveal much about our world. Arguing that our knowledge of social reality is concept determined, value laden and thus pre-interpreted, does not imply that Robinson was a pure relativist, believing that one description of this reality is as accurate as any other. On the contrary, her strong and persistent criticisms of economic orthodoxy led her to develop an alternate way of thinking in economics, one that would not only help us understand the world but also help to make it a better place.

Below, we discuss two methodological issues important to the work of Robinson – the realism of assumptions on which economic theory is built and the methodological categories of equilibrium analysis.

Realism of Assumptions

Robinson's views on economic methodology changed substantially during her life. Her first published work (Robinson 1932) distinguished approaches that emphasize tractable assumptions and approaches that correspond to the real world. She put herself squarely in the former camp: 'I know ... the world to which my techniques apply is not the real world, but I am one of the optimistic economists, and when I have got well used to my two-dimensional technique I will be capable of solving the problems which arise on your assumptions' (Robinson 1932, p. 7).

Economics is a serious subject is subtitled *The Apologia of the Economist to the Mathematician, the Scientist and the Plain Man*. This demonstrates her discomfort with this methodology even at this early stage in her career. There is a certain tension in this work since on the one hand it defends economics against the objections of the mathematician, the scientist and the plain man, while on the other hand it is sympathetic to, and definitely apologetic about the practical complaints of non-economists against economics.

Robinson starts *Economics of Imperfect Competition* (1933a, p. 1) in the same spirit: 'This book is presented to the analytical economist as a box of tools. It is an essay in the technique of economic analysis, and can make only an indirect contribution to our knowledge of the actual world'. Already, Robinson has gone beyond being an optimist. While her aim is still to build a logically consistent theory, her goal is now also to base the theory on a more realistic assumption, namely, 'the generality of monopoly rather than competition as the way forward in the theory of value' (Harcourt 1990, p. 36).

For Robinson, it was the Great Depression that demonstrated the hollowness of a methodology that treats the realism of assumptions as unimportant. It made her more partial towards historical analysis based on realistic assumptions. She began to criticize neoclassical economics as ahistorical, for its methodological reliance on individualism, and for its timeless conception of human nature as self-interested in virtually all situations.

Short-period Equilibrium

From Alfred Marshall, Robinson gained an understanding of partial equilibrium analysis that could not be reconciled with Walrasian general equilibrium. The latter was timeless, while the former discussed entrepreneurs 'operating in ... historical time ... under conditions of uncertainty (as distinct from calculable risk)' (Gram and Walsh 1983, p. 520).

For Marshall, a firm can be in equilibrium for a short period of time at a historically specific productive capacity and with a given set of expectations. Furthermore, the decisions made by entrepreneurs may turn out to be based on a wrong set of expectations, and may not be consistent with the expectations of other entrepreneurs. What was useful in this kind of analysis, as far as Robinson was concerned, was its ability to depict partial equilibria, which were often the closest we could come to explaining economic phenomena such as the formation of relative prices.

On the other hand, as Gram and Walsh (1983, p. 521) point out, the 'analytic perfection of a general equilibrium model evades this problem, concerning itself with the existence of prices compatible with given conditions of static or intertemporal supply and demand'. Robinson is critical of Marshall for ignoring the contradictions inherent in partial equilibria by assuming that a persistent stationary set of conditions in economic life would lead to general equilibrium in the long run. This assumed that long-period equilibrium is achievable at some date in the future. In contrast, for Robinson (1951–79, Vol. 3, p. 101) long-period equilibrium is nothing but 'an imaginary state of affairs in which there are no incompatibilities in the existing situation, here and now'.

While retaining Marshall's notion of partial equilibrium as short period and inherently contradictory, Robinson rejects extending the concept of equilibrium to a future period where economic conditions are 'stationary for a run of time long enough to enable them all to work their full effect' (Marshall 1961, p. 347). This is where Keynes comes into the picture. Keynes argued against the macroeconomic system moving towards general equilibrium. As Gram and Walsh (1983, p. 522) pointed out, Robinson insisted 'on an interpretation of Keynes in terms of the Marshallian short-period, characterized by uncertainty, incompatible decisions, and unrealizable expectations'. This was one of her key contributions.

For Robinson, then, short-period equilibria contain contradictions that may not be apparent in the short period. One such contradiction was a capital stock which 'embodies the consequences of misguided investments made in the past', and which is divided between sectors in such a way that is 'never exactly appropriate to the investment now being planned' (Robinson 1962b, p. 69). A second contradiction was the state of past expectations which, while having not been realized, still forms the basis for future expectations, and may well turn out to be false again. Because of these contradictions, short-period equilibria are not built on the assumption of a past equilibrium, and so are not self-sustaining.

Long-period Equilibrium

After her intense involvement with the Keynesian Revolution, Robinson (1951–79, Vol. 1, p. 155) developed an analysis of the dynamic long-period to supplement Keynes's short-period analysis, and to 'swallow up, as a special case, the long-run static theory in which the present generation academic economists are educated'. This long-period method was an attempt to generalize *The General Theory* by synthesizing Keynes with David Ricardo, Marx, Marshall, Michal Kalecki and Sraffa. Long-period analysis required an understanding of growth and accumulation, the structures of reproduction that generate a surplus, and the nature of capital.

Rethinking the orthodox methodology of the long-period motivated her famous article 'The production function and the theory of capital' (Robinson 1953–54), and initiated the capital controversies (Harcourt 1972). For Robinson, while it was legitimate to ignore the nature of capital in the short period, when the capital stock is held constant, in the long period, with the capital stock changing, the question of how capital is measured becomes relevant.

Robinson's critique of neoclassical capital theory centred on the logical consistency and ideological import of the marginal productivity theory of distribution. Her point was that the marginal productivity of capital (the relative share of profits in distribution) was incoherent if a meaningful quantity of capital could not be identified. Moreover, for Robinson the marginal productivity theory of distribution was not descriptive of real-world phenomena, since it was based on a methodological error and because it ignores real, causal and historical processes. In the end, by defining returns to capital as a reward for waiting, neoclassical economics provides an ideological justification for income from property in capitalism.

Robinson's long-period analysis culminated in the methodological distinction between differences and changes in underlying economic variables. For Robinson, this distinction was linked with her view on the difference between logical and historical time. General equilibrium is the outcome of a long-run process (a sequence of short-run equilibria at the end of which all markets clear), and so we need a satisfactory analysis of how the economy can get into equilibrium. Robinson observes that this process moves in logical time. It can explain differences, but not changes, in the underlying variables. Moreover, this methodology is mechanical in its use of a space metaphor to describe a process through time.

> For mechanical movements in space, there is no distinction between approaching equilibrium from an arbitrary initial position and a perturbation due to displacement from an equilibrium that has long been established. In economic life, in which decisions are guided by expectations about the future, these two types of movement are totally different. (Robinson 1951–79, Vol 5, p. 49)

Neoclassical economists see equilibrium as a position the economy moves towards over time. 'But it is impossible for a system to get into a position of equilibrium, for the very nature of equilibrium is that the system is already in it, and has been in it for a certain length of past time' (Robinson 1953–54, p. 130). But if there is change, 'the position is no longer one of equilibrium, (Robinson 1951–79, Vol. 5, p. 52).

The method of long-period equilibrium deemed useful by Robinson starts in the steady state but quickly moves to the short period to deal with disequilibrium situations and uncertain expectations. This approach is in historical time. It identifies a set of variables with a 'particular set of values obtaining at a moment of time which are not, in general, in equilibrium with each other', and shows 'how their interactions may be expected to play themselves out' (Robinson 1962b, p. 23). Given this methodology, the theory would have to tell a whole new 'story about the behavior of the economy when it is out of equilibrium, including the effect of disappointed expectations on decisions being taken by its inhabitants' (Robinson 1951–79, Vol. 5, p. 52). Gram and Walsh (1983, p. 532) are completely correct when they observe that:

> This is, in a sense, precisely opposite to the neoclassical method of argument which 'moves' (with the aid of perfect foresight or its probabilistic counterpart, rational expectations) through a sequence of momentary equilibria 'towards' a position of long-run equilibrium.

The Nature of Equilibrium

Having been influenced by Keynes and Marx, Robinson argued that economics should examine the real problems faced by individuals. Attempting to understand the high unemployment experienced during the Great Depression 'Keynes had reintroduced the concept of capitalism as a particular economic system, evolving through history' (Robinson 1951–79, Vol. 5, p. 91). Robinson also liked the historical conceptualization of capitalism in Marx. Marx, like Keynes, tried to understand how the world worked. 'His theory formalized what he believed to be the case. He did not "construct" his belief from his theory' (Robinson 1951–79, Vol. 4, p. 25). Robinson felt that Marxists idolized Marx to the point of devaluing his major contribution – his historical perspective. Having a historical perspective and developing Marx's thought into a dogma were mutually exclusive since Marxist dogma, like neoclassical dogma, was supposed to be timeless and applicable to any situation.

Robinson (1951–79, Vol. 5, pp. 48-58) pointed out the major flaws in the concept of equilibrium. First, reliance on equilibrium not only disal-

lows uncertainty, it also requires perfect foresight on the part of producers and consumers. Not only is history ignored, but the future does not
pose a problem because individuals have perfect foresight. Second, the
concept of equilibrium implies the existence of stability, which Robinson
sees as too mechanical to apply to economic life. Even if we assume that
the economy starts at an equilibrium situation that is subsequently
disturbed, the neoclassical story of how a new equilibrium gets re-estab-
lished is far too simplistic since it assumes a change in the pattern of
production and demand devoid of any consideration of uncertainty.
Robinson (1951–79, Vol. 5, p. 48) views expectations as far more uncertain than neoclassical economists, who see them as simple matters of
calculated risk: 'As soon as the uncertainty of the expectations that
guide economic behavior is admitted, equilibrium drops out of the argument and history takes its place'. Finally, since equilibrium is seen as the
end of a series of exchanges between individuals who, until they reach a
final result are presumed to be in a non-equilibrium position, it is not
clear to Robinson how and why the previous non-equilibrium situation
would not continue.

These criticisms of equilibrium have a number of important implications. First, Robinson disagreed with the conclusion of neoclassical
equilibrium theory that individuals are free to pursue their self-interest,
and that society as a whole will benefit and harmony will reign in capitalist economies if there is no interference by the government. Because
neoclassical theory sees the interest of the individual converging with that
of society, the policy prescription of this theory must be *laissez-faire*. If
social harmony reigns when the individual is allowed to pursue self-interest, then the best policy is no policy at all. Social problems will not arise if
everyone simply watches out for him- or herself. Second, having given up
the concept of equilibrium and a belief in social and economic harmony
in favour of history, Robinson sees social and economic conflict as the
rule. In this context, issues of economic and ideological power become
relevant. Third, an emphasis on history rather than equilibrium implies
that diversity can no longer be replaced by homogeneity nor can uncertainty be supplanted by predictability. Robinson was clearly ahead of her
time concerning issues of diversity. Finally, in the context of this dissent,
the whole definition of economics needs to be reconsidered. Economics
could no longer be defined as the science of allocating scarce resources,
but would have to be about growth, accumulation, distribution and providing for the needs of diverse members of society (Robinson 1951–79,
Vol. 5, p. 172).

PEDAGOGICAL DISSENT

Robinson came to insist that economics be capable of dealing with realistic economic problems, accept its historical determinacy, and be capable of providing different theoretical frameworks for the various peoples experiencing different degrees of economic development. These beliefs greatly influenced Robinson as a teacher. Her theoretical critique of the neoclassical paradigm and her pedagogic critique of the economics profession constitute a unified totality.

Robinson wrote two papers on teaching economics. The first was written in 1933 and has never been published. It is in the tradition of *Economics is a Serious Subject* and *Imperfect Competition*, and begins by expressing dissatisfaction with the state of teaching economics. Robinson (1933b) asks, 'If our aim is principally to teach our students to think, how does it come about that the results of our efforts are often so lamentable?'. The problem with economic instruction is that students are expected to 'accept on trust "axioms" and "doctrines" which in so far as they are valid are merely based on common sense, as though they require some esoteric knowledge as yet beyond their grasp'. At the same time the student 'is excused from the smallest effort at rigorous thinking'. Robinson then discusses many concrete ways a teacher of economics can facilitate student learning and interact with students, ways that involve the student as an active learner and not just a passive recipient of knowledge. She advocates a 'do-it-yourself' technique of learning, and rejects teaching students to mouth the principles of economics 'without any understanding of their real basis in common sense and the real limitations of their application in the actual world'.

Even at this early stage in her career, Robinson is quite critical of the economics profession and is uncomfortable with its pedagogy. However, having not yet rejected the Marshallian framework, she confines her criticism to discussing the means of teaching economic theory and does not focus on the theory itself. Robinson objects to teaching and learning a doctrine as the goal of education, and proposes rigorous thinking as the outcome of a meaningful education.

In a second paper on teaching, Robinson (1951–79, Vol. 3, pp. 1–6) combines her earlier interest in learning by doing with criticism of neoclassicism, especially its inability to deal with real-world problems.

> For many years I have been employed as a teacher of theoretical economics; I would like to believe that I earn my living honestly, but I often have doubts. I am concerned particularly for India and other developing countries whose economic doctrines come to them mainly from England and in English. Is what we are giving them helpful to their development? (Robinson 1951–79, Vol. 3, p. 1)

Robinson was also concerned that those studying in England would become teachers in their own countries and perpetuate the same education practices they learned. 'The exam-passer who does well becomes in due course an examiner, and by then he has quite lost any doubt he may once have had to stifle. He has come to believe that this kind of thing really is education. And so the system feeds on itself' (Robinson 1951–79, Vol. 3, p. 1).

What exactly was wrong with economic education? Consistent with her critique of dominant economic doctrine, she objects to a reliance on methodological individualism.

> The serious student is often attracted to economics by humanitarian feelings and patriotism. ... Orthodox teaching deflects these feelings into the dreary desert of so-called Welfare Economics, a system of ideas based on a mechanistic psychology of a completely individualistic pursuit of pleasure and avoidance of pain, which no one believes to be a correct account of human nature, dished up in algebraical formulae which do not even pretend to be applicable to actual data. (Robinson 1951–79, Vol. 3, p. 2)

She then goes on to argue that students cling to methodological individualism because 'no other way has been offered of formulating the vague benevolent feelings with which they began' (Robinson 1951–79, Vol. 3, p. 2).

Moreover, students spend a significant portion of their time learning the theory of relative prices, which leads to *laissez-faire* conclusions. Rather than studying questions of growth and income distribution, which she saw as relevant to every country, students are asked to take the resources of their country as given, assume equitable income distribution, and investigate the question of the distribution of these given resources among alternative uses. 'If the serious student has the hardihood to ask: But are the resources given, and is income distributed equitably? he is made to feel foolish' (Robinson 1951–79, Vol. 3, p. 3).

For Robinson, teachers have a responsibility to help students develop analytical, problem-solving and valuing skills so that they can become independent thinkers. Given her view that economics must respond to actual historical circumstances, it would be inconsistent for her to teach economics as if one all-encompassing theory had been discovered. She saw her responsibility as developing lifetime thinkers who would learn economics by actually doing economics. In asserting that students become actively involved in learning economics, Robinson argues for breaking down the authoritarian nature of the typical classroom and putting the student at the centre of the teaching and learning process.

How would Robinson go about teaching economics? She would begin by discussing various types of economic systems, thus introducing history and diversity at the outset. This approach would show *laissez-faire* capitalism to be only one way of organizing society. It would also show the possibility of improving economic outcomes. On the theoretical level, Robinson would concentrate on analysing reproduction, accumulation and distribution, thus displacing price theory from its central position within economics by making it part of a more general theory of distribution. Finally, Robinson would insist that students actively participate in their own learning. 'I should try to break down the awe that students feel for formulae ... to form the habit of picking them to pieces and putting them together again with the ambiguities cleared off, and keeping them firmly in their place as useful adjuncts to common sense, not as substitutes for it' (Robinson 1951–79, Vol. 3, p. 4).

CONCLUSION

Joan Robinson's dissent from economic orthodoxy was multidimensional and integrated. Her well-known theoretical dissent was part of a sophisticated and thoughtful critique of the foundations and nature of economic knowledge. Her pedagogical dissent and practices were consistent with her theoretical and methodological dissent. Robinson had a keen sense of the limitations and the potential for economic analysis. This made economics both a very serious, and a very alive, subject for her.

REFERENCES

Gram, H. and V. Walsh (1983), 'Joan Robinson's economics in retrospect', *Journal of Economic Literature*, **21**, June, 518–50.
Harcourt, G.C. (1972), *Some Cambridge Controversies in the Theory of Capital*, Cambridge: Cambridge University Press.
Harcourt, G.C. (1990), 'On the contributions of Joan Robinson and Piero Sraffa to economic theory', in Maxime Berg (ed.), *Political Economy in the Twentieth Century*, New York: Phillip Allan, pp. 35–67.
Jensen, H. (1991), 'The role of values in the economics of Joan Robinson', in Ingrid Rima (ed.), *The Joan Robinson Legacy*, Armonk: M.E. Sharpe, pp. 20–34.
Marshall, A. (1961) [1920], *Principles of Economics*, London: Macmillan.
Rima, I. (1991), 'Robinson and the "other half" of the Keynesian Revolution', in Ingrid Rima (ed.), *The Joan Robinson Legacy*, Armonk: M.E. Sharpe, pp. 195–209.
Robinson, J. (1932), *Economics is a Serious Subject*, Cambridge: W. Heffer & Sons.
Robinson, J. (1933a), *The Economics of Imperfect Competition*, London: Macmillan,
Robinson, J. (1933b), 'Teaching economics', King's College Modern Archives, Robinson Papers.
Robinson, J. (1937), *Introduction to the Theory of Employment*, London: Macmillan.
Robinson, J. (1951–79), *Collected Economic Papers*, 5 vols, Oxford: Blackwell.

Robinson, J. (1953–54), 'The Production Function and The Theory of Capital', *Collected Economics Papers*, 2 vols, Oxford: Blackwell.

Robinson, J. (1962a), *Economic Philosophy*, Chicago: Aldine.

Robinson, J. (1962b), *An Essay on Marxian Economics*, second edn, New York: St. Martin's Press.

Robinson, J. (1970), *Freedom and Necessity: An Introduction to the Study of Society*, New York: Pantheon.

Robinson, J. (1973), *After Keynes*, Oxford: Basil Blackwell.

Robinson, J. (1976), 'The age of growth', *Challenge*, **19**, May/June, 4–9.

Sraffa, P. (1926). 'The laws of returns under competitive conditions', *Economic Journal*, **36**, December, 535–50.

15. Thomas Schelling's dissent from the narrow scope of economics

David Latzko

THE NATURE OF DISSENT

Dissent is a synonym for disagreement. Boulding's (1957) distinction between dissent from orthodox economic thought and dissent from economic institutions provides a useful way to begin to understand disagreement in economics. A dissenter disagrees with mainstream academic economic ideas, customs or methodology; or a dissenter disagrees with his or her country's economic system.

Many who disagree with the way an economic system operates do so for profoundly ethical reasons. Socialists see the capitalist system as exploiting the working class and unfair to women and minorities. They complain that unfettered capitalism degrades our values, our environment and our society. Such moral dissent is not based on the practical consideration that a socialist economy would function better than a capitalist economy. Rather, the objection is entirely philosophical. Capitalism exploits workers, even though the living standards of workers may be higher in capitalist countries than in economies professing to be based on socialist principles.

There can also be dissent from an economic system on purely intellectual grounds. This type of dissent is made for practical, utilitarian reasons and lacks the overtly political content of moral dissent. Libertarians believe that our economy is insufficiently *laissez-faire* and that there is far too much government interference with the beneficial, natural workings of the market. Such governmental interference is undesirable because it produces suboptimal results.

The distinction between moral and intellectual dissent is not sharp. Leftists claim that a truly socialist economy, besides being morally superior, would perform better than a capitalist one, while the libertarian dissent against central banking is conditioned by their philosophical distrust of government. In the end, the classification of heterodox thinking as intellectual dissent or moral dissent may be a matter of rhetorical emphasis (see Figure 15.1).

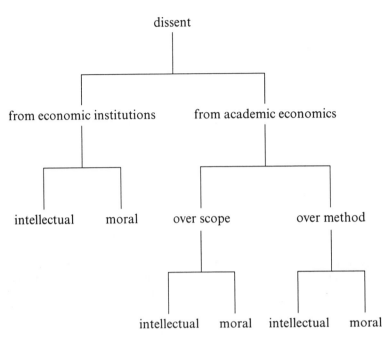

Figure 15.1 Varieties of dissent

The focus of this volume is on dissent from mainstream academic economics. Here, too, an intellectual/moral division is operative. Moral dissent is based on a philosophical or political rejection of mainstream economics. Marxists, for example, see neoclassical economics as justifying a morally objectionable economic system (Green 1977). Intellectual dissent lacks this political content. Instead, the appeal here is to the practical or utilitarian advantages of some alternative approach. Fogel (1964; Fogel and Engerman 1974), with his explicit use of economic methods to study historical questions, engaged in intellectual dissent from the traditional methods of economic history. Writing about his methodology, which weds neoclassical economics and econometrics to pose counterfactual questions, Fogel (1964, pp. vii–viii) argues that 'while most historians will agree that the subject matter ... is drawn from their domain, some will reject the methodology as alien to the spirit and purpose of their discipline. But if history is to attempt to reveal what actually happened in the past, then the methodology ... cannot be dismissed'.

One form of intellectual dissent from mainstream academic economics is over the appropriate models and assumptions or, to crib from John Neville Keynes (1955, p. 2), over method: 'the logical processes specially appropriate to the study – that is, the methods of investigation and proof'. Those who dissent from the method of mainstream economics believe that the economics taught in our universities and colleges does not provide adequate tools for understanding economic reality. The Keynesian Revolution was a revolution in method. John Maynard Keynes (1973, p. 3) argued that

> the postulates of the classical theory are applicable to a special case only and not to the general case ... Moreover, the characteristics of the special case assumed by the classical theory happen not to be those of the economic society in which we actually live, with the result that its teaching is misleading and disastrous if we attempt to apply it to the facts of experience.

So, too, with rational expectations. Lucas and Sargent (1978, pp. 49–50) claim that the predictions of Keynesian economics

> were wildly incorrect, and that the doctrine on which they were based is fundamentally flawed ... The task which faces contemporary students of the business cycle is that of sorting through the wreckage, determining which features of that remarkable intellectual event called the Keynesian Revolution can be salvaged and put to good use, and which others must be discarded.

Dissent from the methods of mainstream economic analysis can also be based on moral or essentially philosophical grounds. The Austrian tradition, as represented by Hayek (1952), has criticized the mechanical application of principles from the natural sciences to the social sciences. The scientific method (formulate and test a hypothesis which is then either rejected or not rejected) is valid only if facts can be verified objectively and externally from human perception. Social scientists, including economists, are concerned with people's perceptions of facts which, by necessity, are subjective. There are no objective facts in the realm of the social sciences. Thus, the application of the scientific method to economics is invalid.

Moral dissent from mainstream methods often has an implicit, if not explicit, political basis. One of the reasons for rapid acceptance of the marginal utility theory of value was its political appeal.

> It was the rise of Marxism and Fabianism in the 1880's and 1890's that finally made subjective value theory socially and politically relevant; as the new economics began to furnish effective intellectual ammunition against Marx and Henry George, the view that value theory really did not matter became more difficult to sustain. (Blaug 1973, p. 13)

It should be emphasized that dissent from mainstream economics need not be accompanied by dissent from capitalist economic institutions. Beginning with Veblen (1919), the Institutionalist literature reads like a series of complaints about neoclassical economics, yet Institutionalist economists do not generally dissent from capitalism.

There is a second form of intellectual dissent from mainstream economics – addressing questions not traditionally studied by mainstream economists. This concern with unorthodox subject matter is dissent over the scope of economics. Scope refers to 'the distinguishing features of the phenomena with which it deals, and the kind of knowledge that it seeks concerning these phenomena' (Keynes 1955, p. 2). Such diverse economists as Gary Becker (1957, 1964, 1976, 1981), with his application of microeconomic reasoning to discrimination, crime and the family and Mancur Olson (1965, 1982), with his rational choice examination of interest group formation, can be classified as practising intellectual dissent from the scope of economics. It is important to emphasize that those who dissent from the scope of mainstream economics do not necessarily disagree with its methodology and conclusions. This type of dissent is strictly over subject matter.

Dissent over the scope of economics can also be morally based. Marxists are concerned with topics generally ignored by the mainstream such as the workplace, the economics of education, sexism, racism and military expansion. They 'seek to illuminate the relationships between capitalist institutions and the various forms of oppression' (Edwards, Reich and Weisskopf 1978, p. xii). Use of the word 'oppression' betrays the moral foundation and political agenda of this dissent.

THE DISSENT OF THOMAS SCHELLING

At first blush, it would appear that Thomas Schelling is included in a volume on dissenting economists solely because of the stunning scope of his research. In general terms, he has made pathbreaking contributions to the theory of bargaining and conflict management and to the theory of interdependent choice and behaviour. Specifically, he has done research on nuclear strategy and arms control (Schelling 1960c, 1966; Schelling and Halperin 1961), organized crime and extortion (Schelling 1967; 1984b, pp. 291–308), addiction and self-control (Schelling 1980, 1992a), racial segregation (Schelling 1971a, 1972), global warming (Schelling 1990b, 1992b), energy policy (Schelling 1979), environmental protection (Schelling 1983), foreign aid (Schelling 1955) and the value of human life (Schelling 1968), and this is only a partial list. Schelling's uniqueness is evident in the fact that he has published in journals as disparate as the *American Economic Review*, the *Bulletin of the Atomic Scientists*, the *American Journal of Public Health* and *Space Times*.

Upon closer examination, there also appears a methodological element to Schelling's dissent. While his dissent from mainstream neoclassical economics is not over the adequacy of its tools for understanding economic reality, Schelling does aim to reorientate consumer demand theory and game theory so that it is more cognizant of the actual behaviour of real people.

This is the essence of Schelling's dissent: he poses new questions and examines unexplored areas in a way that combines dissent over scope and dissent over method. His methodological dissent consists of broadening the scope of mainstream theory to encompass real-world behaviours either by incorporating these behaviours into existing models or by utilizing different modes of analysis.

Self-command

Schelling's (1980; 1984a; 1984b, pp. 84–112) trio of articles on self-command contain all the essential characteristics of his dissent – an unorthodox subject matter; a subtle probing of the deficiencies of mainstream economic theory, and an attempt to remedy them; some memorable illustrations; and an eye towards practical, real-world applications of theoretical analysis. This line of research developed from studying how people try to influence the behaviour of others. Schelling came to see that this situation was similar to how people try to influence their own behaviour (Iglehart 1990, p. 110). Schelling calls on economists to recognize that opting to constrain one's future choices can be a rational choice. He draws our attention to the problem by describing the dilemma of a pregnant woman who requests that anaesthesia be withheld during delivery, pleads for it during delivery and does the same thing again at the next delivery. He also describes his youthful decision to emulate Admiral Byrd and toughen himself by removing one blanket from his bed.

> That decision to go to bed one blanket short was made by a warm boy; another boy awoke cold in the night, too cold to go look for a blanket, cursing the boy who removed the blanket and swearing to return it tomorrow. But the next bedtime it was the warm boy again, dreaming of Antarctica, who got to make the decision, and he always did it again. (Schelling 1984a, p. 8)

Everyday examples of tricks people play on themselves to make them do things they ought to, or to prevent themselves from doing things they should not, include placing the alarm clock across the room, Christmas saving clubs and counting to ten when angry. These examples demonstrate that there may be utility gains from denying freedom of choice and ignoring revealed preferences. A person may act to restrict his or her options in violation of what he or she knows his or her preference will be at the time the behaviour is to take place in order to dictate his or her later behaviour. This phenomenon of attempting to exercise control over one's own future behaviour by frustrating one's future preferences Schelling labels anticipatory self-command. He asserts that

> this phenomenon of rational strategic interaction among alternating preferences is a significant part of most people's decisions and welfare and cannot be left out of our account of the consumer. We ignore too many important purposive behaviors if we insist on treating the consumer as having only values and preferences that are uniform over time, even short periods of time. (Schelling 1984a, p. 5)

Emphasizing the importance of self-control and changing preferences is an attempt to expand the horizons of consumer theory beyond the narrow view represented by Stigler and Becker (1977). Schelling (1980, p. 98) writes that 'we should not be surprised that people act as if they were not quite singular individuals with unique identities and values and memories and sensory perceptions that display smooth continuity over time'. He links the problem of self-command to a struggle between two selves that differ fundamentally over a particular issue for which there is no way to determine which behaviour maximizes their collective utility. Schelling (1980, p. 100) suggests that the art of self-control be recognized as part of economics. Schelling (1984b, p. 93) makes this dissatisfaction with textbook consumer theory explicit:

> the ordinary human being is sometimes ... not a single rational individual. Some of us...are more like a small collectivity than like the textbook consumer ... If we accept the idea of two selves of which usually only one is in charge at a time ... 'rational choice' has to be replaced with something like collective choice.[1]

A complete model of consumer behaviour ought to be able to handle instances of anticipatory self-command. Schelling (1984a) goes on to describe how one's different selves compete for command – relinquishing authority to someone else, arranging rewards and penalties, committing or contracting, or employing a buddy system. Throughout this series of papers, Schelling does not belittle the value of neoclassical demand theory. His purposes are to call attention to a common behaviour it ignores, and to appeal to economists to build that behaviour into their models. As such, Schelling dissents from both the scope and method of mainstream consumer theory.

Schelling also explores the ethical and the social policy implications of exercising self-command. 'If somebody now wants our help later in constraining his later behavior against his own wishes at that time, how do we decide which side we are on?' (Schelling 1984b, p. 87). In the original movie version of *Moby Dick*, Ahab, immediately after losing his leg, begs not to be burned by a blacksmith holding a hot iron to cauterize the stump. Despite his loudly expressed wishes, crewmen hold Ahab down as the iron is applied. The next scene shows Ahab happy to be alive, and no sign that disciplinary action was taken against the blacksmith or the crewmen.

Which Ahab do we help? Do we aid the Ahab being tortured by the hot iron or do we help the Ahab who will contract gangrene and die from an uncauterized wound? Is his life worth the pain? Economic theory provides no basis for us to choose, and nearly all of us lack the personal experience to imagine ourselves in Ahab's place. Such a concern with ethics is unusual for an economist, and is another example of Schelling's dissent from the scope of economics (also see Schelling 1984b, pp. 1–26).

An individual's selves frequently come into conflict over the use of addictive drugs. Nicotine is one of the most addictive substances, and Schelling has done considerable research into cigarette smoking. He notes that cigarettes and nicotine have characteristics distinct among addictive drugs (Schelling 1992a). They are cheap, quickly available, portable and storable. There is no impairment of any faculty, no danger of overdose and the damage is slow in arriving. It used to be appropriate to smoke anywhere. Polls indicate that a majority of smokers would elect to deny themselves the possibility of smoking another cigarette. Yet, the addictive qualities of nicotine explain why the smoking self prevails and efforts to quit often fail. The self who wants to stop smoking asserts itself whenever a smoker wears a nicotine patch, makes a public vow to quit, or supports a smoking ban.[2]

Game Theory Applications

Schelling's most influential work has been the application of game theory to international relations. *The Strategy of Conflict* (Schelling 1960c) uses game theory to analyse bargaining between states, focusing on the exploitation of potential force instead of its actual use. Schelling emphasizes that the same general principles can be used to study any conflict situation in which there are some outcomes that are worse for both sides and the ability of one party to achieve his or her objectives is dependent on the decisions made by the other party such as manoeuvring in traffic, designing an agenda for a meeting or disciplining children.

Schelling (1960c, p. 22) reaches the startling conclusion that 'in bargaining, weakness is often strength, freedom may be freedom to capitulate, and to burn bridges behind one may suffice to undo an opponent'.

It can be an advantage to have bound oneself to a particular negotiating position. A bargain is reached when one side believes that the other will not make any further concessions; one side concedes because he or she thinks the other will not. Bargaining strength rests in convincing your adversary that you will not concede any further. Schelling describes three tactics for binding oneself to a position from which retreat is impossible – an irrevocable commitment, the threat and the promise.

An irrevocable commitment demonstrates a party's reservation price. Suppose one wishes to persuade someone that he or she will not pay more than $16,000 for a house with a $20,000 asking price. 'If both men live in a culture where "cross my heart" is universally accepted as potent, all the buyer has to do is allege that he will pay no more than $16,000, using this invocation of penalty and he wins' (Schelling 1960c, p. 24), unless the seller beats the buyer to it by saying '$19,000 is as low as I'll go, cross my heart'.

A threat of mutual harm can be used to proclaim one's own reservation price to the other party. For example, one oligopolist can threaten to cut his or her price if his or her competitor does. Like an irrevocable commitment to a bargaining position, the threat to carry out a promise of mutual harm needs to be persuasively communicated to the other party in order to have value as a bargaining tactic. It can be useful then for the threat to be carried out in steps, with each step more severe than the previous one, in order to convince the other party of its credibility.

Whenever an agreement leaves any incentive to cheat, a convincing and self-binding promise can make the agreement enforceable. Consider a kidnapper who would like to release his victim if he can be assured that the victim will not turn him in. 'If the victim has committed an act whose disclosure could lead to blackmail, he may confess it; if not, he might commit one in the presence of his captor, to create the bond that will ensure his silence' (Schelling 1960c, p. 44).

Wage bargaining, tariff negotiations, cartels, international treaties, out-of-court settlements, a real estate agent and his or her customer are all obvious face-to-face bargaining situations. However, the set of bargaining games is far richer than these examples of explicit bargaining. Schelling is also concerned with tacit bargaining in which communication is incomplete or impossible:

> You are to meet somebody in New York City. You have not been instructed where to meet; you have no prior understanding with the person on where to meet; and you cannot communicate with each other. You are simply told that you will have to guess where to meet and that he is being told the same thing and that you will just have to try to make your guesses coincide. (Schelling 1960c, p. 56)

The absence of face-to-face communication does not mean that a mutually beneficial agreement cannot be reached. The same principle that generates a stable outcome in explicit bargaining works in tacit bargaining situations. Both require convergence of the participants' expectations on a point from which each expects the other not to concede. An irrevocable commitment provides such a focal point in explicit bargaining. In tacit bargaining, outcomes that enjoy prominence, uniqueness, precedent or some rationale that makes them qualitatively different from other possible outcomes, can bring expectations into convergence. Thus, a majority of Schelling's sample chose to meet at the information booth in Grand Central Station.

Analysing how focal points help coordinate expectations, Schelling (1960c, p. 162) argues that, contrary to methodological fashion, 'the mathematical structure of the payoff function should not be permitted to dominate the analysis' of bargaining games. Rather, 'we have to recognize that the kinds of things that determine the outcome are what a highly abstract analysis may treat as irrelevant detail'. Calling for more empirical study of mixed-motive bargaining games he writes, 'one cannot, without empirical evidence, deduce what understandings can be perceived in a nonzero-sum game of maneuver any more than one can prove, by purely formal deduction, that a particular joke is bound to be funny' (Schelling 1960c, p. 164).

Schelling (1960c) aims to reorientate game theory away from a simple division between zero-sum and nonzero-sum games. He stresses that nonzero-sum games can be either pure coordination games (trying to meet somewhere in New York when any agreement is preferred by both parties to a bargaining failure) or mixed-motive bargaining games, where parties have opposed interests but some outcomes are worse for both of them. By ignoring this distinction, and then abstracting away from communication and enforcement mechanisms, Schelling (1960c, p. 119) argues that formal game theory has 'defined away some of the essential ingredients of typical nonzero-sum games'. It has nothing to contribute to such questions as what determines an efficacious threat, or how do pedestrians crossing the street intimidate automobile drivers. Widening the scope of game theory to address such questions requires a change in method. It also requires a wider scope – we must recognize both cooperative and mixed motive games, and communication and enforcement mechanisms.

Schelling (1960c, p. 161) identifies several strategic moves designed to influence 'the other person's choice in a manner favorable to one's self, by affecting the other person's expectations on how one's self will behave'. These have all been neglected by formal game theory. He also integrates these moves (commitments, threats, promises and relinquishing the initiative) into a game-theoretic framework so that outcomes depend solely on the other party's choice. If situations are set up properly, the other party's optimal choice is also the optimum for one's self.

The principle policy concern of *The Strategy of Conflict* and several subsequent publications is the US/USSR conflict. Schelling begins by noting it is far easier to destroy than to create. 'A house that takes several man-years to build can be burned in an hour by any young delinquent who has the price of a box of matches' (Schelling 1966, p. v). The power to hurt is bargaining power; to exploit that power is diplomacy. In bargaining, there must be some common interest even if it is only to avoid mutual harm. Since neither the United States nor the Soviet Union want a nuclear war, because even the winner would suffer dreadful destruction, the threat of violence can be used to coerce or deter Soviet behaviour. Nuclear weapons increase the costs of following through on a threat, so the United States needs to persuasively commit itself to its deterrent threats. Part of making a credible threat is 'a matter of resolve, impetuosity, plain obstinacy, or ... sheer character ... . But it is hard to make it believed' (Schelling 1966, pp. 42–3).[3]

Deterrence depends on our adversary's expectation that we will do what we threaten to do. Expectations of future behaviour are dependent on past behaviour. If previous threats were not carried out, there is no reason for an adversary to believe that the present threat will be either. Schelling's (1966, p. 56) California principle states that there is no way to let the Soviets take California and make them believe that they cannot have the rest of the country. National boundaries have an all-or-nothing character. Effective deterrence beyond national boundaries hinges on attaching to other areas the status of a California. American troops and their families are stationed in Germany in order to give Germany the status of California in the eyes of the Russians.

'Accidents do not cause war. Decisions cause war' (Schelling 1960b, p. 293). A war that neither side really wants could occur if one side believes that the other is about to launch a surprise attack.[4] As surprise carries an enormous advantage, it is beneficial to preclude it by striking first yourself. The significance of a surprise attack lies in the possible vulnerability of retaliatory forces. 'Thus schemes to avert surprise attack have as their most immediate objective the safety of weapons rather than the safety of people' (Schelling 1960c, p. 233). Deterrence against a surprise attack requires a credible second-strike capability.

With that as the theoretical background, Schelling and Halperin (1961) produced the classic study of arms control. Arms control is possible where there is a 'mutual interest in the avoidance of a war that neither side wants, in minimizing the costs and risks of the arms competition, and in curtailing the scope and violence of war in the event it occurs' (Schelling and Halperin 1961, p. 1). As weapon developments continually enhance the advantage of striking first, the best nuclear configuration is a second-strike destructive potential on both sides, or the absence of a first-strike capability to eliminate retaliatory potential (Schelling 1989b, p. 29). The foundation of peace is reciprocal vulnerability to a second strike (Schelling 1985/86). But since land-based missiles are extremely vulnerable to a first strike, and thus encourage a preemptive attack, Schelling (1987) favours an agreement to abolish land-based missiles, and even a unilateral decision to do so.

The most dangerous aspect of nuclear weapons has been the importance of striking first. Despite years of tension and mistrust, neither the United States nor the Soviet Union seized that advantage. Schelling (1989a, p. 315) identifies three factors that have contributed to preemptive stability. The first is a shared expectation that nuclear war is so unlikely that even during a crisis, negotiation will be preferred to nuclear attack. Second, there is a universal conviction that nuclear weapons are not like other weapons. Third, and most important, is the 50-year tradition of not using nuclear weapons (Schelling 1984b, pp. 291–308; 1989a; 1989b; 1991).

Another example of Schelling's concern with unusual subject matter is organized crime. 'Racketeering and the provision of illegal goods have been conspicuously neglected by economists' (Schelling 1967, p. 61). Since economic principles must operate in the underworld as well as in legitimate enterprises, Schelling (1967) has sought to analyse criminal behaviour from an organizational perspective in order to explain why some criminal activity becomes organized and some does not. The answer turns on how strongly the law against that activity is enforced. There is some optimal degree of enforcement which attracts criminal monopoly. Without this level of enforcement, the criminal activity could not be profitable enough to invite monopolization. 'Organized crime could not, for example, possibly corner the market on cigarette sales to minors. Every twenty-one year old is a potential source of supply' (Schelling 1967, p. 74). When the sale of contraceptives was nominally illegal, but the ban not enforced, the supply was too large and it was too difficult for monopoly to be profitable. Prohibition laws, on the other hand, were enforced to the point at which bootlegging became the province of organized crime.

The Bounded Neighbourhood Model

The interdependence of individuals in an urban society produces a new set of problems that cannot be solved by conventional economic analysis.

One of these is racial segregation. Schelling (1971a) uses a model that translates unorganized individual behaviour into collective results in order to show how some segregation is the natural consequence of individual choices. Individual incentives and perceptions of difference can lead to more racial segregation overall than any single person desires or than society itself finds desirable. If whites and blacks wish to avoid minority status, complete segregation is a stable equilibrium. Using dimes and pennies on a checkerboard, Schelling (1971b, pp. 82–8) shows that even a moderate urge to avoid small-minority status (each person wants at least one-third of his or her neighbours to be his or her race), can cause an integrated pattern to unravel and highly segregated neighbourhoods to form.

Schelling (1971a) concludes that complete segregation is the only equilibrium in societies with a black–white population mix like that of the United States. The model assumes a common definition of the neighbourhood and its boundaries. A person is either inside the neighbourhood or out of it. Everyone is concerned about the racial composition of the neighbourhood, but not the arrangement within the neighbourhood. Everyone also has a threshold proportion of blacks and whites, and he or she will choose another location once the threshold is reached. If the median white and the median black will each live with equal numbers of blacks and whites, the only stable equilibrium when the racial composition ratio surpasses two to one is all white and all black neighbourhoods.[5]

When people's behaviour is influenced by the behaviour of others, or when people care about the behaviour of others, 'there is no presumption that the self-serving behavior of individuals should usually lead to collectively satisfactory results' (Schelling 1978, p. 25). Racial segregation is one example. Choosing whom to send a Christmas card is another example.

> People feel obliged to send cards to people from whom they expect to receive them, often knowing that they will receive them only because the senders expect to receive cards in return. People sometimes send cards only because, cards having been sent for several years, cessation might signal something. People send cards early to avoid the suspicion that they were sent only after one had already been received. Students send cards to teachers believing that other students do. Sensible people who might readily agree to stop bothering each other with Christmas cards find it embarrassing, or not quite worth the trouble, to reach such agreement. (Schelling 1978, pp. 31–2)

Neoclassical economics covers the special case of free market transactions in which everybody affected is a voluntary participant. Extending the scope of economics to cover non-market interactions requires employing different methods of analysis. Schelling (1978) discusses five families of social science models that examine interactive and interdependent behaviours, and which ought to be part of economists' tool-kits. The first is the critical mass model, in which behaviour depends on how many people are behaving a particular way. Once some activity exceeds a certain minimum level, the activity becomes self-sustaining. With open seating on an airline flight, a line does not form at the gate until a few people stand up. At that time, the remaining passengers quickly queue. The market for lemons also illustrates critical mass. Second, there are models of self-fulfilling expectations. These models can be used to explain runs on banks. Self-enforcing conventions and the social contract are models three and four.

Schelling (1978) identifies the commons as a fifth family of social science models. The commons refers to situations in which people, in pursuit of their own interests, so encroach on each other that collectively they would be better off if they could be restrained. The problem is that no one has an incentive to practise individual self-restraint.

Schelling has lately been concerned with policy problems of the global commons, such as the greenhouse effect. A change of three degrees celsius in average temperature is expected to occur within the next 100 years, a variation in average temperature beyond any experienced within the last 10,000 years (Schelling 1992b, p. 3). However, 'no climate changes are forecast that compare with moving from Boston to Irvine, California' (Schelling 1990b, p. 258). The effect of global warming on the economic output of developed countries will be negligible, but undeveloped agricultural economies are much more vulnerable to global warming. So, while developed economies have no self-interest in curtailing carbon emissions, less-developed countries cannot afford the economic cost of slowing down the greenhouse effect. In any event, all nations will likely try to free ride off the fossil fuel emission-reductions of others. Schelling (1990b, 1992b) thinks the likelihood of an international emission rationing regime is zero. Anyway, 'for the developing world, the increasing concentration of people is probably more serious than the increasing concentration of carbon dioxide' (Schelling 1992b, p. 7).

'Space has been mankind's latest frontier, and historically as frontiers became settled what had been freely available without limit becomes scarce' (Schelling 1990a, p. 9). Schelling (1990a) considers whether space will soon become a commons. He doubts that during the next 25 years the geosynchronous orbit above the equator, in which a satellite is stationary in relation to the Earth's surface, will become so crowded with satellites that interference becomes a problem because almost everything that can be usefully placed in that orbit in the next 25 years has already been thought of. He is less sanguine about the 25 years after that, but still expects that what goes into orbit will improve the quality of life.

CONCLUSION

Despite having worked on many problems that fall outside the customary domain of economics, Schelling has never really abandoned the mainstream. He has never denounced economic orthodoxy nor has he constructed an alternative to it. He has, instead, used the standard neoclassical rationality assumption to explore human behaviour in a variety of contexts that have been overlooked by other economists. 'Like most economists I am attracted to this model, at least as a benchmark, because when it works we get a lot of output from minimal input using a standard piece of intellectual machinery' (Schelling 1984b, p. x). He is fascinated by cases where rational behaviour does not seem to explain enough and by seemingly dissimilar situations where similar principles are at work. It is when the standard neoclassical model does not explain enough that Schelling urges that it be broadened to take real-world behaviours into account, such as anticipatory self-command. Failing that, new methods of analysis should be adopted, such as the bounded neighbourhood model of segregation.

Schelling's efforts to broaden the realm of economics, his dissent from its scope, have sometimes required a methodological dissent, but his intellectual dissent from mainstream economics is not a result of intellectual dissatisfaction. Rather, it results from his intellectual curiosity. The narrow economic aspects of a problem fail to hold his interest.

> I have been in studies of smoking and health; the intriguing issues are not the economics of tobacco farming and tobacco taxes. I have been in symposia on medical ethics, like the 'right to die', and it was not the rising costs of hospital care that held my attention. I have helped with studies of biomedical technologies, like selecting the sex of offspring, and the fascination is not in animal husbandry. (Schelling 1984b, pp. vii–viii)

NOTES

1. Schelling (1984b, pp. 328–46) notes that, in addition to being a decision-making organ, much of our consumption takes place in the mind.
2. Schelling has even done research into compliance with no-smoking laws. Rigotti et al. (1992, 1993) found low compliance with local no-smoking ordinances in two Massachusetts communities.
3. Schelling's (1966, p. 33) hunch that wars are more a contest of nerve and risk-taking, and of pain and endurance, than a contest of strength is borne out by Maoz (1983), who found that military capabilities are unrelated to the outcomes of interstate disputes while resolve variables are consistently related to the outcomes.
4. To reduce the possibility of such misunderstanding, Schelling (1960a) proposes forming a surveillance force whose purpose would be to diminish the likelihood of unpremeditated war by observing the enemy's behaviour, at the enemy's invitation, and to report home instantly.
5. Clark (1991) tests the bounded neighbourhood model and finds that while the racial composition preference schedules have a different functional form from that suggested by Schelling, stable integrated equilibria are unlikely. Schelling (1972) models the process of neighbourhood tipping.

Economics and its discontents

REFERENCES

Becker, G.S. (1957), *The Economics of Discrimination*, Chicago: University of Chicago Press.

Becker, G.S. (1964), *Human Capital: A Theoretical and Empirical Analysis, with Special Reference to Education*, New York: National Bureau of Economic Research.

Becker, G.S. (1976), *The Economic Approach to Human Behavior*, Chicago: University of Chicago Press.

Becker, G.S. (1981), *A Treatise on the Family*, Cambridge, MA: Harvard University Press.

Becker, G.S. (1993), 'Nobel lecture: The economic way of looking at behavior', *Journal of Political Economy*, **101** (3), June, 385–409.

Blaug, M. (1973), 'Was there a marginal revolution?', in R.D.C. Black, A.W. Coats and C. Goodwin (eds), *The Marginal Revolution in Economics: Interpretation and Evaluation*, Durham: Duke University Press, pp. 3–14.

Boulding, K.E. (1957), 'A new look at Institutionalism', *American Economic Review*, **47** (2), May, 1–12.

Clark, W.A.V. (1991), 'Residential preferences and neighborhood racial segregation: a test of the Schelling segregation model', *Demography*, **28** (1), February, 1–19.

Edwards, R.C., M. Reich, and T.E. Weisskopf (1978), *The Capitalist System*, Englewood Cliffs, NJ: Prentice-Hall.

Fogel, R.W. (1964), *Railroads and American Economic Growth: Essays in Econometric History*, Baltimore: Johns Hopkins University Press.

Fogel, R. and S.L. Engelman (1974), *Time on the Cross: The Economics of American Negro Slavery*, Boston: Little, Brown.

Green, F. (1977), 'The myth of objectivity in positive economics', in F. Green and P. Nore (eds), *Economics: An Anti-Text*, London: Macmillan, pp. 3–20.

Hayek, F.A. (1952), *The Counter-revolution of Science: Studies on the Abuse of Reason*, Glencoe, IL: Free Press.

Iglehart, J.K. (1990), 'Perspectives of an errant economist: a conversation with Thomas Schelling', *Health Affairs*, **9** (2), Summer, 109–21.

Keynes, J.M. (1973), *The General Theory of Employment, Interest and Money*, Volume VII of *The Collected Writings of John Maynard Keynes*, London: Macmillan.

Keynes, J. N. (1955), *The Scope and Method of Political Economy*, reprint of the fourth edition, New York: Kelley & Millman.

Lucas, R.E. and T.J. Sargent (1978), 'After Keynesian economics' in *After the Phillips Curve: Persistence of High Inflation and High Unemployment*, Boston: Federal Reserve Bank of Boston, pp. 49–72.

Maoz, Z. (1983), 'Resolve, capabilities, and the outcomes of interstate disputes, 1816–1976', *Journal of Conflict Resolution*, **27** (2), June, 196–229.

Olson, M. (1965), *The Logic of Collective Action*, Cambridge, MA: Harvard University Press.

Olson, M. (1982), *The Rise and Decline of Nations: Economic Growth, Stagflation, and Social Rigidities*, New Haven: Yale University Press.

Rigotti, N.A., D. Bourne, A. Rosen, J.A. Locke, and T.C. Schelling (1992), 'Workplace compliance with a no-smoking law: a randomized community intervention trial', *American Journal of Public Health*, **82** (2), February, 229–35.

Rigotti, N.A., M.A. Stoto, M.F. Bierer, A. Rosen, and T. Schelling (1993), 'Retail stores' compliance with a city no-smoking law', *American Journal of Public Health*, **83** (2), February, 227–32.

Schelling, T.C. (1955), 'American Foreign Assistance', *World Politics*, **7** (4), July, 606–26.

Schelling, T.C. (1960a) 'Arms control: proposal for a special surveillance force', *World Politics*, **13** (1), October, 1–18.

Schelling, T.C. (1960b), 'Meteors, mischief, and war', *Bulletin of the Atomic Scientists*, **16** (7), September, 292–6, 300.

Schelling, T.C. (1960c), *The Strategy of Conflict*, Cambridge, MA: Harvard University Press.

Schelling, T.C. (1966), *Arms and Influence*, New Haven: Yale University Press.

Schelling, T.C. (1967), 'Economics and criminal enterprise', *Public Interest*, **7**, Spring, 61–78.

Schelling, T.C. (1968), 'The life you save may be your own', in S.B. Chase, Jr. (ed.), *Problems in Public Expenditure Analysis*, Washington, DC: Brookings Institution, pp. 127–62.

Schelling, T.C. (1971a), 'Dynamic models of segregation', *Journal of Mathematical Sociology*, **1** (2), July, 143–86.

Schelling, T.C. (1971b), 'On the ecology of micromotives', *Public Interest*, **25**, Fall, 61–98.

Schelling, T.C. (1972), 'A process of residential segregation: neighborhood tipping', in Anthony H. Pascal (ed.), *Racial Discrimination in Economic Life*, Lexington, MA: D.C. Heath, pp. 157–84.

Schelling, T.C. (1978), *Micromotives and Macrobehavior*, New York: Norton.

Schelling, T.C. (1979), *Thinking Through the Energy Problem*, New York: Committee for Economic Development.

Schelling, T.C. (1980), 'The intimate contest for self-command', *Public Interest*, **60**, Summer, 94–118.

Schelling, T.C. (1983), 'Prices as regulatory instruments', in Thomas C. Schelling (ed.), *Incentives for Environmental Regulation*, Cambridge, MA: MIT Press, pp. 1–40.

Schelling, T.C. (1984a), 'Self-command in practice, in policy, and in a theory of rational choice', *American Economic Review*, **74** (2), May, 1–11.

Schelling, T.C. (1984b), *Choice and Consequence*, Cambridge, MA: Harvard University Press.

Schelling, T.C. (1985/86), 'What went wrong with arms control?', *Foreign Affairs*, **64** (2), Winter, 219–33.

Schelling, T.C. (1987), 'Abolition of ballistic missiles', *International Security*, **12** (1), Summer, 179–83.

Schelling, T.C. (1989a), 'Are the superpowers moving toward new strategic policies and a new strategic relationship?', in A. Clesse and T.C. Schelling (eds), *The Western Community and the Gorbachev Challenge*, Baden-Baden: Nomos, pp. 314–21.

Schelling, T.C. (1989b), 'From an airport bench', *Bulletin of the Atomic Scientists*, **45** (4), May, 29–31.

Schelling, T.C. (1990a), 'An economist looks at space', *Space Times*, **29** (6), November–December, 9–12.

Schelling, T.C. (1990b), 'Global environmental forces', *Technological Forecasting and Social Change*, **38** (3), November, 257–64.

Schelling, T.C. (1991), 'The thirtieth year', *Daedalus*, **120** (1), Winter, 21–31.

Schelling, T.C. (1992a), 'Addictive drugs: the cigarette experience', *Science*, **225** (5043), 24 January, 430–33.

Schelling, T.C. (1992b), 'Some economics of global warming', *American Economic Review*, **82** (1), March, 1–14.

Schelling, T.C. and M.H. Halperin (1961), *Strategy and Arms Control*, New York: Twentieth Century Fund.

Stigler, G.J. and G.S. Becker (1977), 'De gustibus non est disputandum', *American Economic Review*, **67** (2), April, 76–90.

Veblen, T. (1919), *The Place of Science in Modern Civilization*, New York: B.W. Huebsch.

16. Piero Sraffa and mainstream theory

Heinz D. Kurz and Neri Salvadori

INTRODUCTION

An author might find fault with the scope, or the method, or the content of a particular analysis. As regards the *scope*, she might be of the opinion that it is too narrow or too broad. In the former case she will probably plead for opening up the analysis to incorporate aspects or phenomena hitherto excluded; in the latter she will advocate focusing attention on a smaller number of problems. Dissenters with regard to the scope of analysis generally question the established division of labour within and between disciplines. In recent times, dissenters of this kind in economics frequently asked for more interdisciplinary approaches to given problems. Regarding the *method* of analysis, dissenters question the usefulness of the method conventionally employed to tackle a particular problem and advocate some other method. For example, the traditional long-period method, which was used by both classical and early neoclassical economists to study an economic system in motion in terms of a sequence of different long-period positions (or equilibria), was criticized on the ground that it could not adequately describe the dynamic behaviour of the system; a study of the latter necessitated a proper dynamic method. Finally, in terms of *content*, an analysis may be rejected for trying to explain certain phenomena in terms of independent variables which are considered to be the wrong ones or not the most important ones, postulating relationships among variables that are mistaken in one way or another.

Piero Sraffa was not a dissenter in terms of either scope or method. His dissent concerned the content of received theory. His contributions to the foundations of the theory of value and distribution do not advocate widening the scope of analysis as it was defined by earlier authors, most notably Adam Smith and David Ricardo. Also, he does not question the adequacy of the method of analysis, developed by the classical authors and adopted by the marginalist ones, to deal with the problem of value and distribution. His dissent concerned the content of marginalist or neoclassical theory – the way its advocates attempted to determine relative prices and income distribution. He found fault with the proposed explanation of all prices and distributive variables in terms of supply and demand.

Sraffa's early work criticized the *partial* version of marginalist theory. His 1960 book aimed at long-period *general* equilibrium analysis as advocated by authors such as Léon Walras, Eugen von Böhm-Bawerk, John Bates Clark and Knut Wicksell. It is only since the late 1920s that the latter kind of analysis has also been challenged from within the marginalist camp by the emerging intertemporal and temporary equilibrium models. However, the old long-period neoclassical theory manages to survive in mainstream teaching and research; and more recently, with the boom of 'new' growth models, has shown a remarkable revival. In view of this, it is useful to recall the criticism implicit in Sraffa's 1960 analysis.

EARLY WORKS

In November 1923, Sraffa was appointed to a lectureship in Political Economy and Public Finance at the University of Perugia. The preparation of his lectures stimulated him to analyse (Sraffa 1925) the foundations of decreasing, constant, and increasing returns in Alfred Marshall, and to discuss critically the partial equilibrium approach. F.Y. Edgeworth invited Sraffa to publish a version of this article in the *Economic Journal*. This paper starts with the observation:

> A striking feature of the present position of economic science is the almost unanimous agreement at which economists have arrived regarding the theory of competitive value, which is inspired by the fundamental symmetry existing between the forces of demand and those of supply, and is based upon the assumption that the essential causes determining the price of particular commodities may be simplified and grouped together so as to be represented by a pair of intersecting curves of collective demand and supply. This state of things is in such marked contrast with the controversies on the theory of value by which political economy was characterised during the past century that it might almost be thought that from these clashes of thought the spark of an ultimate truth had at length been struck. (Sraffa 1926, p. 535)

Sraffa dissented from this view, the mainstream view in the English-speaking countries at the time and a view which, surprisingly, still dominates economic textbooks. He found 'one dark spot which disturbs the harmony of the whole'. This 'dark spot' is represented by the supply curve, based upon the combination of the laws of increasing and diminishing returns. Its foundations 'are actually so weak as to be unable to support the weight imposed upon them' (Sraffa 1926, p. 536).

The partial equilibrium argument can be summarized as follows. A change in one market (for example, a shift in the demand for bread) has first an effect on the equilibrium of that market (for example, a change in the price and in the quantity of bread produced) and second an effect on the other markets as a consequence of the change in the price and the quantity determined in the market where the original change took place (for example, a shift in the demand for flour, used to produce bread, and in the demand for biscuits, a bread substitute). If it can be assumed that the effects on the other markets are of a second order of magnitude with respect to the effect obtained on the equilibrium of the market where the original change took place, and if these second order of magnitude effects are assumed to be so small that they can be neglected, at least at a first stage, then the demand and supply curves of a given market can be considered independent both of each other and of the demand and supply curves for all other commodities.

The central issue of Sraffa's criticism concerns variable returns. Three cases can be distinguished: variable returns that are (i) internal to the firm; (ii) external to the firm but internal to the industry; and (iii) external to both the firm and the industry. It was clear that variable returns of type (i) are incompatible with the assumption of perfect competition. Sraffa spent a large part of the 1925 paper and of the first part of the 1926 paper showing that variable returns of type (iii) are incompatible with the method of partial equilibrium. Thus, only variable returns of type (ii), whose empirical importance is dubious, are compatible with Marshall's analysis of the supply curve of an industry in conditions of perfect competition.

Sraffa (1925, 1926) showed that variable returns of type (iii) are incompatible with the method of partial equilibrium because it cannot be excluded that a change in the quantity produced by a variable cost industry *at the same time* entails a change in the costs of firms in *other* industries as it entails a change in the costs of firms in the industry in which the change in the quantity produced took place. A typical example is when the same quality of land is used to produce two different commodities, say apples and pears. An increase in the production of apples, for instance, may lead to a rise in the cost curve for the producers of apples because of an increase in the rent paid for the use of land. But this rise in rent would likewise affect the cost curve of the producers of pears. The changes in costs would be of the same order of magnitude in both industries, so that it would seem to be illegitimate to disregard the changes in the cost curves of firms outside the industry in which the quantity produced has changed (pears), while taking into account only

changes obtained in the cost curves of firms inside the industry in which
the variation in quantity took place (apples).

When a change in the quantity produced by a variable cost industry
does not entail a change in the costs of firms in other industries, the variable costs are said to be *internal to the industry*. A typical example is when
returns are decreasing because land is in short supply and each quality of
land is specific to the production of one commodity only. If the
(dis)economies responsible for variable costs are external to the firm and
internal to the industry, variations in the quantity produced by one industry may affect the cost curves of firms outside that industry only as a
consequence of the change in the equilibrium price and quantity of the
commodity produced by the industry in which the variation took place.
This would be an effect of the second order of magnitude only, whose
presence, it could be contended, is perhaps compatible with using the
ceteris paribus clause (see also Roncaglia 1978; Panico 1991; Kurz and
Salvadori 1995, Chs 1 and 13).

From this, Sraffa (1925) concluded that the assumption of constant
returns is the most convenient one for analysing the supply curve of an
industry under competitive conditions. This conclusion is repeated in the
1926 paper: 'the old and now obsolete theory which makes ... [competi-
tive value] dependent on the cost of production alone appears to hold its
ground as the best available' (Sraffa 1926, p. 541). Yet this did not satisfy
Sraffa. He was confronted with two alternatives: either abandon the
assumption of perfect competition or abandon partial equilibrium analysis. As is well known, Sraffa initially followed the first route, but soon
switched to the second.

His 1926 paper ruled out the second alternative on the grounds that an
examination of 'the conditions of simultaneous equilibrium in numerous
industries' is far too complex: 'the present state of our knowledge ... does
not permit of even much simpler schema being applied to the study of
real conditions' (Sraffa 1926, p. 541). Adoption of the first alternative
was instead motivated by two related arguments. First, the abandonment
of the hypothesis of perfect competition is suggested by '[e]veryday experience ... that a very large number of undertakings – and the majority of
those which produce manufactured consumers' goods – work under conditions of individual diminishing costs'. Second, it is argued that the

> chief obstacle against which [business men] have to contend when they want
> gradually to increase their production does not lie in the cost of production ...
> but in the difficulty of selling the larger quantity of goods without reducing
> the price, or without having to face increased marketing expenses. This ... is
> only an aspect of the usual descending demand curve, with the difference that
> instead of concerning the whole of a commodity, whatever its origin, it relates
> only to the goods produced by a particular firm. (Sraffa 1926, p. 543)

In his 1926 paper, then, Sraffa suggested retaining partial equilibrium analysis. This was possible, however, at the cost of abandoning the concern with the free competition form of markets: in order to preserve the partial framework the analysis had to be limited to the study of economies internal to the firm. Sraffa's proposal was taken up by several authors and triggered a rich literature on market forms which bloomed during the 1930s (see especially Robinson 1933).

Apart from a contribution to the 1930 *Economic Journal* symposium on increasing returns, Sraffa did not participate further in the debate on the Marshallian theory of value. This contribution was considered a 'negative and destructive criticism' by Keynes in the 'Notes by the Editor' introducing the debate. Sraffa's rejoinder to Robertson concludes with the following sentences:

> I am trying to find what are the assumptions implicit in Marshall's theory; if Mr. Robertson regards them as extremely unreal, I sympathise with him. We seem to be agreed that the theory cannot be interpreted in a way which makes it logically self-consistent and, at the same time, reconciles it with the facts it sets out to explain. Mr Robertson's remedy is to discard mathematics, and he suggests that my remedy is to discard the facts; perhaps I ought to have explained that, in the circumstances, I think it is Marshall's theory that should be discarded. (Sraffa, 1930, p. 93)

His analytical work following the 1926 paper, investigated 'the process of diffusion of profits throughout the various stages of production and of the process of forming a normal level of profits throughout all the industries of a country ... [a problem] beyond the scope of this article' (Sraffa 1926, p. 550). This problem constituted the main topic of his *magnum opus*: *Production of Commodities by Means of Commodities.*

THE COLLABORATION WITH KEYNES AND THE CONTROVERSY WITH HAYEK

In 1931 Hayek (1931a) published *Prices and Production*, a book based on four lectures given at the London School of Economics, and the first part of his critical review of Keynes's *Treatise on Money* (Hayek, 1931b). Both contributions rejected the explanation of economic crises in terms of deficient aggregate demand. In his book, Hayek elaborated the Austrian approach to the theory of money and economic fluctuations, tracing crises back to 'misdirections of production' caused by the banking system fixing the money rate of interest below the equilibrium rate.

Keynes tried to answer the challenge, though with little success. Like other Anglo-Saxon and American economists, he had difficulty understanding and countering Hayek because he lacked knowledge of the main building blocks of his analysis – Paretian general equilibrium theory and Böhm-Bawerk's theory of capital and interest. Keynes invited Sraffa, who was familiar with both intellectual traditions, to ward off the attacks from Hayek.

Sraffa (1932a) published a refutation of Hayek in the *Economic Journal*; Hayek (1932) replied, and Sraffa (1932b) then responded to Hayek. Sraffa's criticism was purely internal; he scrutinized the consistency of Hayek's argument in the context of its own analytical framework. He showed that Hayek had committed a number of serious blunders which deprived his analysis of almost any explanatory value. By assuming that money was only a means of exchange (and thus ignoring its role as a store of value), Hayek dealt with an economic system containing 'emasculated' money. How could such an economy behave differently from a barter economy? Apparently, Sraffa argued, Hayek must have introduced an element that is extraneous to the discussion and which causes the difference.

This element became visible in Hayek's treatment of 'voluntary' saving and 'forced' saving. The first case concerns a change in intertemporal preferences. In Hayek's marginalist setting, an increase in voluntary saving means that agents decide to forgo present consumption for future consumption. In an economic system with a given and constant labour supply and a given and constant technical knowledge this means that more 'roundabout', or 'capitalistic', processes of production will be adopted, characterized by a higher consumption output per capita. This, in turn, involves a change in the proportion of gross income spent on consumption and on capital goods (that is, a change in gross savings). Net savings will be positive only during the transitory phase, until a new and stable equilibrium is reached.

While in Hayek's view this case is unproblematic, the other case, forced saving, concerns interventions into the 'voluntary decisions of individuals' and thus infringes upon their 'freedom of action'. A money rate of interest below the equilibrium rate leads to an expansion of producers' or of consumers' credit. In the former case producers will find it now profitable to lengthen the 'average period of production'. This is only possible, however, if labour and non-specific factors of production are shifted from lower stages of production (that is, those close to the 'maturing' of the consumption goods) to higher stages, thereby imposing on agents a reduction in consumption (that is, 'forced' saving). Eventually incomes will rise; and since preferences of agents have not changed, consumption demand will go up. Prices of consumer goods will rise, indicating to producers that it is profitable to adopt less roundabout production processes. As a consequence, capital has to be reduced again – a process that 'necessarily takes the form of an economic crisis' (Hayek 1931a, p. 53). After a costly roundtrip, and on the assumption that the banking system will eventually correct its error, the system is bound to return to its original equilibrium.

For Hayek (1931a, p. 57), while the 'artificial stimulant' of inflation in the shape of producers' credits can do no good, such a stimulant in the shape of consumers' credits is said to do harm, because it tends 'to frustrate the effect of saving'. Inflation through consumers' credits would decrease capital and push the system to a new equilibrium with lower consumption output per capita. Sraffa (1932a, p. 48) dryly comments: 'Thus Dr. Hayek will have it both ways'. Hayek's claim that the two cases are not analogous finally reveals the 'error or irrelevancy' which is responsible for the fact that a rise or fall in the quantity of 'emasculated' money can make a difference. As Sraffa (1932a, p. 49) stressed: 'an extraneous element, in the shape of the supposed power of the banks to settle the way in which money is spent, has crept into the argument and has done all the work'.

Returning to the case of producers' credits, Sraffa (1932a, p. 48) objected that Hayek failed to show that those whose real income was curbed during the inflation will benefit in the end: 'One class has, for a time, robbed another class of part of their incomes; and has saved the plunder. When the robbery comes to an end, it is clear that the victims cannot possibly consume the capital which is now well out of their reach'. Seen from the vantage point of Paretian general equilibrium theory, which Hayek endorsed, Sraffa's criticism amounts to the objection that the process of inflation (as well as that of deflation) is typically associated with a change in the distribution of wealth and thus affects one of the fundamental data determining general equilibrium. To this is added a further objection which shows that Hayek's attempt to identify his two cases as pure cases is ill-conceived. Since it can safely be assumed that those who gain from inflation will be engaged in 'voluntary' saving, the picture gets blurred. Conversely, there will also be a destruction of capital in the case of voluntary saving: 'With or without money, if investment and saving have not been planned to match, an increase of saving must prove to a large extent "abortive"' (Sraffa 1932a, p. 52).

Finally, Sraffa took issue with Hayek's claim that a difference between the actual or money rate of interest and the natural or equilibrium rate is a characteristic of a money economy:

If money did not exist, and loans were made in terms of all sorts of commodities, there would be a single rate which satisfies the conditions of equilibrium, but there might be at any moment as many 'natural' rates of interest as there are commodities, though they would not be 'equilibrium' rates. The 'arbitrary' action of the banks is by no means a necessary condition for the divergence; if loans were made in wheat and farmers (or for that matter the weather) 'arbitrarily changed' the quantity of wheat produced, the actual rate of interest on loans in terms of wheat would diverge from the rate on other commodities and there would be no single equilibrium rate. (Sraffa 1932a, p. 49)

Sraffa illustrated his argument in terms of an example which introduced the concept of the *own rate of interest* or, as he preferred to call it, the 'commodity rate of interest'. Both in the monetary and the barter economy loans are made in terms of all commodities for which there are forward markets. Assume that in the money economy a cotton spinner borrows at time t a sum of money for θ periods (months) and uses the sum to purchase on the spot market a quantity of raw cotton at price p^t, which he simultaneously sells θ periods forward at price $p^{t+\theta}$. This means that the cotton spinner 'borrows' cotton for θ periods. Sraffa (1932a, p. 50) expounded: 'The rate of interest which he pays, per hundred bales of cotton, is the number of bales that can be purchased with the following sum of money: the interest on the money required to buy spot 100 bales, plus the excess (or minus the deficiency) of the spot over the forward prices of the 100 bales'. Let $i_{t,\theta}$ designate the money rate of interest between t and $t+\theta$, then the sum of money, M, referred to equals

$$M = (1 + i_{t,\theta})p^t - p^{t+\theta}.$$

The own-rate of interest of cotton between t and $t+\theta$, $\rho_{t,}^{\theta}$, is then defined as the quantity of cotton which can be purchased with that sum of money at the given forward price, that is,

$$\rho_{t,\theta} = \frac{M}{p^{t+\theta}} = \frac{(1+i_{t,\theta})\,p^t - p^{t+\theta}}{p^{t+\theta}} = \frac{(1+i_{t,\theta})p^t}{p^{t+\theta}} - 1.$$

Sraffa (1932a, p. 50) added:

> In equilibrium the spot and forward price coincide, for cotton as for any other commodity; and all the 'natural' or commodity rates are equal to one another, and to the money rate. But if, for any reason, the supply and the demand for a commodity are not in equilibrium (i.e. its market price exceeds or falls short of its cost of production), its spot and forward prices diverge, and the 'natural' rate of interest on that commodity diverges from the 'natural' rates on other commodities.

Essentially the same can be said of an economy without money: out of equilibrium, 'natural' rates of interest will be different for at least some commodities. Hayek's opinion that in a disequilibrium caused by a sudden increase in money supply (in the propensity to save) the natural rate of interest would be above (below) the money rate does not make sense, because out of equilibrium there is no such thing as *the* natural rate; there may rather be 'as many "natural" rates as there are commodities' (Sraffa 1932a, p. 50).

This observation led Sraffa to the question of how the system gets re-equilibrated. He stressed 'that, under free competition, this divergence of rates is essential to the effecting of the transition as is the divergence of prices from the costs of production; it is, in fact, another aspect of the same thing'. As to the gravitation of market prices to costs of production (inclusive of interest), Sraffa (1932a, p. 50) addressed Hayek's case in which

> there is a change in the distribution of demand between various commodities; immediately some will rise in price, and others will fall; the market will expect that, after a certain time, the supply of the former will increase, and the supply of the latter fall, and accordingly the forward price, for the date on which equilibrium is expected to be restored, will be below the spot price in the case of the former and above it in the case of the latter; in other words the rate of interest on the former will be higher than on the latter.

This will prompt profit-seeking producers of the former commodities to expand output and of the latter commodities to reduce it. In this way production will adjust to demand until a new equilibrium obtains in which all commodity rates of interest are uniform and, in the case of a money economy, equal to the money rate of interest. The concept of equilibrium under discussion was the traditional long-period concept accepted by the earlier classical economists and advocated by all marginalist authors until the late 1920s, including Walras, Böhm-Bawerk and Wicksell. More important, it was precisely the concept adopted by Hayek in *Prices and Production*.[1]

In his reply, Hayek (1932, p. 245) admitted that 'there would be *no single rate* which, applied to all commodities, would satisfy the conditions of equilibrium rates, but there might, at any moment, be as many "natural" rates of interest as there are commodities, *all* of which would be *equilibrium rates*' (emphasis added). In his rejoinder, Sraffa noticed Hayek's admission with satisfaction, but he asked him to draw the consequences for his ideal maxim for monetary policy – the proposition that they '*all* ... would be equilibrium rates'. Sraffa (1932b, p. 251) commented: 'The only meaning (if it be a meaning) I can attach to this is that his maxim of policy now requires that the money rate should be equal to all the divergent natural rates'.

In view of Sraffa's devastating criticism it is hardly surprising that even those sympathetic to Hayek felt that his stature as an economic theorist had been seriously damaged in the debate with Sraffa (compare Lachmann 1986). Keynes, on the other hand, must have been extremely pleased with Sraffa's performance: it effectively countered the assault on his intellectual project launched by Lionel Robbins and his circle, and it allowed him to develop the *General Theory* undisturbed by interventions from Hayek. Chapter 17 of the *General Theory* (Keynes 1936, pp. 222–44) made use of Sraffa's concept of own rates of interest, arguing that the money own rate of interest is determined by liquidity preference, which, in a given time and place, is a conventional datum. As we know from his unpublished papers, Sraffa opposed Keynes's liquidity preference theory. However, his close friendship with and otherwise high opinion of Keynes appears to have prevented him from openly attacking it. Sraffa's main criticism was 'that the advantages involved in *holding* a commodity have no relation to its "own particular rate of interest"; and indeed no properties of that commodity (apart from expected price change) have any relations to the difference between its rate and other rates.' For when someone borrows, whether money or anything else, he normally does not hoard the proceeds but uses them to buy what he needs for production. It is of no import to him whether he starts by paying in money or in wheat. The commodities he buys he normally does not hold, but puts them to productive use, which implies that he is not interested in whether they have carrying costs or advantages. Keynes's misconception is said to be rooted in 'two wrong notions, which have entirely misled him: a) that commodities are borrowed for holding them till the end of the loan; b) that only durable articles can therefore be borrowed. But in fact it is as convenient to make a loan of fresh fish for 100 years, as it is to make it of gold.' The properties considered by Keynes are the properties of investment in fixed capital. In his argument he therefore should have referred to its marginal product. Keynes is therefore taken to be wrong in assuming that the own rates of interest on different articles correspond to the different advantages or disadvantages (yield, carrying cost, liquidity) associated with their possession: 'Nothing of the sort: if no changes in price are expected *all* commodities will have the same rates of interest, whether it be a delight or a nuisance to possess them: the discrepancies can *only* be due to expected change in relative prices.' (see Sraffa's papers in the Wren Library of Trinity College. Shelf mark I 100, sheets 9 and 10).

THE WORKS AND CORRESPONDENCE OF DAVID RICARDO

We know from the manuscript of his lectures on value theory in the late 1920s, and from his characterization of classical value theory as 'the old and now obsolete theory which makes [the competitive value] dependent on the cost of production alone' (Sraffa 1926, p. 541), that Sraffa originally read Ricardo through the lens of Marshall's interpretation. A careful reading of Ricardo eventually convinced him that this interpretation did not stand up to close examination. Sraffa thus dissented from the conventional interpretation of Ricardo; and he elaborated an interpretation of the classical approach to the theory of value and distribution that differed markedly from the then dominant one.

This new interpretation centres around the concept of *surplus*. For Ricardo (*Works*, I, p. 6) income distribution was 'the principal problem in Political Economy'. His main concern was to elaborate a coherent theory of the rate of profit, based on that concept: 'Profits come out of the surplus produce' (*Works*, II, pp. 130–31). According to Sraffa (1951, pp. xxxi–xxxiii), the development of Ricardo's thoughts on the matter can be divided into four steps. These steps reflect consecutive attempts to simplify the problem of distribution.

The first step eliminated the problem of the rent through the theory of differential rent developed in Ricardo's 1815 *Essay on the Influence of a low Price of Corn on the Profits of Stock* (*Works*, IV). This allowed Ricardo to focus attention on marginal (that is, no-rent) land: 'By getting rid of rent, which we may do on the corn produced with the capital last employed, and on all commodities produced by labour in manufactures, the distribution between capitalist and labourer becomes a much more simple consideration' (*Works*, VIII, p. 194). The second step consisted of trying to get rid of the problem of value by assuming the corn model: with seed corn as the only capital good and wages paid in terms of corn, the rate of profit obtained in corn production can be ascertained directly as a ratio of quantities of corn (the surplus product to the corn capital advanced) without any need to have recourse to prices. With corn entering the production of all other commodities (as the only wage good and possibly also as an input) the prices of these commodities would have to adjust so that the same competitive rate of return could be earned in their production. Sraffa stressed: 'Although this argument is never stated by Ricardo in any of his extant letters and papers, he must have formulated it either in his lost "papers on the profits of Capital" of March 1814 or in conversation [with Malthus]' (1951, p. xxxi).

Yet Ricardo had to accept the objection of Thomas Malthus that there is no industry in which the composition of the product is exactly the same as that of the capital advanced. It is here that theories of distribution based on the concept of social surplus are confronted with the problem of value. Therefore, in a third step, Ricardo presented a theory of value according to which the exchange values of commodities are regulated by the quantities of labour needed directly and indirectly in their production. The surplus product and the social capital (the two magnitudes whose ratio gives the general rate of profit) could thus be 'measured' in terms of embodied labour. Hence, what was to become known as the 'labour theory of value' was introduced by Ricardo precisely in order to overcome the analytical difficulty encountered in his attempt to explain profits in terms of the surplus product left after making allowance for the cost of production, including the wages of productive workers.

However, Ricardo (*Works,* I, p. 30) soon realized that the principle that the quantity of labour regulates exchange value cannot be sustained as a general rule: it is 'considerably modified by the employment of machinery and other fixed and durable capital'. For, with different proportions of (direct) labour to means of production in different industries, and with different durabilities of these means of production, relative prices would not only depend on the quantities of total labour embodied in various commodities, but also on the level of the rate of profit, and would change with that level. Sraffa considered the search for a measure of value that is invariable with respect to changes in distribution (that is, variations in the real wage rate and the associated contrary variations in the rate of profits) as the final step in Ricardo's efforts to simplify the theory of distribution. This measure of value was meant to corroborate his conviction that the laws of distribution 'are not essentially connected with the doctrine of value' (*Works,* VIII, p. 194; see also Kurz and Salvadori 1993).

Sraffa deserves credit for having rediscovered the 'classical' approach to the theory of value and distribution. After reconstructing the classical approach, it had to be developed, given a logically coherent formulation, and completed by taking into account phenomena such as fixed capital, joint production and natural resources with which the earlier authors had grappled with only limited success. This constituted one of the tasks of his 1960 book.

PRODUCTION OF COMMODITIES BY MEANS OF COMMODITIES

From the middle of the 1950s onwards Sraffa eventually found time to revise and complete his notes on the classical approach to value and distribution. These were eventually published as *Production of Commodities by Means of Commodities*. Its main aim is a critique of *long-period* marginal theory. In the preface, Sraffa (1960) pointed out that although 'The set of propositions now published ... do not enter into any discussion of the marginal theory of value and distribution, they have nevertheless been designed to serve as the basis for a critique of that theory'. He also stressed: 'If the foundation holds, the critique may be attempted later, either by the writer or by someone younger and better equipped for the task.' (Ibid., p.vi). Since the publication of the book the critique implicit in it has indeed been carried out (see below). Major representatives of the neoclassical school (most notably Paul Samuelson and F.H. Hahn) have admitted that the criticism of long-period neoclassical theory is correct and have advocated abandoning that theory.[2] At the same time it was quite natural to ask whether the critique (or elements of it) carries over from long-period to short-period analysis, that is, theories of intertemporal and temporary equilibrium.

According to some interpreters, Sraffa's book was exclusively designed for a negative task – to serve as the basis for a critique of marginal theory. However, this interpretation cannot be sustained. Sraffa's work was not only critical, it was also constructive. (Sraffa's concern with the constructive task becomes obvious when reading his papers in the Wren Library at Trinity College, Cambridge.) He may be said to have followed Spinoza's famous dictum *determinatio est negatio*: by elaborating a coherent theory of relative prices and income distribution he sought to prepare the ground for a critique of marginalist theory.

In his book, Sraffa was *a dissenter*, but he was also a *consenter*. Sraffa (1960, p. v) made it clear that the standpoint taken in the book 'is that of the old classical economists from Adam Smith to Ricardo, [which] has been submerged and forgotten since the advent of the "marginal" method'. The affiliation of his analysis with the theories of the old classical economists is stressed again in the following remark concerning the concept of 'price' or 'value' adopted in the book: 'Such classical terms as "necessary price", "natural price" or "price of production" would meet the case, but value and price have been preferred as being shorter and in the present context (which contains no reference to market prices) no more ambiguous'. Finally, Appendix D provides additional 'References to the Literature' concerning special ideas and concepts of classical derivation.

Sraffa proceeds as follows. Chapter I deals with an actual economic system, assuming that it is capable of *self-replacement*; that is, it produces of each commodity: (i) at least as much as is needed in order to make good the quantity used up of the commodity under consideration as a means of production across all industries of the economy; (ii) plus the quantity of it needed to provide necessities at a given (minimum) level for those engaged in production. He then assumes that any remaining surplus product (quantities of the different commodities produced in excess of the requirements of self-replacement) disappears, leaving a system which he calls 'Production without Surplus'. Sraffa (1960, p. 3) finds that in such a system the relative exchange values of commodities or price ratios 'spring directly from the methods of production and productive consumption'.

Chapter II brings the surplus back into the picture, assuming that this surplus will be distributed in the form of profits on capital at a uniform rate (that is, in proportion to the capital advanced in each industry). Since the means of production and means of subsistence advanced in each industry at the beginning of the (uniform) production period consist of sets of heterogeneous commodities, the magnitude of each industry's capital can only be ascertained once prices are known. Prices, however, cannot be determined independently of the rate of profit. Hence, Sraffa concludes, prices and the rate of profit must be determined *simultaneously*.[3]

The concept of surplus then leads to the distinction between *basic* and *non-basic* products, and to the assumption that there exists at least one basic commodity. Basic products enter directly or indirectly into the production of all commodities, whereas non-basic products do not. The main aim of Chapter III is to provide a first discussion of price movements consequent upon changes in distribution on the assumption that the methods of production remain unchanged. Sraffa concludes 'this preliminary survey of the subject' by asserting that

> the relative price-movements of two products come to depend, not only on the 'proportions' of labour to means of production by which they are respectively produced, but also on the 'proportions' by which those means have themselves been produced, and also on the 'proportions' by which the means of production of those means of production have been produced, and so on. The result is that the relative price of two products may move ... in the opposite direction to what we might have expected on the basis of their respective 'proportions'; besides, the prices of their respective means of production may move in such a way as to reverse the order of the two products as to higher and lower proportions; *and further complications arise, which will be considered subsequently.* (Sraffa 1960, p. 15; emphasis added)

Chapter VI provides the complete analysis of price movements in the case of single production. This chapter also contains the well-known example of old wine and the oak chest, which shows that the difference between the prices of two commodities can be positive or negative depending on income distribution. The analysis is significantly simplified by using the Standard commodity as *numéraire*. Chapters IV and V introduce this tool of analysis and study its properties.[4]

Part II generalizes the analysis of Part I, which was restricted to single-product industries and circulating capital, to the case of multiple-product industries and fixed capital. It contains impressive counter-evidence to W. S. Jevons's contention that the classical approach is incapable of dealing with this more realistic and complicated case and, as a result, had to be abandoned for a new theoretical approach (see Kurz 1986). Sraffa deserves credit for having demonstrated that the multiple-product industries framework is suited to analyse a wide range of problems and need not be limited to investigating examples of joint production proper – such as wool and mutton, or coke and coal-gas.

The method of treating what remains of *fixed capital* goods at the end of the production period (as a part of the gross output) fits easily into the classical picture and was first introduced by Robert Torrens when criticizing Ricardo (Sraffa 1960, p. 94). The method allows the correct calculation of the annual charge on the fixed capital consisting of the payment of profit at the uniform rate and the depreciation that makes possible the replacement of the durable instrument of production when it is worn out. Most importantly, the method is not restricted to the simplified case of constant efficiency, but has general validity (Sraffa 1960, p. 66; see also Kurz and Salvadori 1995, Chs 7 and 9). It is shown that the depreciation quotas, and thus the price of ageing machinery, cannot be ascertained independently of distribution, contrary to a widespread belief that finds expression in *ad hoc* rules such as linear depreciation, 'radioactive decay' or 'depreciation by evaporation'.

Unlike capital, which consists of produced means of production, natural resources (such as land) can be taken as external elements of production, measured in their own physical units. 'Being employed in production, but not themselves produced, they are the converse of commodities which, although produced, are not used in production' (Sraffa 1960, p. 74); that is, the converse of non-basics that are pure consumption goods. In accord with Ricardo's treatment of the problem, Sraffa starts from a given system of production – given quantities of the commodities produced, given methods of production in use, and a given distribution of income between wages and profits. He then indicates how such a constellation can be conceived 'as the outcome of a process of "extensive" ... [or] "intensive" diminishing returns' (Sraffa 1960, p. 76).

Part III of Sraffa's book is devoted to a discussion of the problem of the choice of technique. Sraffa (1960, p. 83) assumes that the choice between alternative techniques 'will be exclusively grounded on cheapness'. Thus, he is concerned with determining the *cost-minimizing* system(s) of production. In comparing different methods of production to produce the same commodity the phenomena of *extra costs* and *extra profits* make an appearance. Although Sraffa does not provide a formalization of his argument, it is clear that in this context inequalities rather than equations would be appropriate.

CRITIQUE OF LONG-PERIOD MARGINALIST THEORY

Neoclassical economics attempts to explain all prices and quantities, including the prices and quantities of the factors of production or factor services, in terms of demand and supply. These are conceptualized as functions relating the price of a good or factor service to the collective quantity of it demanded or supplied. These functions are derived from the choices of microunits (utility-maximizing consumers and profit-maximizing producers) confronted with alternative sets of relative prices. In order to determine prices and quantities (the endogenous variables), the theory typically starts from the following data (or exogenous variables): (i) the initial endowments of the economy and the distribution of property rights among individual agents; (ii) the preferences of consumers; and (iii) the set of technical alternatives from which cost-minimizing producers can choose.

Factor prices (wages, rents and the rate of profit) are considered to reflect the scarcity of the respective factors of production. In conditions of free competition (that is, the absence of persistent barriers to entry or exit), there will be a tendency towards a uniform rate of profit across industries and a uniform rate of remuneration for each 'original' factor of production. Prices of goods are taken to reflect the marginal importance of the different goods in satisfying consumers' wants and desires, and factor prices are taken to reflect the marginal importance of the different factors in production.

Historically, marginalist or neoclassical theory can be shown to derive from a generalization of the theory of rent in terms of land of uniform quality and 'intensive' margins to all factors of production, including capital (see Bharadwaj 1978; Garegnani 1990). Assume that corn can be produced with unassisted labour and land. Variable proportions of the two factors can then be shown to imply equality between the marginal products and the rates of remuneration of the factor services (that is, the wage rate and the rent rate in terms of the product). A relationship between the wage rate and the quantity of labour employed can be built up in this special case. This relationship is a decreasing one and is commonly called 'the aggregate demand function' for labour. Confronting this demand function with an aggregate supply function of labour derived from the optimal choices of utility-maximizing individuals regarding the desired consumption of corn and leisure time (and consequently the desired labour time), respectively, for alternative levels of the real wage rate, may then give rise to equilibrium values of total employment, L^*, and the real wage rate, w^*, for the economy as a whole.

With flexible wages, these equilibrium levels are assumed to be a *centre of gravitation*. Starting from a level of the wage rate higher than the market-clearing level, the number of labourers employed would be smaller than the number of those seeking employment. Unemployed labourers would then start bidding down the real wage until it reaches the level compatible with full employment. Similarly, with an initial wage rate smaller than the market-clearing level, and hence with the demand for labour larger than the supply, landowners, unable to find additional workers at the going wage rate, would start bidding up wages. Assuming other things to be equal, including the amount of land available for the production of corn, in both cases the system would tend towards an equilibrium position.

Next assume that corn is produced by labour and 'capital' consisting exclusively of corn (seed corn), on homogeneous land that is available in unlimited quantities (that is, a free good). With continuously variable proportions between labour and (corn) capital the argument developed for the labour–land case carries over to the present case. Hence a similar equality would hold between the rate of profit (interest), r, and that of wages on the one hand and the marginal products of (corn) capital and labour on the other. This is the analogy between 'capital' (or land) and labour drawn by the early marginalist authors. The question is whether this analogy holds in less special cases than the one where capital consists exclusively of corn. Neoclassical authors have answered this question in the affirmative. They contended that the simple case carries over to the general case where heterogeneous capital goods are used in production and where land can be in short supply.

Expressing the quantity of capital in value terms is necessitated by the following consideration. Careful scrutiny shows that the advocates of the traditional neoclassical theory of distribution (with the notable exception of Walras, at least until the fourth edition of the *Eléments*), were aware of the fact that to be consistent with the concept of a long-run equilibrium the capital endowment of the economy could not be conceived as a set of given physical amounts of produced means of production. For, if the capital endowment is given in kind, only a short-run equilibrium, characterized by differential rates of return on the supply prices of the various capital goods, could be established by the forces constituting supply and demand. However, with free competition, which would enforce a tendency towards a uniform rate of profit, such an equilibrium could not be considered, in the words of Hicks (1932, p. 20), a 'full equilibrium'. Hence the 'quantity of capital' available for productive purposes had to be expressed as a value magnitude, allowing it to assume the physical 'form' suited to the other data of the theory (that is, the endowment of the economy with factors of production other than 'capital', the technical alternatives of production and the preferences of agents).

Thus the formidable problem for the neoclassical approach in attempting determination of the general rate of profit consisted in establishing the notion of a market for 'capital', the 'quantity' of which could be expressed *independently* of the price of its service – the rate of profit. Moreover, the plausibility of the supply and demand approach to the theory of distribution was felt to hinge upon a demonstration of the existence of a unique and stable ǝquilibrium in that market (see Marshall 1920, p. 665n.). With the 'quantity of capital' in given supply, this, in turn, implied that a monotonically *decreasing* demand function for 'capital' in terms of the rate of profit had to be established.

This inverse relationship was arrived at by the neoclassical theorists through introducing two kinds of *substitutability* between capital and labour (and other factors of production) – substitutability in consumption and in production. According to the former concept, a rise in the rate of profit relative to the real wage rate would increase the price of those commodities whose production exhibits a relatively high ratio of capital to labour. This would prompt consumers to shift their demand towards relatively cheaper labour-intensive commodities. Hence in the economy as a whole the capital–labour ratio, or capital intensity, and the rate of profit are inversely related. The second concept, substitutability in production, we encountered already when discussing the model with corn capital. A rise in the rate of profit (interest) relative to the wage rate would make cost-minimizing entrepreneurs in different industries employ more of the relatively cheapened factor of production (that is, labour). Hence, through both routes capital would be substituted for labour, and for any given quantity of labour employed, a decreasing demand schedule for capital would obtain. The conclusion is close at hand that the division of the product between wages and profits can be explained in terms of the scarcity of the respective factors of production, labour and capital, where the latter is conceived as a value magnitude that is considered independent of the rate of profit.

Sraffa dissented from this theory. His contribution lies in demonstrating the impossibility of establishing in general (i) a notion of capital as a measurable quantity that is independent of distribution and prices and (ii) a *decreasing* demand function for capital.

With respect to the necessity of defining a 'quantity of capital' independently of distribution, the question arises as to whether the prices of the different commodities, and thus the value of the means of production (or capital), remain unchanged when the wage rate (the rate of profit) is hypothetically varied. As mentioned above, the effect of changes in one of the distributive variables on the other, and on the prices of the commodities, assuming that the methods of production remain unchanged, is investigated extensively in Sraffa's book (Chapters III and VI for the case of single production and § 83 for production with fixed capital). Sraffa (1960, Ch. VI) uses the method of the 'reduction to dated quantities of labour' to demonstrate the impact of changes in distribution on relative prices (in single-product systems). The price vector p, in fact, can be seen as the sum of the infinite series

$$p = wl + (1 + r)wAl + (1 + r)^2wA^2l + ... + (1 + r)^nwA^nl + ...$$

where A^sl ($s = 0, 1, 2, ...$) represents the vector of the quantities of labour expended directly in the production of the different commodities at step s or, for short, the respective 'labour terms', w is the wage rate and r is the rate of profit. As Sraffa (1960, p. 37) argues, the labour terms 'can be regarded as the constituent elements of the price of a commodity, the combination of which in various proportions may, with the variation of the rate of profits, give rise to complicated patterns of price-movement with several ups and downs'.

This is demonstrated by means of an example that figured prominently in Austrian capital theory – the maturing of wine and the growing of an oak which eventually is made into a chest. Sraffa (1960, p. 38) stresses that this example is a crucial test for the marginalist notions of a quantity of capital and a period of production:

> the case just considered seems conclusive in showing the impossibility of aggregating the 'periods' belonging to the several quantities of labour into a single magnitude which could be regarded as representing the quantity of capital. The reversals in the direction of the movement of relative prices, in the face of unchanged methods of production, cannot be reconciled with *any* notion of capital as a measurable quantity independent of distribution and prices. (original emphasis)

The radical implication of this result follows: 'One can only wonder what is the good of a quantity of capital or a period of production which, since it depends on the rate of interest, cannot be used for its traditional purpose, which is to determine the rate of interest' (Sraffa 1962, p. 479).

Variations of relative prices corresponding to changes in the rate of profit played an important role in the capital controversies of the 1960s and 1970s (Garegnani 1970, 1990; Harcourt 1969, 1972; Harcourt and Laing 1971; Bliss 1975; Burmeister 1980; Kurz 1987; Ahmad 1991; Kurz and Salvadori 1995, Ch. 14). While earlier authors knew that distribution influenced relative prices, they were not fully aware of all the complications involved. In particular, they thought that with a rise in the rate of profit (that is, a fall in the wage rate) the ratio of prices of any two commodities would, stay constant *or* rise *or* fall, throughout the range of variation of r (w). This opinion was closely related to the hypothesis that capital–labour or capital–output ratios of different industries could be brought into a ranking that is independent of distribution. However, as Sraffa (1960, p. 15) showed, this is generally not possible: 'the price of a product ... may rise or it may fall, or it may even alternate in rising and falling, relative to its means of production'. Therefore, to characterize an industry as capital intensive or labour intensive makes no sense unless the level of the rate of profit is specified at which this characterization is supposed to apply.

It is because marginalist theorists must establish a *decreasing* demand function for capital that reswitching and capital reversing are of crucial importance in a critique of orthodox theory. The possibility of the reswitching of techniques is clearly stated by Sraffa. Considering two alternative methods for the production of one commodity (basic or not), it is possible 'that as the rate of profits rises there may be several intersections between the prices at which the two methods produce, with as many switches backwards and forwards from one method to the other and consequently from one system to the other' (Sraffa 1960, p. 84). The implication of this is that the direction of change of the input proportions cannot be related unambiguously to changes of the so-called 'factor prices'. The central element of the marginalist explanation of distribution in terms of supply and demand is thus revealed as defective. The demonstration that a rise in r may lead to the adoption of the more capital intensive of two systems of production seriously undermines the marginalist concept of substitution in production. Moreover, since a rise in r may cheapen some of the commodities, the production of which at a lower level of r was characterized by a relatively high 'capital intensity', the substitution among consumption goods contemplated by the traditional theory of consumer demand may result in a higher, as well as in a lower, capital intensity (compare Garegnani 1970, p. 424). It follows that the principle of substitution in consumption cannot offset the breakdown of the principle of substitution in production.

We talk of 'reverse capital deepening' when the relationship between the value of capital in terms of the consumption unit (per capita) and the rate of profit is increasing. As Pasinetti (1966, p. 516 n. 5) noted, the idea of reverse capital deepening was suggested to him by Sraffa. The consequences of reswitching and reverse capital deepening for traditional theory are illustrated in Figure 16.1, where the value of capital in terms of the consumption unit corresponding to the full employment level of labour is plotted against the rate of profit. Obviously, if with traditional analysis we conceived the curve KK' as the demand curve for capital, which, together with the corresponding supply curve $K^*K^{*'}$, is taken to determine the equilibrium value of r, we would have to conclude that this equilibrium, although unique, is unstable. With free competition including (as conceived in neoclassical theory) the perfect flexibility of the distributive variables, a deviation of r from r^* would lead to the absurd conclusion that one of the two income categories, wages or profits, would disappear. According to critics of traditional neoclassical theory, this result demonstrates the failure of the supply and demand approach.

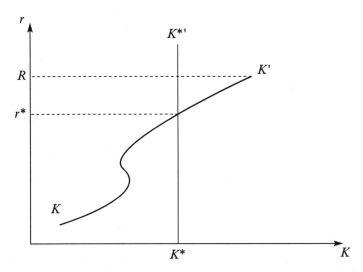

Figure 16.1 'Supply' and 'demand' of capital with reverse capital deepening (the consumption unit being the numerative).

It is hardly surprising that protagonists of the supply and demand approach were so concerned when confronted with this critique. Levhari (1965) claimed to have demonstrated that reswitching was impossible. This claim was shown to be false by Pasinetti (1966), who was encouraged to do so by Sraffa (Baranzini and Harcourt 1993, p. 9).

When the possibility of reswitching and reverse capital deepening could no longer be denied, questions were raised about its empirical significance (see Ferguson 1969). The adopted strategy consisted of playing down the importance of the new results, thereby insinuating that neoclassical theory was a simplified picture of reality, the basic correctness of which could not be endangered by the kind of exceptions analysed in the capital debate. This sort of reasoning was implicitly dealt with by Sraffa in an oral intervention at the 1958 Corfu conference on capital theory. Counterpoising the statistician's measure with measurement in theory, which should be universally applicable, Sraffa emphasized that theoretical measures required absolute precision. ... The work of J.B. Clark, Böhm-Bawerk and others was intended to produce pure definitions of capital, as required by their theories, not as a guide to actual measurement. If we found contradictions, then these pointed to defects in the theory, and an inability to define measures of capital accurately. (Lutz and Hague 1961, pp. 305–6)

Other advocates of the neoclassical approach were conscious that the attempts to avoid reswitching or to play down its importance were defective. Since the phenomenon was irrefutable it had to be absorbed and shown to be compatible with more sophisticated versions of the theory. Thus, the criticism of traditional neoclassical theory is accepted by major representatives of neoclassical general equilibrium theory. Instead of defending what cannot be defended, they examine the alternative, classical theory, claiming that it does not constitute an alternative to *modern* versions of neoclassical theory – those based on the notions of temporary or intertemporal equilibrium (Bliss 1975; Burmeister 1980; Hahn 1975, 1982). Because of rapidly declining health, Sraffa could not enter into a discussion of this kind of defence (see, however, Kurz and Salvadori 1995, pp. 455–67).

CONCLUDING REMARKS

Sraffa launched the revival of the classical approach to the theory of value and distribution and dealt a serious blow to traditional, long-period neoclassical economics, both in its partial and general equilibrium versions. His main concern was with interdependent production systems – the production of commodities by means of commodities. He rejected the marginalist view of production as a one-way avenue leading from the services of original factors of production to final goods as grossly misrepresenting the process of production in developed industrialized economies characterised by a sophisticated division of labour.

The impact of Sraffa's criticism on mainstream economic research and teaching has so far been limited (with the possible exception of his contribution to the theory of imperfect competition). It may be conjectured that this is partly because the economics profession is largely unwilling to face the fact that its foundations are much less solid than is generally believed. Sraffa overthrew the simple messages of textbook economics and deprived the applied economist of a well-entrenched pattern of thought concerning price–quantity relationships that allows quick answers to policy questions. Given the limited success of economic policy recommendations, the profession might want to ask whether that has anything to do with the analytical core from which these recommendations are derived.

NOTES

1. The view that Sraffa's criticism misses its target because he argued from the point of view of traditional long-period theory, whereas Hayek presupposed intertemporal equilibrium, cannot be sustained (see Kurz 1995).
2. Hahn (1982, p. 354) admitted that the Sraffa-based critique is correct with respect to 'many writers whom we regard as neoclassical who have either made mistakes of reasoning or based themselves on special assumptions which have themselves nothing to do with neoclassical theory'. Hahn (1982, p. 353) also wrote that 'Sraffa's book contains no formal propositions ... I consider to be wrong although here and there it contains remarks which I consider to be false'.
3. In this regard Sraffa dissents from all 'successivist' approaches to the problem under consideration, the most famous of which is perhaps Marx's transformation problem. See on this especially Steedman (1977).
4. For a detailed analysis of the role of the Standard commodity, see Roncaglia (1978), Schefold (1986), Kurz and Salvadori (1993; 1995, pp. 116–21).

REFERENCES

Ahmad, S. (1991), *Capital in Economic Theory: Neo-classical, Cambridge and Chaos*, Aldershot: Edward Elgar.

Baranzini, M. and G.C. Harcourt (1993), 'Introduction', in M. Baranzini and G.C. Harcourt (eds), *The Dynamics of the Wealth of Nations: Growth, Distribution and Structural Change: Essays in Honour of Luigi Pasinetti*, New York: St. Martin's Press, pp. 1–42.

Bharadwaj, K. (1978), *Classical Political Economy and Rise to Dominance of Supply and Demand Theories*, New Delhi: Orient Longman.

Bliss, C.J. (1975), *Capital Theory and the Distribution of Income*, Amsterdam: North-Holland.

Burmeister, E. (1980), *Capital Theory and Dynamics*, Cambridge: Cambridge University Press.

Ferguson, C.E. (1969), *The Neo-Classical Theory of Production and Distribution*, Cambridge: Cambridge University Press.

Garegnani, P. (1970), 'Heterogeneous capital, the production function and the theory of distribution', *Review of Economic Studies*, **37**, 407–36.

Garegnani, P. (1990), 'Quantity of capital', in J. Eatwell, M. Milgate and P. Newman (eds), *Capital Theory*, London: Macmillan, pp. 1–78.

Hahn, F.H. (1975), 'Revival of political economy: the wrong issues and the wrong argument', *Economic Record*, **51**, 360–64.

Hahn, F. H. (1982), 'The Neo-Ricardians', *Cambridge Journal of Economics*, **6**, 353–74.

Harcourt, G.C. (1969), 'Some Cambridge controversies in the theory of capital', *Journal of Economic Literature*, **7**, 369–405.

Harcourt, G.C. (1972), *Some Cambridge Controversies in the Theory of Capital*, Cambridge: Cambridge University Press.

Harcourt, G.C. and N.F. Laing (eds) (1971), *Capital and Growth*, Harmondsworth: Penguin Books.

Hayek, F.A. (1931a), *Prices and Production*, London: Routledge & Kegan Paul.

Hayek, F.A. (1931b), 'Reflections on the pure theory of money of Mr. J.M. Keynes', *Economica*, **11**, 270–95.

Hayek, F.A. (1932), 'Money and capital: a reply', *Economic Journal*, **42**, 237–49.

Hicks, J.R. (1932), *The Theory of Wages*, London: Macmillan.
Keynes, J.M. [1936] (1964), *The General Theory of Employment, Interest and Money*, New York: Harcourt, Brace & World.
Kurz, H. D. (1986), 'Classical and early neoclassical economists on joint production', *Metroeconomica*, **38**, 1–37.
Kurz, H.D. (1987), 'Capital theory: debates', in J. Eatwell, M. Milgate and P. Newman (eds), *The New Palgrave: A Dictionary of Economics*, London: Macmillan, Vol. 1, pp. 357–63.
Kurz, H.D. (1995), 'Über "natürliche" und "künstliche" Störungen des allgemeinen Gleichgewichts – Friedrich August Hayeks monetäre Überinvestitionstheorie in *Preise und Produktion*', in B. Schefold (ed.), *Klassiker der Nationalökonomie: Friedrich August Hayeks Preise und Produktion*, Düsseldorf: Verlag Wirtschaft und Finanzen, pp. 67–119.
Kurz, H.D. and N. Salvadori (1993), 'The "Standard commodity" and Ricardo's search for an "invariable measure of value"', in M. Baranzini and G.C. Harcourt (eds), *The Dynamics of the Wealth of Nations: Growth, Distribution and Structural Change: Essays in Honour of Luigi Pasinetti*, New York: St. Martin's Press, pp. 95–123.
Kurz, H.D. and N. Salvadori (1995), *Theory of Production: A Long-Period Analysis*, Cambridge, Melbourne and New York: Cambridge University Press.
Lachmann, L.M. (1986), 'Austrian economics under fire: the Hayek–Sraffa duel in retrospect', in W. Grassl and B. Smith (eds), *Austrian Economics: Historical and Philosophical Background*, London: Croom Helm, pp. 225–42.
Levhari, D. (1965), 'A non substitution theorem and switching of techniques', *Quarterly Journal of Economics*, **79**, 98–105.
Lutz, F.A. and D.C. Hague (eds) (1961), *The Theory of Capital*, London: Macmillan.
Marshall, A. (1920) [1890], *Principles of Economics*, London: Macmillan.
Panico, C. (1991), 'Some notes on Marshallian supply functions', *Economic Journal*, **101**, 557–69.
Pasinetti, L.L. (1966), 'Changes in the rate of profit and switches of techniques', *Quarterly Journal of Economics*, **80**, 503–17.
Ricardo, D. (1951–73), *The Works and Correspondence of David Ricardo*, 11 volumes, ed. P. Sraffa with the collaboration of M.H. Dobb, Cambridge: Cambridge University Press (referred to as *Works*).
Robinson, J.V. (1933), *Economics of Imperfect Competition*, London: Macmillan.
Roncaglia, A. (1978), *Sraffa and the Theory of Prices*, New York: John Wiley.
Schefold, B. (1986), 'The Standard commodity as a tool of economic analysis: a comment on Flaschel', *Journal of Institutional and Theoretical Economics*, **142**, 603–22.
Sraffa, P. (1925), 'Sulle relazioni fra costo e quantità prodotta', *Annali di Economia*, **2**, 277–328.
Sraffa, P. (1926), 'The laws of returns under competitive conditions', *Economic Journal*, **36**, 535–50.
Sraffa, P. (1930), 'A criticism' and 'rejoinder', *Economic Journal*, **40**, 89–93.
Sraffa, P. (1932a), 'Dr. Hayek on money and capital', *Economic Journal*, **42**, 42–53.
Sraffa, P. (1932b), 'Rejoinder', *Economic Journal*, **42**, 249–51.
Sraffa, P. (1951), 'Introduction', in Ricardo (1951–73), *Works* I, pp. xiii–lxii.
Sraffa, P. (1960), *Production of Commodities by Means of Commodities: Prelude to a Critique of Economic Theory*, Cambridge: Cambridge University Press.
Sraffa, P. (1962), 'Production of commodities: A comment', *Economic Journal*, **72**, 477–9.
Steedman, I. (1977), *Marx after Sraffa*, London: New Left Books.

17. Thorstein Bunde Veblen: the quintessential dissenter

Charles M.A. Clark*

INTRODUCTION

Dissenting economists present an interesting and unique problem for historians of economic thought. Some will dismiss them as a lunatic fringe – the economics profession's equivalent to the flat earth society. Yet such a dismissal abdicates the responsibilities of a historian.

Dissenting economists persist throughout the history of economic thought; and dissent is a phenomenon that needs to be understood for a complete understanding of the history of economic ideas. This is the case for at least four reasons. First, today's dissenting economist occasionally becomes the foundation of tomorrow's orthodoxy, John Maynard Keynes being one good example.[1] Second, dissenters often generate competing schools of thought and achieve lasting influence. Moreover, economic dissenters often influence disciplines other than economics. Karl Marx is the obvious example here. Third, dissenters often influence orthodoxy. This occurs when their ideas come to be accepted; it also occurs when orthodox economists respond to their attacks (as in the case of Joan Robinson and John Kenneth Galbraith). Finally, one should understand dissenters for the simple reason that often the dissenters are correct and orthodoxy is wrong.

This chapter examines Thorstein Veblen, who in many ways is the quintessential dissenting economist, with no close equal in this century. The next section explains what it is to be a dissenting economist and examines the phenomena of dissent from the perspective of the sociology of knowledge. Next, we examine Veblen as an example of a dissenting economist, looking at both why and how he dissented from orthodoxy. Then we briefly survey how Veblen's dissent influenced his own positive contributions to economic and social analysis.

FROM DISAGREEMENT TO DISSENT

Economists are notorious for disagreeing. This trait is highlighted in Winston Churchill's famous quip 'Whenever I ask England's six leading economists a question, I get seven answers'.[2] Yet we must distinguish dissent from mere disagreement. Economists disagree for a variety of reasons, many of which have nothing to do with dissent from the reigning orthodoxy. The fact that economics is a social science and not a hard science allows a great deal of room for disagreement within a particular economic theoretical paradigm. While often this is seen as a methodological problem, the real problem is that economics lacks the invariants necessary to develop a hard science. The existence of invariants, where one can abstract from time and space in the search for natural laws, allows for repeatable experiments that can settle disputes within a paradigm. In the social world, historical and social context are everything. They define the problem by setting the parameters of human action; thus they should not be abstracted from. Furthermore, economists attempt to understand the behaviour of humans who have free will, unknown and unknowable motivations, intentions and expectations. Therefore, the subject matter of economics is not bound by fixed laws and economists cannot hope for the type of certain knowledge possessed by the natural sciences.[3] Since there is never conclusive data, and since the factors we cannot measure and quantify frequently outnumber those we can, it is easy to derive more than one interpretation to derive from a set of circumstances. Thus, although economists frequently disagree on economic issues, this does not entail dissent, for dissent is something fundamentally different.

To be a dissenting economist one must reject at least some of the fundamental tenets of economic orthodoxy. It is not merely holding a different view on policy or a contrary interpretation of economic events. True dissent stems from a different perspective from which to view the economy or a contrary conception of what is the proper object of analysis for understanding the economy. What is noteworthy about dissenting economists is not that they give different answers to questions posed by orthodoxy; rather, dissenters question the questions. They question the logic of a ruling economic theory, its fundamental theories and postulates (the 'hard core' of the theory) and not just its conclusions. They question how economists arrive at their opinions more than what those opinions are. In Joseph Schumpeter's terminology, dissenters have a different vision of how society and the economy function.

DISSENTING ECONOMISTS AND THE SOCIOLOGY OF KNOWLEDGE

'The sociology of knowledge' according to Werner Stark (1967, p. 475), 'is concerned with determining whether man's participation in social life has any influence on his knowledge, thought, and culture and, if it does, what sort of influence it is'. Stark's *Sociology of Knowledge* (1991) presents a very strong argument that social life is *the* most significant influence on the creation of ideas, particularly social ideas. Social life generates the subject matter of social theory as well as the social theory itself. As a mode of inquiry for the history of ideas, the sociology of knowledge attempts to understand systems of thought in the context in which they were created. This allows historians to better understand the object in question (past ideas), as well as to evaluate the validity of such ideas, by testing whether these ideas correctly reflect the circumstances they seek to explain. But most importantly for the historian of ideas, the sociology of knowledge presents a method to explain the origins and development of systems of thought by linking them to their social and historical context.

As an approach to the history of ideas, the sociology of knowledge should be contrasted with what might be called 'the philosophy of science approach'. The philosophy of science approach holds that the purpose of theory is to depict the natural laws of the universe. Whereas the sociology of knowledge expects to find relative truths, the philosophy of science can only accept absolute truths.

What serves as absolute truth for the philosophy of science approach is most often the accepted views.[4] From this perspective, past economic theories are understood in relation to current dogmas. They are either in agreement with current ideas, which means that they are part of the discipline's progressive march towards current orthodoxy, or they are contrary to current theory. If a theory fits into the latter category it is either dismissed or shown to be wrongheaded through its disagreement with accepted theory. Progress in economics is movement towards currently accepted ideas and the purpose of this type of economic historiography is most often to demonstrate such progress. Hence, these rational reconstructions exist more to legitimate than to illuminate.[5] It should be obvious that this approach would have no reason to analyse the phenomena of dissenting economists.

The sociology of knowledge approach attempts to explain what past theorists said, why they said it, and lastly, if it was an adequate representation of their reality. Like the philosophy of science approach, the sociology of knowledge approach evaluates the 'truthfulness' of past theories; yet it does so with a relative, and not an absolute, yardstick.

The sociology of knowledge adheres to the position that all social theory is socially constructed; that is, all social ideas are created and not discovered. This is a fundamental difference with the philosophy of science approach, where discovery implies something that is independent from the observer. For Christopher Columbus to discover the new world it was necessary that the new world be there. The same cannot be said for ideas.[6]

Four factors play a role in the social construction of economic ideas – intellectual milieu, material conditions, micro-sociology of knowledge and ideology. All observation presupposes a perspective, and in the social creation of ideas this perspective comes from the intellectual milieu. At one level the intellectual milieu provides what Stark referred to as the 'axiological layer of the mind'. This is the '*a priori* system of social valuations or prejudgements which enable us to form, out of the infinitude of the knowable, the finite and hence comprehensible universe of the known' (Stark 1991, p. 113). It gives the theorist a basic conceptual framework, and provides a guide for selecting what is essential and what is to be ignored in his or her theoretical system.

The intellectual milieu also provides the theorist with the concepts necessary for theory development – the metaphors and analogies from other systems of knowledge which act as heuristic guides in the construction of new theories (Schon 1963; Clark 1992, Ch. 1). Thus, the intellectual milieu teaches the theorist how to think, provides a guide for selecting what to think about, and lastly, provides tools for developing new perspectives from which to view the objects of theoretical analysis.

Material conditions provide what Stark called the 'objects of knowledge'. The material conditions refer to the economy and the economic activity of the members of society; that is, the process by which the society provides for its material reproduction.

The economy also influences theoretical activity in many other ways. The creation of a social surplus is essential for the development of an intellectual discipline, for the obvious reason that theorists must eat. Furthermore, the economic process has a great socializing effect. This will influence perceptions, and work its way into the axiological realm. Marx noted this in his analysis of the factory system on proletarian consciousness, as did Veblen in his analysis of how the machine process influences habits of thought.

The micro-sociology of knowledge refers to the social processes and institutions that influence theoretical activity. Numerous historians of economic thought have written about the professionalization of economics and how it has shaped theory development. This is a topic of the micro-sociology of knowledge. Since theoretical activity is always a social activity, carried out in social groups and under the influence of social institutions, we cannot ignore the influence that the socialization of the theoretical class has on the development of theory. Certainly much of the mathematization of economic theory can be traced to these types of influences.

Finally, we come to the topic of ideology. As Stark (1991) notes, it is unfortunate that the origins of the discipline of the sociology of knowledge were so closely tied up with the concept of ideology. We shall define ideology as the individual's value system. It serves to guide the theorist's interests and provides the final terms for ethical criteria. All theoretical activity, as with all human activity, has a goal-attaining aspect. For the theorist, this is most often his or her vision of a just society. The ideal always influences conceptions of the real. These value judgements always influence theoretical work at many levels.

One common criticism of the sociology of knowledge has been that if ideas are socially created, how can conflicting ideas exist at the same time? This criticism is positivistic in nature. It is not directed at the internal consistency of the sociology of knowledge research programme, but an outright rejection of the social construction of knowledge. None the less, it raises an important question about the social construction of dissent that must be addressed.

As the above analysis suggests, economic theory has developed and changed because of changes in the intellectual milieu, material conditions, institutions controlling theoretical activity and ideology. All four factors can and do produce effects on individual theorists. As a result, we often get a wide variety of theoretical explanations. We should thus expect the existence and persistence of dissenting economists.

We now turn to Veblen as a dissenting economist, examining why he rejected the economic orthodoxy of his day and how this led him to develop a different explanation of economic activity.

VEBLEN AS A DISSENTING ECONOMIST

Two questions naturally arise regarding Veblen as a dissenting economist. First, in what ways was he a dissenting economist? Second, how did he dissent from the orthodoxy of his time, and why did he reject the conventional wisdom of the twentieth century? We shall deal with these queries in reverse order.

When writing about Veblen it is hard to steer clear from his personal story. There are so many quirky tales about Veblen's habits and exploits that it is almost impossible to resist the temptation to explain Veblen's ideas as the result of his atypical biography. As Rosenberg (1956, p. 3) has written: 'Veblen *was* the Marginal Man, the Alien, the Intellectual, the

Stranger' (original emphasis). Veblen's social non-conformity is often correlated with his intellectual non-conformity. Support for this line of analysis comes from two very prominent sources.

In his biography on Veblen, Dorfman (1934) clearly and in great detail demonstrates Veblen's outsider qualities. Although more recent evidence suggests that Dorfman exaggerated the social isolation of Veblen's childhood,[7] Dorfman did not invent Veblen's history; it seems he merely exaggerated the individual circumstances which produced Veblen's original mind. Moreover, Wesley Mitchell reinforces the depiction of Veblen's childhood by Dorfman. After noting Veblen's agricultural and rural upbringing, Mitchell (1969, p. 619) states:

> He came out of that background and was thrown at Carleton into the midst of people who came from a money-making New England background. ... The contrast between the life seemingly devoted to making useful things and the life of money-making where it was not so easy to see that the activities of the shrewd businessman might really be contributing to the satisfaction of human needs struck him very forcibly, and interested him when he was young and impressionable in questions of cultural differences.

Another source adding credence to the influence of Veblen's 'not fitting in' as a factor in his dissent comes from Veblen himself. Veblen's (1934) famous essay 'The intellectual pre-eminence of the Jews in modern Europe' is often cited as autobiographical in spirit, and with much justification.[8] In this essay, Veblen states that the marginal status of Jews in gentile European society was one reason they made disproportionate contributions to Western intellectual history in general and modern science in particular. Pioneering work, Veblen states, requires a sceptical mind, which is often the byproduct of a marginal or outsider status.

Yet one cannot derive Veblen's economic dissent from his personality traits, or from his childhood, alone. One must understand both the particular individual and the cultural circumstances. In his penetrating book on Veblen, John Diggins has shown how Veblen was a man of his times. At the turn of the nineteenth century, 'the various recent protest movements – free silver, the single tax, populism, socialism, and progressivism – strongly suggest that the majority of citizens felt themselves the victims of new, menacing economic forces they could neither comprehend nor control' (Diggins 1979, p. 3). Diggins lists three major problems of the era: (1) the loss of individual freedom to organizational power (the Robber Barons); (2) 'the affront of wealth and status' brought about by the gilded age; and (3) the inability of contemporary moral and ethical systems and theories to reign in excessive abuses of power of modern business. From this list we can see how Veblen was shaped by his times.

None the less, a major reason why Veblen did not accept the orthodoxy of his day was because it could not explain contemporary problems.
Material conditions had evolved while economic theory had not.
Economic theories based on natural law had a certain adequacy for
the early stages of capitalism, what Veblen called 'the era of free
competition'. But the economy of the late nineteenth and early twentieth
centuries was quite different from that examined by Adam Smith. *The
Theory of Business Enterprise* (Veblen 1904) is an attempt to explain
the dominant features of the economy during this period, an industrial
economy dominated by the machine process, pecuniary principles, credit
and the existence and persistence of the business cycle. These topics were
either ignored in the then reigning orthodoxy or were understood from
the natural law perspective as universal and unchanging concepts.
An economic theory that starts and ends with fixed and universal natural
laws cannot hope to grasp the reality of cumulative change and
social evolution.

We can see that Veblen's personal history, and the cultural circumstances in which he lived, helped shape his theories and partially explain
his status as a dissenter. Yet the change in the intellectual milieu contributed most to Veblen's dissent from mainstream economic theory. The
two intellectual developments which influenced Veblen greatly, and which
form the basis of his critique of neoclassical economic theory and the
foundation of his own views, are the evolutionary theory of Charles
Darwin and the developments taking place in anthropology. Veblen's
critique of neoclassical economic theory stems from his delineation of
theories as either pre-Darwinian or Darwinian. His positive contributions
to social science stem from the economic–anthropologic perspective he
took towards economic phenomena. We shall demonstrate the importance of these two factors by turning to how Veblen dissented from the
orthodoxy of his time.

VEBLEN'S CRITIQUE OF ECONOMIC THEORY

Veblen wrote extensively about the theories making up the accepted economics of his day; yet here we shall look only at his overall objection to
neoclassical economics. This critique is not based on the logical inconsisten-
cies of neoclassical theory, or on erroneous empirical statements and
assumptions – however numerous these may be and however frequently
Veblen pointed them out. Rather, his critique centred on the neoclassical
view of how the world works.

Veblen's criticism of economic theory, past and present, rested on the central distinction between pre- and post-Darwinian science. For Veblen this

was tantamount to the distinction between mythology and science. Veblen criticized the reigning orthodoxy of his time because it adhered to a pre-Darwinian view of how the universe worked. Veblen (1919, pp. 36–7) notes:

> there is a significant difference in the point of view between the scientific era which preceded and that which followed the epoch to which his [Darwin's] name belongs. Before that epoch the animus of a science was, on the whole, the animus of taxonomy; the consistent end of scientific inquiry was definition and classification, as it still continues to be in such fields of science as have not been affected by the modern notion of consecutive change. The scientists of that era looked to a final term. ... [T]he center of interest and attention ... was the body of natural laws governing phenomena.
>
> [Post-Darwinian theory is] substantially a theory of the process of consecutive change, which is taken as a sequence of cumulative change, realized to be self-continuing or self-propagating and to have no final term.

Veblen advocates changing from the equilibrium, natural law view derived from the Newtonian world view to the emerging evolutionary world view.[9]

The significance of the evolutionary perspective in economic theory was highlighted in Veblen's essay 'Why is economics not an evolutionary science?'. Veblen (1919, p. 58) defines an evolutionary science as 'a theory of a process, of an unfolding sequence'. He notes that when classical economists deal with process and development, they conceived of 'their theory in terms alien to the evolutionist's habit of thought' (Veblen 1919, p. 59). For the classical and neoclassical economist what is important is the equilibrium position towards which the economy is tending whereas the evolutionist is interested in the process, maintaining that there is no predetermined point towards which the economy is tending.

Foreshadowing recent work on metaphors, Veblen notes that much of the influence of the natural law outlook on economic theory stems from their terminology.

> With later writers especially, this terminology is no doubt to be commonly taken as a convenient use of metaphor. ... But it is precisely in this use of figurative terms for the formulation of theory that the classical normality still lives its attenuated life in modern economics. ... The metaphors are effective, both in their homiletical use and as a labor-saving device. ... By their use the theorist is enabled ... to construct a theory of such an institution as money or wages or land-ownership without descending to a consideration of the living terms concerned, except for convenient corroboration of his normalised scheme of symptoms. By this method the theory of an institution or a phase of life may be stated in conventionalized terms of the apparatus whereby life is carried on, the apparatus being invested with a tendency to an equilibrium at the normal, and the theory being a formulation of the conditions under which this putative equilibrium supervenes. ... In all this the agencies or forces causally at work in the economic life process are neatly avoided. (Veblen 1919, pp. 66–7)

The importance of the natural law outlook is further elaborated by Veblen in 'The preconceptions of economic science'. This essay examines the extent to which natural law preconceptions influence neoclassical economic theory. It notes that many neoclassicals, most notably Alfred Marshall, attempted to account for some of the issues raised by an evolutionary perspective. In the case of Marshall, this is seen in his call for biological metaphors to replace mechanical metaphors and his emphasis on processes, change, the problem of time, and his allowance for the development of human nature. Yet Marshall cannot escape natural law preconceptions, and thus his doctrines ultimately fall back on equilibrium outcomes.

> Marshall's work is, in aim, even if not always in achievement, a theoretical handling of human activity in its economic bearing. ... And still it remains an inquiry directed to the determination of the conditions of an equilibrium of activities and a quiescent normal situation. It is not in any eminent degree an inquiry into cultural or institutional development as affected by economic exigencies or by the economic interest of the men whose activities are analysed and portrayed. (Veblen 1919, p. 173)

Veblen (1919, p. 70) contrasts this equilibrium, natural law approach with an evolutionary approach:

> There is the economic life process still in great measure awaiting theoretical formulation. The active material in which the economic process goes on is the human material of the industrial community. For the purpose of economic science the process of cumulative change that is to be accounted for is the sequence of change in the methods of doing things, the methods of dealing with the material means of life.

According to Veblen (1919, p. 77) 'an evolutionary economics must be the theory of a process of cultural growth as determined by the economic interest, a theory of a cumulative sequence of economic institutions stated in terms of the process itself'. The main objective of the preconceptions essay was to demonstrate how natural law preconceptions have shaped and, even more significantly, limited the scope and content of economic theory. By assuming the 'normal' case, theorists must either force actual economic data to fit the theory, or they must label it a temporary and transient factor and exclude it from theoretical consideration. Either way it is theory that defines what the economist is considering and not actual economic activity. Veblen contends that what the neoclassical economist takes for granted or assumes away is of primary theoretical interest if one wants to understand economic activity in a non-teleological manner. The primary institutions of a modern capitalist economy – money, credit, property ownership, business principles and activities, and most importantly the institutions that shape and determine economic behaviour – are either reconceptualized to fit the rational economic man model or they are excluded from the analysis. Veblen (1919, p. 250) writes:

> [S]ince it is in just this unhedonistic, unrationalistic pecuniary traffic that the tissue of business life consists; since it is this peculiar conventionalism of aims and standards that differentiates the life of the modern business community from any conceivable earlier or cruder phase of economic life; since it is in this tissue of pecuniary intercourse and pecuniary concepts, ideals, expedients, and aspirations that the conjunctures of business life arise and run their course of felicity and devastation; since it is here that those institutional changes take place which distinguish one phase or era of the business community's life from any other; since the growth and change of these habitual, conventional elements make the growth and character of any business era or business community; any theory of business which sets these elements aside or explains them away misses the main facts which it has gone out to seek.

Neoclassical economists, according to Veblen, have not only assumed away what makes capitalism capitalism; they have assumed away what makes theoretical activity possible – the forces in the economy that generate economic order. *Sans* institutions there would be no economy. Veblen (1946, pp. 85–6) makes a similar point in *The Vested Interests and the Common Man*:

> there are certain saving clauses in common use among persons who speak for that well-known order of pecuniary rights and obligations which the modern point of view assumes as 'the natural state of man'. Among them are these: 'Given the state of the industrial arts'; 'other things remaining the same'; 'in the long run'; 'In the absence of disturbing causes'. ... [T]he state of the industrial arts has at no time continued unchanged during the modern era; consequently other things have never remained the same; and in the long run the outcome has always been shaped by the disturbing causes.

The crux of neoclassical economic theory is that one can explain the market economy based on human nature and scarcity, that economic order is merely the outward manifestation of the interactions of the multitude of human natures, spontaneously created and based on universal laws and principles. Veblen rejects this notion. Furthermore, Veblen ardently rejects the neoclassical conception of human nature.

Veblen objected to the neoclassical view of human nature primarily because of the hedonistic psychology upon which it was constructed. He thought this approach was outdated, discredited by recent work in psychology (especially that of William James) and anthropology. Veblen was always fascinated by the wide variety of human behaviours (both between cultures and within cultures). Such diversity would not be likely if there were a universal and fixed human nature.

Veblen especially objected to depicting humans as passive reactors. In a famous passage he (Veblen 1946, p. 74) writes:

In all the received formulations of economic theory ... the human material with which the inquiry is concerned is conceived in hedonistic terms; that is to say, in terms of a passive and substantially inert and immutably given human nature. ... The hedonistic conception of man is that of a lightning calculator of pleasures and pains, who oscillates like a homogeneous globule of desire of happiness under the impulse of stimuli that shift him about the area, but leave him intact. He is neither antecedent nor consequent. He is an isolated, definitive human datum, in stable equilibrium except for the buffets of the impinging forces that displace him in one direction or another. Self-imposed in elemental space, he spins symmetrically about his own spiritual axis until the parallelogram of forces bears down upon him, whereupon he follows the line of the resultant.

Furthermore, Veblen (1964, p. 157) notes that the hedonistic view of human nature goes hand in hand with the natural law outlook. According to Veblen (1964, p. 74), man is an active force, 'a coherent structure of propensities and habits which seeks realization and expression in an unfolding activity'. The habits and propensities come not from a given, universal human nature. Rather, they are the result of the socialization process, the influence of social institutions on the individual.

FROM DISSENT TO CONTRIBUTION

From the above analysis it should be clear that Veblen's dissent from neoclassical economic theory was complete and comprehensive. He rejected the final terms upon which it rested – the idea of underlying natural laws, the existence and tendency towards equilibrium, and the hedonistic view of human nature. By freeing himself from this intellectual baggage, Veblen was able to see economic phenomena from a new and original perspective. Bringing the idea of evolution to economic and social phenomena allowed him to examine questions of process and change. Rejecting the natural law outlook let him look towards culture as the order bestowing force in the economy and in society. Rejecting all notions of a universal hedonistic human nature allowed Veblen to develop the idea of cultural relativity. Applying the notions of evolution, culture and relativity to economic and social phenomena enabled Veblen to develop instrumental valuation. These four ideas – evolution, culture, cultural relativity and instrumental valuation – become the four pillars of institutionalism (Mayhew 1987).

Bringing the idea of evolution to economic phenomena, and making culture (rather than human nature) the order-creating force, is the beginning of economic anthropology. As Mayhew (1987, p. 976) notes, 'Veblen was the first economic anthropologist, and what makes it so remarkable is that he did not study exotic peoples – it is always easier to see customs when they look foreign and therefore funny – but rather his own culture'. In his most famous work *The Theory of The Leisure Class*, Veblen was able to see that consumption, both in its manifestations and in its underlying motivations, was socially determined and not an act of individual utility maximization. Furthermore, consumption was placed in its institutional context, as part of the overall scheme by which those in power, the leisure class, gain the acquiescence of, and exercise power over, the rest of society. Conspicuous consumption is a fundamental aspect of this power system. Emulation of the leisure class's consumption habits implicitly accepts their system of values, and hence the existing social order.

> All canons of reputability and decency, and all standards of consumption, are traced back by insensible gradations to the usages and habits of thought of the highest social and pecuniary class – the wealthy leisure class. It is for this class to determine ... what scheme of life the community shall accept as decent or honorific; and it is their office by precept and example to set forth this scheme of social solution in its highest, ideal form. (Veblen 1908, p. 104)

Neoclassical economists make the satisfaction of needs and desires the basis of all economic activity, and the utility-maximizing individual the cornerstone of their theoretical investigations. For Veblen, pecuniary emulation was the heart of all economic activity, the desire to draw invidious distinctions in order to achieve social status. Such distinctions first come in the form of predatory prowess, the conspicuous display of the trophies of war and hunting. These eventually evolve into the conspicuous display of wealth and leisure. Thus, the creation and display of wealth become the basis of status and the social order.

Only by taking an evolutionary perspective (that is, examining existing habits and institutions as evolutionary by products of what existed in the past) can we hope to critically understand the economy. As we saw above, such an approach provides a deeper understanding of the economic and social function of consumption, a perspective which is impossible if one takes seriously the notions of universal natural laws in the social universe and fixed human nature. Yet, Veblen wanted not only to provide better explanations of economic activity by adopting a different perspective; he also sought to answer different questions, and to understand the process of cumulative and institutional change. Veblen (1899, p. 188) writes:

> The life of man in society ... is a struggle for existence, and therefore it is a process of selective adaptation. The evolution of social structure has been a process of natural selection of institutions. ... Institutions are not only themselves the result of a selective and adaptive process which shapes the prevailing or dominant types of spiritual attitude and aptitudes; they are at the same time

special methods of life and of human relations, and are therefore in their turn efficient factors of selection. So that the changing institutions in their turn make for a further selection of individuals endowed with the fittest tempera-ment, and a further adaptation of individual temperament and habits to the changing environment through the formation of new institutions.

One would be hard pressed to find a better statement of the view that society is a process, resulting from the interaction of individuals and social institutions, with individuals being shaped by institutions and with new institutions emerging from the actions of individuals.[10]

Veblen does not attach teleological significance to this process, for the evolution of the community has no predetermined path. He asserts that there are two dominant institutional factors in this process of cumulative change: 'institutions ... may be roughly distinguished into two classes or categories ... they are institutions of acquisition or of production ... [and] they are pecuniary or industrial institutions; or in still other terms, they are institutions serving either invidious or the non-invidious economic interests' (Veblen 1899, p. 208). This distinction is fundamental for Veblen and for institutionalist thought. Known as 'the Veblenian dichotomy', it posits forces that promote the well-being of the community and that pro-mote invidious distinctions, and notes that these two institutions (or aspects of a single institution) usually conflict. Most social institutions are inherently conservative and support the status quo. But the dynamic of life never stops. One important institution – the community's collective knowledge (technology) – is always disturbing the status quo. Social evo-lution can be seen as the interaction of these two types of institutions, yet there is no method of predicting what will come out of this interaction.

Yet the Veblenian dichotomy is not merely a tool for understanding cumulative change; it is also a tool for instrumental valuation. The indus-trial, non-invidious institutions promote the life of the community; while the acquisitive, pecuniary, invidious institutions support those in power and frequently retard the interests of the community. Some examples will help illustrate Veblen's normative use of the dichotomy:[11]

salesmanship	workmanship
business	industry
ceremonial	technological
free income	tangible performance
vested interest	common man
sabotage	community serviceability
pecuniary employment	industrial employment
invidious emulation	technological efficiency
competitive advertising	valuable information
business prosperity	industrial efficiency

The left-hand column contains activities harmful to the life process of the community, while terms in the right-hand column promote the 'largest and most serviceable output of goods and services' and the 'most economical use of the countries material resources and man-power, regardless of pecuniary consequences' (Veblen, quoted in Tool 1986, p. 37).

Central to Veblen's economic analysis was his contention that business principles (that is, the pecuniary motives and institutions) retard economic development and keep the community well below its potential. Veblen rejected economic orthodoxy because it shielded this fact. By treating business categories and concepts as universal and natural, neoclassical economic theory acted as an enabling myth. It presented a story which purported to explain the operations of the economy, but in fact prevented such an understanding. Thus, it protected those in power, and it served to legitimate more than to illuminate.

VEBLEN'S RELEVANCE TODAY

Veblen remains an inspiration for current dissenting economists. His disdain for the artificial boundaries separating intellectual disciplines, and his willingness not only to cross them but to shatter them, gives his successors the freedom to examine economic activity in its full social and historical context.

Yet it is the contemporary relevance of Veblen's message that makes reading Veblen so enlightening. A walk through the 'rust belt' of the United States gives ample evidence of the continued conflict between the pecuniary and the industrial. One need only watch the evening news to see the 'honorific' status given to financiers and speculators (today's predators who live by 'force and fraud'). This is likely to be followed by something like 'Lifestyles of the Rich and Famous', which demonstrates that conspicuous consumption is alive and well. Even more telling, however, are the commercials which television programmes periodically interrupt. The appeals to status and conspicuous consumption are ever present; yet they hide what underlies the whole social order. Veblen's theory of pecuniary emulation concluded that the whole social order required waste – the conspicuous display of wealth and leisure. In our demand-constrained economy the necessity of waste, be it short product cycles, planned obsolescence, disposable lifestyles, new and improved packaging, changing fashions, or the military–industrial complex and its need to create enemies, is obvious. No one should doubt that eliminating this conspicuous waste would mean the end of capitalism and the leisure class it supports. Also, no one should doubt that ethically, socially and environmentally, such a social system is not sustainable, much less justifiable. For the leisure class, Veblen remains a most dangerous man.

NOTES

*The author would like to thank William Dugger, Rick Tillman, Charles Whalen and Steven Pressman for their comments and suggestions.

1. Jevons and Menger are also good examples. Both felt themselves to be dissenting from the ruling orthodoxy of their day – Mill for Jevons, the Historical School for Menger.
2. The quotation ends with the jab: 'two from Mr. Keynes'.
3. John Stuart Mill understood this problem of knowledge as a limit to our understanding of economic activity; however, he was so dominated by the natural law outlook that he assumes that if we could ascertain enough information, economic activity would be mechanical and predictable (see Clark 1992, Ch. 5).
4. Usually it is the accepted view of the dominant theory, yet it could easily be that of any accepted orthodoxy.
5. For a lengthy discussion of the issues raised by the historiography of economics, see Stark's postumously published *History and Historians of Political Economy* (1994), a short summary of which is given in Clark (1994). Also see the symposium on this topic in the December 1994 issue of the *History of Economic Ideas*.
6. A good example of this is how the creation of the principle of marginal utility is treated in most history of economic thought texts as a discovery, on a par with those made in the natural sciences.
7. See Tilman (1992, pp. 1–10).
8. Diggins (1978, p. 40) calls the essay 'the closest thing to a self-portrait that Veblen ever committed to print.'
9. For an excellent history of the rise in evolutionary social thought, see Burrow (1966).
10. See Stark (1963) for a detailed description and analysis of the 'society as a process' view.
11. Taken from Tool (1986, pp. 36–7).

REFERENCES

Burrow, J.W. (1966), *Evolution and Society*, Cambridge: Cambridge University Press.

Clark, C.M.A. (1992), *Economic Theory and Natural Philosophy*, Aldershot: Edward Elgar.

Clark, C.M.A. (1994), 'Werner Stark and the historiography of economics', *History of Economic Ideas*, 2, December, 97–108.

Daugert, S.M. (1950), *The Philosophy of Thorstein Veblen*, New York: King's Crown Press.

Diggins, J.P. (1978), *The Bard of Savagery: Thorstein Veblen and Modern Social Theory*, New York: Seabury Press.

Dorfman, J. (1961) [1934], *Thorstein Veblen and His America*, New York: Augustus M. Kelley.

Jaffé, W. (1971) [1924], *Les Théories Économiques et Sociales de Thorstein Veblen* (The Economic and Social Theories of Thorstein Veblen), New York: Burt Franklin.

Mayhew, A. (1987), 'The beginnings of institutionalism', *Journal of Economic Issues*, 21, September, 971–98.

Mitchell, W.C. (1950), *The Backward Art of Spending Money and Other Essays*, New York: Augustus M. Kelley.

Mitchell, W. C. (1969), *Types of Economic Theory*, New York: Augustus M. Kelley.

Rosenberg, B. (1956), *The Values of Veblen*, Washington, DC: Public Affairs Press.

Schon, D.A. (1963), Invention and Evolution of Ideas, London: Associated Book Publishers.

Stark, W. (1963), *The Fundamental Forms of Social Thought*, New York: Fordham University Press.

Stark, W. (1967), 'The sociology of knowledge' in *The Encyclopedia of Philosophy*, New York: Macmillan, pp. 478–8.

Stark, W. (1991) [1958], *The Sociology of Knowledge*, New Brunswick: Transaction Publishers.

Stark, W. (1994), *History and Historians of Political Economy*, ed. Charles M.A. Clark, New Brunswick: Transaction Publishers.

Tilman, R. (1992), *Thorstein Veblen and His Critics*, Princeton: Princeton University Press.

Tool, M.R. (1986), *Essays in Social Value Theory*, Armonk: M.E. Sharpe.

Veblen, T. (1908) [1899], *The Theory of the Leisure Class*, New York: The Macmillan Company.

Veblen, T. (1914), *The Instinct of Workmanship and the State of the Industrial Arts*, New York: B.W. Huebsch.

Veblen, T. (1946) [1919], *The Vested Interests and the Common Man*, New York: Viking Press.

Veblen, T. (1964) [1934], *Essays in Our Changing Order*, ed. Leon Ardzrooni, New York: Augustus M. Kelley.

Veblen, T. (1978) [1904], *The Theory of Business Enterprise*, New Brunswick: Transaction Books.

Veblen, T. (1990) [1919], *The Place of Science in Modern Civilization*, New Brunswick: Transaction Publishers.

Index

Economics and its Discontents

Dissenters have a common dissatisfaction with economics as it is currently practised, and they recognise that twentieth century economics has failed to explain real world economic phenomena. This major book focuses on the work and lives of seventeen of the most influential dissenting economists who have shaped twentieth century economics and who continue to make economics more relevant.

In *Economics and its Discontents* each chapter explains what it means to be a dissenting economist and examines how and why the work of the featured economist constitutes dissent. It demonstrates that dissent in the profession extends beyond ideology and that dissenters can come from radical, liberal or conservative backgrounds. Dissent is considered in many respects, including how economics is taught, the methodology of economic analysis, the lack of attention economists pay to the real world behaviour of individuals, the narrow and limited assumptions made by economists, the inappropriate attempt of economics to dominate all social sciences, and the policy conclusions reached by standard economic analysis. The dissenters featured in this book suggest that there is a better way to do economics, and a better way to be an economist, and each has helped keep economics honest by constantly questioning traditional thinking. This book salutes and celebrates these dissenters who exemplify the very best of the discipline. If economics is again to be a respected field and a highly regarded profession, we must look to these dissenters to point the way forward.

This book will be welcomed by professional economists, researchers and postgraduate students, especially those interested in the history of economic thought, and economic methodology and philosophy.